THE CULTURAL LIFE OF
THE AMERICAN COLONIES

The

New American Nation Series

EDITED BY

HENRY STEELE COMMAGER

AND

RICHARD B. MORRIS

THE CULTURAL LIFE OF THE AMERICAN COLONIES

1607 ★ 1763

By LOUIS B. WRIGHT

ILLUSTRATED

NEW YORK

HARPER & BROTHERS · PUBLISHERS

THE CULTURAL LIFE OF THE AMERICAN COLONIES

Library of Congress catalog card number: 56–11090

Contents

EDITORS' INTRODUCTION ix

PREFACE xiii

1. AGRARIAN SOCIETY AND LEADERSHIP 1

2. THE GOSPEL OF WORK AND THE ARISTOCRACY OF
   TRADE 23

3. NON-ENGLISH ELEMENTS AND THEIR INFLU-
   ENCE 45

4. DIVERSITY OF RELIGIONS 72

5. ZEAL FOR EDUCATION 98

6. BOOKS, LIBRARIES, AND LEARNING 126

7. LITERARY PRODUCTION: NORTH AND SOUTH 154

8. DRAMA, MUSIC, AND OTHER DIVERSIONS 176

9. ARCHITECTURE AND THE DECORATIVE ARTS 196

10. SCIENTIFIC INTEREST AND OBSERVATION 216

11. THE PRESS AND COMMUNICATIONS 238

BIBLIOGRAPHY 253

INDEX 275

Illustrations

*These photographs, grouped in a separate section,
will be found following page 144*

1. The Hart Room
2. Pine kitchen
3. The title page of John Smith's *Generall Historie of Virginia*
4. "Grand Rehearsal of the Anniversary Ode of the Tuesday Club"
5. "Drinking" tobacco
6. The title page of William Barriffe's *Military Discipline*
7. A cottage spinner
8. Colonial school texts
9. Female costume of the early period
10. A soldier of the early period
11. A colonial tobacco wharf
12. View of Charleston, 1739
13. Benjamin Franklin's printing press
14. Sassafras and tobacco
15. Processing of indigo
16. Mrs. Gabriel Manigault

17. WILLIAM PEPPERRELL

18. GEORGE WHITEFIELD

19. A colonial factory yard

20. Harvard College

21. Colonial craftsmanship

22. Frontispiece to Dilworth's *New Guide to the English Tongue*

23. The title page of Ovid's *Metamorphoses*

24. ANN POLLARD

25. THOMAS SMITH

26. THE REVEREND SAMUEL JOHNSON

27. EZRA STILES

28. Plan of Boston, 1728

29. The Capitol, Williamsburg, Virginia

30. The Wren Building, College of William and Mary

Editors' Introduction

THE twentieth century has rediscovered the cultural life of the colonial period. The reconstruction of colonial Williamsburg, the skillful assemblage of such superb collections as those housed in the American Wing of the Metropolitan Museum of Art and the Henry Francis du Pont Winterthur Museum, and the innumerable restorations of the homes of planters and merchants, of village communities, and historic shrines are tangible evidence of a yearning to recapture the chaste simplicity of an earlier day. The popular enthusiasm for such enterprises attests the strong appeal to our own age of the tastes and style and goals of living of colonial times.

To this rediscovery of our colonial past Dr. Wright's volume makes a significant and original contribution. His book is concerned not with traditional political history but with depicting how the colonists lived, the faiths and goals that inspired them, and the manner in which their lives were enriched. His lively and sympathetic story incorporates the results of the most recent scholarship but shows a nice discrimination in rejecting unproven assumptions. Dr. Wright is a man of strong convictions and he tears the veil off a number of myths about colonial culture. He strips Southern plantation life of a good deal of glamour, treats the New England Puritans with welcome objectivity, and provides many illuminating insights into the new aristocracy of trade.

The society which Dr. Wright examines is refreshing in its diversity and astonishing for the amount of social mobility that it encouraged. There was a mercantile and a metropolitan way of life, a Chesapeake society, a Carolina society, and a back-country society. The peasant

culture of the Pennsylvania Germans differed as sharply from the
Scotch-Irish modes of living in the upper valley of Virginia as did
upcountry from tidewater. Each society differed in tastes, in manners,
and in morals. Nor was it a closed society. More than one indentured
servant married a planter's daughter and won a place for himself
among the landed gentry. Indeed, it is one of the numerous virtues of
this volume that it spells out some fascinating and in many ways
typical early American success stories, for the achievements of the
Henry Laurenses and the Thomas Hancocks, of the Robert Livingstons and the Richard Derbys could be matched by a host of other
ambitious colonists.

It is also a virtue of this book that it gives us a balanced account
of the national origins of colonial cultural life. While a majority of
the population were of English stock, the proportions are not as overwhelming as has so often been depicted. The important cultural contributions of immigrants and their descendants of non-English origin
deserve the fresh retelling found in this volume. Dr. Wright reminds us
of the contribution to the crafts of such distinguished artisans as Paul
Revere, Henry William Stiegel, and Myer Myers, and to education
and politics of immigrants like William Smith and John Witherspoon.

The social mobility of colonial times should not be mistaken for
democracy. The pioneer wealthy class, whether the planters of the
South or the merchants of the North, dominated political life, but that
domination was tempered by a strong sense of social and civic responsibility and a respect for the dignity of labor. The "gospel of work"
was part of the fundamental social doctrine of Puritans, Quakers, and
others who reflected ideas that had received emphasis among the rising
commercial classes of England during the late sixteenth and seventeenth centuries. The cult of the self-made man had its American
beginnings in the colonies, where success early came to be measured
in the accumulation of property, but wealth was rarely an end in
itself. The upper classes encouraged cultural activities and, for persons
often lacking in systematic education, were surprisingly well-read and
articulate.

The cultural life of the colonies produced no Shakespeare, no Rembrandt, no Newton, and no Handel. Benjamin Franklin stands alone
as the cultural giant of colonial times. But much of this age was
devoted not to thought but to action, to clearing the wilderness and
establishing military security. Once these basic goals were achieved the

level of cultural attainment rose extraordinarily fast, as evidenced by the expansion and quality of the literary output, the notable level of achievement in the household and decorative arts, the widening horizon of scientific interests, and the advance of higher education. In the cultural story geography and technology play crucial roles. Improvement in transportation and communication by the eve of the Revolution served to make the colonies more unified, both politically and culturally, than they were in the seventeenth century, and at the same time less isolated in mind and spirit from the rest of the world than were some of the more remote countries of England. By the eve of the Revolution the British colonies of North America had become a significant part of the Atlantic cultural community.

This volume is one of The New American Nation Series, a comprehensive co-operative survey of the history of the area now known as the United States from the days of discovery to the mid-twentieth century. Since the publication a half century ago by the House of Harper of the American Nation series under the editorship of the distinguished historian Albert Bushnell Hart, the scope of history has been broadened and a new approach has been developed to deal with the problems of historical interpretation and presentation. The time has now come for a judicious appraisal of the new history, a cautious application of the new techniques of investigation and presentation, and a large-scale effort to achieve a synthesis of the new findings with the traditional facts, and to present the whole in attractive literary form.

To this task The New American Nation Series is dedicated. Each volume is part of a carefully planned whole, and co-ordinated with other volumes in the series; at the same time each volume is designed to be complete in itself. Some overlapping is doubtless inevitable, but it has seemed to the editors that overlapping is less regrettable than omissions, and from time to time the same series of events and the same actors will be seen from different points of view. While for the most part the series follows a chronological organization, separate volumes or groups of volumes will be devoted to cultural history, constitutional history, and foreign affairs.

HENRY STEELE COMMAGER
RICHARD BRANDON MORRIS

Preface

THE PRESENT volume attempts to provide a brief insight into the cultural developments of the thirteen British colonies which later became the United States during the period from 1607 to 1763. The year 1763 completes an era. The Peace of Paris, which gave the illusion of inaugurating an age of stability, actually saw the beginning of a period of domestic controversy and turmoil which would end in Revolution and Independence. This period of turbulence saw many developments and changes in the cultural attitudes of the colonies which are treated elsewhere in the series and are not within the scope of this volume.

Space limitations have prevented detailed study of cultural manifestations in all their aspects during a span of more than one hundred and fifty years. The decision on what to include in a survey of this type must necessarily be subjective, and I have tried to indicate the trends and developments that seemed to me most significant and important. If readers find their favorite areas of interest scantily treated, they will of course attribute the shortcoming to the bad judgment of the author, and he will plead the Procrustean necessity of sawing the material to fit the space.

In titles and quotations, I have consistently modernized both spelling and punctuation in the interest of smoother reading.

My indebtedness to countless authors of books, monographs, and articles I have tried to acknowledge in the footnotes and Bibliography, but the Bibliography has also had to be selective. I have tried, however, to suggest other bibliographical resources for more detailed references than space will permit here.

For criticism of the entire manuscript, I am particularly grateful to Richard B. Morris, one of the editors of the series. For suggestions and help with the chapter on "Architecture and the Decorative Arts" I am indebted to Charles F. Montgomery, director of the Henry Francis du Pont Winterthur Museum, and his colleagues. In gathering material for several chapters of the present volume I have had the help of Mrs. David Haynes, for whose assistance I am grateful. For help with the entire book I am under heavy obligation to Mrs. Virginia Freund, executive secretary of The Folger Library, whose painstaking care has saved me from many errors that I might otherwise have made.

Louis B. Wright

June 15, 1956

THE CULTURAL LIFE OF
THE AMERICAN COLONIES

CHAPTER 1

Agrarian Society and Leadership

FOR TWO hundred and fifty years after the first settlement at Jamestown in 1607, life in America was profoundly influenced by the nearness of the people to the soil. During the colonial period, even the largest cities were never very far removed from the back country that supported them, and town dwellers were in close contact with the farmers. In many instances they shared a large proportion of the interests and some of the activities of country folk. A prosperous trades- man of Boston might graze his cows on Boston Common and drink milk from his own dairy. A New York or Philadelphia merchant would expect to eat vegetables grown in his own kitchen garden, and he might own a nearby farm upon which he kept a watchful eye. In Charleston, South Carolina, even the wealthiest shipping magnates frequently owned plantations on which they lived during the cooler parts of the year. The highly organized division of labor which we know in a modern urban society did not exist. The country was close to the town, and the town knew country ways. The impact of the country was subtle and far-reaching upon both social and political life. Even yet many Americans will not concede that an urban civilization is superseding the mores and habits of an agrarian state, and many political clichés carry over from the time when America was pre- dominantly a nation of farmers. At the beginning of settlement and for many generations thereafter, agrarian society and the leadership that an agrarian society developed played a paramount part in the civilization of North America.

Tales about the New World and propaganda for settlement overseas convinced many of the colonists who came to Jamestown that they would find a land flowing with milk and honey. Consequently most of the settlers were ill prepared for the realities of life, but those who survived learned to adapt themselves to wilderness conditions. Although the newcomers showed little initial enterprise and skill in coping with nature, they gradually learned how to live off the land, even to eat Chesapeake Bay oysters, a hardship that brought complaints from some of them. In 1614 John Rolfe, famous for his marriage to Pocahontas, made a more notable contribution by shipping to London a cargo of tobacco and pointing the way to a money crop that would establish the colony's prosperity. By 1617 the inhabitants were planting tobacco even in the streets of Jamestown, and from this time onward the Chesapeake Bay area was committed to a one-crop system that determined the quality of its society. By chance the colonists had discovered a commodity that fitted perfectly into the mercantilist theories of the day. They were able to produce a raw product that could be shipped to England, processed there, and distributed at home and abroad at a profit.

The relative ease with which tobacco could be grown and transported, thanks to the country's innumerable waterways, made Virginia and Maryland a land of planters whose commercial interests focused on London and Bristol. And since it was discovered that tobacco exhausted the soil in about seven years, planters had to be sure of a succession of fresh soil, a fact that accentuated the normal land hunger. Much of the subsequent social history of the region may be explained in terms of this obsession with land.

A society of farmers, scattered over a wide area, labored under an immense handicap in developing the normal amenities that we associate with a civilized life. The maintenance of schools and churches, for example, posed a particular problem in a region where the principal method of transportation was along the waterways. Roads were poor and travel in the interior was slow and difficult. In times of bad weather the churches were often so inaccessible that funeral parties could not reach them, a condition that accounts for the development of family burying grounds so unlike anything in England. The isolated lives of the planters explain in part their openhanded hospitality, for any chance visitor might bring a bit of news from the world beyond the borders of the host's plantation. These planters could not ride to the nearest trading post, as the pioneers in the West were wont to do, and trade products of the land for manufactured goods. Although the larger planters frequently imported small quantities of goods for barter with their less prosperous neighbors, not until near the end of the colonial period would the Chesapeake Bay region have merchants with adequate stocks. The Virginian and the Marylander in the seventeenth and early eighteenth centuries had to depend upon ship captains from England for their merchandise, and London and Bristol were their nearest market towns.

As the settlers in the agrarian colonies pushed up the rivers and waterways into the interior and drove the Indians farther into the back country, the plantations in the older regions began to take on some of the look of a settled society instead of frontier outposts. Slowly the amenities of a cultivated way of life softened the crudities of the earlier days as the planters found time and opportunity for social intercourse. The quality of their houses improved; they imported more luxurious furnishings; they dressed better; a few had carriages or simpler horse-drawn vehicles; those who could imported books and hired schoolmasters for their children; they entertained their neighbors and friends with a little more attention to formality; they began to observe social "occasions"—the sovereign's birthday, the governor's ball, or some particular local holiday—and in time communities like Williamsburg, Virginia, Annapolis, Maryland, or Charleston, South Carolina, developed coherent social groups and a social season when planters and their families got together for entertainment, gaiety, and matchmaking.

In general, the upper planter class in Virginia, Maryland, and South Carolina made a conscious effort to imitate the county families of England. Land had always been the symbol of aristocracy in England. When rich merchants of London wanted to improve their social status, they sought to buy freeholds in the country, and to marry their sons or daughters to country gentlemen who could assure their heirs of being landed proprietors. In time the grocer's son, or at least the son's son, would graduate into the ranks of the gentry himself. In the colonies the transition in some respects was even easier. Land, the *sine qua non* of aristocracy, was easier to come by. Anybody with a little capital, or a large family, for each of whom he could claim fifty acres as headrights, could become a landowner. Land was the key to social status, and the more land a planter controlled, the greater was his chance of being a person of importance. The status that land conferred helps to explain the land hunger of colonists in all those regions where agriculture was the principal occupation. Planters wanted sufficient acreage to assure to each of their heirs adequate holdings. The law of primogeniture rarely operated in the colonies to exclude the younger sons and daughters from inheriting some portion of their father's estates.[1] Indeed, it was the hope of every provident father to make certain that each of his heirs had a piece of land as his portion. The eldest son might inherit the home place and its appurtenances, but the others might expect to receive farms that would permit them to continue to live in a style befitting their station.

It would of course be a grave mistake to assume that most of the planters were imitators of the English gentry, or incipient aristocrats. The numerical majority were plain farmers with holdings ranging from fifty to a few hundred acres. The work of the farm was performed with their own hands and those of their immediate family. Thomas J. Wertenbaker estimated on the basis of a quitrent roll of 1704 that only one Virginian in fifteen owned more than a thousand acres of land and the greater number depended on no help outside their families.[2] A few of the smaller farmers had one or two indentured laborers but most had none. They were yeomen farmers much like the independent yeomen of England. In the first seventy years of the seventeenth century, the yeoman farmer by his own exertions could farm successfully in the tobacco colonies and hope to compete with the larger planter. But with increasing production, tobacco prices slumped and the yeoman found it ever more difficult to make a profit by the labor of his own hands. He could subsist in reasonable comfort on the products of his farm and he could sell enough tobacco to provide for the necessities that he had to buy, but he could not expect to achieve any spectacular prosperity through his own individual labor,

[1] Cf. Thomas J. Wertenbaker, *The Old South: The Founding of American Civilization* (New York, 1949), pp. 328–329. A discussion of the operation of the law of primogeniture and of entails will be found in Richard B. Morris, *Studies in the History of American Law, with Special Reference to the Seventeenth and Eighteenth Centuries* (New York, 1930), pp. 73–82. For evidence of the small effect of the law of primogeniture in Virginia, see Clarence R. Keim, "Influence of Primogeniture and Entail in the Development of Virginia," University of Chicago *Abstracts of Theses,* Humanistic Series, 1926–27, V (Chicago, 1928), 289–292.

[2] Thomas J. Wertenbaker, *The Planters of Colonial Virginia* (Princeton, N.J., 1922), pp. 183–247.

as had happened to a few in the earlier days when tobacco was scarce and brought as much as sixpence a pound. When the price went down to a penny a pound or less, the advantage was all with the large planter who had white bond servants and black slaves to cultivate his acres, and a factor in London to look after the sale of his crop and purchase the supplies that he needed.

The growth of slavery from 1670 onward had a profound effect on the social structure of the southern colonies. It was responsible for a chasm between large planter and small freeholder, a chasm that grew wider as the eighteenth century wore on. Most of the economic and political power was in the hands of the great landowners. The small farmers sometimes accepted the situation silently, sometimes grumbled, and occasionally stirred themselves to overt hostility. But throughout the colonial period, the wealthier planters maintained political and economic control. In Virginia and Maryland they built great houses along the rivers, the James, the Rappahannock, the Potomac, the Patuxent, and other deepwater outlets to the sea. In South Carolina they established themselves at first along the Ashley and Cooper rivers, and later occupied the land along the other navigable streams. Unlike the Virginians, wealthy South Carolina planters also maintained town houses in Charleston, where they took refuge in the summer from the heat and the mosquitoes which made life unbearable inland.

Thanks to romantic novels, motion pictures, and amateur history written by ancestor worshipers, we have sometimes conjured up a picture of plantation life in the South, especially in Virginia, that rarely existed except in the imagination.[3] The very perfection of the restoration of colonial Williamsburg, with its fresh paint, polished floors, and handsome furnishings, has helped to confirm a belief in the myth of a land of gallant gentlemen and lovely ladies forever idling in a glossy paradise. In reality the members of the ruling class in Virginia, imitators of the county families of England, succeeded in establishing for a time a remarkable aristocracy that contributed some of the most effective leaders at the time of the American Revolution, but it was a hard-working aristocracy that tolerated little or no romantic nonsense.

The planters who made up this aristocracy were a diligent lot, intent upon the architecture of their own fortunes, determined to procure the means to be landed gentlemen in the English manner. Many

[3] Portions of this section are taken from a previously published essay, "Less Moonlight and Roses," *The American Scholar*, XII (1943), 263–272.

of them had come from simple origins, but land and wealth enabled them to acquire the accomplishments and qualities of the gentry of the mother country. Most significant of all, these planters carried over into Virginia not merely the outward forms of aristocracy but a sense of social responsibility that had characterized the English county families for many generations. The so-called cavaliers of Virginia had no time to be idle fops; they were too busy making a living, establishing families, and governing the country. The best of them also felt an obligation to cultivate their minds, pay some attention to religion, and see that their children got the rudiments of a classical education.[4] Though they were far from perfect in either manners or morals, they had the strength and ambition to establish an orderly society. The notion sometimes expressed by cynics that the wealthy planters monopolized all the civil and military power exclusively for their personal aggrandizement is demonstrably false. They had inherited from an earlier period a sense of obligation to serve the state, and they often filled tedious and unremunerative public offices without complaint. When militia duty was required, they served as a matter of course, even when it meant personal hardship and loss of valuable time.[5] Of the heroics dear to popular romance, there was next to none. Dueling was practically unknown.[6] That refinement of chivalry had to wait until our ancestors had steeped themselves in the tales of Sir Walter Scott.

The planters who made up the upper class in Virginia were not a numerous body, but they were enormously influential. From their group came the principal county officers, the judges, the colonels of the militia, the revenue officers on the rivers, the majority of the members of the House of Burgesses, and all of the members of the Council of State, which served as an upper house of the legislative body as well as a supreme court for the colony. These planters also

[4] Louis B. Wright, *The First Gentlemen of Virginia* (San Marino, Calif., 1940), *passim.*

[5] Charles S. Sydnor, *Gentlemen Freeholders: Political Practices in Washington's Virginia* (Chapel Hill, N.C., 1952), *passim.*

[6] Only a very few cases of dueling are recorded anywhere in the colonies and most of these date from the Revolutionary period. In some instances the men involved were Englishmen in the army, or in the naval service. See Evarts B. Greene, "The Code of Honor in Colonial and Revolutionary Times, with Special Reference to New England," *Publications of the Colonial Society of Massachusetts, Transactions,* 1924–26, XXVI (1927), 367–388.

served as vestrymen in the churches and as social arbiters in their respective communities.

Their economic power exceeded the mere land that they controlled and cultivated, for they often acted as agents for their poorer neighbors in the sale of their tobacco and the purchase of commodities abroad. Ship captains from England, it is true, came up the Virginia rivers and traded on their own accounts with tobacco farmers of all degrees; but since the acceptable unit of tobacco at a river landing was a hogshead of about five hundred pounds, farmers often found it more satisfactory to barter smaller quantities to the great planters who maintained regular factors abroad and imported supplies to trade with their neighbors. The rich planters thus became middlemen and made a profit on the transactions.

No colonial Virginian, however rich and grandiose, held any nonsensical notions about the taint of trade. William Byrd I laid the foundation of his prosperity by trading pots and pans, guns, and rum with the Indians in the interior. He also conducted a lively business in both Indian and Negro slaves. Charles Carter of Cleve and Nathaniel Harrison of Wakefield made money from the sale of ship biscuit to the captains of the tobacco fleet. William Fitzhugh of Stafford got rich as much from bartering commodities left with him by the ship captains as from growing tobacco.[7] The only trade that these wealthy planters despised was that carried on by seagoing peddlers in coasting ships from New England, traders who were willing to barter even with slaves for small quantities of tobacco and other produce.

One of the most ornamental planters of the early eighteenth century was William Byrd II of Westover, who conferred a favor on posterity by keeping an intimate diary giving a daily record of life on a large Virginia plantation. Byrd's diary destroys many of the romantic delusions that lovers of fiction have treasured.[8] He himself was one of the

[7] Wright, *First Gentlemen of Virginia*, pp. 47, 49, 52, 314–316, 343–344. See also John Spencer Bassett, "The Relation between the Virginia Planter and the London Merchant," *Annual Report of the American Historical Association for the Year 1901* (Washington, 1902), I, 553, 575.

[8] Two volumes of the diary are in print: *The Secret Diary of William Byrd of Westover, 1709–1712*, ed. Louis B. Wright and Marion Tinling (Richmond, Va., 1941), and *Another Secret Diary of William Byrd of Westover, 1739–1741*, ed. Maude H. Woodfin and Marion Tinling (Richmond, Va., 1942). A third portion of the diary, owned by the Virginia Historical Society and covering the years 1717–21, is now being edited for publication by Louis B. Wright and Marion Tinling.

most cultivated Americans of the first half of the eighteenth century. He had received his education in England and had been a member of the Middle Temple. His father had also sent him to Holland to learn something about business methods there, and he had served a brief apprenticeship with Perry & Lane, merchants of London. During his residence in London, Byrd became the familiar friend of writers like Wycherley and Congreve and tried his own hand at literary exercises. In due time he was invited to become a member of the Royal Society and contributed a paper on observations of an albino Negro.

Byrd gathered one of the finest collections of books in the colonies, a library of more than 3,600 volumes, and he brought home portraits of his noble acquaintances in England, painted by some of the better artists. Throughout his life he kept up a correspondence with the Earl of Orrery, the Duke of Argyle, and other noblemen. His ancestral seat at Westover on the James was baronial in extent and luxurious in its appointments. The lord of Westover belonged to the ruling clique which controlled the colony, and he himself at one time or another held most of the important public offices. Surely here, if ever, was to be found the storybook cavalier.

Actually, Byrd was a hard-working man, so heavily invested that he was often in want of ready cash. To his dying day he was constantly revolving schemes of real-estate promotion to increase his revenues, for speculation in land, which would play such an important part in later American life, had already begun. From early morning until late at night he gave his attention to a thousand and one details concerned with the operation of his plantations. He personally superintended the planting of his orchards and gardens and the planning of his crops; and although he had overseers to carry out his orders, he supervised the management of farms from Westover to Richmond, a town which he laid out because he foresaw a time when the headwaters of the James would be a focal point of shipping. He operated a sawmill and a gristmill; prospected for coal, iron, and copper; bought up tobacco and shipped it to London; and continued his father's trade with the Indians and the traffic in slaves. When illness befell his family, his slaves, or his neighbors, Byrd personally dosed them, for he fancied himself something of a doctor and scientist. Because he believed that a gentleman should be a learned man, he set himself a discipline of study that would have shamed a cloistered monk: often he got up at three in the morning and read Hebrew, Greek, or Latin till breakfast, which consisted of a bowl of warm milk. In the evening he sweetened his reading with a sermon, usually one of Archbishop John Tillotson's.

Though Byrd—like most of his contemporaries—had little time for gaiety, he was no recluse and saint. If his frivolities lacked the dainty grace of Arcadian romance, they were infinitely more real and effective. When he went to Williamsburg to attend meetings of the Council of State, he and his fellow planters relaxed in the evenings. They drank deep and played late, and Byrd usually lost a tidy sum at dice or cards. He worried over his losses and periodically resolved to quit gambling unless his luck improved. He had an eye for every woman who passed, whether chambermaid or planter's wife, and he missed few chances to solicit their affections. A surprising number of chambermaids turned him down. Not even the presence of his wife dampened his ardor. One evening, after an exciting game of cards with Mrs. Chiswell, wife of a Williamsburg citizen, he "kissed her on the bed till she was angry and my wife also was uneasy about it and cried as soon as the company was gone." Not even fastidiousness, which one associates with the romantic concept of the cavaliers, restrained Byrd —a fact that is made evident by many episodes in his diary, written down with complete lack of regret.

Plantation life was not the smooth, well-ordered existence of conventional legend. Westover, which one can visit today and think of an the perfection of aristocratic elegance, knew much disorder and crudeness. Servants more often than not were untrained, ignorant, and slatternly. Indeed, the servant problem was one of Byrd's trials. On one occasion when his patience was exhausted he rose from the table and kicked the cook out of the dining room for bringing in the bacon half raw. But Westover was probably better run than many other planters' houses. Byrd frequently complains about the quality of the food and drink at the home of his brother-in-law, John Custis, and he remarks that the beds at Colonel Dudley Digges' smelled so bad that he could hardly sleep. Even Governor Spotswood had trouble keeping his servants in order. To be certain that house servants would be sober enough to look after guests attending a great ball in the Governor's Palace in celebration of the Queen's birthday in 1711, Spotswood allowed them to get drunk the next day by permission.

Manners among the upper planters in colonial Virginia were courtly, but not so courtly as we have been led to suppose. Men and women quarreled publicly and occasionally railed like fishwives. The noblest ornaments of society were sometimes drunk in public. If we may believe Byrd's statement, Mrs. James Blair, a member of the Harrison family and wife of the highest-ranking official of the Church of England, was habitually tipsy. She it was whom Daniel Parke, Byrd's father-in-law (and grandfather of Martha Washington's first husband), threatened to drag bodily from her pew in Bruton Church because of her gossip and her husband's sermon condemning Parke's adultery. The Reverend Arthur Blackamore was dismissed from his teaching post at William and Mary College for repeated drunkenness. George Mason, grandfather of the author of the Virginia Declaration of Rights, was drunk in the House of Burgesses, but that fact would have gone unobserved had he not betrayed Byrd as the author of a scurrilous lampoon on his fellow members.

The record of the daily routine of men and women who ruled Virginia destroys many illusions about their grandeur, but it also reveals another aspect of their lives—a stronger, more rugged side that gives a clue to an understanding of the leadership which they and their sons assumed. When we see these Virginians in their everyday clothes, without the silks and brocades worn when their portraits were painted, we realize that they were determined, forceful men, creating in the wilderness a society that one day would make a great nation. Often they worked under tremendous handicaps, handicaps that agrarian society still suffers: low prices, overproduction, high freights, a wasteful economy. But they succeeded in establishing themselves as independent, fearless citizens of a commonwealth that prized its heritage of the common law, the traditions and rights of free Englishmen. With all their ambition to acquire land and wealth—amounting at times to inordinate greed—they never made wealth an exclusive end in itself. Property they accumulated to establish their families that they might take their proper place as leaders in society. They enjoyed the emoluments and prestige of ruling, to be sure, but they had inherited from the past a tradition that obligation and responsibility went with privilege, something that was notably lacking in the men of great wealth in the Gilded Age of the nineteenth century. With all of their shortcomings, the gentlemen-planters of the early eighteenth century created a society that could produce Washington, Jefferson, Marshall, and other statesmen who shaped a new nation.

The most striking evidence in the documents that have come to light is the revelation of how hard the planter-aristocrats themselves worked. Few businessmen today slave longer hours at their desks than did these men in the management of their estates. Yet somehow they contrived to salvage time to cultivate their minds and to accept their share of civic responsibility.

One of the best examples of the "working gentleman" was Robert Carter of Corotoman, called "King" Carter because of his pride and the magnitude of his landed holdings. Like Byrd, his contemporary, Carter is traditionally remembered as a grandee, as a silken gentleman, engaging in the gaieties of tidewater society. Actually, Carter, the progenitor of the most numerous clan of Virginia aristocrats, spent most of his time in the exacting duties of managing his own estates and serving as agent for the Fairfax proprietary. A thin little manuscript volume of his letters, written between 1720 and 1727, now preserved in the Huntington Library,[9] provides a revealing description of his struggle to make a profit from growing and trading in tobacco. Not for a minute was Robert Carter negligent of business, as the cavaliers are traditionally supposed to have been. He was observant of every item of expense and every opportunity to make a profit. When his London factors were caught up in the speculative fever that culminated in the South Sea Bubble, Carter wrote urgent reproofs and warned against wildcat schemes of getting rich quickly. If other businessmen had taken his advice, fewer would have been ruined in the South Sea crash.

But Carter, like others of his Virginia colleagues, had vital interests outside of business. Perhaps that typical quality accounts for the distinction achieved by this group of colonials. Although the planter of Corotoman amassed great wealth and died in possession of 300,000 acres, money did not usurp his mind. He was interested in classical learning and in religion. One finds scattered through his letters observations that showed concern for intellectual and spiritual matters. To his agents in England he sent careful instructions about the supervision of his sons' education: they were to be placed in good English schools where they could learn the Latin tongue in the manner taught by Comenius, and they were to be brought up in the Church of England. In his own well-selected library, Carter, his family, and his friends could read not only the best of the classics but sound works of history, law, and religion. If his personal piety did not achieve per-

[9] *Letters of Robert Carter, 1720–1727: The Commercial Interests of a Virginia Gentleman,* ed. Louis B. Wright (San Marino, Calif., 1940), *passim.*

fection, he nevertheless believed that good government and a decent way of life demanded respect for religion, and he set an example to his community by regular attendance at Christ Church, where he occupied the best pew. Nor was he too busy to read extensively in sermon literature. Dr. John Scott's *Christian Life* was one of his favorite works.

On occasion Robert Carter could celebrate merrily with bottle and cards with his fellow councilors in Williamsburg, but neither he nor any of the others were idle dandies, living lives of flippant pleasure. That kind of aristocrat would have quickly suffered bankruptcy and ruin in colonial Virginia.

Robert Carter of Corotoman and William Byrd II of Westover, in their virtues as well as their faults, were typical of the ruling class of colonial Virginia. There were other founders of family dynasties who might be mentioned: William Fitzhugh, Ralph Wormeley II, Robert Beverley, Richard Lee II, and a score of others; but though they all had strongly marked individual qualities, they lived according to the same social pattern.

As the eighteenth century wore on, the dependence of the great planters on their English agents became more marked. Almost invariably they were in debt to the factors who sold their tobacco and managed their affairs, and almost invariably they were short of cash, a prevailing characteristic of southern agriculture from the beginning to the present day. The great planters found that they could not operate without slave labor, and yet that type of labor required such an outlay of capital and so much supervision that the planters themselves were in bondage to an unwieldy and inefficient system. To escape bankruptcy a planter required skill, diligence, and the capacity to adapt to changing conditions. Not all of them possessed these qualities. Toward the end of the eighteenth century, the grandson of Robert Carter of Corotoman, himself named Robert Carter, of Nomini Hall, realized the plight that he and his fellow planters were in and tried to do something about it. Carter tried many experiments. When tobacco proved unprofitable, he turned to grains, especially wheat, and to hemp, flax, and even cotton. Finding slave labor wasteful, he developed a system of tenantry and hired laborers. Not content with merely growing agricultural products, he bought and sold wheat in large quantities, milled his own grains, sold flour and meal, and baked bread on a commercial scale in his own ovens. He manufactured textiles on his plantation, invested in a textile mill in Baltimore, owned an interest in the Baltimore Iron Works, and for several years operated a salt works profitably.

Carter was a man of immense versatility, like many another of his class. He read the best Latin and Greek authors, and especially delighted in history, philosophy, law, religion, science, and the theory of music. He was a musician, a skilled performer on several instruments. Of a philosophic turn of mind, he was eternally searching for an abiding faith and was by turns an Episcopalian, a deist, a Baptist, and a Swedenborgian. Yet despite his diversity of accomplishments, there was not a suggestion of the overly polished gallant of eighteenth-century portraiture. A plantation was no place for the imitation of the manners and habits of a Georgian court. Thanks to Philip Fithian, a Princeton tutor who kept a diary covering his stay at Nomini Hall during 1773–74, we have a vivid picture of life in Carter's household, and Carter's own letters and account books reveal the complexity of life on a large plantation.[10]

Though Virginia's aristocracy has loomed largest in the public imagination in modern times, Virginia had no monopoly of aristocratic society. Other colonies, particularly Maryland, South Carolina, and New York, had clearly defined aristocratic elements, sometimes with even more of the trappings of feudal splendor than the Virginians could boast. Maryland, for example, a proprietary colony, with the Calverts as lords proprietors, saw an attempt to establish a manorial system of the traditional type. The Calverts in part succeeded, and in theory all landholders in Maryland were the Calverts' tenants, but the degree of tenantry differed. The Calverts gave to their friends and relatives vast estates which they tried to administer as English manors with all of the rigmarole of manorial courts. These estates might remain in the possession of the landholders for three lifetimes or longer, or for as long as they paid quitrents to the proprietors. The Calverts also leased smaller farms to yeomen who peopled the back country. The system of land tenure was a fruitful cause of disputes throughout the colonial period, but in effect there came to be very little difference between leasehold and freehold. Many settlers on the

[10] *Journal and Letters of Philip Vickers Fithian, 1773–1774: A Plantation Tutor of the Old Dominion,* ed. Hunter Dickinson Farish (Williamsburg, Va., 1943). See also Louis Morton, *Robert Carter of Nomini Hall: A Virginia Tobacco Planter of the Eighteenth Century* (Williamsburg, Va., 1941), *passim.*

frontier held their land by squatters' rights and succeeded in evading the payment of quitrents.

The great baronial estates in tidewater Maryland were similar to those in tidewater Virginia. The tobacco economy was identical and the quality of life was much the same. The labor system in this region in the eighteenth century was based more and more on Negro slavery as white indentured servants became scarcer. A few families in all of the tidewater counties acquired holdings that often comprised many thousands of acres. Charles Carroll of Carrollton, for example, in 1764 held 40,000 acres, 285 slaves, two houses in Annapolis, and much other property.[11] The greatest landholders, in addition to the Carrolls, were the Bennetts, the Lloyds, and the Dulanys, though every county had its quota of gentry who imitated in some degree the English county families.

The rise of the Dulany family is characteristic of the development of many American family dynasties in the colonial period and later. Daniel Dulany the immigrant was a Protestant youth from Queen's County, Ireland, who arrived in Maryland in 1703 with his two brothers. All three came as indentured servants. Daniel, who had spent some time at the University of Dublin, had the good fortune to be sold to Colonel George Plater, who needed a clerk in his law office. As so often happened, the law proved an avenue to advancement, and young Dulany in less than ten years was a practicing lawyer and a landowner in Prince George's County. He had made a good marriage to Rebecca, daughter of well-to-do Colonel Walter Smith. Dulany, like many Americans after him, grew wealthy, not merely from the dual activities of lawyer and planter, but from shrewd investments in land. He was one of the first to realize that the rich bottomlands in the interior—what was then the West—represented potential wealth, and he was a forerunner of the land speculators of the later eighteenth and nineteenth centuries. Dulany's son Daniel was a worthy successor to his father, and his other children, both sons and daughters, made up a dynasty of social significance in the colony.[12]

Annapolis was the social as well as the political capital of Maryland and by the mid-eighteenth century it was the center of such cultural

[11] Charles A. Barker, *The Background of the Revolution in Maryland* (New Haven, 1940), p. 37.

[12] For an excellent account of the Dulanys and their milieu, see Aubrey C. Land, *The Dulanys of Maryland* (Baltimore, 1955).

life as the colony had. There in 1727 William Parks established the *Maryland Gazette,* which lasted until 1734, to be followed by a second *Gazette* in 1745 published by Jonas Green, a durable and jolly printer. There from the mid-century onward could be seen an occasional play. There during the meetings of the legislative assembly came members of the wealthier families with their wives and daughters for balls and other festivities. Particularly gay was the celebration of the lord proprietor's birthday, when the governor entertained the elite at a ball and broached a barrel of punch for the common sort. The governor and his friends also gave their blessing to horse racing at Annapolis, one of the colony's favorite sports.

The Maryland planters prided themselves on their familiarity with the principles and practice of law, for legal knowledge was regarded as a necessary accomplishment of a gentleman. Charles Carroll wrote his son in 1759 to stick to his studies at the Middle Temple, for "It is a shame for a gentleman to be ignorant of the laws of his country and to be dependent on every dirty pettifogger." [13] The great interest in legal procedures helps to account in part for the popularity of the social clubs which had a particular place in Maryland life, especially in that portion of society based on Annapolis, for one of the favorite entertainments of the club was the mock trial. The most famous of these social gatherings, exclusively reserved to men, was the Tuesday Club, founded at Annapolis on May 14, 1745, under the leadership of a Scot, Dr. Alexander Hamilton, remembered also for his *Itinerarium,* the record of a journey through the colonies in 1744.[14] The Tuesday Club, limited to fifteen men, emphasized good conversation, raillery, good drink, and good fellowship, and elected Jonas Green to be its "poet, printer, punster, purveyor, and punchmaker." One subject, politics, was forbidden in the precincts of the club. Other clubs similar in purpose and quality flourished in Maryland.

The intellectual interests of the Maryland planters did not differ much from those of the Virginians. Many of them collected libraries of significance and gave evidence in their letters of having read their books; they occasionally wrote essays and verse for the *Maryland Gazette;* and they made a diligent effort to see that their sons and

---

[13] Barker, *Background of the Revolution in Maryland,* p. 41.
[14] *Gentleman's Progress. The Itinerarium of Dr. Alexander Hamilton, 1744,* ed. Carl Bridenbaugh (Chapel Hill, N.C., 1948), pp. xvi–xvii.

daughters acquired the kind of mental furniture that would keep them from being uncouth provincials.

In their religion, the upper planting group differed from the Virginians in that the Church of England was not the only faith of the aristocrats. Since the Calverts had intended for Maryland to be a refuge for distressed Catholics, some of the oldest and wealthiest families, such as the Carrolls, remained Catholic. In some of the northern counties, and in those areas chiefly populated by Scots, the wealthier planters were Presbyterian. But by the mid-eighteenth century, the Anglicans occupied the predominant place of social influence. It is perhaps significant that the Presbyterian Scot, Dr. Hamilton, under the influence of his aristocratic friends in Annapolis, decided to join the Church of England. The Anglicans were coming to occupy the place they would retain in large areas of the country, the faith of the socially elect.

The social structure of Maryland was more diverse than that of Virginia. Despite the relative homogeneity of the planter class in tidewater Virginia and tidewater Maryland, there were other elements in Maryland that made it anything but a replica of its southern neighbor. A large population of industrious Germans in Frederick County and other areas of the back country produced a variety of agricultural products, particularly grain and livestock, which found a market via overland roads in Baltimore, a port that by the mid-eighteenth century was showing signs of developing into a town of commercial importance. The sources of Baltimore's prosperity lay not in the tidewater plantations but in the growing back country where even the aristocrats were beginning to take up land as a speculation. Baltimore and Annapolis had little in common. Instead of the easy social life of Annapolis with its clubs and congenial gatherings of aristocratic planters, Baltimore had a bustling trade more characteristic of Philadelphia or Boston than of the South. Some of its richer citizens, to be sure, partook of the qualities of both planter and merchant, but the merchant would soon dominate in that area.

Far to the south in South Carolina, an aristocracy developed that combined with notable success the agrarian life of the plantations with the business activities of a city. The ruling class of South Carolina in the eighteenth century converged on Charleston. Indeed, as one historian has commented, the low country "focussed in Charleston to such a degree as to make the whole district in some sense a city-state." [15]

A part of Charleston's peculiar development may be attributable to the climate. The wealthy planters who built great houses along the rivers and made money growing rice and indigo could not endure the heat and mosquitoes on their plantations in the summer. They soon discovered that they could mitigate the tropical humidity in the country and perhaps save themselves from the chills and fever of malaria by taking refuge in a town house in Charleston during the worst months. Cooled by breezes from the Atlantic and cheered by a sufficient quantity of mint juleps, South Carolina planters found Charleston in the summer a gay and active place.

But the South Carolina planters were no more idle and frivolous than their Virginian counterparts. Indeed, they combined agriculture and business in a remarkable fashion and achieved prosperity that was in most cases economically sounder than that of the tobacco planters on the Chesapeake. Like the upper class in the other colonies, most South Carolina aristocrats were self-created. Not many of them with certainty could claim highborn ancestry, but they made the most of their opportunities once they came into possession of land and grew prosperous. Some of the more substantial settlers in South Carolina had come from Barbados with capital, slaves, and the knowledge of how to make their way in a new society. They were an enterprising group with no scruples against trade. Indeed, some of the best families engaged in the slave trade, selling African slaves to their fellow countrymen and exporting Indian captives to slave markets in the West Indies. They also found an important commodity in naval stores —rosin, turpentine, and ship spars—which the South Carolina long-leaf pine forests supplied in abundance. Many merchants were also the owners of plantations which received their personal attention. There was no social distinction between the upper planter group and the wealthy merchant group in Charleston. Indeed, frequently the same individual combined both interests. Despite the fantastic social hierarchy devised by John Locke and incorporated in the Fundamental Constitutions, this artificial hereditary system had little if any effect on the development of the South Carolina aristocracy. As in the other agrarian colonies, the families who established themselves with landed holdings and slave labor acquired in time the accomplish-

[15] Ulrich B. Phillips, *Life and Labor in the Old South* (Boston, 1948), p. 52.

ments and the recognition accorded the gentry, whatever their origins may have been.

One of the best examples of social evolution in South Carolina is afforded by the Manigault family, in the late eighteenth century one of the most polished and "acceptable" dynasties in the colony. The foundation of this family's fortunes was laid by Pierre Manigault, a Huguenot refugee craftsman, who arrived in Charleston in 1695, accompanied by his brother Gabriel, a carpenter. Gabriel died from injuries incurred when he fell off a scaffold. Pierre married Judith Giton, and after trying their hands at farming on the Santee, where Judith worked beside her husband in the fields, the couple moved to Charleston and opened a tavern. Pierre soon branched out and acquired a distillery and a factory for making barrels; he also built a warehouse and kept a shop on the docks. At his death he was well-to-do and bequeathed to his son Gabriel a comfortable fortune. Gabriel made the most of his inheritance and became South Carolina's wealthiest citizen, a planter, merchant, and slave trader. He had also made a good marriage and was accepted by the best families as one of them. In short, he had become an aristocrat and a patron of the arts. His son Peter, born in 1731, received a European education, learned the elements of law at the Inner Temple, made the grand tour, and returned to Charleston one of the most polished gentlemen of his time. The Manigaults and their family connections constituted one of the most important of the aristocratic dynasties in South Carolina. Like the Manigaults, other Huguenots married into English families in South Carolina, and in time their families became influential in the social structure of the colony.

The fact that Charleston was in effect a city-state and that the most cultivated group in South Carolina society spent a part of the year in the town, which was far more citylike than Williamsburg or Annapolis, inevitably gave an urban polish to the South Carolina upper class that could not be easily attained by the planters of Virginia and Maryland. By the end of the eighteenth century, though Charleston had a population of hardly more than fifteen thousand people, half of whom were slaves, it was, says Ulrich B. Phillips, "perhaps the most urbane of American cities, with a notable semi-public library, thriving bookstores, excellent newspapers, mantua makers and milliners in touch with Paris fashions, a thronged race course, dancing assemblies, and easy-mannered men's clubs." [16] The peninsula that projected into the harbor where the water was too shallow for commercial wharves was the site of the fashionable residential quarter. There well-to-do planters and merchants built great houses designed for comfort. Usually the houses had their ends to the street with the front facing a garden, and were so placed that sea breezes would cool their broad piazzas.

Possessed of the greatest per capita wealth of any city in North America, Charleston did its best to imitate the beau monde of Augustan London. Its leading citizens kept up with the fashions and the news of the English metropolis, and by the middle of the eighteenth century their punctiliousness of manners gave them an air of gentility hardly equaled by the English aristocracy in the same period. The Charleston nabobs were soon making a profession of being genteel and imitating the English gentry with a sedulousness characteristic of a society on the make. Wealthy families hired tutors and governesses for their children and frequently sent them to England or the Continent to finish their education. When they returned, insofar as they could, they tried to make Charleston a replica of the London of the Hanoverians. They established and supported a theater, they imported and read the latest books from London, and they organized concert groups and enjoyed music; in short, they established an urban culture of polish and sophistication.

But in the back country, up the rivers from Charleston, beyond the swamps and the sandhills, another society developed, a society dominated by small farmers, chiefly Presbyterian Scots from Ulster, with a sprinkling of Germans who had found their way from Pennsylvania and Maryland. They were a sturdy, thrifty lot who worked the land with their own hands and had as little as possible to do with the wealthy Anglican gentry of the low country. Indeed, from the beginning, a rift between the up country and the low country was discernible, a rift that widened until modern times. The low country during the colonial period maintained its political control, but the up country was biding its time. One day it would rule the aristocrats of Charleston who now regarded it with far-off faint disdain.[17]

[16] *Ibid.,* p. 52.

[17] The most accurate discussions of the Carolina back country will be found in Robert L. Meriwether, *The Expansion of South Carolina, 1729–1765* (Kingsport, Tenn., 1940); David Duncan Wallace, *South Carolina, A Short History* (Chapel Hill, N.C., 1951); and Verner W. Crane, *The Southern Frontier, 1670–1732* (Durham, N.C., 1928).

The back country of North Carolina was peopled by a variety of simple folk: refugees from competition with the slaveholding planters of Virginia, Quakers from here and there, Scots from both Ulster and Scotland, Germans from Pennsylvania, and various other folk who had little except their own labor to advance them. Only on the coastal fringe, chiefly in the Cape Fear region around Wilmington, was there an extension of the aristocratic planter group like that of South Carolina.

In the North an aristocracy small in numbers but powerful in political influence developed in New York. The Dutch had laid the foundations for a landed upper class by the patroon system, a system, it is true, that produced only one fully developed example, Rensselaerswyck; but that vast barony was a vivid reminder, if any were needed, of what land speculators might hope to attain in the period after the English occupation of New Netherland. A few powerful families succeeded in acquiring enormous holdings of land in New York, holdings that surpassed in size the estates of the aristocracy of the southern colonies. In 1693, Colonel William Smith, the easygoing chief justice of New York, received a grant of fifty miles on Long Island and established himself on the Manor of St. George.[18] Godfrey Dellius received in one grant 1,400,000 acres. Stephanus van Cortlandt bought up enough land from the Indians to establish his Manor of Cortlandt with approximately two hundred square miles in the Croton valley. Frederick Philipse had analogous holdings and was established in the Manor of Philipsburgh between the Hudson River and the Bronx.[19] Robert Livingston and Peter Schuyler also had vast tracts of land. In 1702, Caleb Heathcote became the possessor of the Lordship and Manor of Scarsdale under letters patent granted by King William III, "according to the tenure of our Manor of East Greenwich." [20] Sixteen of these baronial manors were granted in the colony of New York, and six were in the county of Westchester.[21] Heathcote's was the last and in some respects the most interesting because of the owner's reincarnation of the English gentleman with all the appurtenances that went with manorial rights. From all the

---

[18] Dixon Ryan Fox, *Caleb Heathcote, Gentleman Colonist: The Story of a Career in the Province of New York, 1692–1721* (New York, 1926), p. 83.

[19] *Ibid.,* p. 101.

[20] *Ibid.,* pp. 105–106.

[21] *Ibid.,* p. 99.

evidence, Heathcote took seriously his duties as lord of the manor. He had the right to hold courts leet and courts baron, and as justice of the peace he also presided over the county court. In short, Heathcote, like "Judge" Bean in the country west of the Pecos in a later day, was the "law" in that corner of Westchester County. The difference was that Heathcote received his rights and privileges as the symbol of law and justice through a formal tradition that crystallized in the Middle Ages.

Though the great landlords of New York were influential in politics, they never gave to New York the kind of aristocratic government that their counterparts in Virginia developed. From the beginning, New York society was too complex and contained too many hostile elements to permit the growth of a paternalistic aristocracy like that of the Virginia planters. In general the New York landlords showed more interest in trade and the legal profession than in the agrarian activities of the landed gentry to the south. The New Yorkers looked upon land as a form of capital investment while they followed vocations in business and in the law; whereas the planters of Virginia and Maryland looked to the products of the soil for their incomes. Merely living in the country and owning land does not make an agriculturist, and the great landowners of New York were concerned less with agriculture than with the investment aspects of their land. For example, Robert Livingston, the Scottish progenitor of a distinguished clan in New York, became town clerk of Albany in 1674 and within a few years had utilized so successfully his office and his opportunities for trade that he could acquire a manor in Dutchess and Columbia counties of 160,000 acres, but Governor Fletcher observed acrimoniously that "his being a little book-keeper, he has screwed himself into one of the most considerable estates in the province." [22] The great New York landlords represented a powerful and conservative influence in politics, though the Livingstons and some of their allies did lead a Whig faction which opposed the De Lanceys after the middle of the eighteenth century. William Livingston, grandson of Robert the founder of the manor, was a moderate Whig who exercised an intelligent leadership and tried to restrain the firebrands in the popular party.[23] Though public-

[22] See the *Dictionary of American Biography, sub* Robert Livingston. Further details will be found in Edwin B. Livingston, *The Livingstons of Livingston Manor* (New York, 1910).

[23] Dorothy R. Dillon, *The New York Triumvirate* (New York, 1949), *passim.*

spirited citizens like William Livingston were not unknown among the great New York landholders, most of them showed more interest in feathering their nests than in the service of the commonwealth. Though the families of these wealthy landowners produced many cultivated and polished members, their influence on New York's culture was far less than one would suppose. One can discount John Adams' sour observation that at the beginning of the Revolution New York had not a single cultured man,[24] but it is true that even early in the eighteenth century it was already apparent that the market place and material concerns would be determining factors in the quality of that colony's civilization.

[24] *Ibid.*, p. 15.

CHAPTER 2

The Gospel of Work
and the Aristocracy of Trade

I N THE tradition of American life, few ideas have received greater prominence than the notion of the dignity of labor and the virtue of diligent application to one's job, whatever it might be. From the earliest times to the latest lecture on "successful living" those related themes find expression in infinite variety and provide emphasis to the lesson that earnest industry is unfailing in its rewards. In colonial America this gospel was a part of the fundamental social doctrine of Puritans, Quakers, and others who reflected ideas that had received particular emphasis among the rising commercial classes of England during the late sixteenth and seventeenth centuries. One significant fact gave it greater pertinence in the New World than in the Old: in the New World, from the beginning of European settlement, labor was scarce, the returns from an individual's work were unusually high, and the opportunities to rise from a lower to a higher economic and social status were relatively constant. The cult of the self-made man had its American beginnings in the colonies, where success early came to be measured in material prosperity.

Countless treatises, handbooks, guides to conduct, sermons, and proverbs emphasized the value of sobriety, diligence, and thrift. The maxims of Benjamin Franklin, which summarized middle-class doctrines in the eighteenth century, had a long background which went back to the sixteenth and seventeenth centuries. For at least two centuries apprentices had been hearing the wise saws that Franklin put into the mouth of Father Abraham in *Poor Richard's Almanac* of

23

1758, an epitome of advice on how to get ahead that has come to be known by the title "The Way to Wealth." No book except the Bible has had a more continuous popularity in America or has exerted a greater influence on social ideas.[1]

The prudential virtues emphasized by the Puritans and Quakers [2] and their repeated injunctions against waste, extravagance, and ostentatious vanities were conducive to material prosperity and the development of a capitalistic milieu, but neither Puritans nor Quakers had a monopoly of these attitudes. They were characteristic of the rising middle class in England and they were translated to America to become a dominant influence in the English colonies. Max Weber's famous thesis that capitalism was an outgrowth of Calvinistic ideology was an oversimplification and a distortion of an idea that had more than a germ of truth. The Protestant ethic glorified those virtues that induced men to apply themselves to their earthly callings with cheerful diligence, that enjoined them to sobriety and thrift, and that urged them above everything else to avoid the waste of God's precious time lest idle hands find work for the devil. Sedulous observance of this doctrine made success almost inevitable in a country like America offering so many rich resources for exploitation. If a youth followed all the injunctions to work hard, to avoid extravagant spending, and to use his savings thriftily, there was little else for him to do except prosper materially.[3] He might not have time or opportunity to enjoy

[1] Louis B. Wright, "Franklin's Legacy to the Gilded Age," *The Virginia Quarterly Review*, XXII (1946), 268–279. For the background see also Louis B. Wright, *Middle-Class Culture in Elizabethan England* (Chapel Hill, N.C., 1935), pp. 170–200.

[2] The Quakers' attitude toward the virtues that induced material prosperity is admirably discussed by Frederick B. Tolles, *Meeting House and Counting House: The Quaker Merchants of Colonial Philadelphia, 1682–1793* (Chapel Hill, N.C., 1948), *passim*.

[3] See A. Whitney Griswold, "Three Puritans on Prosperity," *The New England Quarterly*, VII (1934), 475–493.

Much has been written about Weber's thesis, which has sometimes been misunderstood and misinterpreted. An adequate introduction to the controversy will be found in the following: Max Weber, *The Protestant Ethic and the Spirit of Capitalism*, trans. Talcott Parsons, with a Foreword by R. H. Tawney (London, 1930); R. H. Tawney, *Religion and the Rise of Capitalism* (rev. ed., London, 1936); H. M. Robertson, *Aspects of the Rise of Economic Individualism: A Criticism of Max Weber and His School* (Cambridge, 1933); Talcott Parsons, "H. M. Robertson on Max Weber and His School," *The Journal of Political Economy*, LXIII (1935), 688–696. This essay is one of the best balanced discussions of the subject. Other aspects of the religious attitude toward

his success, but it would accrue to him anyway as the blessing of God for his pious diligence.

If the Protestants, especially the Puritan elements in Protestantism, did not invent the gospel of work, they adopted it with such enthusiasm that it became a cardinal point in their social doctrine. One reason for the Puritans' insistence upon education was the fear that ignorance would beget idleness, and idleness, which was the waste of God's precious time—a recurring phrase in Puritan writing—was one of the worst of sins.[4] The Puritans were convinced that education increased piety and "piety bred industry," a desirable end in itself.[5] Judge Samuel Sewall, mindful of the waste of time on April Fools' Day, wrote to Ezekiel Cheever the schoolmaster on April 1, 1708, complaining about the foolish doings: "If men are accountable for every idle word, what a reckoning will they have that keep up stated times to promote lying and folly," he fumes. "What an abuse is it of precious time; what a profanation! What an affront of the divine bestower of it." [6] Sewall hoped that Cheever would warn his pupils against idleness and idle pleasures. Thomas Shepard, writing to his son at Harvard in 1672, warned him against wasting time: "Abhor therefore one hour of idleness as you would be ashamed of one hour of drunkenness." [7] Cotton Mather in numerous passages expounds the gospel of work and inveighs against the iniquity of idleness. When he looked about Boston at the turn of the century, he saw a relaxation of the early strenuousness that saddened him. "Idleness, alas!" he sighed, "idleness increases in the town exceedingly; idleness, of which there never came any goodness! idleness which is the 'reproach of any people.'" To Mather's distress, beggars had been seen on the streets of Boston, beggars whom "our Lord Jesus Christ himself hath expressly forbidden us to countenance." [8] If they refuse to work, the poor must not eat, Mather believed, for refusal to work was a sin against God himself.

industry, thrift, and related problems will be found in Ernst Troeltsch, *The Social Teaching of the Christian Churches* (2 vols., London, 1931), and Talcott Parsons, *The Structure of Social Action: A Study in Social Theory with Special Reference to a Group of Recent European Writers* (New York, 1937).
[4] Samuel E. Morison, *The Puritan Pronaos* (New York, 1936), pp. 63, 186.
[5] Samuel E. Morison, *Builders of the Bay Colony* (Boston, 1930), p. 169.
[6] *Massachusetts Historical Society Collections*, 6th Ser., I (1886), 365.
[7] Frederick L. Gay, "Letter of Thomas Shepard, 1672," *Publications of the Colonial Society of Massachusetts*, XIV (1911–13), 191–198.
[8] Cotton Mather, *Magnalia Christi Americana* (Hartford, 1853), I, 102.

The Puritan emphasis upon the value of incessant industry as evidence of godliness, and upon its corollary that God would reward pious diligence with prosperity, inevitably resulted in a doctrine that the indigent poor brought their poverty upon themselves; that they were culpable and a disgrace to a well-ordered society. An English historian, commenting on the social attitudes of the mid-seventeenth century, observes that the employer of a laborer "felt a glow of positive righteousness in making it difficult for him to fritter away his time in unproductive amusements. Long hours and low wages were a kindness to him if he did but know it. Even up to recent times the sight of a poor man amusing himself aroused a feeling of moral indignation in his superiors." [9] A Massachusetts law of 1646 prohibited certain amusements, such as "the use of shuffleboard and bowling in and about houses of common entertainment whereby much precious time is spent unprofitably," [10] and in 1715 a Connecticut regulation sought to prevent drunkenness and the "expense of precious time needlessly at taverns." [11] These prohibitions were designed to keep the poor from unprofitable leisure. The very fact that the poor had not prospered was indicative of their failure to live in accordance with Christian injunctions, and it was doubtful whether charity toward them was a virtue. The best thing that could be done for the indigent poor was to establish workhouses where the law could enforce the kind of incessant industry for which they had shown no liking. In England during the period of the Puritan Revolution, the debates on poor relief illustrated a growing attitude of illiberality toward the poor. "During the Commonwealth there were many schemes for ameliorating unemployment, but nearly all of them bore traces of a growing disposition to regard poverty as a crime and disgrace," observes Miss Margaret James. "Vagrants were to be treated with the utmost severity. . . . Few writers doubted that the idle poor were idle through choice." [12] This attitude was accentuated if possible in New England in the same period, and in part it helps to explain the reputation that New Eng-

[9] Margaret James, *Social Problems and Policy during the Puritan Revolution, 1640–1660* (London, 1930), p. 22.

[10] G. F. Dow, *Every Day Life in the Massachusetts Bay Colony* (Boston, 1935), p. 110.

[11] Charles J. Hoadly (ed.), *Public Records of the Colony of Connecticut, from August 1689 to May 1706* (Hartford, 1868), p. 502.

[12] James, *Social Problems*, p. 18.

land had for inhospitality toward strangers. Who knew but that the stranger within the gates tomorrow would be a charge on the township and a problem for the magistrates? Only diligent workers were welcome, and the authorities always wanted to be certain that a newcomer had an acceptable intent to work. If so, work was available and in the sweat of his brow he might attain the blessing of God and material prosperity.

The governments of all of the English colonies were concerned lest the indigent poor should become a burden. In general they followed the pattern of law laid down by English Parliaments for poor relief, but the administration of law varied from region to region. In New England it was under the supervision of the townships; in the South it usually came under the jurisdiction of the parish. "In the Middle colonies," Richard B. Morris points out, "poor relief administration combined features of the New England town system and the parish system of the Southern colonies. Persons obtaining relief were required to wear a badge. In New Jersey the pauper had to wear on the shoulder of the right sleeve a large blue or red 'P' together with the first letter of the name of the city or county in which he resided." [13] The purpose of the laws was to make poverty so disgraceful that a man would labor to the extent of his capacity to avoid such a stigma.

Laws, public opinion, religion, and opportunity all combined to encourage diligence and thrift. If not everybody prospered in the colonies, the great majority of honest hard-working men made their own way and improved their lot. From the first settlements to the end of the colonial period, wages were prevailingly high. Indeed, the high cost of labor accounts for the failure of certain industries like silk growing, which required a steady supply of highly skilled workers, a type always scarce in the colonies. Throughout the colonial period, local authorities were constantly struggling with regulations designed to protect employers from exorbitant charges for duties performed by porters, draymen, smiths, millers, ferrymen, and similar servants of the public; but in general the effort to fix maximum wage rates in the manner that had prevailed in England before the Statute of Artificers of 1563 failed because of the pressing demand for skilled labor.[14]

[13] Richard B. Morris, *Government and Labor in Early America* (New York, 1946), p. 16.
[14] *Ibid.*, p. 20.

"The colonial workman commanded real wages which exceeded by from 30 to 100 per cent the wages of a contemporary English workman," Mr. Morris asserts. "All authorities agreed on the relatively high wages prevailing in the colonies. John Winthrop records the answer made by a servant to a master who had been obliged to sell a pair of oxen to meet his wages. The master told the servant that he saw no prospect of being able to continue to pay him. 'Sell more cattle,' said the workman. 'What shall I do when they are gone?' 'You can serve me and get them back' was the reply. John Winter wrote from Maine in 1639 that if the current high rate of wages continued, 'the servants will be masters and the masters servants.' " [15]

The opportunities for economic independence that this situation offered to skilled artisans and craftsmen persisted throughout the colonial period. The worker with a special skill, such as the cabinetmaker, the shipwright, the carpenter, the shoemaker, the tailor, and in fact almost any craftsman that ministered to the perennial needs of man, occupied a favored position. By his own hard work he could accumulate money, hire journeymen, and establish a business for himself. Even the unskilled worker could in time acquire land and by the labor of his own hands and those of his wife and children gain a competence. By the practice of the virtues laid down by Franklin in his *Autobiography,* any craftsman might hope to become well-to-do and to occupy a position of respect in society.

Conditions were not identical in all of the colonies, of course. In the northern and middle colonies, where towns had a greater development and there was more division of labor and diversity of occupations, the artisan and the skilled craftsman had larger opportunities. Furthermore, the white worker, whether he was a farm laborer or an artisan, did not have to compete with slave labor in these colonies. It is true that all of the colonies had some Negro slaves, but in the colonies north of Maryland they were not numerous enough to be a problem. South of Pennsylvania, however, the competition of white worker and Negro slave from an early date created a social problem that has persisted to the present day. Thousands of small farmers in the southern colonies depended upon the labor of their immediate families for their prosperity, and they quickly found that the great planters of the tidewater regions, with gangs of slaves to cultivate their tobacco or rice plantations, to cut their timber, gather rosin and make

[15] *Ibid.,* p. 45.

naval stores in the pine forests, and do all of the heavy work requiring little skill, were in a favored economic position. The political division evident in later periods between the up country and the tidewater regions had its beginning in the economic competition of the colonial period. On the lowest level, the least successful of white workers, nondescript itinerant laborers, sometimes transported convicts, sometimes ne'er-do-wells that crop up in any society—those denominated "poor white trash"—hated their Negro competitors with a virulence known only among those who struggle for survival in the jungle. That conflict of interest between "poor white" and Negro slave, which began in colonial days, resulted in an abiding hatred that developed into the most corrosive influence bequeathed to later times.

Although plantation masters tried with some success to train slaves in many crafts, white artisans were in great request in the South and commanded high wages. The newspapers of the southern colonies are filled with notices of services and advertisements for skilled help. Although competition with slaves brought a certain loss of prestige to the white worker in the South, we are likely to forget the great numbers of respectable and often prosperous craftsmen in the South, particularly in centers like Charleston. In our preoccupation with the great planters we are also likely to forget the large proportion of independent small farmers, especially in the upland regions. They hung on, worked hard, and the best of them prospered moderately. Their condition improved as transportation to market towns grew easier. By the end of the colonial period, food grains and cattle from the up country were becoming profitable commodities and were bringing increased prosperity to the small farmers of that region. Thus, even in the slaveholding sections, the industrious worker, either farmer or craftsman, might hope to prosper far beyond the possibilities in the Old World.

In contrast to the Old World, the colonies offered the poor man who was industrious and thrifty the opportunity of acquiring land and a house of his own. The rising economy also tended to increase the value of his property and made it possible for him to add to his landed possessions and improve his status. The increase in the value of real estate, especially in the towns, produced a situation that became characteristic of America, that of descendants reaping a large increment of value from land obtained for a small price by their fathers. In the urban areas, particularly in New England, the poor man's children could also obtain the rudiments of an education in the town schools, for opportunities for higher education were not restricted to the well-to-do. Nobody in colonial America, to be sure, believed that society owed every child the ultimate in education, but intelligence, industry, and thrift combined with ambition got many a poor man's son into the colonial colleges. From the beginning, American society was flexible and fluid. Nowhere did society harden into a caste or even into rigid classes. Though the Virginia planters, the South Carolina aristocrats, and the great merchants of New England had family pride in a superabundance, not even they were able to fix upon the colonies a rigid and lasting class stratification. Not that colonial Americans understood the meaning of democracy as we interpret the term, not even in New England with its town meetings, for differences in economic status quickly produced distinctions in social position, but always there was opportunity for the industrious and thrifty to rise to the surface and take their places as men of property—and prestige.

Early in the development of the port towns of New England and the middle colonies, enterprising merchants laid the foundation of commerce and business that would permanently affect the course of American history and have a profound influence on the quality of American civilization. Within two generations after the settlement of Boston, Newport, New York, Philadelphia, and other towns, merchants and traders were adding ships and warehouses to their possessions, accumulating working capital, building comfortable and sometimes imposing houses, and establishing family dynasties. They were the mercantile aristocracy, a powerful and proud group, who would grow in greatness throughout the colonial period and would give over their power only when the *nouveaux riches* from among the Civil War profiteers overthrew them in the Gilded Age of the later nineteenth century. Some of them developed a pride of family and place that equaled if it did not exceed the pretensions of the planter aristocracy in the southern colonies.

New England was as class-conscious as any other section and boasted among its original settlers families of aristocratic pretensions like the Winthrops, Saltonstalls, Downings, Johnsons, Dudleys, and many others.[16] Also among the founding fathers were representatives

[16] Charles M. Andrews, *The Colonial Period of American History: The Settlements* (New Haven, 1935), I, 500–501; Samuel E. Morison, "Precedence at

of the merchant and tradesmen classes of London with capital enough to make a sound start in the new country, men who quickly established themselves and set about improving their status. Within the first generation some of them had made money enough to go back to England and live out their lives in ease, but most of those who prospered, choosing to cast their lots with the new country, became the ruling aristocracy, an aristocracy who represented often a fusion of families of ancient lineage with the new mercantile fortunes. Something of the same sort was happening in Old England, as had long been the case in that flexible society, but the transformation took place more quickly in the New World and the development was less hindered by entrenched landholders and the encrustation of local customs and prejudices.

Puritanism had gained a great hold on the tradesmen and mercantile classes of seventeenth-century London, and a concern about the dominance of bishops, coinciding with the depressions of the early years of Charles I, persuaded many of them to emigrate to Massachusetts Bay. On arrival they turned to the occupations that they knew best and set up shop in Boston, Salem, Roxbury, or some other town. Many of the merchants who first rose to prominence in New England had their beginnings as London tradesmen of one kind or another.[17]

The succinct and vivid account of the career of John Hull, goldsmith and mintmaster of Boston, in Samuel Eliot Morison's *Builders of the Bay Colony* provides a classic statement of the development of seventeenth-century trade in New England. Hull's success, like that of many of his contemporaries, may be attributed to his ingenuity, his everlasting industry, and that quality of imagination which Americans like to think is characteristic of business enterprise. Son of a blacksmith of Market Harborough, Leicestershire, who brought him to Massachusetts Bay in 1634, John Hull as a child helped his father with the farm work; but by the time he was eighteen he was already

Harvard College," *Proceedings of the American Antiquarian Society,* XLII (1932), 371–432; and *Builders of the Bay Colony,* pp. 83–84, 162.

[17] Bernard Bailyn, *The New England Merchants in the Seventeenth Century* (Cambridge, Mass., 1955), pp. 101–102. A recent book, Allen French, *Charles I and the Puritan Upheaval* (Boston, 1955), discusses the quality of the emigrants in the Great Migration with somewhat too great an emphasis on the religious motivation.

a goldsmith's apprentice, a trade that he was to follow for the rest of his life, albeit combined with multifarious business affairs.

Hull came to manhood at a time when New England had to change its business habits to avoid bankruptcy. During the decade of the heavy migrations from England, 1630–40, a combination of farming and local trade had been profitable, for many of the new arrivals came well stocked with money and goods and were eager to buy the wherewithal to start life in the colony. Sale, barter, and exchange between old and new inhabitants, and shipment of surplus stocks of furs and fish to England, made up most of the early trade. But with the beginning of the Puritan Revolution and the reduction of emigration to New England, the colonists had to think of some other way of living. The drying up of the flow of new money from England brought on a crisis that forced the settlers to turn to fresh avenues of trade. They developed shipbuilding and even set up an ironworks. Yankee ingenuity first demonstrated its promise in these critical years as the colonists turned to foreign trade. From the 1640's onward, New England found in the Caribbean and the Mediterranean an outlet for the abundant produce of its fisheries, and the products of its forests as well as its farms. Codfish, barrel staves, wooden ware, food grains, salt pork, salt beef, ships' stores, and even the sturdy oak vessels themselves, built in dozens of New England shipyards, became articles of commerce. Horses to haul the cane and propel the grinding mills of the sugar factories in Barbados and the other sugar islands were in demand. The shippers brought back wine from Spain and the Madeiras, iron and salt from Spain, and a variety of luxuries including Seville oranges and Malaga grapes, for already by the mid-seventeenth century many New Englanders were prosperous enough to indulge their tastes and fancies.

The details of the trade and the routes varied but the principles were the same. New Englanders learned that money was to be made not merely from their own products but from the transport of products wanted by the rest of the world, whether those products originated in some other colony of the New World, in the West Indies, the coast of Africa, or Europe. By the end of the seventeenth century, two new elements came into the trade to enrich New Englanders: these were the manufacture of rum and the traffic in slaves. Newport slavers exceeded those of all the other port towns engaged in the latter traffic, but Boston was one of the largest producers of rum, a *sine qua non* in the barter for slaves on the Gold Coast. The famous triangular trade between New England, the West Indies, and the coast of Africa, which was the basis of New England's prosperity in the eighteenth century, had its beginnings in the experimental trading ventures of Puritan merchants like John Hull in the preceding century.

Hull was too early for the full-blown rum-and-slave trade, but, though he inveighed against "man-stealing" of Indians, on one occasion he did ship two Negro slaves to Madeira in exchange for red wine.[18] God-fearing and pious, he was much troubled in mind when a shipment of logwood, a tropical dyewood much in request in England, turned out to be the wood of plum trees.[19] To his ship captains he issued instructions that they were to leave no debts behind them; they were to be mindful of the decent behavior of their men; and they should be "careful to see to the worship of God every day on the vessel and to the sanctification of the Lord's day and suppression of all profaneness that the Lord may delight to be with you and his blessing upon you. . . ."[20] Here was a man careful of his credit and reputation in a way that would have pleased Franklin—or the preachers of Hull's own day. Here too was a man imaginative in exploring all the avenues of commerce: trade with Virginia for tobacco for shipment to Ireland or England in small vessels which brought back textiles and other manufactured products, some of which he sold in New York. He had vessels in the wine and sugar trade between Boston, the West Indies, and Spain and Madeira. He shipped horses raised on his own farm to Barbados. Indeed, there was scarcely any type of legitimate trade that his small vessels, the *Seaflower, Hopewell, Dove, Society, Tryall, Friendship,* and others, did not engage in, for honest John Hull was as resourceful as the best of the Yankee businessmen.

More than that, he was a skilled craftsman who turned out handsome silver cups, pitchers, bowls, pins, buttons, buckles, and in fact anything required by the inhabitants of growing Boston and its environs. His reputation and skill made him the natural choice for mintmaster, and with his partner, Robert Sanderson, they coined the famous pine-tree shillings as well as sixpence and threepence pieces.

[18] Morison, *Builders of the Bay Colony,* p. 173.
[19] *Ibid.,* pp. 173–174.
[20] *Ibid.,* p. 171. Letter of Hull to John Alden, shipmaster of the ketch *Friendship,* dated Sept. 18, 1671.

So profitable was this venture that a legend grew up that Hull gave his daughter Hannah her weight in silver shillings when she married Samuel Sewall the diarist, an amount magnified in the telling to £30,000, though actually it was £500 paid in installments.[21] Through his own diligence and ingenuity, Hull had become one of the first citizens of Boston, the owner of a fine house, of many ships, of town lands and farms, and of riches sufficient to warrant such a legend as that of his daughter's dowry. If not the first self-made man of wealth in America, he at least typified the cult of success that was to dominate so much of American thinking in the generations to come.

The business success of John Hull was paralleled in greater or lesser degree by countless craftsmen, tradesmen, shipmasters, and merchants in the maritime regions from Maine to Maryland. The wealthiest and the proudest were the great merchants, those who owned ships and had business with the ends of the earth. They became the aristocrats of the colonial business world, and many of them looked down on lesser folk, but they had no monopoly either of prosperity or of pride. A spirit of independence permeated all ranks of business and many a craftsman rose to prominence. As in all societies, there was an ebb and flow of fortunes and social positions as new people accumulated money. A Boston record of December 6, 1644,[22] disclosing the merchant Valentine Hill's foreclosure of a mortgage on John Winthrop's "mansion house," is symbolic of the social rise of the men of trade. Hill, incidentally, was one who placed great faith in the doctrines of William Perkins and held in high regard Perkins' *A Cloud of Faithful Witnesses Leading to the Heavenly Kingdom,* a favorite work of the merchant classes, which showed by scriptural examples how faith in the Lord led to worldly success.[23]

The art of getting ahead, set forth in many a tract, was exemplified in hundreds of families who began as humble artisans, farmers, or fishermen and rose to wealth and prominence. Nobody was so foolish as to speak scornfully of trade, no matter to what high eminence he came, for trade was the means by which men attained to leadership and prestige in the northern and middle colonies. Examples of this climb to success can be picked almost at random from the leading

[21] *Ibid.,* pp. 138, 153–154.
[22] *Massachusetts Historical Society Collections,* 2nd Ser., XI (1896–97), 185–186.
[23] Wright, *Middle-Class Culture,* p. 282.

families of nearly any town. For example, particularly notable was the Burrill family of Lynn, Massachusetts, called for its prominence "the Royal Family of Lynn." [24] The first of the line was a farmer, George Burrill, who received a grant of two hundred acres of land in 1638. From him sprang a numerous progeny listed in the next two generations as shoemakers, tailors, coopers, tanners, maltsters, sailmakers, seamen, and almost every other trade common in Massachusetts. Gradually Burrills acquired more and more property and attained to posts of increasing responsibility. John Burrill, who died in 1703, a maltster and tanner, was a lieutenant of militia; his son John, a well-to-do farmer, was a captain in King Philip's War, speaker of the legislative assembly of Massachusetts for ten years, a justice of the peace and a judge of Essex County, and the holder of sundry other offices. When he died in 1722 he willed his silver-headed rapier to his brother Colonel Theophilus Burrill. The latter, described as tanner, yeoman, and finally esquire, married as his second wife the sister of the Reverend Edward Holyoke, president of Harvard College. A swarm of other Burrills throughout the eighteenth century played useful and often prominent roles in Massachusetts, earnest, hard-working, and highly respected as the first citizens of their communities.

The career of Robert Sedgwick, a tradesman, who arrived in Boston in 1636 and settled at Charlestown, throws light on the general attitude toward the retail shopkeeper, sometimes looked down upon, it is supposed, by the greater merchants. Nobody appears to have scorned Robert Sedgwick, who kept a clothing shop, though he was admonished once by the magistrates for selling goods at too high a price. His shop prospered and he built wharves and warehouses, bought ships and land, and joined John Winthrop, Jr., in establishing the first furnace and ironworks at Lynn. A venture probably closer to his heart even than his business was the Ancient and Honorable Artillery Company which he helped organize in imitation of the famous London company. He became its captain in 1641. On a visit to England in 1654, he attracted the favorable attention of Oliver Cromwell, who appointed him and Captain John Leverett to lead an expedition against the Dutch on the Hudson. Though peace with the Dutch was made before Sedgwick had time to earn any glory, he did lead a successful expedition against the Acadians in 1654 and in 1656 was made

[24] Frank A. Gardner, "The Burrill, Burrell Family of Essex County," *Essex Institute Historical Collections,* LI (1915), 271–281.

commander of the troops ordered to the recently captured island of Jamaica. There, unhappily the erstwhile shopkeeper died, full of piety and honors, a soldier after the Lord Protector's own heart.[25]

More spectacular was the rise of the Pepperrell family. The first William Pepperrell, a native of Tavistock, came to Sable Island in 1676 as a fisherman, but soon moved to Kittery on the mainland and had the good judgment to marry Margery Bray, daughter of a prosperous citizen. Continuing to fish, he added lumber to his interests and built up a good business in fish, lumber, provisions, and ships' stores. His son William, born in 1696, in time became a partner in the business, which multiplied until the Pepperrells controlled the largest mercantile operations in Maine with ships carrying lumber, fish, and other products to the West Indies and Europe.[26] Investing their profits in lands, they soon possessed a vast territory. The family business often took young William Pepperrell to Boston, where he met and married Mary Hirst, granddaughter of Samuel Sewall. Governor Jonathan Belcher took a liking to him and in 1730 appointed him Chief Justice of Massachusetts, a post which induced him to order a supply of law books from London so that he could inform himself on the intricacies of the law. For his services as commanding officer in the expedition that captured Louisbourg in 1745, he was created the first American baronet. When he visited London in 1749 the King received him and the City of London presented him with a service of silver plate. Thus had the son of a Maine fisherman risen in wealth and honor.

Another New England maritime trader who rose to prominence, got himself knighted, and lived in high style was Charles Hobby, a shipmaster of Boston, who dealt in slaves, West Indian sugar, and molasses. Happening to be in his sloop the *Sea-Flower* off Jamaica when that island suffered a disastrous earthquake in 1692, he gained a reputation by his rescue work. Back in Boston he became in 1701–3 captain of the Ancient and Honorable Artillery Company and so im-

---

[25] Henry Dwight Sedgwick, "Robert Sedgwick," *Publications of the Colonial Society of Massachusetts,* III (1895–97), 156–173.

[26] An excellent study of the two Pepperrells is Byron Fairchild, *Messrs. William Pepperrell: Merchants at Piscataqua* (Ithaca, N.Y., 1954), which has useful bibliographical references for the history of colonial trade. See also John Austin Stevens, "The First American Baronet, Sir William Pepperrell," *The Magazine of American History,* II (1878), 673–684; Luther Dame, "Life and Character of Sir William Pepperrell," *Essex Institute Historical Collections,* XXI (1884), 161–184; C. H. C. Howard, "The Pepperrells in America," *ibid.,* XXXVII (1901), 265–280.

pressed the Mather faction that they intrigued to get him appointed governor in place of Joseph Dudley, who had incurred their disfavor. When he went to London in 1705 bearing recommendations from that disgruntled faction, Queen Anne received him and dubbed him a knight, but she did not appoint him governor. A year later Sir Charles was back in his Boston countinghouse watching his business and taking an active interest in military matters and local politics.[27] The knighthood did not diminish his concern about trade.

Perhaps the most romantic success story in colonial New England was that of Sir William Phips, who began as an obscure Maine frontiersman and remained a ship's carpenter in Boston until he was past thirty. After his marriage to the widow of John Hull, who brought with her enough capital to enable Phips to become a shipbuilder on his own account, he began to prosper. Not content with building ships, he took command of one, and during a trading voyage to the West Indies picked up stories of treasure to be had in sunken Spanish galleons. In 1683 Phips managed to induce Charles II to give him command of H.M.S. *Rose* to try for a prize off the Bahamas, but nothing came of it. Still hopeful, he next gained the support of the Duke of Albemarle, and this time the venture succeeded. He and his crew found a hulk off Haiti and from it took a hoard of gold and silver, enough to make Phips wealthy and to win a knighthood in 1687 from James II. In the days of his poverty, Phips had yearned for a "fair brick-house" in the fashionable quarter of Boston. Four days after his knighthood, Lady Phips bought a mansion in Green Lane so that Sir William could live in the style to which he was not accustomed. Seeing in the colorful Phips a useful instrument for his cause, Increase Mather, who was in London trying to regain the old charter for the theocracy, succeeded in having Phips named royal governor of Massachusetts. As the Mathers expected, he proved a pliant tool for the theocracy, but not always an edifying example of Christian grace. On one occasion he dragged a customs officer off a wharf and publicly caned a captain in the Royal Navy, and he annoyed the pious and conservative aristocrats by consorting with some of his former shipmates and fellow carpenters. Samuel Sewall observed that he hoped Lady Phips' new mansion in Green Lane would not prevent

[27] Rollin G. Hubby, "Sir Charles Hobby, Early Knight and American Merchant Adventurer," *Journal of American History*, III (1909), 91–111.

her from inheriting a heavenly abode. But at length Phips attained that pantheon of the pious, Cotton Mather's huge compilation of biographies, the *Magnalia Christi Americana,* and was held up to the youth of New England as a glorious example of how God would crown "heroic virtue" with success.[28] If in actuality he was something less than a paragon of thrift, diligence, and sobriety, he was represented as having all these virtues in Mather's apotheosis.

Upon the varied trade carried on by New England shippers, many families grew to wealth and importance. In Salem, William Browne, who arrived from England in 1635, acquired enough money as a merchant to become a dominant figure in the commerce of the town and a notable benefactor of Harvard. One of his descendants of the same name married a Virginia woman, built a house in 1740 so grandiose that it was known as "Browne's Folly," and maintained a style that would have been the envy of most tobacco planters.[29] The Browns of Providence became an even more prominent family. Founded by Chad Browne, a pious Baptist who combined business with the vocation of preaching, the family flourished in Christian grace and gained in prosperity and influence. Chad Browne arrived in Boston in 1638, a little later moved to Salem, and eventually went to Providence for the sake of his conscience. From Chad descended numerous Browns in the next two centuries who became shopkeepers, mariners, traders, distillers, shipping magnates, merchants, and manufacturers. It would be hard to imagine Providence without the influence of the Browns, who throughout the colonial period maintained a prominent place in civic as well as commercial enterprises. The two brothers, James and Obadiah, in the first part of the eighteenth century, expanded the outlook and activities of the Providence Browns. James varied the life of a shopkeeper with going to sea and in 1727 we find him the master of the sloop *Truth and Delight,* surely a proper craft for a Baptist deacon, headed for Martinique with a cargo of corn, tobacco, cheese, tar, shingles, lumber, and eleven horses. On the return trip his cargo consisted of sugar and molasses for the rum distilleries which he was beginning to operate. Not only did he trade with the West Indies but

[28] Viola F. Barnes, "The Rise of William Phips," *New England Quarterly,* I (1928), 271–294; and "Phippius Maximus," *ibid.,* pp. 532–553.

[29] Ezra D. Hines, "A Stately Pleasure House," *Essex Institute Historical Collections,* XXXI (1895), 205–212; and also "Browne Hill in History," *ibid.,* XXXII (1896), 201–238.

his sloops carried on a coastwise traffic with ports as far afield as Charleston, South Carolina. Pious as was Captain Brown, he felt no pangs of conscience about smuggling to evade the payment of the sixpence-per-gallon tax on foreign molasses after the passage of the Molasses Act of 1733, and he gave his shipmasters careful instructions on ways to avoid the customs agents.[30] From this time onward, much of the trade carried on by enterprising American shippers was technically illegal, and the avoidance of the Molasses Act became a fine art in the colonies.

Obadiah Brown followed in his brother's footsteps and continued to expand the family trade. He added a "chocklit" mill to his enterprises and imported and ground chocolate beans. About the middle of the century he began the manufacture of spermaceti candles which became one of the important industries in Rhode Island.[31] During the Seven Years' War, when British men-of-war made trade with the French West Indies more difficult, Obadiah's vessels were constantly loading French sugar and molasses at the neutral Spanish port of Monte Christi in Hispaniola,[32] for the Rhode Island traders were adepts at trading with the enemy through neutral ports. Obadiah Brown's sons died before they reached maturity, but his four nephews, Nicholas, Joseph, John, and Moses, sons of his brother James, lived to carry on and multiply the Brown enterprises until the Providence Browns were among the important business dynasties of colonial America.

Every local history in New England and the middle colonies lists families of importance who owed their eminence to trade. Boston and Newport had numerous grandees who by the end of the colonial period were living in a magnificence that equaled if it did not surpass that of their counterparts in London or Bristol. They had fine houses, furnished in excellent taste, and the portraits of their wives, children, and themselves, done in oils by the best painters they could find, hung on their walls. Most of them had not begun as day laborers and artisans, it is true, but the majority of these families owed their start to a small shopkeeper, a shipmaster, a craftsman with a little capital, or a small landowner who had invested shrewdly. The Hancocks of

[30] James B. Hedges, *The Browns of Providence Plantations: Colonial Years* (Cambridge, Mass., 1952), p. 5. The spelling of the Providence Browns varied between Brown and Browne, with the e-less Browns apparently in the majority.
[31] *Ibid.*, p. 9.
[32] *Ibid.*, p. 8.

Boston, one of the most important mercantile families of the eighteenth century, looked back to an ancestor, Nathaniel Hancock of Cambridge, the town's shoemaker and the father of thirteen children. One son of Nathaniel, John, managed to get through Harvard and become a preacher at Lexington. He begot Thomas, who elected business instead of the learned professions, and was apprenticed to a bookseller of Boston. By 1735, he had prospered to such an extent that he had a thriving overseas trade in general merchandise and was rich enough to build Hancock House on Beacon Hill, which he filled with the best furniture obtainable in London. For his library he ordered the classics, well bound with gilt edges, and to one of his agents in London he wrote asking him to "look into the Herald'[s] office and take out my arms. Let it be [a] well cut crest and arms in silver fixed to ivory for the use of a counting room." [33] In this fashion the grandson of the village cobbler of Cambridge demonstrated his rise in the world. One way in which he had enriched himself was by the deliberate evasion of the British Navigation Acts, or in other words, smuggling. His nephew and heir, John Hancock, grew even richer, with an inherited distaste for the Navigation Acts and a zeal for patriotism that made him a signer of the Declaration of Independence. The Derby family of Salem, which rose to eminence in the eighteenth century, had a progenitor, Richard Derby, who started out as a soap boiler and proprietor of a small shop that sold among other things Bibles and psalmbooks.[34] Like the Hancocks, the eighteenth-century Derbys got rich in international trade and prospered in part by flouting the Navigation Acts. Many of the merchant families had members located at strategic points, one at Newport, let us say, another in the West Indies, and perhaps one in Charleston or in England. They maintained a close liaison with each other and watched their business with all of the care that the handbooks to success counseled.

Although Boston for a long time overshadowed New York in the ramifications and volume of its commerce, New York from the earliest days was noted for its singular devotion to business. An Anglican clergyman, John Miller, writing in 1695, commented that "merchandizing in this country [New York] is a good employment, English goods

[33] William T. Baxter, *The House of Hancock: Business in Boston, 1724–1775* (Cambridge, Mass., 1945), pp. 67–69.

[34] James Duncan Phillips, *The Life and Times of Richard Derby, Merchant of Salem, 1712 to 1783* (Cambridge, Mass., 1929), p. 2.

yielding in New York generally 100 per cent advance above the first cost and some of them 200, 300, yea sometimes 400 [per cent]. This makes so many in the city to follow it that whosoever looks on their shops would wonder where there are so many to sell there should be any to buy." [35] New York was already establishing its preoccupation with trade, a preoccupation that dominated every other interest and left little time for the arts, letters, or scientific speculation. By the middle of the eighteenth century, New York had many families of importance engaged in international trade, and they were already noted for their love of comfort and the increasing luxury evident in their households.

Large landholders, prosperous merchants, and influential lawyers made up the ruling aristocracy in New York. There was constant intermarriage in these groups and many of the leading families had members in all three categories. For example, the De Lanceys and the Livingstons, the great eighteenth-century rivals for political power, both could count among their relatives merchants, landowners, and lawyers. Stephen De Lancey, a French Huguenot merchant, married Anne van Cortlandt, who was descended from Oloff van Cortlandt, the Dutch founder of a rich merchant family. Stephen's son James became chief justice and lieutenant governor, and married Anne Heathcote, daughter of the landowner Caleb Heathcote. The De Lanceys continued to mix trade, landowning, law, and politics until the Revolution, when their Loyalist affiliations brought ruin upon them. Philip Livingston, grandson of Robert who founded the Livingston fortune, was an aristocratic merchant, a graduate of Yale in the class of 1737, a philanthropist, and a signer of the Declaration of Independence. Though the Livingstons were moderates and frowned on the goings-on of the radical "Sons of Liberty," their long fight against the reactionary De Lanceys made their sponsorship of the patriot cause inevitable. Philip Livingston, who married Christina Ten Broeck, lived the life of a lordly aristocrat with a splendid town house on Duke Street and a country house overlooking New York Harbor

[35] Victor H. Paltsits (ed.), *New York Considered and Improved, 1695,* by John Miller (Cleveland, 1903), pp. 45–46. An excellent discussion of the background of the New York merchants in the eighteenth century is Virginia D. Harrington, *The New York Merchant on the Eve of the Revolution* (New York, 1935). See also Dorothy R. Dillon, *The New York Triumvirate* (New York, 1949), which treats the careers of William Livingston, John Morin Scott, and William Smith, Jr.

on Brooklyn Heights. Few prouder citizens could be found than these aristocrats of trade.

Philadelphia in the eighteenth century surpassed Boston and New York as a center of commerce, and near the end of the colonial period, when it had become the second city of the British Empire, it boasted some of the most powerful commercial families in America. Many of these were Quakers who in their incessant industry equaled the Puritans. As the dominant political influence in the colony, the Quakers maintained a tolerant attitude toward all sects that encouraged other businessmen to settle in Philadelphia. As that port became the principal gateway for immigrants entering the colonies in the eighteenth century, the diligent Quakers could hardly fail to profit from local as well as international trade, and the increasing opportunities of the port attracted Quakers and others from various parts of British America.

From Barbados came Samuel Carpenter, the richest man in early Philadelphia [Frederick Tolles points out]; from Jamaica, Samuel Richardson, reputedly second only to Carpenter in the amount of his worldly goods. Isaac Norris and Jonathan Dickinson (1663–1722), great merchants and active figures in early Pennsylvania politics, also hailed from Jamaica. From Boston came Edward Shippen (1639–1722), who was reputed to be worth at least ten thousand pounds sterling, and who was known as the owner of the biggest house and the biggest coach in Philadelphia; and from New York, Humphrey Morrey (d. 1715/16), Philadelphia's first mayor, and William Frampton (d. 1686), owner of one of the first wharves on the Delaware river front. William Fishbourne (d. 1742), Samuel Preston (1663–1743), and Richard Hill, all substantial traders, removed to Philadelphia from Maryland, and Anthony Morris (1654–1721), a wealthy brewer, mayor of Philadelphia, and provincial councillor, crossed over from Burlington, New Jersey . . .[36]

Among these names are some who founded wealthy Philadelphia dynasties.

Men of Puritan background found themselves at home in the business atmosphere of Philadelphia, as young Benjamin Franklin discovered when he came as a lad from Boston. From all over the colonies craftsmen, traders, shopkeepers, shipmasters, and merchants of many kinds flocked to Philadelphia to share in the business that Quaker tolerance had made possible. Quakers and non-Quakers flourished together and grew rich.

[36] Tolles, *Meeting House and Counting House,* pp. 43–44.

They did not always live in complete harmony, however. Non-Quakers asserted that the Quakers were a closed corporation with secret communications and secret intelligence in all parts of the world that gave them an advantage over other folk, a belief that was in part true, for Quakers did maintain a wide correspondence and were inclined to do business with their own kind. The Quakers also adhered to a somewhat stricter code in regard to the Navigation Acts [37] than the Puritans of New England and the Presbyterians of Philadelphia, who had little compunction about smuggling or discreet trading with the enemy in time of war.

The increase of wealth in Philadelphia softened in some degree the Quaker resolution to adhere to a simple life. Under the impact of prosperity Quaker merchants built commodious houses, furnished them luxuriously, and lived in much the same style that other grandees affected. The love of finery in household furnishings and even in dress disturbed some of the stricter Quakers, who at intervals in the monthly meetings made objections that had no visible effect. Quakers like James Logan, Jonathan Dickinson, and others had houses as fine as any Anglican in Philadelphia. Dickinson had a great quantity of silver plate engraved with his coat of arms and maintained a coach similarly emblazoned. When Isaac Norris in 1713 ordered a coach "like Jonathan Dickinson's," he felt squeamish about having a crest painted on it and settled for his initials. When it came to liveries for his coachman and footmen, he blamed his wife for this ostentation and compromised by ordering liveries "strong and cheap, either of a dark gray or sad color." [38]

Great as was the concern of the Quakers for business, they did not let it monopolize their activities. They collected libraries, read good books, took an interest in scientific activities, and helped in making Philadelphia a focal point of intellectual activity that surpassed Boston by the end of the colonial period. The notion that the Quaker merchants were laggards in cultural matters is not borne out by the facts. One has only to mention James Logan, Isaac Norris, and a notable group of enlightened Quaker physicians to disprove this belief. [39]

As the main avenue to success in the Middle Ages had been through the church, so the surest road to prosperity and prestige in British

[37] *Ibid.*, p. 79.
[38] *Ibid.*, p. 131.
[39] *Ibid.*, pp. 101–204, 222–224.

America was through the merchant's countinghouse. In the southern colonies, it is true, the agrarian aristocracy attained to great social significance and contributed importantly to the intellectual leadership of the colonies and of the new nation after 1776, but they also respected trade. No Virginia planter of the eighteenth century was too proud to turn an honest penny in the way of business. Henry Laurens, one of the most distinguished leaders in South Carolina during the Revolution, was the son of a French Huguenot saddler who made money in his trade and acquired substantial property in and around Charleston. Henry became a prosperous merchant dealing in rice, deerskins, indigo, and slaves. This last branch of trade he disliked and gave up. His profits he invested in lands and he became one of the influential planters of the coast country. Henry Laurens, merchant and planter, was as much an aristocrat as the best of the South Carolina grandees, and nobody would have thought of denying his standing and prestige in the community. Thus it was that trade brought not only wealth but an honored place in the social hierarchy even in those colonies where planter families predominated.

The rise of men like Henry Laurens or Thomas Hancock or Richard Derby, or a thousand others throughout the thirteen colonies, is characteristic of the American success story. Colonial men of business took pride in their prowess, and they gloried in their ability to achieve a success often in the face of hardships. If they were not so blatant as their nineteenth-century counterparts in proclaiming that they were self-made men, it was perhaps a result of their piety which made them give greater credit to God for blessing their virtues of thrift, diligence, and sobriety. During the eighteenth century particularly a new emphasis is discernible, an emphasis upon daring and audacity in business, qualities that became a *sine qua non* in the legendary of the nineteenth-century industrialists. The glorification of trade and the apotheosis of the successful businessman, which reached their culmination when the American public finally placed a halo on the brows of Andrew Carnegie and John D. Rockefeller, had their beginning in the colonial period when Cotton Mather could see only virtue in William Phips and other Bostonians took off their hats to Peter Faneuil, the successful slave trader, and to Thomas Hancock, dealer in contraband molasses and other illegal wares. Colonial Americans began the tradition of giving the highest awards of prestige to their fellows whose diligence and audacity succeeded.

CHAPTER 3

Non-English Elements and Their Influence[1]

THE CONCEPT of the United States as a great melting pot of all nations and races was a favorite theme for essayists and orators in the heyday of foreign immigration a generation or more ago. Near the end of the colonial period, Hector St. John de Crèvecoeur, a Frenchman naturalized in New York, commented on this melting pot out of which came a new man, an American, changed and different from the Englishman, Dutchman, Frenchman, German, or Jew who had arrived as an immigrant on these shores. The metaphor coined by de Crèvecoeur and used by countless writers since that time suggests an extraordinary power of assimilation possessed by the civilization developed in British North America, an assimilative process that has taken a mass of polyglot material and created from it a relatively homogeneous people. From the earliest times, the New World attracted all sorts and kinds of men, some of whom left their impression upon their adopted country. If the melting pot fused them all into something new, nevertheless these new Americans could not help bearing evidence of their complex origins.

Social historians of late have shown a growing interest in analyzing the various ores that went into the melting pot and of demonstrating that not all of it fused completely. Nevertheless the metaphor is essentially an accurate one.

What analyses have shown is that the percentage of English in the

[1] This chapter will exclude consideration of the American Indians and African slaves, who are treated in other volumes in this series.

colonial population is not so overwhelming as was formerly believed. The most careful study of the distribution of population on the basis of national origins was that made in 1927 by a group of scholars under the auspices of the American Council of Learned Societies, using the statistics of the first federal census of 1790.[2] This study, employing linguistic techniques in the analysis of family names, revealed that of the total white population of 3,172,444 in the United States, 60.9 per cent were English; 14.3 per cent were Scotch and Scotch-Irish from Ulster; 8.7 per cent were German, 5.4 per cent were Dutch, French, and Swedish; 3.7 per cent were South Irish; and 7 per cent were unassignable and miscellaneous.[3] Thirty years before, in 1760, the proportion of English stock was probably slightly higher, but the figure for 1790 will provide at least an indication of the distribution according to national origins near the end of the colonial period.

A few non-British foreigners found their way to England's first permanent colony. Among the Jamestown settlers as early as 1608 were Poles and Germans who were induced to come as experts in the erecting of sawmills and the making of glass, tar, pitch, and potash, but their presence and skill were not sufficient to make a success of these ventures. In 1621, the Virginia Company of London again made an effort to promote glass manufacture at Jamestown by sending out four Italian craftsmen who proved so intractable and difficult that George Sandys, the colony's secretary, declared that "a more damned crew hell never vomited." [4] Though at least two of these Italians were still living in Virginia in 1625, they made no further impression upon the colony. In 1619, the Company sent over several Frenchmen skilled in vine culture in the hope of establishing an industry in wines, but that, like the silkworm culture promoted at the same time, failed, and the French workers disappeared from history.

The first successful non-British people to establish themselves in what would become one of the original thirteen colonies were the Dutch who settled New Amsterdam in 1624. Almost symbolical of

[2] *American Council of Learned Societies Report of the Committee on Linguistic and National Stocks in the Population of the United States,* printed in the *Annual Report of the American Historical Association for the Year 1931* (Washington, 1932), pp. 103–441.

[3] *Ibid.,* p. 307.

[4] Quoted from a letter of Sandys by Philip A. Bruce, *Economic History of Virginia in the Seventeenth Century* (New York, 1907), II, 443.

New York's later development as the greatest port of entry for foreigners was the make-up of the settlers whom the Dutch encouraged to come to New Netherland, for they were a mixed and polyglot people. Most of the families in the first contingent were French-speaking Walloons, refugee Protestants from the Spanish Netherlands. Though the charter granted the West India Company for the settlement of New Netherland specified that the colonists had to be Protestant Christians, the rule was not strictly observed. One reason was the difficulty of finding emigrants in Holland, for the Dutch were happy at home and felt no compulsion to try their luck in the New World. Since Holland had been hospitable to both political and religious refugees, however, some of these were recruited and went out to seek their fortunes in New Netherland. Among the diverse people who were counted in the early stages of development were Frenchmen, Germans, Danes, Norwegians, Swedes, Finns, Portuguese, Spaniards, Italians, Bohemians, Poles, and Jews. In addition, all segments of the British Isles were represented. That section of New York known as the Bronx took its name from a Dane, Jonas Bronck, who received a patent to a farm there. A contemporary reported counting eighteen languages spoken in New Amsterdam.[5]

It would be a mistake, however, to assume that foreigners outweighed the Dutch in influence. Actually, the Dutch established their language and characteristics in New Netherland and only the English were able to infiltrate with sufficient success to supersede them. Before the formal English occupation in 1664, the Dutch had made solid contributions to colonial culture that would persist for well over another century, though in a diminishing degree.

Politically, the Dutch occupation of the Hudson Valley had an enormous and unforeseen value to the English. To the superficial observer, it would appear that they had divided and therefore weakened the English colonies. Actually, the Dutch in the Hudson Valley served as a shield to protect the English to the north and south from the French, who otherwise might have come down from Canada and outflanked the English colonies before they were strong enough to protect themselves. A strong French segment in the Hudson Valley might have changed the whole course of American history. This the Dutch forestalled.

[5] Marcus L. Hansen, *The Atlantic Migration, 1607–1860* (Cambridge, Mass., 1940), p. 39.

Of the Dutch cultural contributions, some were visible and concrete, while others were intangible. The most obvious Dutch influence was in architecture. The towns built at New Amsterdam and Fort Orange (Albany) had the look of towns in Holland. Farmhouses and even haystacks equipped with movable shed roofs also revealed unmistakably their Dutch origins. The Dutch were fond of brick walls and tile roofs, a type of construction that saved many a house from fire, the great destroyer where clapboard and shingles were the prevailing material. Because plank and shingles were cheap in a land of trees, however, even the Dutch frequently abandoned their traditional brick and red and black tiles for the cheaper construction, but New York and Albany had enough sturdy Dutch houses of brick and stone to arouse the admiration of travelers. In the middle of the eighteenth century, Peter Kalm, the Swedish botanist, describes Dutch farmhouses in New York with clapboard weatherboarding to protect inner walls of unfired brick. In Albany he found houses of the same style except that the gable ends facing the street were made of fired brick, giving the impression that the whole house was brick. Perhaps the characteristic that made the houses look "Dutch" to most observers were these gable ends turned to the street, gables that might be of the stepped construction familiar from old houses in Haarlem and Alkmaar, or some variation of this form.[6] In the better houses of Albany and New York, the fireplaces were decorated with blue and white figured tiles. Kalm was particularly impressed by Dutch cleanliness, the floors of the houses being scrubbed by the women "several times a week." [7] Adaptations and variations of Dutch farmhouse and city construction passed into the tradition of American architecture and persist to the present day.

In the household arts, the Dutch craftsmen and Dutch taste made a contribution that also persisted. The use of colorful tiles, though not strictly confined to Holland, was a characteristic of Dutch interiors in the seventeenth and eighteenth centuries. Dutch cabinetmakers turned out well-made tables, chairs, beds, and cradles that have become valued heirlooms in many a New York family. Their hardware, ironwork, kitchenware, and pottery were well designed, simple and

[6] For a discussion, with illustrations, of characteristic Dutch architecture in colonial America, see Thomas J. Wertenbaker, *The Founding of American Civilization: The Middle Colonies* (New York, 1949), pp. 40–51.

[7] Adolph B. Benson (ed.), *The America of 1750. Peter Kalm's Travels in North America* (New York, 1937), II, 612–613.

utilitarian rather than ornate, intended to last for more than one generation.

Throughout the Hudson Valley, Manhattan, parts of Long Island, and the fringe of New Jersey across the Hudson, the Dutch language gained a foothold and for many years stubbornly held its own against the overwhelming odds of English. The great conservative influence was the Dutch Reformed Church, which held its services in Dutch as long as the predominant group of church members could understand the language. Until the middle of the eighteenth century, the church maintained schools in New York City where children were taught Dutch. But by 1762, so many church members in New York City could no longer understand Dutch that influential members of the congregation petitioned for a preacher who could speak English. So angry were some of the conservatives that they left the Reformed Church and joined the Church of England. If they had to hear a sermon in English, they would at least not have their ears disturbed by the old service in an alien tongue.[8] Though English gradually superseded Dutch in the city, Dutch remained the prevailing language in some country communities of the Hudson Valley until the early years of the nineteenth century. Its influence upon later American English is best remembered in such words as *cruller, cooky, boss, crib* (for a child's bed), *stoop* (for porch), and *spook.*

The tremendous power of assimilation that English was to exert in the years to come was already evident in Dutch New York in the mid-eighteenth century. This capacity, which in the nineteenth century was sufficient to transmute in one generation millions of immigrants speaking scores of languages and dialects into a people of one tongue, was observed by Peter Kalm:

Dutch was generally the language which was spoken in Albany [he reports]. In this region and also in the places between Albany and New York the predominating language was Dutch. In New York were also many homes in which Dutch was commonly spoken, especially by elderly people. The majority, however, who were of Dutch descent, were succumbing to the English language. The younger generation scarcely ever spoke anything but English, and there were many who became offended if they were taken for Dutch because they preferred to pass for English. Therefore it also happened that the majority of the young people attended the English church, although their

[8] Wertenbaker, *Founding of American Civilization,* p. 111.

parents remained loyal to the Dutch. For this reason many deserted the Reformed and Presbyterian churches in favor of the English.[9]

Among the intangible qualities that the Dutch transmitted to New York was a commercial spirit that was to become the dominant characteristic of the city they founded on the Hudson. Though the Dutch had no monopoly of the zeal for business, and they could hardly equal the Puritans of Boston for thrift and diligence in pursuit of money, they gave to New York an earthy sort of materialism that it has magnified rather than diminished. The difference between Boston and New York was the latter city's greater concentration upon commerce to the exclusion of other activities. If the burghers of New Amsterdam had any profound concern about the arts, letters, or learning, they concealed it in their preoccupation with trade and with the pleasures of the fleshpots.

The conviviality of the Dutch and the exigencies of a port town resulted in a surprising number of taverns in New Amsterdam. Thirteen years after the Dutch landed on Manhattan, one-fourth of the houses were grogshops or shops devoted to the sale of tobacco and beer. Smoking his pipe, drinking his flagon of beer, making merry in his tavern, the burgher of New Amsterdam was as convivial as his counterpart in Jan Steen's paintings. He established a pattern of conviviality that in later days would become one of New York's best-known characteristics. Some traditional customs the Dutch transmitted to a later period in New York. One of these was the habit of making calls on New Year's Day, and another was the attribution to St. Nicholas of holiday gifts for children, a custom that is supposed to have resulted after the colonial period in the corruption of St. Nicholas into Santa Klaus. To the Dutch of New Netherland we are also indebted for a certain amount of folklore that includes the sources for the legend of Rip Van Winkle.

South of the Hudson on the Delaware, another group from northern Europe struggled to found a colony, but they were doomed to be absorbed by the Dutch and English. They were the Swedes, who, like the Dutch, had to depend on other people to fill up their quotas of colonists. The first Swedish settlement on the Delaware in 1638 had as its leader Peter Minuit, a former director at New Amsterdam, and for colonists the Swedes had to supplement their numbers with Finns.

[9] Benson, *America of 1750*, II, 626–627.

Though the Swedes and the Finns were few in number, they maintained an independent colony on the Delaware for sixteen years. They established the Lutheran Church in the Delaware Valley, and, what made an even more obvious contribution to the American scene, they introduced the notched-log construction in housebuilding. To the Swedes, and perhaps later to the Germans, the American frontiersman owed the model of the log cabin that would become the easiest type of house to build in the woods to the West. Some few bits of folklore may have their origins in the belief that the Finns were given to traffic with witches and devils.[10]

Peter Kalm found many people of Swedish extraction in the Delaware region, and he observed an even greater eagerness among them to forget their origins than he had noticed among the Dutch of New York. "Since English is the principal language of the land all people gradually get to speak that and they become ashamed to talk in their own tongue because they fear they may not in such a case be real English. Consequently many Swedish women are married to Englishmen, and although they can speak Swedish very well, it is impossible to make them do so, and when they are spoken to in Swedish they always answer in English. The same condition obtains among men; so that it is easy to see that the Swedish language is doomed to extinction in America."[11]

The non British people who exerted the most pervasive influence in proportion to their numbers throughout the North American colonies were the French. Though France was actively at war with Britain through much of the eighteenth century, and hostile Frenchmen and their Indian allies were a constant threat to the very existence of the English colonies, French Huguenots and other French refugees were finding a welcome and a home in British America.[12] Some of the Huguenots came via England, Switzerland, or Holland, where their families had taken refuge during the persecutions of the sixteenth century. England had received a large number of Frenchmen after the massacre of St. Bartholomew's Eve in 1572, and descendants

[10] For a discussion of Swedes and Finns, see Amandus Johnson, *The Swedish Settlements on the Delaware* (2 vols., Philadelphia, 1911), and *The Swedes and Finns in New Jersey*, American Guide Series (Bayonne, N.J., 1938).

[11] Benson, *America of 1750*, II, 683.

[12] Cf. Gilbert Chinard, *Les Réfugiés Huguenots en Amérique* (Paris, 1925), and Charles W. Baird, *History of the Huguenot Emigration to America* (2 vols., New York, 1885).

of these families were among the emigrants to the New World. During the persecutions that followed the revocation of the Edict of Nantes in 1685, many other Huguenots fled France and found their way to America. They came to all of the colonies, but South Carolina, Virginia, Pennsylvania, and New York received more than the others. A few Catholic French also came in the eighteenth century, the most numerous group being exiles from Acadia, but they were not numerous enough in the colonies of the Atlantic Coast to exert a great influence.[13] The greatest non-Huguenot French influence upon the country came in a later time from the French of Louisiana.

Although a few French Huguenots came in the earlier period of settlement, the heaviest immigration was in the 1680's and later. South Carolina, for example, in 1680 received a group of forty-five French refugees from England. By 1699, the French refugees in and around Charleston had increased to a total of 438, and small groups continued to arrive during the remainder of the colonial period. In 1732, Jean Pierre Purry, a French Swiss, brought in 600 Swiss Protestants, more than half of them French, and settled them on the Savannah River. Another large group of French immigrants came in 1764 and settled in South Carolina at a place which they called New Bordeaux.[14] But the French were never as numerous as they seemed —or as their enthusiastic descendants have made them appear. They brought with them a diversity of skills, trades, and accomplishments. A South Carolina petition of 1697, listing the names of sixty-three persons of whom fifty-nine were Huguenots, classified the group into occupations as follows: twelve planters, twelve weavers, eleven merchants, four shipwrights, three coopers, three smiths, two goldsmiths, two gunsmiths, two joiners, two leather workers, one apothecary, one blockmaker, one brazier, one doctor, one gardener, one saddler, one sailmaker, one silk throwster, one watchmaker, and one wheelwright.[15] The Huguenots had long been celebrated for their thrift, industry, and sobriety, and these qualities, added to their skills, gave them a

[13] Oscar W. Winzerling, *Acadian Odyssey* (Baton Rouge, La., 1955), pp. 18–19.

[14] Robert L. Meriwether, *The Expansion of South Carolina, 1729–1765* (Kingsport, Tenn., 1940), pp. 252–254.

[15] David Duncan Wallace, *South Carolina, A Short History* (Chapel Hill, N.C., 1951), p. 63. For a general discussion of the Huguenots, see Arthur H. Hirsch, *The Huguenots of Colonial South Carolina* (Durham, N.C., 1928), but note a criticism of Hirsch's accuracy by Wallace, pp. 63–65.

greater significance in the cultural development of the new country than their numerical proportion in the population might indicate. The Huguenots had the energy and drive of the Puritans without the angularity that often characterized the English Calvinists.

So industrious, intelligent, and adaptable were the Huguenots as a group that by the second generation many of them occupied places of prominence. They often married into non-French families and were readily assimilated into the dominant society. One of the most notable examples in South Carolina of the rise to prominence of a Huguenot family is to be found in the history of the Manigaults. Other Huguenots were equally successful and contributed immensely to the prosperity and development of South Carolina. Family names like Huger, Gaillard, DeSaussure, DuPre, Guerard, LeGaré, Izard, Laurens, LeConte, Lesesne, and Porcher, all prominent in South Carolina since the colonial period, attest to the place the French immigrants took in the life of the colony. Huguenot names were to be found in nearly every business and profession. Benjamin Franklin picked Louis Timothée, son of a French refugee, to go to Charleston in 1734 and revive the *South Carolina Gazette*. Another Frenchman, Andrew DeVeaux, improved the process of making indigo, which had been introduced by Eliza Lucas, and quickly surpassed her. To the French immigrants, the English looked for help in trying to establish the wine and silk industries, two will-o'-the-wisps that the Board of Trade continued to pursue throughout the eighteenth century. If the high cost of labor had not made silk making unprofitable, the French might have succeeded with their silkworms. They planted mulberry trees for the worms and actually produced silk at various places, including Charleston and Abbeville, but the supply of skilled labor was never sufficient to make it a practical operation. Wherever there was any enterprise requiring skill, industry, intelligence, and ingenuity, Huguenots were likely to be involved.

The Huguenots showed a great capacity for assimilation. They adapted themselves to local conditions and made the best of them. Though they were Calvinists in theology and therefore more akin to the Presbyterians than to the Anglicans, they saw the wisdom of affiliating with the Anglicans in South Carolina, for the Anglicans were the controlling group and their church was supported by taxation. Of the six churches that the Huguenots founded, all except one, which still exists in Charleston, became a part of the Anglican establishment.[16] Indeed, many of the most distinguished ministers of the Episcopal Church at a later period were of Huguenot descent.

South Carolina in 1755 received another increment of French settlers, in this case suspect and unwelcome, for they were Catholic French peasants being deported from Acadia by the British authorities. More than six thousand Acadians were dumped without notice in various Atlantic ports, and of these approximately 1,200 reached Charleston. Because of the war with France, the Charlestonians regarded the Acadians as enemy aliens, and rumors spread through the town that they were trying to incite a rebellion of the slaves. Homeless and without any means of livelihood, some were sold as indentured servants, while others managed to make their way to Haiti or Louisiana. Few settled permanently in South Carolina, but to the family of Lanneau, one of those that did remain, the distinguished Greek scholar, Basil Lanneau Gildersleeve, traced his ancestry.[17]

In contrast to the reception of the Acadians was the welcome given the Huguenots from the late seventeenth century to the end of the colonial period. So prized were they as immigrants that promoters and land speculators were constantly scheming to induce them to come to British America. Several Virginia planters with large landholdings attempted to settle their estates with French refugees. William Fitzhugh, for example, between 1680 and 1690 busied himself with a plan to develop a 21,000-acre tract in Stafford County with Huguenot tenants. He persuaded a few to come, but his dream of a populous tenantry was never realized. Ralph Wormeley in 1686 entertained a French traveler, a certain Monsieur Durand, and showed him a 10,000-acre tract which he hoped to settle with Huguenots. About 1690, William III gave his royal support to a project to send Huguenot refugees to the southern colonies in the hope of stimulating wine and silk production. Within a few years seven or eight hundred men, women, and children had come to Virginia. Most of these settlers took up fertile land on an abandoned Indian tract known as Manakin Town, about twenty miles above the site of Richmond. When Robert Beverley was writing his *History and Present State of Virginia,* they had already demonstrated their thrift, industry, and ingenuity in making wine and brandy, in manufacturing their own cloth and making

[16] Wallace, *South Carolina,* p. 64.
[17] *Ibid.,* pp. 174–175. Cf. Winzerling, *Acadian Odyssey,* pp. 17–35.

clothes, and in cattle raising. "I have heard that these people are upon a design of getting into the breed of buffaloes," Beverley reports, "to which end they lie in wait for their calves that they may tame and raise a stock of them." [18] If they did not succeed in raising tame buffaloes or in making Virginia into a source of palatable wine, it was not for lack of trying. Certainly they contributed to the development of the colony, though not as conspicuously as in South Carolina. They did scatter through the tidewater region, and a considerable number of French names of distinction in Virginia go back to these refugees.

Beverley's *History*, if not purposely written as propaganda to attract Frenchmen to Virginia, at least was used for that purpose, for it had four printings in French. The first French version was brought out in 1707 at Amsterdam by the stationer Thomas Lombrail. In the same year, a Parisian bookseller, Pierre Ribou, had printed at Orléans a pirated edition of Lombrail's version; in 1712 and 1718, two reprintings of the Lombrail edition occurred at Amsterdam. Beverley himself was much interested in the bringing to Virginia of French vignerons, and his father-in-law, William Byrd I, received high praise in the *History* for his activities in behalf of Huguenot refugees. Clearly, Beverley hoped that his favorable account of the fruitfulness of the colony and the charity of Virginia planters would appeal to French readers.

Like many other settlers in Virginia, some of the French from Manakin Town made their way over the border into North Carolina in search of more extensive lands which they might obtain on better terms. Under the leadership of their minister, the Reverend C. P. de Richbourg, a group in 1707 settled on the Neuse River. So distressed were the Virginians at the loss of the French that they prompted the Board of Trade to begin an investigation which provoked Governor Henderson Walker to make a heated denial that North Carolina was soliciting runaways from Virginia.[19]

After South Carolina, Pennsylvania appears to have received the largest number of Huguenot refugees.[20] Mingled with Swiss and Germans who entered at Philadelphia in increasing numbers were many

[18] Robert Beverley, *The History and Present State of Virginia* (1705), ed. Louis B. Wright (Chapel Hill, N.C., 1947), p. 282.
[19] Hugh T. Lefler and Albert R. Newsome, *The History of a Southern State: North Carolina* (Chapel Hill, N.C., 1954), pp. 49–50.
[20] W. F. Dunaway, "The French Racial Strain in Colonial Pennsylvania," *The Pennsylvania Magazine of History and Biography*, LIII (1929), 322–342.

French families, some of whom took Germanic names, a fact that makes it difficult to trace the French as a separate group. As elsewhere, the French assimilated easily with other stocks in the area. Nevertheless, from the large number of French names dating from the late seventeenth and early eighteenth centuries, it is obvious that Pennsylvania, and particularly Philadelphia, had a significant infusion of French blood. Huguenot craftsmen played an important part in developing the arts and crafts in Philadelphia. They also became prominent in the business and social life of the city, and some of their descendants occupied conspicuous places in the later life of the country. Names like Girard, Boudinot, Hillegas, and Roberdeau stem from the Huguenot group in Philadelphia.

French names occur in New York from the time of the Dutch onward, too. Among the early settlers recruited by the Dutch were French Huguenots who made common cause with the Walloons. A small body of French Protestants were mingled with the Flemings who settled New Paltz, New York, in 1677. This community, composed mostly of artisans and farmers, unlike other Huguenots, kept to themselves and remained French in language and characteristics for fifty years.[21] Another French group at New Rochelle, which was settled about 1695, retained certain distinctive characteristics for nearly a century. New Rochelle was famed for the polite manners of its citizens, and its French schools were patronized by New York families who wanted their children to learn not only the French language but polished behavior as well. In short, New Rochelle became fashionable and a resort of the socially prominent or the socially ambitious.[22] In New York City, many families with French names rose to prominence and importance in both business and society. Among the New York families of French origin were such names as De Lancey, de Forest, Vassar, Gallaudet, and Delano (from de La Noye).

Many Huguenots landed in New England in the 1680's, and in 1687 a French settlement, somewhat like that at Manakin Town in Virginia, was established in Massachusetts on the Manexit or French River, where it flourished until the Deerfield Massacre of 1704.[23] In the early years of the eighteenth century, Huguenot refugees were

---

[21] Howard Mumford Jones, *America and French Culture* (Chapel Hill, N.C., 1927), p. 87.

[22] *Ibid.*, pp. 222–223.

[23] *Ibid.*, p. 89.

to be found throughout New England. In Boston they were strong enough to maintain a church until 1748, when its members scattered to join English-speaking churches of their liking. Among the French names of historical interest in New England are the families of Allaire, Faneuil, Revere, Sigourney, Bowdoin, and DuPuy. As elsewhere, many of the better craftsmen were French. Perhaps the best remembered is Paul Revere, the silversmith and patriot, whose craftsmanship is known to some who never heard of his famous ride.[24]

Wherever they went the French Huguenots contributed to the intellectual and artistic life of the community as well as to the economic and social development. Many of them became teachers of the arts, the social graces, the classics, the sciences, navigation, and almost every other subject then required. In actual numbers the French Huguenots who emigrated to the Atlantic coastal region were never a numerous company. By the census of 1790, the estimated number of people of French descent was 54,900.[25] But they were widely disseminated and they assimilated quickly with the rest of the population. Their extraordinary dispersal and the multiplicity of their activities made them a potent force in cultural progress throughout the British colonies.[26]

[24] On being shown a statue of Paul Revere in Boston, a silver collector from France is reported to have said, "I suppose it is proper to erect a monument to a silversmith, but why the horse?" Cited by Carl Bridenbaugh, *The Colonial Craftsman* (New York, 1950), p. 87.

[25] *ACLS Report,* p. 397.

[26] "The Huguenots," says Howard Mumford Jones, "helped to teach the colonists how to live. Bringing them the arts, the accomplishments, the graces of the most polished civilization in the world, together with a gaiety and good humor in strong contrast to the New England or Pennsylvania temperament, the Huguenot ameliorated the conditions of colonial life, softened the hard edges of existence. The French at New Rochelle were, according to tradition, the first to utilize the remnants of worn-out garments by cutting them into strips and weaving them into carpets; they brought in better spinning wheels; better grafts and roots from the fruit-growing and wine-making districts of France; they imported hangings, mirrors, china, and furniture; and whereas the English and Dutch dyed linen yarn and wove it into ugly stripes and checks for beds and window curtains, the French used white linen or dainty colors, usually in one shade, with light designs. Their homes, in fact, were more attractive and dainty, their skill in dress and color, with needle and bobbin, more commendable, and withal, they were thrifty—admirable models for the growing leisure class." *America and French Culture,* pp. 224–225. If Professor Jones somewhat overemphasizes the good taste of the French at the expense of other nationalities, nevertheless he is essentially correct in the appraisal of French qualities and the peculiar contribution made by them to society in the British colonies.

In contrast to the small numbers of French, the German immigrants were far more numerous, but they were inclined to keep to themselves, to retain their peculiar characteristics, and to create Germanic communities rather than to assimilate with the other nationals. At the outbreak of the Revolution, it is estimated that Pennsylvania alone had a population of 100,000 Germans,[27] and many thousands more were to be found on the frontiers of Maryland, Virginia, and the Carolinas. They made important contributions to the development of the country, chiefly in agriculture and the handicrafts. Indeed, without the labor and the skill of the German farmers in the back country, Philadelphia could not have attained its pre-eminence in the export of grains and foodstuffs.

William Penn's promotional tracts describing the fruitfulness of Pennsylvania were translated into German and widely distributed in the towns and villages of the Rhine Valley, particularly in the Palatinate on the Upper Rhine. Beginning with the Thirty Years' War, the Rhine Valley had been repeatedly devastated and the populace had been reduced to miserable poverty. Many of the inhabitants had broken away from the Lutheran State Church and had joined various Pietist sects. Of these perhaps the Mennonites are the best known. Since most of these people were pacifists and held views not unlike the Quakers, they were easily persuaded to come to a Quaker colony that held out the hope of both peace and prosperity.

The first German group to arrive in Pennsylvania was led by Francis Daniel Pastorius, a lawyer and head of a body of Frankfurt Pietists. He obtained from Penn a plot of land just north of Philadelphia, and in October, 1683, he brought over a company recruited principally at Frankfurt and at Crefeld on the Lower Rhine. This settlement, known as Germantown, quickly became a flourishing village noted for the weaving of flax and for other handicrafts. The diversity of occupations of the German immigrants is indicated in a statement made by Pastorius himself a year after their arrival: "My company consisted of many sorts of people. There was a doctor of medicine with his wife and eight children, a French captain, a Low Dutch cake-baker, an apothecary, a glassblower, a mason, a smith,

---

[27] Frank R. Diffenderffer, *The German Immigration into Pennsylvania through the Port of Philadelphia from 1700 to 1775,* Pennsylvania German Society *Proceedings and Addresses at Ephrata, October 20, 1899,* X (Lancaster, Pa., 1900), 102–103.

a wheelwright, a cabinet-maker, a cooper, a hat-maker, a cobbler, a tailor, a gardener, farmers, seamstresses, etc., in all about eighty persons besides the crew." [28] Three craftsmen from Arnhem, Holland, Wilhelm Ruttinghausen (anglicized to Rittenhouse) and his two sons, Claus and Gerhard, in 1690 established a highly successful paper mill on a branch of the Wissahickon, the first in the colonies. The Germantown settlers planted peach and apple trees, set out vineyards, cleared land for farms and gardens, engaged in beekeeping, and showed others how to conduct a model self-sustaining community.

Through his writings and advice, Pastorius, a man of broad learning and sound common sense, exerted a beneficent influence on prospective German immigrants. Though the land was fertile, he warned, no one need come who did not expect to work hard. *"Hic opus, hic labor est,"* he asserted, "and it is not enough to bring money hither without the inclination to work, for it slips out of one's hands. . . . Working people and husbandmen are in the greatest demand here." [29]

During the next two decades, in the wake of the Germantown settlers, many hundreds of other sectarians came from the Rhineland: German Quakers, Mennonites, many German Baptist Brethren, sometimes called Dunkers, and various other sects, including some with such strange names as the New Mooners, the River Brethren, and the Society of the Woman in the Wilderness. From the neighborhood of Germantown they pushed out into Lancaster County, and from there they spread to the Delaware on the north and to Maryland on the south, forming compact communities of farmers and craftsmen. Most of these sectarians came with sufficient money or financial backing to set up as independent farmers or to establish themselves in their particular crafts.

Early in the eighteenth century, however, another German element began to swarm into Pennsylvania. They were chiefly Lutherans and members of the German Reformed Church, and since many of them came from the Palatinate, the English applied the name "Palatines" to all of them. These later immigrants are also sometimes referred to as "church people" to distinguish them from the earlier sectarians. In 1719, Jonathan Dickinson wrote: "We are daily expecting ships from

[28] From Pastorius' *Sichere Nachricht* (1684) in Albert C. Myers (ed.), *Narratives of Early Pennsylvania, West New Jersey, and Delaware, 1630–1707* (New York, 1912), p. 395.

[29] *Ibid.*, p. 397.

London which bring Palatines, in number about six or seven thousands," [30] and between 1737 and 1746, sixty-seven ships arrived at Philadelphia, bringing approximately 15,000 Germans, most of whom had embarked at Rotterdam. Many of these later arrivals were so desperately poor that they sold themselves into bondage for from three to five years, or occasionally for longer periods, to pay their passage. These indentured servants were known as "redemptioners." But whether they worked independently or at first as indentured servants, their industry helped make Pennsylvania prosperous, and as soon as the redemptioners were independent, they were ready to push on to the frontier where they could get cheap land for themselves. Throughout the eighteenth century there was a steady migration of Germans filtering through Pennsylvania into Maryland, and eventually down the Shenandoah Valley into the Carolinas.

Philadelphia, of course, was not the only port of entry for Germans, but more came through Philadelphia than through all the other American ports put together. Nevertheless, many Germans landed elsewhere, and promoters and land speculators eagerly competed for German settlers. A considerable number of Germans and German Swiss landed at Charleston, South Carolina, and settled in what was then the back country at Amelia township, Orangeburg, the Dutch Fork between the Broad and Saluda rivers, and at other places. Usually they kept to themselves and retained their language and customs throughout the colonial period. A few Germans even tried to settle in Maine, but the New England colonies proved less hospitable than other regions.

Some of the Germans who came to Pennsylvania and the other colonies were of Swiss origin. A settlement at New Bern, North Carolina, in 1710, promoted by the Baron Christopher de Graffenried, a Swiss himself, was composed partly of Germans from the Palatinate and partly of German Swiss. In the group of settlers that Jean Pierre Purry brought to South Carolina in 1726 to establish a silk industry, were many German Swiss. William Byrd II of Virginia was eager to procure "Switzers" for his large landholdings on the Roanoke River and was bitter because someone lured one group to North Carolina instead. In order to persuade them of the value of his territory, he provided the notes for a promotional tract published in 1737 at Berne

[30] Diffenderffer, *German Immigration,* pp. 32–33.

by Samuel Jenner as *Neu-gefundenes Eden.* In the following year, 250 German Swiss embarked for Virginia to settle Byrd's land, but their ship wrecked and only a handful got ashore alive. Byrd was eager for the Swiss because, he said, "I had much rather do with the honest Switzers than the mixed people that come from Pennsylvania." [31] Never were there enough Swiss or Germans to satisfy speculators with vacant land, for these people were regarded as the hardest-working and thriftiest settlers available.

A third German group who exerted a great cultural influence was the United Brethren or Moravians. This group of religionists had fled from Moravia in Austria and taken refuge on the estates of Count Zinzendorf in Saxony. They were a pietistic and pacifistic sect who claimed to be Lutherans but gradually broke away from orthodox Lutheranism, much as the Methodists separated from the Episcopal Church. Under the leadership of Count Zinzendorf, who eventually came to America, they planned to emigrate, and in 1736 an advance body of forty-seven Moravians took up land in Georgia near a settlement of Lutherans from Salzburg. But the danger of war with the Spaniards on this frontier soon persuaded them to move on to Pennsylvania, where about 1741 they established themselves and settled towns at Bethlehem, Nazareth, and Lititz. Although by the time of the Revolution they still numbered hardly more than 2,500, they had already attained a great reputation for their religious and educational activities. Their missionaries to the Indians met with considerable success and they also supplied religious instruction to many a lonely settlement on the frontier. The Moravian schools and the Moravian emphasis on music had a lasting effect on colonial society. Their choral music was a particular feature of their schools and churches. A young ladies' seminary, established at Bethlehem in 1749, provided a better education for women than was generally available, and this was followed a decade later by an excellent boys' boarding school at Nazareth. Counting both day schools and boarding schools, the Moravians founded ten educational institutions in Pennsylvania. In 1753, Moravians who had difficulty in acquiring land in Pennsylvania bought a tract of nearly one hundred thousand acres in North Carolina, which they named "Wachovia" in honor of one of Count Zin-

[31] R. C. Beatty and W. J. Mulloy (eds.), *William Byrd's Natural History of Virginia or The Newly Discovered Eden* (Richmond, Va., 1940), p. xxi.

zendorf's titles, and established several settlements there before the Revolution.

By the outbreak of the Revolution, every British colony had some German settlers, but the heaviest German populations were in Pennsylvania and in the colonies adjacent. So concentrated were the Germans in some areas, as in Lancaster County, Pennsylvania, and in Frederick County, Maryland, that the German language predominated. In 1738 at Germantown, Christopher Sauer and his son established a German-language printing press which lasted until the Revolution. Their publications numbered approximately 150 books and pamphlets, including three editions of the German Bible. Though Franklin was the first to print German books in America, Sauer was the first to use German type face.[32] From 1739 to 1777, the Sauer press also issued under various titles a German-language newspaper which circulated among the German settlements as far away as Georgia.

German industry, thrift, and capacity for hard work made the German settlements prosperous within one generation, and their sense of family solidarity made for economic stability. Showing a preference for the strong limestone soils in Pennsylvania, Maryland, and Virginia, they continually improved their land and added to their houses and buildings. German communities could be identified by the huge barns, the sleek cattle, and the stout workhorses. Flour mills and sawmills dotted their territory. In their great covered wagons, they hauled flour, meat, fruit, and vegetables to town markets that other farmers would have considered too distant or difficult to reach. So productive were the German farms that it is said that Pennsylvania alone could have fed the rest of the colonies.

In the mechanical crafts, German workmen also proved their value. In addition to the manufacture of the Conestoga wagons which were the ancestors of the "prairie schooners" of a later day, Germans developed the long rifle that became the indispensable companion and safeguard of the frontiersman. The gunsmiths of Lancaster, Pennsylvania, were actively at work as early as the 1720's, and the rifles produced at Lancaster and other Pennsylvania German towns played an important part in the Indian wars. German craftsmen were also the first organ builders in the colonies. Glassmaking, which the James-

[32] Albert B. Faust, *The German Element in the United States* (New York, 1927), I, 144.

town settlers had tried, met with its first success when the German, Caspar Wistar, set up a furnace in 1738 near Alloway Town in New Jersey. Later, a picturesque figure, Henry William Stiegel, sometimes called "Baron" Stiegel because of his expansive way of life, also made glass of remarkable quality. Germans were noted as ironworkers. Between 1714 and 1720, Governor Spotswood encouraged Germans to settle at Germanna, Virginia, to operate one of the earliest ironworks in the colonies. In 1750, Johann Huber founded an ironworks in Lancaster County, Pennsylvania, that lasted for a century. Baron Stiegel about 1758 opened an ironworks and a stove factory at Mannheim, in Lancaster County, that proved successful, though Stiegel ruined himself by his extravagance—a notorious exception to the general thriftiness of the Germans. Germans were also makers of furniture, some of which they decorated with colorful designs. Solid, well-made furniture, clever needlework, bright-colored pottery, and ingenious kitchenware were characteristic of the Pennsylvania German household, and, indeed, of German households throughout the colonies. The Germans believed in the creature comforts and were willing to work hard to surround themselves with the material evidence of what to them was the good life.

Among the non-British immigrants from Europe who would have a great influence in later periods were a few Jews who arrived in the colonial period. Most of them were Sephardic Jews, descendants of the Jews exiled from Spain in 1492, and many of them came from Holland. The first group arrived in New Amsterdam in 1654 and despite some opposition from the Dutch authorities in New Netherland soon made a place for themselves in the business life of the town. By the beginning of the Revolution, there were Jews in all thirteen colonies, though not all colonies made them equally welcome. Georgia, for example, despite its philanthropic origins, was distinctly cool to the Jewish immigrant.[33] Rhode Island, however, with its tolerance for all sects, attracted many Jews, and Newport had a number of important families and became the center of Jewish life in the northern colonies. As early as 1759, the Jews of Newport were making plans to build a synagogue. They employed Peter Harrison to design it and

[33] A succinct discussion of the attitude of the various colonies toward the Jews is to be found in Abram V. Goodman, *American Overture: Jewish Rights in Colonial Times* (Philadelphia, 1947), *passim*. Goodman also provides useful insights into other aspects of Jewish life in the colonies.

solicited funds from Jews scattered through the British colonies. After much effort, the synagogue at last was completed and dedicated on December 2, 1763.[34] Important congregations were located in Charleston, South Carolina, Philadelphia, and New York. Although most of the Jews in colonial America were Sephardim, or Spanish-Portuguese Jews, there were a few Ashkenazim, or Germanic and East-European Jews.

The colonial Jews took a prominent part in commercial enterprises. Aaron Lopez, for example, came to Newport from Portugal about 1754 and made a fortune. When he died in 1782, Ezra Stiles observed that "he was a merchant of the first eminence, for honor and extent of commerce probably surpassed by no merchant in America." [35] Lopez' father-in-law, Jacob Rivera, is said to have introduced the making of spermaceti candles.[36] Another Jew, James Lucena, began the manufacture of castile soap in Rhode Island.[37]

The first Jew in British America to receive a college degree was Judah Monis, who in 1720 submitted to the Harvard faculty a Hebrew grammar that he had prepared and received an M.A. degree. Two years later he was baptized a Christian and became an instructor in Hebrew at Harvard, where he continued to teach until 1760. In 1735 he published the first Hebrew grammar in America. One of the most talented silversmiths in New York in the mid-eighteenth century was Myer Myers, who was so highly thought of that he was made president of the Silversmiths' Society.[38] From the mid-eighteenth century onward, the Jews were an increasing influence in the commercial, intellectual, and artistic life of the colonies.

Peter Kalm in the middle of the century was astonished at the prosperity, freedom, and the privileges of the Jews in New York, a condition that generally prevailed in all the colonies. ". . . many Jews

[34] *Ibid.*, pp. 48–49. The estimates for the Jewish population in Newport have sometimes been vastly exaggerated by overly enthusiastic historians. Cf., e.g., Rufus Learsi [Israel Goldberg], *The Jews in America* (Cleveland and New York, 1954), p. 31. Goodman points out that a Newport census of 1774 listed 121 men, women, and children of Jewish extraction. A detailed discussion of the Jews in Newport is Morris A. Gutstein, *The Story of the Jews of Newport* (New York, 1936).

[35] Franklin Bowditch Dexter (ed.), *The Literary Diary of Ezra Stiles* (New York, 1901), III, 24.

[36] Goodman, *American Overture*, p. 50.

[37] Jacob R. Marcus, *Early American Jewry* (Philadelphia, 1951), I, 89.

[38] Goodman, *American Overture*, p. 107.

have settled in New York, who possess great privileges. They have a synagogue, own their dwelling-houses, possess large countryseats and are allowed to keep shops. They have likewise several ships, which they load and send out with their own goods. In fine, they enjoy all the privileges common to the other inhabitants of this town and province." [39] The freedom and opportunities that Kalm observed in New York also prevailed in Philadelphia and in Charleston, South Carolina, at the end of the colonial period. New York, Rhode Island, Pennsylvania, and South Carolina had the distinction in this period of showing the greatest hospitality to the Jews. [40]

In the cultural development of colonial America, the Scots were among the most significant groups of the non-English elements of the population after the turn of the eighteenth century. These Scots were of various kinds: Lowland Scots, Highlanders, and Ulster Scots. Interest in the Scots in America has produced a vast and growing literature in which there is much confusion of both fact and terminology, much romance, and not a little nonsense. First of all, the term Scotch-Irish has sometimes led to misunderstanding. Many otherwise well-informed Americans assume that Scotch-Irish means people of mixed Scottish and Irish blood, whereas historically it means people of Scottish descent resident in Ireland before their emigration to America. In many colonial records these people frequently were simply called "Irish," a designation that has misled more than one unwary genealogist. They had little or no Celtic Irish blood in their veins, and almost invariably they were Protestants, and usually Presbyterians. During the whole of the colonial period, only a handful of Catholic Irish came to America, and at the end of the Revolution Catholics of all nationalities in the new nation numbered hardly more than 24,000. [41] The great influx of true Irish into the United States was a nineteenth-century phenomenon. Because of this confusion of terminology, the term "Ulster Scots" will make clearer the origins of the people now commonly denominated as "Scotch-Irish."

Following rebellions by Irish chieftains in Northern Ireland, King James I confiscated their lands and about 1608 began what is known as "the Great Plantation" in counties composing the ancient province

---

[39] Benson, *The America of 1750*, I, 129.

[40] Goodman, *American Overture*, pp. 47–68, 96–114, 115–132, 150–167.

[41] Wayland F. Dunaway, *The Scotch-Irish of Colonial Pennsylvania* (Chapel Hill, N.C., 1944), p. 41.

of Ulster by inducing large numbers of Scots from the Lowlands to settle there. They pushed the native Irish into the more backward areas on the worst land and were careful not to mingle with them. More Scots came after the Great Rebellion of 1641, and still more came in 1690 after the Battle of the Boyne. One contemporary estimated that more than 50,000 families from the Scottish Lowlands came into Ulster between 1690 and 1715.[42] During the seventeenth century, the whole of Ulster, or what is now Northern Ireland, became a domain of Lowland Scots, though many native Irish remained and some English and a few French Huguenots also settled there. The Scots intermarried with the English and the French Huguenots, but there was almost no intermarriage between the Presbyterian Scots and the Catholic Irish. Such unions were anathema to both.

Had the English shown more wisdom in the administration of Ulster, they might have avoided many later calamities. But in 1699 Parliament passed the Woolen Act making it illegal for the weavers of Ulster to export their cloth to any foreign country. The effect of this was to ruin the export trade of the Scottish weavers in order to protect the industry in England. Not content with bringing economic ruin upon Northern Ireland, Parliament in 1704 put through a Test Act for Ireland which disfranchised the Scottish Presbyterians unless they conformed to the Established Church. These actions embittered the Scots, who had never loved the English anyway, and they brought this bitterness with them when they migrated to America.

Some Scots had come to the colonies in the seventeenth century, but the migration did not reach large proportions until about 1717. The years of heaviest emigration were 1717–18, 1727–28, 1740–41, and 1771–73.[43] Agents for ships in the Atlantic trade went about Northern Ireland recruiting emigrants, and in the summer of 1717 more than a dozen ships loaded with Scottish passengers landed at Philadelphia. In the summer of 1729, a resident of Londonderry reported twenty-five ships with emigrants for North America leaving that port, not to mention many more sailing from Belfast and other Irish ports. Between 1700 and 1776, one writer estimates that 200,000 Scots emigrated from Ulster alone, and Wayland F. Dunaway, after weighing all the evidence that he can find, thinks that the total num-

[42] *Ibid.*, p. 25.
[43] *Ibid.*, p. 34.

ber of Scots coming to North America in the eighteenth century amounted approximately to 250,000.[44] The principal port of entry was Philadelphia, but Charleston, South Carolina, also received many of them, and nearly every American port got its quota of Scots. Some of them went to New England, but New England was a little too much like Old England for their tastes, and they found freer opportunities in the back country of Pennsylvania, New Jersey, Maryland, Virginia, and the Carolinas.

The Ulster Scots nearly all came from the Lowlands and the Western Isles, and almost invariably they were Presbyterians. After the Jacobite rebellions of 1715 and 1745, many Highlanders also came to America. Some were fugitives, but the majority accepted exile to America and took the oath of allegiance to the House of Hanover as the price of their freedom. Like the Ulster Scots, these Highlanders were chiefly Presbyterians. When the Revolution came, the majority of the Highland Scots remained loyal to the King. Two reasons seem to account for their action. They had taken a solemn oath of allegiance which they were loath to break, and the British government sent over two Highland recruiting officers empowered to promise all Highlanders who joined the King's army two hundred acres of land free, exemption from taxes for twenty years, and remission of quitrents already owed.[45]

In the conquest of the back country from the Indians, the Ulster Scots played a decisive part. Restless, energetic, tough, and fearless, they continually pushed on in search of more and better land. Always just beyond the horizon a new hope beckoned, and the Scots, rarely content for long with what they had, always believed a better fortune lay before them. Armed with an invincible text from the Old Testament that told them to smite the heathen and seize their lands, the Scots had no compunction about driving the Indians from their traditional hunting grounds. Though peaceful German gunsmiths made the frontiersman's long rifle, the Scots made the most effective use of it. From the Cumberland through the Shenandoah Valley into North

[44] *Ibid.*, p. 41. *The ACLS Report*, p. 231, estimates the total Scottish element in 1790 at 263,330, or 8.3 per cent of the population. But it also adds another 6 per cent of what the *Report* describes as "Ulster Irish contributions resulting from fairly distinct streams of Scotch-Irish, English-Irish, and native Irish from Ulster." The proportion of South Irish in 1790 is estimated at 3.7 per cent.

[45] Lefler and Newsome, *North Carolina*, p. 199.

and South Carolina, the Ulster Scots poured into the frontier wilderness. There they met other Scots who had landed at southern ports and had found their way inland, and together they laid the foundations of civilization in the back country from Pennsylvania to Georgia.

The Scots early demonstrated a love of freedom combined with political acumen, a quality important in a nascent democracy. They were frequently agitators for political reform and in Pennsylvania, for example, they fought against the tight control of the Quaker minority. This conflict was the key to most political issues in Pennsylvania until the Revolution. Similarly, Scots in the back country of Virginia, North Carolina, and South Carolina were repeatedly in conflict with the older landed aristocracy. The readiness of the Scots to demand their rights and to fight for them, to insist upon equality of representation, and to protest the encroachments of vested interests represented by the older and more conservative elements in colonial society had an important influence in the colonies, especially from Pennsylvania southward. In Virginia and South Carolina particularly, the lines drawn in the eighteenth century between the up-country folk and the conservative element in the tidewater regions persisted down to recent times and has not yet altogether disappeared. It was not a mere coincidence that Patrick Henry was a back-country politician of Scotch Presbyterian descent, as were many others who led the fight against George III.[46]

The economic contributions of the Ulster Scots were less conspicuous than those of other less restless people, and they were not especially

[46] Though their ruthless courage made the Ulster Scots excellent frontiersmen, their stubbornness and their dogmatic Presbyterianism sometimes antagonized other folk, who found it hard to see their virtues. For example, the Reverend Charles Woodmason, a prejudiced Anglican missionary whose own violent bigotry makes his *Journal* suspect as a factual document, commented in 1767 of the Ulster Scots who had populated the Waxhaws district in South Carolina: "A finer body of land is nowhere to be seen. But it is occupied by a set of the most lowest, vilest crew breathing—Scotch-Irish Presbyterians from the north of Ireland. They have built a meeting house and have a pastor, a Scotsman among them, a good sort of man. He once was of the Church of England. . . . [These people] in his breast he heartily contemns. They will not suffer him to use the Lord's Prayer. He wants to introduce Watts' Psalms in place of the barbarous Scotch version but they will not admit it." Richard J. Hooker (ed.), *The Carolina Backcountry on the Eve of the Revolution: The Journal and Other Writings of Charles Woodmason, Anglican Itinerant* (Chapel Hill, N.C., 1953), p. 14. Elsewhere Woodmason refers to "an herd of vile Irish Presbyterians," his usual designation for these theological adversaries. *Ibid.*, p. 141.

noted for any craft except weaving of woolen and linen cloth, in which they developed home industries of some consequence. But the Scottish frontiersman was characteristically a jack-of-all-trades because he had to be to survive.[47] He made the simple furniture and kitchenware that necessity required; he raised flax and sheared wool from his sheep, and his wife carded, spun, and wove both into cloth for bedding and clothing, with sometimes a surplus for barter. Although the Scots had no monopoly of distilling, they were adepts at the making of rye and bourbon whisky, which they used as a convenient medium of exchange. Whisky was a normal beverage which everyone drank, and the Presbyterian minister not only drank it but took it in part payment of his salary.

Much of the Indian trade on the frontier was in the hands of the Scots, who developed a natural aptitude for bargaining. They traveled far into the back country in search of skins and furs and transported them to market towns. In South Carolina, some of the most hard-bitten characters of colonial times were Scotsmen who practically monopolized the trade in furs and deerskins with the Cherokees. From the mountains, they brought their goods on packhorses to Charleston and sometimes included Indian slaves whom they had bought from their Cherokee captors. These they sold to the Charleston merchants for shipment to the West Indies.

After the Act of Union in 1707, many Scottish businessmen came to the colonies, and from then until the Revolution they exerted an important influence on the economic development of the country. All of the colonies received agents for Scottish shipping firms and mercantile houses, but in none were they more important than in Virginia and Maryland. There they established tobacco warehouses and stores at strategic points, and before the end of the colonial period, they absorbed so much of the tobacco trade that Glasgow surpassed Bristol and all the other ports of the United Kingdom except London in the importation of tobacco.[48] The Scottish merchants in the colonies were not invariably loved, for they were hard traders and in some areas, as in the Chesapeake region, they stifled native competition. During the period of controversy with Great Britain, they sympathized with the

[47] Dunaway, *The Scotch-Irish*, p. 171.

[48] See Jacob M. Price, "The Rise of Glasgow in the Chesapeake Tobacco Trade, 1707–1775," *The William and Mary Quarterly*, 3rd Ser., XI (1954), 179–199.

colonies; but when war became inevitable, they remained loyal to Britain and tried to prevent the outbreak, which in the end ruined their businesses.

Another influential group of Scotsmen were teachers and private tutors. During the last half of the eighteenth century, these teachers were found in most of the colonies, sometimes as permanent residents of a community, sometimes as itinerant teachers. They helped to civilize isolated regions, and in localities without organized schools the peripatetic Scottish teacher and the circuit-riding Scotch Presbyterian minister often provided the only means for frontier children to obtain a modicum of education. During the mid-eighteenth century, Scots almost monopolized teaching on Virginia and Maryland plantations. Philip Fithian of Princeton, one of the few native American tutors in Virginia, commented on the large number of Scots among the merchants, shopkeepers, and teachers in the circle of acquaintances whom he met at Nomini Hall.[49]

The greatest cultural contribution of the Scots was in their dogged insistence upon the necessity of a classical education, in the premium which they placed upon a learned ministry, and in their equating of godliness with a knowledge of Latin and Greek. If they did not literally believe that Latin and Greek would provide the passwords into heaven, Scotch schoolmasters and ministers managed to convey the suspicion that St. Peter would be more impressed by a learned man than a barbarian. The schools, academies, and colleges which they founded in all the areas where Scotch Presbyterians were dominant stand as a monument to their cultural ideas. The College of New Jersey, later Princeton, was their greatest colonial achievement in education, and John Witherspoon, sometime minister of the Presbyterian Church in Paisley, Scotland, was Princeton's most effective president in this period.

Witherspoon was an excellent example of the type of Scot who combined piety and classical learning, godliness and patriotic zeal for his adopted country. Among the Lowland Scots in the colonies, there were many other Presbyterian preachers and teachers who shared these qualities, but few had them in such a conspicuous degree as Witherspoon. From the time when he landed in Philadelphia in 1768, he

[49] Hunter D. Farish (ed.), *Journal and Letters of Philip Vickers Fithian, 1773–1774: A Plantation Tutor of the Old Dominion* (Williamsburg, Va., 1943), p. 39. See in Chapter V, p. 112.

considered himself a citizen of the new land. Equally zealous for his church and his country, he proved a statesman in both realms. He won the respect of both Old Side and New Light factions in the Presbyterian Church and united them in behalf of Princeton. He also was so highly regarded that he was drafted to serve in the first Continental Congress and was one of the signers of the Declaration of Independence. When the British occupied Princeton and burned Witherspoon's personal library, a contemporary wrote: "It grieves him much that he has lost his controversial tracts. He would lay aside the cloth to take revenge on them. I believe he would send them to the devil if he could." [50] These Scots, from the circuit rider on the outermost periphery of civilization to John Witherspoon of Princeton, were a tough-minded lot ready to fight the Prince of Darkness with pen or musket as occasion demanded.

The churches and schoolhouses built by the Scotch Presbyterians during the colonial period were lighthouses of religion and learning. It would be hard to overestimate their influence in reducing the frontier to a civilized way of life. This influence would persist and increase until the Scots had carried their religion and their learning to the distant Pacific Coast.[51]

[50] Quoted by Lyman H. Butterfield, *John Witherspoon Comes to America* (Princeton, N.J., 1953), pp. ix–x.

[51] This subject is treated in some detail in Louis B. Wright, *Culture on the Moving Frontier* (Bloomington, Ind., 1955), *passim*.

CHAPTER 4

Diversity of Religions

W HEN a dweller in the mid-twentieth century tries to project himself into the period of his colonial ancestors, one of his greatest difficulties is a comprehension of the pervasiveness of religion and its universal influence upon men, women, and children of the earlier age. Religious beliefs were almost as varied then as now; but whatever men believed, they believed with greater devotion than most of their descendants display today. That is not to say that our ancestors were more virtuous than we, but that they were more God-fearing. When the wicked sinned, more of them trembled in fear of eternal damnation.

Religion was not merely a Sunday ritual; in the seventeenth century it was an enveloping influence seven days in the week, and its all-pervading vitality lasted throughout the colonial period and affected all shades of opinion, Puritan, Anglican, Quaker, or Catholic. The seventeenth century was an age of faith, and the eighteenth saw only a relative weakening of ancient beliefs; indeed, among some groups like the Presbyterians the eighteenth century in America was an age of crusading devotion.

The land of opportunity beckoning from the New World offered privileges that minority groups in the Old World had not known, and they hastened to take advantage of them. The privilege of setting up one's own kind of religion in the new country, and of maintaining it there, made a strong appeal to devoted groups. Let no one imagine, as school children have sometimes been taught to believe, that our ancestors came in search of "religious toleration." Toleration was a concept that few of them recognized or approved. What they wanted was freedom from interference by opposing religious sects or unfriendly official authorities. Once firmly in the saddle themselves, sects that had been persecuted in England became equally zealous to root out heretics from their own order.

But North America was a vast land where men of every belief might hope to find refuge. Some of the colonies owed their inception to this search for a religious haven. As everyone knows, Massachusetts Bay began as a Puritan theocracy, Maryland as a home for persecuted Catholics, Pennsylvania as a destination for Quakers and quietists of all nations. Although we should remember that religion was not the primary motive that led most emigrants to brave the North Atlantic, we should not underestimate its importance in their thinking and planning, and its significance in the propaganda for the settlement of British America.

Popular books have said little about religion as one of the motivations for the colonial ambitions of Raleigh and his immediate successors, the promoters of the Virginia colony. But all of the early imperialists emphasized the necessity of establishing a Protestant bulwark against Catholic Spain. If England was to have a place in the sun of the New World, the argument ran, it must make haste to settle Protestants at strategic points on the American coast where they could block the further advance of Spain. Raleigh, Richard Hakluyt, Humphrey Gilbert, and a score of others made this argument vocal. Other Protestants used similar reasoning. A Calvinistic refugee from Antwerp, Willem Usselinx, in 1606, proposed that the Dutch West India Company should serve God and country—and at the same time enrich itself—by establishing bases on the flank of Spain's lines of communication to the New World. A battery of high-powered English preachers, including John Donne, the dean of St. Paul's, set themselves up as propagandists of the Virginia Company's activities.[1]

Preachers who accompanied the early settlers furthered the work by sending back accounts of the enterprise. One of the most interesting of these clerical narratives is Alexander Whitaker's *Good News from Virginia* (1613), published by authority of the Virginia Company, with an introduction almost as long as the original, by another

[1] Louis B. Wright, *Religion and Empire: The Alliance Between Piety and Commerce in English Expansion, 1558–1625* (Chapel Hill, N.C., 1943), *passim*.

parson, William Crashaw. Because of God's favor to the English, Crashaw pointed out, not all of the devil's machinations had been able to destroy the Company's work. God had taken special care, for example, to deliver Sir Thomas Gates and Sir George Somers from shipwreck and to reveal to them the Bermudas, a garden spot kept from other people until then that the English might enjoy it. Whitaker in his part of this essay insisted that to doubt the success of the Virginian enterprise was to doubt God's promises.

Other Anglican ministers were as emphatic as Crashaw and Whitaker in their assertion of God's interest in English colonization. Although the Puritans conceived of themselves as God's chosen instruments to establish a godly commonwealth in the New World, they had no monopoly of the sense of destiny in these matters. Lewis Hughes, one of the first Anglican ministers in Bermuda, sent back in 1615 *A Letter . . . from the Summer Islands* in which he declared that as God had placed cherubim before the Garden of Eden, so he had "terrified and kept all people of the world from coming into these islands to inhabit them" until the English were ready for their occupation.[2] In a later pamphlet published in 1621 Hughes further emphasized "the goodness of God in reserving and keeping these islands ever since the beginning of the world for the English nation, and in not discovering them to any to inhabit but to the English." God was clearly on the side of the English, whether they were Puritans or Anglicans.

In promotional tracts urging the advantages of colonization, clergymen and laymen alike emphasized the obligation of Englishmen to spread the Gospel among the heathen. They also pointed out that such soul-saving would be profitable in this world's goods, but that attitude is not proof of cynicism. Seventeenth-century Englishmen believed that God's promises included tangible assets. The concern of the early promoters for the salvation of the Indians was undoubtedly genuine, for they believed that the fulfillment of the scriptural injunction to go into all the world and preach the Gospel would insure the success of their enterprises. As a sort of insurance, they took care to send along preachers with the emigrants.

The Virginia Company of London sent a minister of the Church of England with the first group who settled Jamestown, and from that day until the Revolution the Established Church was the official re-

2 *Ibid.,* p. 113.

ligion of the colony. Although Dissenters, Quakers, and even a few Catholics found their way to Virginia, the Anglicans remained dominant. Robert Beverley, writing in 1705, observed that Virginia had "no more than five conventicles amongst them, namely three small meetings of Quakers, and two of Presbyterians," and "as for the Quakers, 'tis observed by letting them alone, they decrease daily." [3] Presbyterians and other nonconformists increased during the next seventy years, but the Established Church retained its official authority. During the seventeenth century the House of Burgesses from time to time enacted laws aimed at conformity, but with landowners eager for servants and settlers, nobody inquired too closely into the religion of a newcomer.

The Established Church as it developed in Virginia varied somewhat from the church in England. Perhaps the most important difference lay in the control by vestries instead of by patrons. Although the twelve vestrymen of each church were originally chosen by vote of the parishioners, the vestry soon became a self-perpetuating body exercising virtually independent control of its church. The Bishop of London, who had general oversight of ecclesiastical matters in the colonies, was a long way off; and even when he appointed an officer known as a commissary to represent him, that official had difficulty exercising authority over the vestries. The law provided that the governor had the right of inducting ministers into office, a ceremony which gave them privileges of tenure. To get around that, the vestries rarely presented ministers for induction but employed them from year to year, or for a term of years. Nevertheless, ministers could feel reasonably secure, for, as Beverley comments, they were "very rarely turned out without some great provocation." [4]

Throughout the colonial period, churches in Virginia had difficulty attracting able ministers. Salaries were paid at a fixed rate in pounds of tobacco, which meant that the minister's income varied with the fluctuation of the tobacco market and the quality of the crop. The plantation system also made Virginia a region of country churches with the hardships that a flock of widely scattered parishioners imposed upon a conscientious minister in the performance of his pastoral duties.

[3] Robert Beverley, *The History and Present State of Virginia,* ed. Louis B. Wright (Chapel Hill, N.C., 1947), pp. 261–262.
[4] *Ibid.,* p. 264.

The informality of the Virginia churches was something of a scandal to High-Church ecclesiastics back home, who from time to time urged more regard for "decency and order" in worship, forgetting that country churches, without trained choirs and equipment, could not sustain a ritual designed for a different order of society. Even the custom of burial in the churchyard had to be modified because many planters found the church inaccessible and buried their dead in plantation graveyards. In Virginia, as elsewhere on the frontier, the Episcopal ritual naturally followed Low-Church practice. Most Virginians probably shared the views of Robert Carter, who in 1720 wrote to his London agent concerning his sons: "I resolve the principles of our holy religion shall be instilled into mine betimes; as I am of the Church of England way, so I desire they should be. But the high-flown up-top notions and great stress that is laid upon ceremonies, any farther than decency and conformity, are what I cannot come into the reason of. Practical godliness is the substance—these are but the shell." [5]

The religion of Virginia's neighbor Maryland was more diverse— and more vexing to the authorities. When George Calvert, the first Lord Baltimore, was projecting the colony, he undoubtedly hoped to make it a refuge for his Catholic coreligionists, but there is no evidence that he dreamed of founding an exclusive Catholic commonwealth. He was wise enough to realize that he could not get enough settlers without making conditions attractive to immigrants of other religions. When the colony was finally launched in 1633 under Calvert's son, Cecil Calvert, the Proprietor was glad to welcome Protestants as well as Catholics. The first formal piece of legislation on the subject, called "An Act Concerning Religion," was not passed until 1649. This act specified that all who believed in the Trinity might have freedom of worship, Protestants and Catholics alike, but it imposed severe penalties for blasphemy against the Trinity; specified fines for those who spoke reproachfully of the Virgin Mary, the Apostles, and the Evangelists; and prescribed punishments for those who reviled each other by opprobriously applying the name of heretic, Papist, Puritan, or Jesuit. The intention of the act was apparently not toleration for all people, as we understand it, but to ensure peace in the settlement. When the Puritans gained the upper hand in 1654,

[5] Louis B. Wright (ed.), *Letters of Robert Carter, 1720–1727* (San Marino, Calif., 1940), p. 25.

however, they repealed this act and substituted another which extended freedom of worship only to those Protestants who were clear of any taint of "popery or prelacy." [6] This Act of 1654 disfranchised both Catholics and Anglicans. The Lord Proprietor regained his authority in 1658 and restored religious freedom. After the Revolution of 1688 in England, Maryland became a royal province, and Anglicans in the colony began to agitate for an Established Church, which was finally accomplished in 1702 through the efforts of Commissary Thomas Bray.

Meanwhile in New England Puritanism in various forms had established a dynamic religion which was to exert a profound influence on the future history of America. Puritanism was a crusading faith, originally intent upon purging the Church of England of elements believed inimical to its primitive purity. Some sectarians gave up hope of purifying the Established Church and separated from it. Others remained within the Establishment and continued to agitate for reforms. The Pilgrims who settled Plymouth were Separatists. The Puritans who founded the colony of Massachusetts Bay refused to admit that they were outside the church, but, finding themselves unable to conform to the ritual as prescribed by the bishops in England, they removed to New England where they sought to re-establish the true church pure and undefiled.

The Pilgrims who came over in the *Mayflower* and established themselves at Plymouth in 1621 influenced later American imaginations out of all proportion to their numbers or contemporary importance. The courage of William Bradford, the historian, of John Carver, the governor, and of others in that little company, which by 1637 still numbered only 549 souls, passed into legend and poetry. They became a symbol of simple virtue and strict ethical behavior rather than an active force in the developing life of America. In church government, it is true, the Pilgrims established the principle of independence for each congregation. But though this characteristic form of church government in New England may have owed something to the Pilgrims, other influences were more directly responsible for its widespread acceptance among the Puritans in the colonies.

Unlike Plymouth, the Massachusetts Bay Colony developed into a center of power for American Puritanism. Its influence was felt

[6] Charles M. Andrews, *The Colonial Period of American History: The Settlements* (New Haven, 1936), II, 310–311, 318.

throughout New England and its evangelical zeal affected regions as far afield as South Carolina. In the thirteen years between 1629 and 1642, approximately 20,000 English settlers came to New England, and most of them settled in the Bay Colony.[7] Although many of these immigrants were lukewarm in their religious professions, as the behavior of some of them vividly demonstrated, the ruling group were earnest and zealous Puritans who created in Massachusetts Bay a Christian commonwealth that profoundly influenced not only colonial development but later history. The dynamic energy of these immigrants made them a potent force in further expansion. When they found themselves out of harmony with local authorities, or ambitious for further opportunities, they sometimes moved on to adjacent territory. For generations, Massachusetts Bay was a hive from which Puritan sectarians swarmed.

John Winthrop and the other leaders, who procured the charter for the Massachusetts Bay Colony in 1629 and organized the movement to remove to the New World, were greatly troubled by the religious state of England. Charles I and his advisers, notably William Laud, who became Archbishop of Canterbury in 1633, were determined to root out nonconformity. In the opinion of many Puritans, their ultimate intention was to restore what the Puritans described as "popery." The growing emphasis upon ritualism and the increasing power of the bishops gave small encouragement to Winthrop and his kind to believe that they could purify the church at home. But in a new environment overseas, far removed from Laud and his minions, they might restore the church to its primitive virtues and set an example to the rest of Christendom. Furthermore, an economic depression had stimulated a desire to move to greener fields, and prospective emigrants were easily convinced that they could improve their lot by removing to New England.

Adhering to a modified form of Calvinism in theology, certain of their righteousness, and earnest in their zeal, the leaders of the Massachusetts Bay Colony believed that they could find the answer to all their questions, civil and religious, in the Bible. With the word of God as their guide, they set up a holy commonwealth which they felt

---

[7] Cf. Allen French, *Charles I and the Puritan Upheaval: A Study of the Causes of the Great Migration* (Boston, 1955), p. 15 *et passim*. Although Mr. French does not prove his thesis that religion was the dominant motive in this mass movement, he presents much useful information in readable form.

compelled to keep free from contaminating influences. That meant that they had to be even more zealous than Archbishop Laud—or the Spanish Inquisition—to enforce conformity to *their* beliefs. But Puritan conformity was even harder to enforce than conformity in other faiths because of its own doctrine that everybody should read the Bible to discover the truths revealed therein. Revelations naturally varied with individual readers, and the divisive effect of this personal interpretation of the Scriptures, implicit in all Protestantism, was a problem which perpetually vexed the leaders of Massachusetts Bay.

In the beginning they maintained the fiction that they had not separated from the Established Church, but their best casuists were unable to contradict the realities of their practice. Their polity departed from that of the Church of England, for despite what they said, Congregationalism prevailed from the outset. Indeed, the individual congregation became the essential unit of organized society and of local government. Towns developed around the church. As Massachusetts became thickly populated, migratory groups moved out as congregations to settle other towns in more distant territory. Church flocks, led by their chosen ministers, migrating as units, carried the religion and polity of Massachusetts Bay far beyond its borders. Self-government in the churches, and in the towns established around the churches, became a principle of New England ecclesiastical and political policy. Though democracy as we know it was a doctrine often vigorously disapproved by the leaders of the Massachusetts Bay Colony, the polity that they established prepared the way for the growth of democratic processes.

Under the influence of a sequence of English preachers, notably William Ames, William Perkins, John Preston, Richard Sibbes, and others contemporary with them, the Puritans developed a coherent body of ideas and doctrines.[8] In New England, the Puritans modified certain inherited doctrines, nowhere more significantly than in the development of their "Covenant Theology," which distinguished three covenants: The Covenant of Grace, or the invisible church of saints, God's body of elect; the Church Covenant, or the visible church composed of those who believe themselves elected to salvation and, because

[8] The best studies of Puritan thought are to be found in William Haller, *The Rise of Puritanism . . . 1570–1643* (New York, 1938) and *Liberty and Reformation in the Puritan Revolution* (New York, 1955).

of their virtuous lives and conviction of salvation, are accepted as members; and the Civil Covenant, or ruling body of civil authority.[9]

As applied to life in Massachusetts Bay, the three covenants led to the virtual identification of Church and State. If the ministers were the interpreters of God's will and the magistrates were the instruments for enforcing it, the distinction in their offices made very little difference in the administration of discipline. During the early days of the colony the civil magistrates carried out the instructions of the clergy, who managed to establish an effective theocracy. As one historian has expressed it, "in practice, and to a large extent even in theory, the three covenants were really one. The Church Covenant gave form to the Covenant of Grace, and the Civil Covenant gave power to the Church Covenant. Society in New England was actually organized, as Baxter said it should be, into a Holy Commonwealth." [10]

Membership in the Church Covenant was not for everyone. To be accepted by the congregation of God's saints, the individual had to give proof of a blameless life and make a statement that he had experienced a sense of his personal salvation. The elders in the church might cross-examine the candidate if they themselves were unconvinced that God had called him. Church membership was highly desirable, for it carried special privileges. In 1631, the General Court of Massachusetts Bay decided that "No man shall be admitted to the freedom of this body politic, but such as are members of some of the churches within the limits of the same." [11] Thus church membership became a requisite for being made a freeman of the commonwealth, and only freemen had the right to vote and participate in the government of the colony. It has been argued that Massachusetts Bay was not a theocracy because ecclesiastics were not technically the rulers,[12] but the influence of the clergy upon the magistrates was such that the effect was the same.

[9] The clearest and most concise statement of the Covenant Theology is to be found in Herbert W. Schneider, *The Puritan Mind* (New York, 1930), pp. 19 ff. A synthesis of the doctrines of the principal theologians who discussed the subject will be found in Perry Miller, *The New England Mind: The Seventeenth Century* (Cambridge, Mass., 1954), *passim;* and "The Marrow of Puritan Divinity," *Transactions of the Colonial Society of Massachusetts*, XXXII (1933–37), 247–300.

[10] Schneider, *The Puritan Mind*, pp. 24–25.

[11] Quoted by William W. Sweet, *Religion in Colonial America* (New York, 1942), p. 88.

[12] *Ibid.*, pp. 88–89.

Restriction of church membership to those who could give proof of their conversion, with a corollary restriction of suffrage to the saints, looked like a perfect plan to keep the Holy Commonwealth in the hands of the righteous. Unhappily for the pious, Massachusetts Bay prospered beyond the dreams of its founders, its population multiplied with new people who were not always saints, and, worst of all, the children of church members frequently were unable to testify that they had experienced conversion. By the mid-seventeenth century, the churches faced a dilemma. If they admitted the children of church members who could not testify that they were conscious of God's grace, they would destroy one of the pillars of their faith; if they did not admit them, they foresaw the rapid diminution of their numbers and power. To meet this problem, the Synod of 1662 ratified a proposal of the ministers to admit to membership, subject to certain reservations, the children of members who professed a belief in Christian principles and wished to affiliate with the church. Without satisfactory proof of conversion, however, they could not take communion and enjoy all the privileges of full membership in the church. But they could vote. This arrangement, called in derision the Half-Way Covenant, did little to stave off increasing secularism and precipitated a controversy in the New England churches.

The saints worked hard to keep the Holy Commonwealth unspotted from the world and clear of heretics, but, try as they might, they could not confound the hosts of Satan, nor could they prevent perverse and unorthodox ideas from invading the minds of men, even among the clergy. For example, the Reverend Roger Williams, who arrived in Massachusetts in 1631, proved a disappointment and a sore trial to his brethren. Because the Massachusetts Puritans still asserted that they were in communion with the Church of England, Williams declared that they were compounding corruption. After a spell as minister at Salem he moved over to Plymouth in search of a Separatist church. But soon he was back in Salem, annoying the brethren by complaining that the association of the clergy threatened the freedom of individual congregations. He also raised an even graver problem by questioning the right of the settlers to take land from the Indians. Such opinions required drastic action, and the magistrates in October, 1635, sentenced him to banishment, giving him six weeks to arrange his affairs. But when they learned that he was recruiting followers to form a settlement on Narragansett Bay, they forced him to flee in the dead of winter to the protection of the Rhode Island Indians.

Williams' recalcitrance was only the beginning of trouble. In September, 1637, a controversy over what was known as "Antinomianism" came to a climax with the heresy trial of Mrs. Anne Hutchinson before the General Court, held at Newtown (Cambridge) where the judges would not be influenced by the more liberal minds of Boston. Mrs. Hutchinson was a mystic who held meetings in her home, discussed the sermons of the ministers, and expounded her own belief in sanctification through grace as opposed to salvation through works. Her views were not unlike those held by the Quakers and other evangelical pietists. By declaring that an inner light was more important in salvation than moralism, law, and external demonstrations of piety, she came into conflict with the orthodox clergy and was sentenced to banishment. When she asked the reason for her punishment, Governor Winthrop ordered her to be silent: "Say no more, the court knows wherefore and is satisfied." [13] Mrs. Hutchinson's conviction did not receive unanimous approval even in Massachusetts Bay. She was not the only Antinomian. Shortly before her own trial the Reverend John Wheelwright had received a sentence to exile for similar views, and their cases won many sympathizers.

Even more obnoxious than Mrs. Hutchinson and John Wheelwright were the Quakers who began to invade the colony in the summer of 1656. The first to arrive in Boston were two women from Barbados, Mary Fisher and Ann Austin. On the pretext of looking for signs of witchcraft, the authorities stripped them naked and examined their bodies minutely. They then threw them into an unlighted cell for five weeks before shipping them back to Barbados. Fearful of Quakers' entering the commonwealth, the General Court tightened the laws to make it a crime for shipmasters to bring them to Massachusetts or for other individuals to aid them. In 1658, the General Court ordered the death penalty for Quakers returning after banishment. An old man, Nicholas Upsall, was fined and banished for aiding the two Quaker women. Another old man, a Quaker named William Brend, was so cruelly punished that the Boston populace made a disturb-

[13] A detailed account of Mrs. Hutchinson's trial is available in Charles Francis Adams, *Antinomianism in the Colony of Massachusetts Bay*, The Prince Society (Boston, 1894), pp. 285–336. For a recent analysis, see Richard B. Morris, *Fair Trial* (New York, 1953), pp. 3–32.

ance. To the people in the street it seemed hard that he should have his head and heels locked together with irons for sixteen hours and then be given 117 lashes with a tarred rope until he was unconscious. The Reverend John Wilson, however, assured the public that this was the will of Jehovah and that the jailer had only done his duty. The clergy were willing to be more merciful in some cases. When two Quakers could not pay their fines, the ministers agreed that it was equitable to sell their children into bondage and ship them away. Thus they could turn a profit and rid the Bay Colony of potential Quakers. Others required sterner treatment. Judge John Endecott and his fellow magistrates in October, 1659, sentenced William Robinson, Marmaduke Stevenson, and Mary Dyer to hang, but at the last minute they commuted the woman's penalty to banishment. Having seen her companions executed before her face, however, Mary Dyer was imbued with a spirit of martyrdom and returned the next year; such stubbornness met with quick retribution and she too was hanged.[14]

Though the clergy searched the Scriptures for warning texts, inveighed against heresy, and spurred the magistrates to punish all who deviated from the true faith, they could not keep the Bay Colony uncontaminated. Commerce brought Bostonians into contact with people of diverse beliefs and broke down the old religious isolationism. Young people drifted away from the faith of their fathers until gradually the power of the clergy was broken. Though Increase and Cotton Mather might rage, by 1684, when the Massachusetts Charter was forfeited, the colony was forced to tolerate Anglican worship. In the spring of 1687 Governor Edmund Andros arranged for Anglican services to be held in Old South Meeting House in Boston when it was not being used by its regular Congregational members. In the meanwhile, plans were afoot for the erection of King's Chapel, the first Anglican church in Boston. When a revolution in Massachusetts Bay, coinciding with the Glorious Revolution of 1688, drove out Governor Andros, some of the Congregationalists began an agitation to pull down the new church; Increase Mather published a tract on the unlawfulness of using the Book of Common Prayer; and a few opponents of Anglicanism broke windows in King's Chapel.[15] But the days of the Holy Com-

14 James T. Adams, *The Founding of New England* (Boston, 1911), pp. 263–274, gives a succinct account of the trouble with the Quakers in Massachusetts Bay. A more circumstantial treatment is that by Rufus M. Jones, *The Quakers in the American Colonies* (London, 1911).

15 Sweet, *Religion in Colonial America*, p. 48.

monwealth of Massachusetts Bay were over. When a new charter was granted, no longer was the right to vote determined by church membership, nor could the Congregationalists any longer exclude Anglicans.

Although the political power of Congregationalism was broken, Puritanism continued to be a vital and dynamic faith. In Massachusetts, Connecticut, and in other parts of New England, Congregationalism remained the dominant religion. In some communities, notably New Haven, it was even stricter and more conservative than in Massachusetts Bay. Migrating congregations tried to maintain their purity. In 1695 a congregation moved from Dorchester, Massachusetts, to South Carolina, where they named their settlement after the town of their origin. To support them in the faith and prevent their straying into Anglicanism, Cotton Mather kept them supplied with sermons of his own composition.

In contrast to the emphasis upon the visible church and its authority in Massachusetts was the extreme individualism of Roger Williams and his followers in Rhode Island. So great was their insistence upon the freedom of the individual that no formal church was organized until March, 1639, when a group in Providence united into a fellowship which Baptists claim as the first of their denomination in the New World.[16] As might have been expected from the tenets of these religious individualists, they could not agree among themselves. The Providence church was not even certain it should be called Baptist; because its members could agree that it was Baptist, the church at Newport, organized in 1644, also has a claim to being the first Baptist church in the colonies. Baptists of various shades of belief and many other sectarians found a haven in Rhode Island. Even Quakers and Jews were permitted to survive and worship as they pleased. Though Roger Williams personally detested Quakers and carried on a violent controversy with George Fox, no law placed them under a ban. When the rest of New England objected to Rhode Island's gentleness toward Quakers and commended Massachusetts' "prudent care" in eliminating them, the Narragansett colonists replied that they had no law "whereby to punish any for only declaring by words, etc. their minds and understandings concerning the things and ways of God as to salvation and an eternal condition." [17] Furthermore, where the Quakers

---

[16] *Ibid.*, pp. 128–129.

[17] John Russell Bartlett (ed.), *Records of the Colony of Rhode Island and Providence Plantations, in New England* (Providence, 1856), I, 336.

were let alone, they made small progress. Such were the tolerance and worldly wisdom which Rhode Island had learned.

Roger Williams' most famous letter, that written to the town of Providence in 1655, explains in simple terms without any theological hairsplitting his notions of liberty of conscience:

There goes many a ship to sea, with many hundreds of souls in one ship, whose weal and woe is common, and is a true picture of a commonwealth or a human combination or society. It hath fallen out sometimes that both Papists and Protestants, Jews and Turks, may be embarked in one ship; upon which supposal I affirm that all the liberty of conscience that ever I pleaded for turns upon these two hinges—that none of the Papists, Protestants, Jews, or Turks be forced to come to the ship's prayers or worship, nor compelled from their own particular prayers or worship, if they practice any. I further add that I never denied that, notwithstanding this liberty, the commander of this ship ought to command the ship's course, yea, and also command that justice, peace, and sobriety be kept and practiced both among the seamen and all the passengers. . . .[18]

The Dutch who settled New Netherland on the southern and western flanks of New England brought along with them another brand of Calvinism, the Dutch Reformed Church, which they established as the official religion of their colony, forgetting the tolerance of the mother country and prohibiting the public worship of other faiths. The one religion for which they made an exception was the Congregationalism of the New England Puritans who infiltrated Long Island and other Dutch territory.

Piety was not a characteristic quality of the early Dutch traders and farmers, but the Dutch West India Company, which ruled the colony, did not intend for its settlers to lapse into paganism. The Company sent along Reformed ministers and lay officials known as "comforters of the sick." The first minister, Domine Jonas Michaëlius, found at New Amsterdam a mixed group containing so many French Walloons that for their benefit he had to conduct some services in French.

[18] *The Letters of Roger Williams, 1632–1683,* ed. John Russell Bartlett, Narragansett Club, *Publications,* VI (1874), 278–279. Recent scholarship attempts to make a differentiation between the public acts of Roger Williams and his theological views. Cf. Mauro Calamandrei, "Neglected Aspects of Roger Williams' Thought," *Church History,* XXI (1952), 239–258, which makes out Williams to be an orthodox Calvinist imbued with theocratic authoritarianism. See also Perry Miller, *Roger Williams* (Indianapolis, 1953), which includes carefully chosen selections from Williams' writings with the author's own interpretations.

Michaëlius was a dour man who quarreled with Peter Minuit, the director, and wrote to a friend in Holland that the director was a compound of lies and iniquity. Michaëlius apparently had dreamed of ecclesiastical authority like that enjoyed by his fellow ministers in New England and was enraged when Minuit blocked his ambitions. The next minister, the Reverend Everardus Bogardus, was no happier over the state of affairs in New Netherland than Michaëlius had been. Like Michaëlius, Bogardus quarreled with the director, Wouter Van Twiller, and his successor, Willem Kieft. A master of invective, Bogardus described Van Twiller as a child of the devil and an incarnate villain and Kieft as a fountain of evil. The parson's enemies replied that he himself was guilty of habitual abuse in his language and of being drunk in his own pulpit.

Later ministers proved more tractable and did more to advance religion in New Netherland. For example, the Reverend Johannes Megapolensis served faithfully for six years in the patroonship of Kiliaen Van Rensselaer and organized a second Dutch Reformed church at what is now Albany. At the expiration of his term there in 1648 he was persuaded to become a minister in New Amsterdam. Megapolensis like other Dutch ministers complained of the drunkenness of his countrymen and their weakness for Indian women, two sins that kept him in a state of discouragement.

An effort to improve the morals of the community and to enforce the observance of religion was made by Peter Stuyvesant when he became director in 1647. As part of his reform movement, he tried to restrict the sale of liquor and forbade drinking on the Sabbath during the hours of religious service. He also required the clergy to preach twice on Sunday, morning and afternoon, and he ordered the populace to attend. By the end of his regime in 1664, eleven congregations of the Dutch Reformed Church had been organized in New Netherland under the ecclesiastical authority of the Classis of Amsterdam in Holland.

Encouraged by the clergy, Stuyvesant made an attempt to enforce conformity to the Reformed Church. Acting under a law of 1640 prohibiting public worship by other faiths, the director sought to keep out Quakers and Jews and to prevent the establishment of a Lutheran church. A Lutheran minister, John Ernest Goedwater, in 1658 was arrested and shipped back to Holland. When Stuyvesant and his leading minister, Megapolensis, began a campaign to prevent Portuguese

Jews from entering New Netherland, the West India Company over-ruled them and permitted Jews to settle and carry on their business, provided they conducted their religious services in private. In similar fashion, the Company ordered Stuyvesant to cease his persecution of Quakers and commended the example of Amsterdam in providing a haven for men of all faiths. Despite the desire of the Reformed clergy and the help of local authorities, New Netherland never became a Calvinistic commonwealth. The settlers who made up the popula-tion were of a great variety of religions, and the actual rulers in Hol-land were more concerned about trade than about enforcing religious conformity.

After the conquest of New Netherland by the English in 1664, Anglicans grew more numerous, and in 1693 they contrived to get through the Assembly a Church Act which in effect gave the Anglican Establishment legal status in six parishes. Trinity Church, which be-came the richest and most fashionable in colonial New York, re-ceived a charter in 1697. New York was too polyglot and too varied in religions, however, to permit any one faith to dominate. A cele-brated trial in 1707 helped to establish the principle of religious free-dom. In that year Governor Cornbury had a Presbyterian minister, the Reverend Francis Makemie, arrested and jailed for six weeks for preaching without a license. The court freed the minister and the Assembly soon passed legislation to prevent a recurrence of religious persecution. Before the end of the colonial period, New York boasted houses of worship of diverse faiths, including one congregation of Jews.

The settlers who came to the two Carolinas were also varied in their religious interests. Although the lords proprietors had promised religious freedom, they did not ban the eventual establishment of the Church of England. Efforts of the Church party to procure such an establishment were the cause of bitter political feuds in the early eighteenth century.

By 1704 the population of South Carolina was slightly more than half Anglican, and in that year they succeeded in passing a law mak-ing membership in the Church of England a requisite for election to the legislative assembly, an act which the Board of Trade vetoed. Nevertheless, two years later, the Board of Trade approved a new law establishing the Church of England with support from the public funds. The Calvinistic French Huguenots, who settled in the coastal region where the Anglicans were most numerous, in time overcame their scruples and thriftily joined the church supported by taxation. In the up country, however, where Scotch Presbyterians became the most numerous sect, there was constant agitation against the Anglican establishment, and the animosity between up-country Presbyterians and low-country Anglicans made a political rift so deep that it persisted until the twentieth century.

The Anglican element in North Carolina, in spite of strenuous opposition, succeeded finally in 1715 in getting through a law establishing the Church of England, but not until 1732 did the colony have a regular minister of that faith. The efforts to set up the church had been discouraging. The Society for the Propagation of the Gospel sent the Reverend John Blair in 1704 as a missionary to the North Carolinians, but he departed in gloom declaring that Quakers, Presbyterians, and some others "like Presbyterians" outnumbered the better sort of people who belonged to the Church of England.[19] William Byrd, with characteristic Virginian contempt of the region to the south, also commented in 1728 on the irreligious condition of North Carolinians, who were "not troubled with any religious fumes" and "did not know Sunday from any other day, any more than Robinson Crusoe did." [20] Throughout most of the colonial period, it must be remembered, however, North Carolina was a frontier region with a mature and decorous society at only a few points on the coast. In the interior, as elsewhere in the colonies, evangelical Dissenters, for the most part Presbyterians, along with some Baptists and Quakers, predominated.

As was natural from the conditions of its settlement, Pennsylvania, of all the colonies, came to be the most conglomerate in religion. Distressed at the persecution of religious groups in England and elsewhere in Europe, William Penn conceived of his proprietary grant on the Delaware as a refuge for oppressed peoples of all kinds, especially for persecuted Quakers. Already Quakers had made settlements in East and West Jersey and Penn had interested himself in those undertakings. Pennsylvania promised to be a haven for Quakers and related sects on a much larger scale. Philadelphia, first settled by Quakers of Penn's choosing, quickly became a port of entry for thousands of

[19] Hugh T. Lefler (ed.), *North Carolina History Told by Contemporaries* (Chapel Hill, N.C., 1934), pp. 45–46.

[20] William K. Boyd (ed.), *William Byrd's Histories of the Dividing Line* (Raleigh, N.C., 1929), p. 72.

immigrants attracted by the promise of rich lands and complete freedom of religious beliefs.

The Quakers, for many years the controlling group in the colony, were strict moralists, not unlike the Puritans in some of their social doctrines. Although they never condoned the enforcing of a man's conscience, they did not confuse freedom of conscience with license to behave as one wished. Consequently they often set themselves up as censors of behavior. For example, since they regarded stage plays as vanities and temptations to evil, the Quakers of Philadelphia banned theatrical performances under penalty of hard labor. When a theater was eventually established outside Philadelphia, Quakers and Presbyterians both complained of the neighboring iniquity. Although no civil laws forbade extravagance and frivolity, the Quakers through their monthly meetings exercised a strict control over their own members and frowned on worldly behavior in others.

Among the early arrivals in Pennsylvania were Germans representing various Pietist groups. Under the leadership of Francis Daniel Pastorius, a lawyer of Frankfurt, German Quakers of Swiss Mennonite background emigrated from the Rhineland in 1683 and settled Germantown. They were soon followed by other related sectarians who all shared with the Quakers a deep-seated pacifism. Coming principally from the Rhineland, which had been periodically devastated by war, they looked upon Pennsylvania as a land of peace where they could work out their own salvation untouched by marching armies. Since their religion frowned on worldly vanities and encouraged its adherents to regard themselves as a people set apart, they naturally developed a clannishness that has persisted among their descendants to this day. Their extreme individualism in Biblical interpretation led to a great range in the shades of their religious opinions. The core of their doctrine, like that of the Quakers, was a belief in the guidance of an inner light.

Even among the first waves of settlers, men of varied beliefs came to Pennsylvania and found a welcome. Pastorius, for instance, remarks that in his mess on shipboard he counted a Catholic, a Lutheran, a Calvinist, an Anabaptist, an Anglican, and a Quaker. French Huguenots found Philadelphia a promising city in which to ply their trades and crafts. The German settlers who came after the turn of the century were frequently Lutherans or members of the German Reformed Church. The Lutherans discovered that the Swedes in Delaware had already introduced their mode of worship to the region. In Lancaster County early in the eighteenth century Mennonites and German Baptist Brethren, sometimes called Dunkers, made up the majority of the population.

In the light of later history, perhaps the most significant group who came to Pennsylvania in the eighteenth century were the Scotch-Irish Presbyterians who entered the port of Philadelphia, filtered through the German settlements, and finally reached the back country, where they became typical frontiersmen. They became the vanguard of westward expansion, carrying with them always a devotion to education and religion. Presbyterian churches dotted the frontier, and the church and the blockhouse were the symbols of advancing civilization. The Scotch Presbyterians, frequently immigrants from the Scottish settlements in the North of Ireland, hated the Anglican establishment and the English government which had tried in Ireland to make them conform. This animosity was an important factor in the growth of hostility toward Great Britain in the later eighteenth century.

Like Pennsylvania, Georgia, the last of the English colonies settled, permitted men of all religious opinions to own land and worship as they pleased. Though the authorities at first sought to exclude Catholics and Jews, the initial prohibition was soon abandoned and immigrants of both religions found a place in Georgia.[21] Some of the earliest immigrants were Lutherans from Salzburg, Austria, who in 1736 settled at Red Bluff on the Savannah River. They were soon followed by German Moravians, but these pacifists found the nearness of the Spanish border and the consequent threat of war so disturbing that in 1740 they migrated to Pennsylvania. Scotch Presbyterians, Congregationalists, Anglicans, Baptists, Jews, and a few Catholics were among the other faiths represented by the immigrants.

Miscellaneous preachers and humanitarians came to Georgia as missionaries and doers of good. In 1736, John Wesley, the founder of Methodism, arrived in Savannah, accompanied by his brother Charles, the hymn writer. Their visit was not too happy either for the Wesleys or the Georgians. Charles soon departed, but John stayed long enough to fall in love with Sophia Hopkey, one of his congregation. When his

[21] E. Merton Coulter, *Georgia: A Short History* (Chapel Hill, N.C., 1947), p. 31.

conscience—supplemented by the advice of some of his Moravian friends—bade him discourage the girl, she married a Georgian who sued Wesley for defaming his wife's character. So unpleasant were the proceedings that Wesley fled to Charleston, South Carolina, and sailed from there to England.

More successful was one of Wesley's followers, George Whitefield, who reached Savannah in 1738 on the first of seven visits to the American colonies. One of his early philanthropic enterprises was an orphanage which he established at Bethesda near Savannah. The orphanage was supported partially out of profits from a plantation in South Carolina which Whitefield acquired and worked with slave labor. His preaching journeys thoughout the colonies were prompted in part by efforts to raise money for this orphanage. Whitefield, one of the most dramatic and moving preachers of the eighteenth century, played a major role in the religious revival known as the Great Awakening, which reached a crescendo in 1740. The emotionalism demonstrated in his preaching became a characteristic of American revivals from that day to this, and Whitefield's activities accelerated the trend toward mass hysteria in religion, signs of which were already evident when he first set foot on this continent.

Although it is conventional for preachers in every age to lament the current decline of religious zeal, their complaints in the 1720's and 1730's had a basis in fact. The older colonies had attained a certain degree of maturity and had prospered. Increased urbanity and ease brought a relaxation in earlier religious rigor. Moreover the growth of towns, the increase of commerce, and the expansion of trade overseas introduced distracting influences which the preachers observed as evidence of iniquity. Verily the young people were forgetting God and following the broad highway to destruction. In the emergency, preachers in various localities began to call their flocks to repentance and warn them of the yawning depths of hell. Frontier preachers, as always, urged their congregations to avoid the snares and pitfalls prepared for them in the towns and cities. Nor did they spare their own backwoods communities. Satan was waiting behind every cabin and lean-to ready to snatch the unwary to destruction.

One of the earliest of the revivalists to make a stir was Theodorus J. Frelinghuysen, a New Jersey preacher of the Dutch Reformed Church. Up and down the Raritan valley and elsewhere in that region, Frelinghuysen preached a doctrine of hellfire and damnation. With the assistance of lay exhorters, he worked his congregations into a fever of excitement. More conventional preachers of the Reformed Church objected to Frelinghuysen's methods and by 1726 he had already brought about a split in the Reformed Church.[22]

A revival movement among the Scotch-Irish Presbyterians also resulted in a division in that sect. The Presbyterian revival was led by Gilbert Tennent, son of William Tennent, who had established a backwoods school, known as the Log College, for the training of preachers, at Neshaminy, Pennsylvania. When Gilbert Tennent became minister of the Presbyterian church at New Brunswick, New Jersey, he had an opportunity to observe the harvest of souls reaped by Frelinghuysen and he was soon emulating the Reformed preacher. Tennent and other graduates of the Log College who joined in the revival were so violent in their denunciation of sin and sinners that they too produced an emotional hysteria in their congregations. They were scarcely less restrained in denouncing ministers who gave no manifestation of conversion. Tennent's sermon on "The Danger of an Unconverted Ministry," first preached in 1739 and printed in 1740, alienated the less extreme ministers and fostered a schism.[23]

Before the Great Awakening, the ground had already been prepared in New England for a revival of religion. Moved by the eloquence of a preacher here and there, revivals had briefly called people to repentance, but it remained for Jonathan Edwards to stir the embers and set aflame the souls of his congregation at Northampton, Massachusetts. Between 1733 and 1735, Northampton underwent a religious convulsion. Children organized into prayer groups and trembled at the thought of the blackness of their sins. Their elders openly confessed their sins and repented. Stricken by remorse, one man of weak mind tried suicide, and another, Joseph Hawley, Edwards' own uncle, cut his throat and died. Others, according to the preacher, heard voices saying, "Cut your own throat. Now is a good opportunity." [24] At last

[22] Charles H. Maxson, The Great Awakening in the Middle Colonies (Chicago, 1920), pp. 11–20. Still valuable is an older book, Joseph Tracy, The Great Awakening: A History of the Revival of Religion in the Time of Edwards and Whitefield (Boston, 1842). See also Wesley M. Gewehr, The Great Awakening in Virginia, 1740–1790 (Durham, N.C., 1930).

[23] Maxson, The Great Awakening, pp. 21–39.

[24] Ola Elizabeth Winslow, Jonathan Edwards, 1703–1758: A Biography (New York, 1941), p. 165. Emphasis on the thought of Jonathan Edwards will be

the fever ran its course and Northampton for a time returned to normal.

Edwards preached a return to the religion of his fathers. He opposed the new latitudinarianism and emphasized afresh the sovereignty of God, the depravity of man, and the necessity of experiencing a sense of election if one would be sure of his salvation. In short, Edwards set out to rehabilitate Calvinism and to deny the validity of Arminianism,[25] which had been making inroads in more than one New England congregation. He also knew how to magnify the terrors of hell. Although his most famous sermon, "Sinners in the Hands of an Angry God," based on the text, "Their feet shall slide in due time," was preached in 1741 at Enfield, Connecticut, after the furor of the first Northampton revival was over, it illustrates the type of fear-provoking homily which struck whole congregations to their knees in paroxysms of fear.

Revivalism reached a new intensity in 1739–40 when George Whitefield made a journey through the colonies preaching as he went. His visitation had the violence of a hurricane as he swept throngs of sinners prostrate with the power of his words. Landing at Philadelphia in August, 1739, he at first went south to Georgia and then returned for a northern journey which took him into New England. During his ten days in Boston and its environs in September, 1740, he shook that town to its foundations. A publicity campaign equal to any devised by his modern counterparts prepared the way. Wherever he went, crowds preceded him. When he preached, solid citizens openly wept and confessed their sins; many fell into faints and some groveled on the floor.

Whitefield was not an imposing figure and he had a definite squint in one eye, but his voice had a magnetic power and his dramatic ability made even David Garrick once declare that he would give a hundred guineas if he could say "oh" with the intensity of the

---

found in Perry Miller, *Jonathan Edwards* (New York, 1949). "The real life of Jonathan Edwards," Mr. Miller comments, "was the life of the mind. Hence, in order that the emphasis may fall in the proper measure, this book is focussed upon the drama of his ideas, and the external biography is restricted to basic essentials," p. xi.

[25] Arminianism, the belief accepted by the Methodists and related groups, opposed the notion of absolute predestination with a doctrine of conditional election, universal redemption, belief in regeneration through the operation of the Holy Spirit or being "born again," and the doctrine that man may resist grace and "backslide" or fall from grace.

preacher. Lord Chesterfield testified that Whitefield could cause men to weep merely by the way he rolled the syllables of "Mesopotamia" under his tongue, and Chesterfield himself was so moved by a description of a blind beggar walking over a cliff that he involuntarily started and exclaimed, "My God, he's gone." [26] Benjamin Franklin, certainly not one to lose his head at a revival, wrote down in his *Autobiography* a famous passage which describes how he emptied his pockets into the collection plate under the influence of the evangelist.

Whitefield, like Tennent, Edwards, and most of the other revivalists of the Great Awakening, was Calvinistic in the tenor of his theology; he and many of the others preached what can be described as an old and conservative doctrine of God's complete sovereignty and the depravity of man, but their congregations were little concerned with theology as such. That was for preachers who knew about such things. The listeners were concerned with the fear of hell, and the sermons of the revivalists scared them out of their wits. Whitefield's preaching had the effect of making men feel that they stood naked and alone, exposed to the gaze of an angry God who knew their innermost thoughts and motives. In imminent peril of their souls, they fell down and begged for mercy.

The Great Awakening raged on for a few years, but by 1744 zeal for revival preaching had dwindled. Ministers who had doubted the good of such religious excesses now openly opposed a renewal of evangelistic activity. Harvard College, which had welcomed Whitefield in 1740, passed a resolution four years later in opposition to him and his conduct. Pamphlet wars raged as both sides argued their merits in anger. Jonathan Edwards found himself under attack and in such disfavor at his alma mater, Yale, that he henceforth attended commencement at Princeton. At Yale, certain members of the senior class thought the time propitious to attempt the publication of Locke's *Essay on Toleration,* and for his part in so revolutionary an enterprise one senior was refused his diploma. Churches were rent asunder. Tennent's group in the Presbyterian Church, known as New Lights, broke away from the group known as the Old Side, which opposed revivalism. The Congregationalists in New England suffered losses. Many

[26] For a succinct account of Whitefield's part in the Great Awakening, see Winslow, *Jonathan Edwards*, pp. 175–193. Still valuable as a repository of information about Whitefield is L. Tyerman, *The Life of the Rev. George Whitefield* (2nd ed., 2 vols., London, 1890).

conventional folk, disgusted with the unrestrained excesses of the evangelists, went over to the Anglican communion where respectable people might worship with decorum, untroubled by a noisy preacher shouting that they were damned. Other Congregationalists, however, displeased at the "coldness" of their churches after the first fervor of evangelism had died, strayed off to the New Light Presbyterians, the Baptists, or to some other faith more to their liking.

The revivalists, who based their doctrine on an old conservative theology, achieved the paradoxical effect of stimulating radical political movements in colonial society, especially in frontier communities. The Great Awakening, like other Protestant upheavals, was a disrupting influence. However conservative the theology of the evangelists, their manner was that of rabble-rousers. Moreover, by condemning the clergy who did not share their enthusiasms for the outpouring of the spirit, Tennent and his group brought older ecclesiastical jurisdictions into disrepute and helped increase the spirit of religious individualism and resistance to external authorities. Hostilities between sects were magnified. The New Light Presbyterians, for example, looked with increased suspicion upon the Anglicans, and their animosity was not diminished by the political controversies developing with Great Britain. Radical sectarian groups multiplied and frequently found themselves in conflict with established political authorities. Not only did the Great Awakening bring about religious confusion, but it had subtle repercussions on politics in the next decades.

The growth of the Anglican Church in the various colonies resulted in a renewal of a proposal to appoint an American bishop. Since there was no bishop resident in the colonies, the Anglican Church suffered certain handicaps. Young men seeking holy orders had to journey to England to be ordained, and even formal confirmation of church members required the ministrations of a bishop. From the beginning of colonization, the Bishop of London had the oversight of the colonial church, and from time to time he appointed a commissary to represent him in the colonies, but the commissary did not possess the ecclesiastical functions of a bishop. After the organization of the Society for the Propagation of the Gospel, the missionary efforts of the Anglican Church increased and the officers of the Society began a fresh agitation for an American episcopate.

The reasons that prevented the appointment of a bishop were

political.[27] In most of the colonies, Dissenters, for whom bishops had become the symbol of tyranny, predominated. Even though the law required colonies like Massachusetts Bay to tolerate the Established Church, the appearance of an American bishop would have caused political unrest and probably mob violence. In Virginia, where the Established Church was strongest, there was no great demand on the part of church members for a bishop. The Virginians felt that they were doing very well without episcopal interference; their children could grow up in the church and share in its sacraments without formal confirmation; a bishop would mean a burden of added expense; and the vestries were of no mind to invite both expense and trouble and to diminish their own authority. Dr. James Blair, who had been appointed commissary in the late years of the seventeenth century, was not the kind of personality to make the prospect of a bishop more appealing. Dr. Blair was a stiff-necked Scot who appeared to find as much comfort in a quarrel as he did in his religion. If a bishop were appointed, Dr. Blair would certainly be a candidate. That possibility was enough to make influential planters cool to the idea, at least during his lifetime.

As the political controversies with Great Britain became more acute after the middle of the eighteenth century, the effort to set up an American bishop looked to anti-British agitators as merely one more effort of the Tories to fasten imperial authority on the colonies. Although New England and New York Anglicans felt the need of a bishop to strengthen their positions, they were unable to persuade the southern Anglicans to support their memorials to the government in England. After the passage of the Stamp Act in 1765, the controversy over the episcopate became a burning issue displaying much of the bigotry on both sides that would be characteristic of American religious controversies for generations to come.

Dissenters loudly asserted that the Church of England sought to renew the tyranny of Archbishop Laud and Charles I. Furthermore, they maintained, the Established Church in England was rapidly falling under the sway of Rome, and Thomas Hollis of London, a Baptist benefactor of Harvard College, wrote friends in New England that the "foulest Hydra Popery" was receiving the encouragement of

[27] The details of the long controversy over an American bishop will be found in Arthur L. Cross, *The Anglican Episcopate and the American Colonies* (New York, 1902). Cf. Evarts B. Greene, "The Anglican Outlook on the American Colonies," *American Historical Review*, XX (1914), 64–85.

the higher clergy and would soon dominate the Establishment. Moved by this threat, the Reverend Jonathan Mayhew sounded a tocsin for New England: "Is the infernal Gun-Powder Plot, are other treasonable and execrable conspiracies of English papists forgotten? . . . Are all their diabolical treacheries and cruelties buried in oblivion?" [28] Clearly they were not, and propagandists against Great Britain found it easy to correlate the movement to bring over an Anglican bishop with the danger of popery and threats to American liberty. Congregationalists in Connecticut and Presbyterians in New York, Pennsylvania, and other colonies set up committees of correspondence to bring the problem to the attention of Dissenters influential in politics in England. They might have saved their energy, because the King's party had no intention of appointing an American bishop. The King's men were intent upon concentrating power in London instead of diffusing it.

Religion, which was such a significant influence in the settlement of the colonies, had an important part in the controversies that finally resulted in American independence. Over a long period, dissenting faiths had waged war against efforts of the British government to control them. After 1765, most of these groups were ardent propagandists for the patriot cause. Congregational and Presbyterian pulpits rang with condemnations of the Tories. In the northern colonies, the Anglicans fought the King's cause; but in Virginia, Maryland, and South Carolina, where Anglicans had long been dominant, they were frequently as zealous in their opposition to the Crown as were the Dissenters. Not all of the minority faiths were anti-British. For example, the Quakers of Pennsylvania, who had grown prosperous and conservative, were naturally opposed to the violent propaganda emanating from Samuel Adams and his radicals in Boston. Likewise the Baptists, who had found New England Congregationalists and Virginia Anglicans ready to invoke statutes against them, found much of the talk about liberty merely sounding brass. Though they had no love for British rule, they had found that local tyrannies might be worse. But wherever Scotch-Irish Presbyterians gathered, in the towns or on the frontiers, they shouted about injustice and demanded freedom. In the years of controversy, the pulpit, as always in America, took sides and exerted a powerful influence.

[28] Jonathan Mayhew, *Remarks on an Anonymous Tract* (Boston, 1764), pp. 72–73. Cf. John C. Miller, *Origins of the American Revolution* (Boston, 1943), p. 191.

CHAPTER 5

Zeal for Education

TWENTIETH-CENTURY Americans have become so accustomed to thinking of secondary education as universally free, a responsibility of the state, that it is difficult for them to realize that three centuries ago free schooling was the exception and not the rule in the British colonies. Indeed the notion that the government had an obligation to supply free schools to every child was a matter of slow development and did not gain general acceptance until within the memory of men living today. Yet from the beginning of the English settlements on this continent, there is evidence of persistent concern lest the children of the settlers should grow up barbarous in the wilderness. This concern was no monopoly of any group. Anglicans in Virginia and the Carolinas, Catholics in Maryland, Puritans in New England, and Quakers in Pennsylvania were constantly discussing the means of ensuring some degree of education for the children of their particular areas. The kind and quality of education varied from region to region, but nowhere was there consistent neglect or a lapse into the barbarism so much feared by the new inhabitants of a wild country.

The emphasis upon reading the Bible and pious books characteristic of the English Puritans was shared in some degree by most Protestants who had made the personal interpretation of the Scriptures a tenet of their religion. The ability to read the Scriptures therefore was a way to salvation, and men and women had a religious obligation to teach their children this essential art. In most areas, those who had the means to pay for instruction were expected to provide for their children. What to do about orphans and poor children was the subject of discussion in all the colonies. The New Englanders succeeded best in creating schools in which children of both the prosperous and the poor could gain the minimum essentials of education, but the other colonies also struggled with the problem. New England, however, had the great advantage of a compact town life, which more than any other factor made possible its educational progress. The agrarian colonies, especially those with widely separated plantations, as in Virginia and Maryland, had the greatest difficulty in establishing schools. Regardless of good intentions and pious hopes, geography is hard to transcend.

The Puritans of Massachusetts Bay also had the initial advantage of a strong centralized government dominated by a clergy who had firm opinions about training the young in a knowledge of the Bible and "other parts of good learning." By persuasion or authority, Massachusetts Bay could see that every child had an opportunity to learn to read. Connecticut and the other New England colonies except Rhode Island followed the example set by Massachusetts. In the remainder of British North America both the authority and the will to establish schools were weaker, but even so a surprising number of schools provided at least a modicum of learning to the increasing population, and in some fashion a great number of colonial boys learned to read. When one surveys the difficulties, the amazing fact is not that schools were few and poor but that so many colonial Americans somehow acquired the basic elements of an education.

Within ten years after the first settlement at Jamestown, the colonial authorities were taking steps to found a school. King James himself sent instructions to the bishops to collect money in their dioceses for this undertaking, and the treasurer of the Virginia Company in 1619 reported approximately £1,500 on hand for "that pious work." [1] The Virginia Company set aside ten thousand acres of land to support "the university to be planted at Henrico" and one thousand acres to support a "college for the conversion of infidels." Nothing came of this or other early plans for education in Virginia because the Indian massacre of 1622 nearly annihilated the colony and such settlers as

[1] More details of the attitude of the colonial Virginians toward education will be found in the chapter entitled "The Planters' Concern over Education" in Louis B. Wright, *The First Gentlemen of Virginia* (San Marino, Calif., 1940), pp. 95–116.

were left alive had no enthusiasm for educating the infidels' children or for any other educational projects. Learning would have to wait until the colony recovered from the massacre.

The earliest school in Virginia to survive was established by Benjamin Symmes, a local planter, who left by will in 1635 two hundred acres of land and the increase and milk of eight cows to provide for the education of children from Elizabeth City and Kiquotan parishes. Thomas Eaton in 1659 founded another school in Elizabeth City with a gift of five hundred acres of land, two Negro slaves, and cattle. Both the Symmes Free School and the Eaton Free School lasted until 1805, when they were united in Hampton Academy. They gave instruction in reading, writing, arithmetic, and perhaps some Latin.

The wills of other Virginia planters showed a concern for the elementary education of children too poor to have instruction supplied by their parents. For example, Richard Russell, a Quaker of Lower Norfolk County, in 1667 set aside a part of his estate for the education of six poor children, "and after these six are entered, then if six more comes, I give a part also to enter them in like manner." [2] The Reverend John Farnefold, minister of St. Stephen's parish in Northumberland County in 1702 bequeathed one hundred acres of land and the schoolbooks in his study to found Winchester School, which would be required to teach free four or five poor children of the parish and to give them their diet, lodging, and washing, "and when they can read the Bible and write a legible hand to dismiss them and take in more." [3]

In general, the practice of the so-called free schools in the southern colonies was to collect fees from parents able to pay and admit free only orphans and children too poor to pay their own way. How many such schools were available in Virginia during the first century of colonization cannot be estimated, for the records are vague and scanty. But many wills did provide something for charitable schooling of this kind.

The great distances that separated plantations scattered along the bays and rivers of Virginia and Maryland made most of them inaccessible to such schools as were established. Every planter of means tried to hire a tutor for his children. In some cases two or three planters in

[2] *The Virginia Magazine of History and Biography,* I (1893–94), 326–327.
[3] "Schools in Virginia," *The William and Mary College Quarterly,* 1st Ser., XVII (1908–09), 244–247.

reach of one another joined together to procure teachers for their children. In many instances, these teachers were indentured servants. More than one Virginia or Maryland father sought to "buy" a servant well seen in Latin to serve as tutor in the household. One observer reported that two-thirds of the schoolmasters in Maryland just before the Revolution were either indentured servants or convicts.[4]

The children of the poorer farmers remote from schools had to make shift as best they could. Occasionally the parson gave a little instruction in reading. More often the parents, when they were themselves literate, taught their children the rudiments of learning. At best, children on isolated farms in the agrarian colonies received little instruction beyond the ability to spell out the catechism and to scrawl their names. Only rarely did a slave learn to read.

Conditions were far more favorable to learning in the compact towns and villages of the northern colonies. When a school was established, every child in the community could get there in some fashion, and the cost of hiring teachers was either a civic responsibility or could be shared by the parents. This economic factor alone made education available to children in New England whose parents would have been unable to pay the higher costs of schooling in the agrarian colonies.

Massachusetts Bay also had another advantage. No other colony had such a high proportion of university graduates among its leaders. They immediately set about establishing a pattern of education as nearly like the one they had known in England as they could make it, for they conceived of the new land of promise as another England purged of its errors and shortcomings. Their children would be brought up to be virtuous and educated men and women, and success was assured, Samuel Eliot Morison observes, "in a community so well provided with ministers, schoolmasters, and birch trees." [5]

Within five years of its settlement, Massachusetts Bay had set about founding a grammar school with a basic Latin curriculum like the grammar schools of England. To that end, the inhabitants of Boston in April, 1635, held a meeting and elected "our brother Mr. Philemon Pormort" to "become schoolmaster for the teaching and nurturing of

---

[4] Marcus W. Jernegan, *Laboring and Dependent Classes in Colonial America, 1607–1783* (Chicago, 1931), p. 53, quoting Jonathan Boucher.

[5] Samuel Eliot Morison, *The Founding of Harvard College* (Cambridge, Mass., 1935), p. 157.

children with us," and the next year a group described as some of the "richer inhabitants" raised money to hire Daniel Maude, late of Emmanuel College, to teach. Thus began the Boston Latin School which has enjoyed a distinguished reputation from that day to this.[6] Almost simultaneously the little town of Charlestown hired a schoolmaster, and soon other New England towns were establishing schools: Dorchester, Salem, Lynn, New Haven, and others. The most famous schoolmaster of the early period, Ezekiel Cheever, began his career at New Haven in 1642. In addition to grammar schools with the traditional Latin curriculum, there were writing schools where both penmanship, reading, and arithmetic could be learned. These ranged from the most elementary dame schools to slightly more advanced schools where apprentices could learn the rudiments of ciphering and bookkeeping.

Whether the term "free school" meant precisely what it means today—a tax-supported public school open without cost to all—has been questioned. "The name 'free school,' which was applied not only to the Latin School but to the writing schools," says the historian of the Boston Latin School, "meant a democratic, public institution not restricted to any class of children. . . . The schools were also free, in the modern connotation of the term, because tuition fees were not charged to residents of the town but only to non-residents. A small amount was expected for 'entrance and fire money,' but this fee was not required."[7] Certainly the founders of New England set out to ensure that schooling should not be denied to any child because of poverty, and legislation enacted in various New England colonies throughout the colonial period indicates an acceptance of responsibility by the local governments for elementary education. The wording of the act passed by the General Court of Massachusetts Bay in 1642 is significant. It required the selectmen in every town to make periodic inquiries of parents and masters concerning the training of children and apprentices, "especially their ability to read and understand the principles of religion and the capital laws of the country."[8] In cases of negligence the selectmen were instructed to impose fines and to apprentice children where they might gain the rudiments of an education. In 1647, the General Court of Massachusetts again passed a law

[6] Pauline Holmes, *A Tercentenary History of the Boston Public Latin School, 1635–1935* (Cambridge, 1935), p. 3.

[7] *Ibid.*, p. 28.

[8] *Ibid.*, p. 6.

looking toward universal literacy in the colony, because, the preamble
to the act observed, "that old deluder, Satan," had as one of his chief
projects, a plan "to keep men from the knowledge of the Scriptures
. . . by keeping them in an unknown tongue." To circumvent Satan,
every town of fifty householders was required to hire a schoolmaster
"to teach all such children as shall resort to him to write and read."
Every town of one hundred householders was ordered to establish a
Latin grammar school where students could be prepared "as far as
they may be fitted for the university." Failure of a town to comply
with this law might result in a fine, and though the fine might be
small, most towns would want to avoid the stigma of being penalized.
A further amplification of the laws in 1648 required the selectmen to
be vigilant lest any of their neighbors should "suffer so much barbarism
in any of their families as not to endeavor to teach by themselves or
others their children and apprentices" to read the English tongue, to
understand the laws, and to learn some honest trade or calling.[9]
Motivated by religion and sound economic reasoning, Massachusetts
Bay proposed to breed up a literate and industrious citizenry.

Not every community obeyed the laws, of course, and there are
frequent complaints of the neglect of towns to provide schoolmasters;
the chain of grammar schools was never so complete as the laws of
1648 envisioned; but Massachusetts Bay did set an example in education. Among the New England colonies, Rhode Island, because of its
decentralized government, fell somewhat behind Massachusetts Bay
and Connecticut in public education; but even in Rhode Island, local
groups and individual benefactors established private schools in considerable numbers. As early as 1640, the town of Newport set aside
one hundred acres "for the encouragement of the poorer sort to train
up their youth in learning." [10]

How far the early schools in New England went in the education of
girls is a moot point.[11] A large proportion of New England women
were literate, and they learned to read somewhere. Many of them
were trained in the dame schools. Some of these dame schools were
private, supported by tuition; others received support from the towns.

[9] *Ibid.*, pp. 7–8.
[10] William Howe Tolman, *The History of Higher Education in Rhode Island,*
U.S. Bureau of Education Circular of Information No. 1, 1894 (Washington,
1894), p. 25.
[11] Walter Herbert Small, *Early New England Schools* (Boston, 1914), p. 14.

In many instances, mothers who had children of their own to instruct took in a few neighborhood children as well. Such a school was kept in New Haven in 1651 by a certain Goodwife Wickham. It is known to history because a little girl, brought before the New Haven magistrates for swearing, testified that she learned naughty words at Goodwife Wickham's where she went to school.[12]

The training of children in some honest calling to live by was a matter of great concern to colonial citizens. The growing influence of middle-class thinking in sixteenth- and seventeenth-century England had helped to emphasize the virtue of industry, of work for work's sake, and the necessity of having a vocation and laboring in it. William Perkins, the Elizabethan preacher, whose influence on both sides of the Atlantic lasted for a century after his death in 1603, in a treatise entitled *A Treatise of the Vocations* had expounded a gospel of work and elaborated the doctrine that the surest way of serving God and attaining happiness in this and the next world is by laboring diligently in some honest trade or vocation.[13] This highly acceptable dogma was embraced enthusiastically by both Puritans and Quakers, as well as by other seventeenth- and eighteenth-century Englishmen, and it helps to explain an emphasis upon vocational training in New England and Pennsylvania. Instruction in writing and ciphering given poor boys was designed to make them proficient in keeping accounts so that they could serve as secretaries and bookkeepers. Dame schools frequently taught girls sewing and embroidery; such training, provided for orphan girls, it was hoped, would help to make them self-supporting. As early as 1720 a Boston committee met "to consider about promoting of a spinning school or schools for the instruction of the children of this town, in spinning." [14] Though there was agitation off and on for spinning schools, nothing seems to have come of it.

During the eighteenth century Boston papers carried advertisements of private schools of various kinds. At least seven "ladies' boarding schools" announced courses designed to teach accomplishments and skills ranging from music and dancing to needlework and art. The

[12] *Ibid.*, p. 162.

[13] See Louis B. Wright, *Middle-Class Culture in Elizabethan England* (Chapel Hill, N.C., 1935), pp. 170–187; and also "William Perkins: Elizabethan Apostle of 'Practical Divinity,' " *The Huntington Library Quarterly*, III (1940), 171–196.

[14] Holmes, *Tercentenary History of the Boston Public Latin School*, pp. 16, 416.

latter included japanning and painting on glass. Boys' schools taught everything from Greek to navigation, with a considerable number advertising such practical courses as shorthand, bookkeeping, and surveying. Caleb Philipps in 1728 advertised correspondence courses in shorthand for persons living outside of Boston, and after 1720 at least eight teachers advertised evening classes in a variety of practical subjects.[15] These night classes were designed particularly for the benefit of apprentices.

Concerned as the colonials were about vocational training, they did not delude themselves into substituting it for education. It remained for the twentieth century to achieve that confusion. Colonial grammar schools remained schools of classical instruction to teach youths who might go on to college and become learned men.

Like their Puritan contemporaries in Massachusetts Bay, the Dutch in New Netherland were concerned lest their children should forget the decency and order of a civilized life. In a remonstrance to the States General in Holland in 1649, the Nine Tribunes, or Nine Men, as they were generally called, recited the sad state into which learning had fallen in the colony and recommended a public school "with at least two good teachers, so that the youth in so wild a country where there are so many dissolute people may first of all be well instructed and indoctrinated, not only in reading and writing, but also in the knowledge and fear of the Lord. Now the school is kept very irregularly, by this one or that, according to his fancy, as long as he thinks proper." [16] Actually, as early as 1637, a schoolmaster, one Adam Roelantsen, is listed among salaried officials of the Dutch West India Company, and even before that, in 1629, the Company had instructed patroons who intended to settle colonists in New Netherland to "endeavor to find out ways and means whereby they may supply a minister and schoolmaster." [17] The earliest schoolmasters sometimes combined the functions of teacher, precentor, sexton of the church, and comforter of the sick. This last office was peculiar to the Dutch Reformed Church, which shared with the West India Company responsibility for licensing and supervising teachers. The school over which Adam Roelantsen presided came to be known, about 1647,

[15] Robert Francis Seybolt, *The Private Schools of Colonial Boston* (Cambridge, Mass., 1935), *passim*.

[16] Daniel J. Pratt, *Annals of Public Education in the State of New York from 1626 to 1746* (Albany, N.Y., 1872), pp. 8–9.

[17] *Ibid.*, p. 3.

as the Collegiate School, and has had a continuous existence from that day to this under the auspices of the Dutch Reformed Church.

Within the next few years, the youth of New Amsterdam increased to such a point that the officials of the town in September, 1658, petitioned the West India Company for a Latin school; they complained that the nearest Latin school was at "Boston in New England, a great distance from here." If the Company would send them a Latin master, the city would undertake "to have constructed a suitable place or school." [18] With speed unusual in these times, the Company secured the services of Alexander Carolus Curtius, "before a professor in Lithuania," and in the spring of 1659 sent him out to New Amsterdam to conduct a Latin school. Soon he was dismissed and another Latin master, Aegidius Luyck, reigned in his place. Luyck, who had come out in 1662 as tutor to the children of Peter Stuyvesant, became a wealthy and respected citizen; in 1674, when the English occupied the country for the second time, he was burgomaster and had to sign the capitulation.

Although the Dutch in New Netherland were too concerned over their material welfare to live up to their reputation in the old country for literacy, they did manage to found a number of schools during their regime, and on the whole the Dutch Reformed Church showed more interest in education than the Anglicans who replaced them in authority after the English took over. The Dutch established public schools not only in New Amsterdam, but in Brooklyn, Flatbush, Flatlands, Bushwyck, Wiltwyck, Harlem, Bergen, and elsewhere. Besides these schools many private schoolmasters received licenses to teach. Emphasis in all of the public schools was upon piety. One of their ministers prepared a special catechism for use in the schools, and reading books contained the Lord's Prayer, the Ten Commandments, the Proverbs of Solomon, prayers, and other pious matter.

In education, New York lagged behind other colonies under the English. Its citizens were notably negligent of public schools. Two bills were introduced in the legislative assembly, in 1691 and 1696, to establish schools, but neither passed. Governor Cornbury in 1702 recommended an improvement in the schools, but beyond the establishment of a short-lived grammar school in New York City, nothing happened. A few towns, principally those with a preponderance of settlers from New England, set up schools; but in 1713, the Reverend

[18] *Ibid.*, p. 22.

John Sharpe commented that "there is hardly anything more wanted in this country than learning." [19] In 1732, the legislative assembly passed an act establishing a grammar school for Latin, Greek, and mathematics in New York City, and in 1736 another act was passed to encourage the establishment of grammar schools. But these acts were little more than hopeful gestures. Education remained in the hands of private schools which sprang up, flourished for a time, and died. In 1741 New York City boasted six private English schools; in 1762 it had ten English schools, two Dutch, one French, and one Hebrew school. Only parents able to pay tuition could send their children to these schools. In 1709 the Society for the Propagation of the Gospel in Foreign Parts aided Trinity Church in establishing a free charity school which was the forerunner of the modern Trinity School. Elsewhere in the colony, notably at Rye, the S.P.G. established charity schools. Despite these efforts, New York before the Revolution had little cause to be proud of its provisions for the education of the poor.

The key to Pennsylvania's attitude toward education may be found in a statement made by William Penn, who was an early advocate of adapting schools to the practical needs of humanity instead of slavishly following outworn methods.

We are in pain to make them [the youth of his day] scholars but not men, to talk rather than to know, which is true canting . . . We press their memory too soon, and puzzle, strain, and load them with words and rules to know grammar and rhetoric, and a strange tongue or two that is ten to one may never be useful to them, leaving their natural genius to mechanical, physical, or natural knowledge uncultivated and neglected. . . . To be sure languages are not to be despised or neglected; but things are still to be preferred. . . . It were happy if we studied nature more in natural things, and acted according to nature, whose rules are few, plain, and most reasonable. . . . It is pity, therefore, that books have not been composed for youth by some curious and careful naturalists, and also mechanics, in the Latin tongue, to be used in schools, that they might learn things with words: things obvious and familiar to them, and which would make the tongue easier to be obtained by them.[20]

The Quaker founders of Pennsylvania wanted to insure against indigency and to make certain that every community provided the

[19] Alexander C. Flick (ed.), *History of the State of New York* (New York, 1933), III, 73.

[20] William Penn, "Reflections and Maxims," reprinted in James P. Wickersham, *A History of Education in Pennsylvania* (Lancaster, Pa., 1886), pp. 35–36.

elements of education for the young. Though they emphasized practical education as opposed to classical learning, they did not despise the traditional Latin grammar school. The Friends Public School, established in Philadelphia in 1689, eventually became the William Penn Charter School, an aggregation of schools, which had the Latin school as the apex of the educational hierarchy, Penn's first Frame of Government ordered the Governor and Council to erect public schools and to see that "all children within this province of the age of twelve years shall be taught some useful trade or skill, to the end that none may be idle, but the poor may work to live, and the rich, if they become poor, may not want." [21] If the Quakers never quite succeeded in eliminating ignorance and poverty, they managed in some fashion to teach their children to read, write, and cipher. They did not follow Penn's instructions closely and they never established a public school system free to all comers. Such schools as they established were free only to those unable to pay. But though they did not make education a matter of public concern, as did Massachusetts Bay, the social pressures were such that Quaker parents made shift to provide their children with the fundamentals of learning. An illiterate Quaker child was rare.

Unlike the Quaker mystics, who were an intensely practical people and saw the utilitarian value of education, the German mystics who made up the early waves of settlers cared little for learning. Daniel Pastorius, it is true, established a Latin school at Germantown in 1702, but he was an exception. Later German settlers of the Reformed and Lutheran churches were for the most part peasants with only a slight interest in education. Of the German settlers, the Moravians were alone in establishing schools and promoting learning.

In contrast, the Scots from Ulster, who swarmed into Pennsylvania during the first half of the eighteenth century, brought with them a respect for their learned Presbyterian ministers, who saw to it that classical education was not forgotten in the wilderness. To these hard-working and hard-traveling preachers, Pennsylvania owed some of its best schools. William Tennent's school at Neshaminy, known as the Log College, was in reality a classical grammar school in the wilderness designed to give hopeful young ministers the elements of the education they needed in their profession, but it also taught laymen.

[21] For a somewhat more detailed treatment of this theme, see Louis B. Wright, *The Atlantic Frontier* (New York, 1947), pp. 244–251.

This school flourished from 1726 to 1742 and encouraged the foundation of other schools. The Presbyterian Latin Grammar School of New London, founded in 1743 by Francis Alison, was so good that the wealthier families of Philadelphia patronized it. The Scottish Presbyterians outstripped all others in Pennsylvania during the eighteenth century in their zeal for learning.

Because of its commercial prosperity and increasing population, Philadelphia early developed a variety of private schools, especially schools stressing utilitarian subjects. A youth could find a school in Philadelphia where he could learn mathematics, bookkeeping, navigation, surveying, and the rudiments of natural science. One of the most popular of the private teachers was Andrew Lamb, who escaped hanging in London by being sold in Philadelphia as a transported convict. He set up a school in 1733, and his skill as an instrument maker made him an especially authoritative teacher of navigation as well as other useful subjects. Many of the private schools ran at night for the benefit of apprentices and workers. For women and girls there were schools where they could learn needlework, plain sewing, and various handicrafts.

But the private schools did not confine themselves to vocational subjects. Despite the frowns of the stricter Quakers, many schools taught music and dancing to both sexes, as well as drawing and painting. More foreign languages were taught in the private schools of Philadelphia than could be learned anywhere else on the continent. By the mid-eighteenth century, one could get instruction in English, German, French, Spanish, Italian, Portuguese, Latin, Greek, Hebrew, and Arabic. So cosmopolitan had Philadelphia grown by the third quarter of the eighteenth century that an ambitious student could find a teacher of sorts in most of the subjects likely to excite his fancy.

In the colonies south of Pennsylvania throughout the colonial period, the efforts to establish schools where children could learn the rudiments of learning were persistent, but more frequently than not they met with indifferent success. The geographical difficulties which baffled the early settlers were not the only problems. In some areas the inhabitants were indifferent and negligent. This was especially true in the back country of the Carolinas. In other areas religious factionalism tended to discourage efforts to found schools.

The first schools in Maryland were under the direction of the Jesuits. A Catholic named Ralph Crouch, who was in Maryland between 1639 and 1659, is reported to have opened "schools for teaching humanities." [22] But with their political ascendancy, the Protestants began to make life difficult for Catholic teachers and to dominate education. Near the end of the seventeenth century Governor Francis Nicholson proposed to the Legislative Assembly that "a way be found out for building of a free school, and the maintenance for a schoolmaster and usher and writing master that can cast accounts." In writing to the Bishop of London, who had ecclesiastical jurisdiction over the Anglican Church in the colonies, Nicholson assured him that they had "attempted to make learning a handmaid to devotion" and he was confident he would favor these pious plans "wherein in instructing our youth in the orthodox religion, preserving them from the infection of heterodox tenets and fitting them for the service of the church and state in this uncultivated part of the world are our cheerful end and aim." [23]

An act of 1696 devised a plan for the establishment of schools, the first to be King William's School at Annapolis, which would have for their aim "the propagation of the gospel and the education of the youth of this province in good letters and manners." [24] In addition to teaching such elementary subjects as reading and writing, the schools would offer instruction in Latin and Greek. A building for King William's School was completed in 1701, but other schools envisioned in the act were never established. There is considerable evidence, however, that several schools existed. Acts were passed in 1717 and later to provide taxes for schools, and in 1723 an act ordered the erection of one school in each county. Schoolmasters should be "members of the Church of England, and of pious and exemplary lives and conversations, and capable of teaching well the grammar, good writing, and the mathematics." [25] These plans were never carried to completion. A few schools like one in Kent County attained considerable reputation. Chestertown advertised a school in 1745 that offered to board boys and teach them writing, arithmetic, merchants' accounts, surveying, navigation, the use of globes, several branches of mathematics, Latin, Greek, fencing, and dancing. The master was

[22] Bernard C. Steiner, *History of Education in Maryland*. U.S. Bureau of Education Circular of Information No. 2, 1894 (Washington, 1894), p. 16.
[23] *Ibid.*, pp. 19–20.
[24] *Ibid.*, pp. 22–23.
[25] *Ibid.*, pp. 24–25.

Charles Peale, father of the artist, Charles Willson Peale. In 1750 the Reverend Thomas Bacon established a charity school in St. Peter's Parish which sought to give elementary education to orphans, poor children, and Negroes, but it did not survive the founder. The Society for the Propagation of the Gospel in Foreign Parts, organized in 1701 to promote the Anglican cause, lent its aid to education until the Revolution. Private schools and tutors supplied the needs of the more prosperous elements in the population. No institution of higher learning was established in Maryland until after the Revolution.

With the growing wealth of Virginia in the eighteenth century came an increasing concern on the part of the more prosperous planters for the education of their children. But the colonial government had not succeeded in making any adequate provision for the education of the poor, and the Society for the Propagation of the Gospel in Foreign Parts had little influence upon education in Virginia. Secondary education therefore remained a problem for parents to solve as best they could. The answer for the planters of means was the family tutor, who often taught children of less prosperous neighbors who were in reach of the plantation schoolhouse.

Some parents, however, were so eager to have their children escape a rustic upbringing that they sent them to England almost as infants. William Fitzhugh of Stafford in 1690 was planning to send his eldest son and namesake, then aged four, to London when he discovered a French Huguenot minister in Virginia who took the child and began his instruction in both French and Latin.[26] Robert "King" Carter of Corotoman sent his five sons, and William Byrd I sent young William, aged nine, and Susan, aged six, to school in England. Carter was constantly writing his English agents to look to the proper education of his sons in the old Latin tradition. Concerning his wards, the sons of Colonel Ralph Wormeley, he wrote in 1702 to Francis Lee, a Virginia merchant in London:

Am glad to learn my cousins Ralph Wormeley and John Wormeley thrive so fast in their learning; no doubt the continuance of careful education will render them accomplished men qualified to preserve the character of their father, and fit for the service of their country, which, to my sorrow I will complain to you, having drawn your first breath here, does at this time labor

26 Wright, *First Gentlemen of Virginia*, pp. 168–170.

under a very thick cloud of ignorance. Pray God send in the next generation it may flourish under a set of better polished patriots.[27]

There were hazards of many sorts in sending children to England: the danger of the long sea voyage, the mortality from smallpox and diphtheria, and the possibility that an English education would unfit them for life in the colony, as sometimes happened.

Numerous as were the children who went to England, the majority stayed at home and learned under tutors. Many of these teachers were Scots, graduates of the Scottish universities, who found favor because of their learning, their sound Protestantism, and their normally stern code of behavior. Philip Fithian, a young Princeton divinity student, who kept a diary of his experiences as a tutor in the household of Robert Carter of Nomini Hall in 1773–74, remarked that "it has been the custom heretofore to have all their tutors and schoolmasters from Scotland, though they begin to be willing to employ their own countrymen." [28] Carter himself, unlike most of his fellow Virginians, preferred native-born teachers "on account of [their] pronunciation in the English language . . . in which he allows young gentlemen educated in good schools on the [American] continent to excel the Scotch young gentlemen & indeed most of the English." [29] Robert Carter did not propose to have his offspring brought up to speak with a Scottish burr or even an English accent.

The conditions that Fithian described must have been similar to those prevailing in Virginia through most of the eighteenth century. An entry in the diary for August 9, 1773, describes the post which Dr. John Witherspoon, president of Princeton, was trying to fill for Robert Carter:

Waited on Dr. John Witherspoon, about nine o'clock, to hear his proposal for my going to Virginia. He read me a letter which he received from Col. Carter, & proposed the following terms—To teach his children, five daughters & three sons, who are from five to seventeen years old. The young ladies are to be taught the English language. And the boys are to study the English language carefully & to be instructed in the Latin & Greek. And he proposes to give thirty-five pounds sterling, which is about sixty pounds currency, pro-

[27] Ibid., p. 285.
[28] Hunter D. Farish (ed.), Journal and Letters of Philip Vickers Fithian, 1773–1774: A Plantation Tutor of the Old Dominion (Williamsburg, Va., 1943), p. 39.
[29] Ibid., p. 125.

vide all accommodations, allow him the undisturbed use of a room and the use of his own library, find provender for a horse, & a servant to wait. By the advice of the Dr. & his recommendation of the gentleman & the place, I accepted the offer & agreed to go in the fall into Virginia.[30]

Though the young Presbyterian divine went into that land of pleasure-loving Anglicans with misgivings, he learned almost at once to respect and like the people and to admire the love of learning evident in many of the Virginians. He found too that as a man of learning and cultivation, he had a respected place in planter society. Perhaps Fithian was more fortunate than some tutors, but his experiences indicate a devotion to traditional learning more widespread than is commonly believed.

South Carolina planters and merchants of the more prosperous group followed much the same pattern as did their contemporaries in Virginia in educating their children. Private schools in Charleston and other towns and private tutors supplied the major part of the instruction. More than four hundred advertisements relating to schools and schoolmasters have been counted in the *South Carolina Gazette*.[31] Many of the wealthier South Carolinians also sent their children overseas for education, usually to England, but in some instances to France.

The colonial government of South Carolina also made a more vigorous effort to foster education than did the government of Virginia. In 1710 and again in 1712, the Legislative Assembly passed acts providing for the establishment of "a free school . . . for the instruction of the youth of this province in grammar and other arts and sciences and useful learning, and also the principles of the Christian religion." [32] These acts set up a board of commissioners to hire schoolmasters and to administer moneys bequeathed by charitable persons for the use of schools. The act of 1712 actually appointed John Douglas "to be master of the said school [in Charleston], by the name and style of preceptor or teacher of grammar and other the arts and sciences," and specified that he and his successors should be "capable to teach the learned languages, that is to say, Latin and Greek tongues, and to catechise and instruct the youth in the principles of the Christian religion as professed in the Church of England." [33] To stimulate

[30] *Ibid.*, p. 8.
[31] Edgar W. Knight, *A Documentary History of Education in the South before 1860* (Chapel Hill, N.C., 1949), I, 573.
[32] *Ibid.*, I, 671.
[33] *Ibid.*, I, 681.

gifts to the school, any donor of twenty pounds or more could nominate a pupil to be taught free for five years. Other free pupils would be nominated by the commissioners. Nobody, apparently, thought of a "free school" as open to every child who might want to attend. An act of 1722 authorized justices of the county and precinct courts to purchase land, erect schools, and assess the expenses upon the property holders in their jurisdictions. Ten poor children were to be taught free each year. Fairly numerous bequests for educational purposes helped to spread the opportunities for learning.[34] Perhaps the most famous of the South Carolina schools was that founded by the Winyaw Indigo Society at Georgetown in 1756, a school which flourished until 1861. It resulted from the philanthropy of the Society, which met on the first Friday of each month "to hold high discourse over the growth and prosperity of the indigo plant, and to refresh the inner man, and so keep up to a proper standard the endearing ties of social life by imbibing freely of the inevitable bowl of punch." [35] The school founded by this cheerful and optimistic group accepted about twenty-five children each year.

The South Carolina back country, dominated by Scotch Presbyterians, had few schools; but ministers, missionaries, and itinerant schoolmasters managed to provide the rudiments of learning for a considerable portion of the population.

North Carolina was the most backward of the colonies in matters of education, and for that reason the Society for the Propagation of the Gospel in Foreign Parts made a particular effort to send teaching missionaries into the back country. These Anglicans were greatly disturbed at the number of Quakers and other unorthodox folk, in whom they could see little good. Though few in number, the missionaries struggled to baptize children and teach the catechism and the rudiments of reading and writing. Reports in the colonial records of North Carolina concerning their activities show mixed reactions. For example, James Adams complained in 1709 that one Mr. Griffin, "reader and schoolmaster," had "fallen into the sin of fornication and joined with the Quakers' interest, which has proved a great stumbling block to many of our persuasion"; but William Gordon gave a contrary

[34] Edward McCrady, Jr., "Education in South Carolina Prior to and during the Revolution," *South Carolina Historical Society Collections*, IV (1887), 7–15.

[35] Knight, *Documentary History*, I, 276.

view that Griffin was a devout and industrious man who had succeeded so well with the people of Pasquotank that he (Gordon) was
"surprised to see with what order, decency, and seriousness they performed the public worship, considering how ignorant people are in
the other parishes." [36] Evidence shows that the missionaries had only
a moderate degree of success in teaching. Nevertheless they provided a
certain amount of instruction, and even labored to teach reading to
Negro slaves. The religious instruction of Indians and Negroes was
one of their special objectives. For the most part, the education of
Negroes was neglected if not specifically forbidden, as in South Carolina, where an act of the General Assembly for 1740 made it a penal
offense for anyone to teach slaves to write or to employ a slave as a
scribe.[37]

From the beginning of the eighteenth century to the Revolution,
the Society for the Propagation of the Gospel in Foreign Parts sent
more than three hundred missionaries to the colonies, and established
a number of parish libraries. In some instances, however, they seem to
have done more harm than good. Stephen B. Weeks, historian of
colonial North Carolina, declared that the backwardness of the colony
in education was directly attributable "to the pernicious activities" of
the missionaries.[38] The missionaries themselves were often unhappy
over their reception. John Urmstone, for example, wrote to the Society
headquarters from North Carolina in 1721 that he could not collect
his money, was plagued by the Quakers, could not hear any news from
England, and was "buried alive in this hell of a hole." [39]

In Georgia, various humanitarian efforts to teach the poor met with
indifferent success. The Associates of the Late Dr. Bray sought to
make good Anglicans out of the Negro slaves and to teach them to
read and write, but in both undertakings their success was meager.
George Whitefield, the evangelist, erected the Bethesda Orphan House
near Savannah in 1739 and combined vocational training and elementary education in an institution that lasted until about the time of the
Revolution. As elsewhere in the South, the children of the more prosperous inhabitants received their education from private teachers,

[36] *Ibid.*, I, 82.
[37] *Ibid.*, I, 705.
[38] *Ibid.*, I, 63. Quoted from Weeks, *Church and State in North Carolina*,
p. 22.
[39] Knight, *Documentary History*, I, 89.

some of whom advertised their readiness to teach Latin, Greek, the modern languages, mathematics, and utilitarian subjects.

The very poverty and inadequacy of opportunities for schooling in most of the colonies placed upon parents a responsibility to see that their children did not grow up in illiteracy. On the lowest economic levels, parents were frequently negligent or incapable of ensuring any instruction to their children, but the moderately well-to-do usually saw to it that their children escaped complete illiteracy. Most of the provisions for the care of orphans and regulation of apprenticeship specified that children must be taught to read and write.

Higher education in English America begins with the founding of Harvard College in 1636. That story has been told by Samuel Eliot Morison in an academic history that is a model of its kind. The passage descriptive of the founding of Harvard from *New England's First Fruits* (1643) has been often quoted, but deserves repeating:

After God had carried us safe to New England and we had builded our houses, provided necessaries for our livelihood, reared convenient places for God's worship, and settled the civil government, one of the next things we longed for and looked after was to advance learning and perpetuate it to posterity, dreading to leave an illiterate ministry to the churches when our present ministers shall lie in the dust. And as we were thinking and consulting how to effect this great work, it pleased God to stir up the heart of one Mr. Harvard . . . to give the one half of his estate (it being in all about £1,700) towards the erecting of a college, and all his library. After him another gave £300, others after them cast in more, and the public hand of the State added the rest. The college was by common consent appointed to be at Cambridge (a place very pleasant and accommodate) and is called (according to the name of the first founder) Harvard College.[40]

As the author of *New England's First Fruits* asserts, one of the primary considerations in establishing a college was to ensure a learned ministry. The college was to be a seminary of preachers. But that was not all. It was to "advance learning and perpetuate it to posterity," not merely through the preachers but through the laymen who would have available the classical education of the English universities. Harvard College was established by a people determined to reproduce the best of traditional learning and make it accessible to their sons. This learning of course inherited much from the ancient scholastic tradition, but

[40] Quoted from the reprint in Morison, *The Founding of Harvard College*, p. 432. Spelling and punctuation have been modernized.

it added something new, the modification of scholasticism that came with the Christian humanism of sixteenth-century scholars, especially the great Protestant humanists. And it early showed the influence of the new spirit in science.

Almost from the beginning, Harvard was a distinguished institution of classical learning. By 1650 it had about forty students in residence and ten graduate students, and Puritan families in England were beginning to send their sons to Harvard to be educated in a purer environment than they could find at Oxford and Cambridge. These youths were not an unalloyed blessing, and their riotous and extravagant ways caused the magistrates much concern.[41] Another group, this time native Indians, from time to time caused something of a problem. The delusion persisted that Indians were merely awaiting the opportunity to embrace classical scholarship and learn Cicero's orations. This belief resulted in the erection in the mid-fifties of a building in the Harvard Yard known as the Indian College. In 1663 John Winthrop, Jr., sent to Robert Boyle, head of a missionary society interested in Indian education, two papers in Latin "composed by two Indians now scholars in the college." Winthrop assured Boyle that he had questioned the Indians in Latin and received good answers in the same language, and heard them both express several sentences in Greek also." [42] Clearly, classical learning had become firmly implanted in New England, and if the scions of English families were not always receptive, natives would set an example. Actually the Indian College was a rank failure, but the effort did produce a remarkable example of scholarship and printing, John Eliot's Indian Bible in the Algonquin language, published in 1663. Some scholars have expressed doubt as to whether the Indians of Eliot's day could comprehend the language of his translation.[43]

Harvard's first effective president, Henry Dunster, who took office in 1640, dreamed of making Harvard College into a university for all of the English-speaking colonies, but religious differences in colonies outside New England prevented that. In the period from 1673 to 1707, 360 students received their education at Harvard, and of the 324 whose homes are known, "fifty-two came from the Connecticut Colony

---

[41] Samuel Eliot Morison, *Harvard College in the Seventeenth Century* (Cambridge, Mass., 1936), I, 76–77.

[42] *Collections of the Massachusetts Historical Society,* 5th Ser., VIII (1882), 84–85.

[43] Morison, *Harvard College in the Seventeenth Century,* I, 347.

and Valley, eight from New Hampshire, seventeen from the Plymouth Colony, and but one from Rhode Island; the remainder were from Massachusetts Bay." [44] Not one came from the Hudson Valley and the region to the south.

In Virginia, the College of William and Mary was established by charter issued in 1693, with aims similar to those of Harvard. Efforts to found a college seemed near success in 1661 when the Virginia Assembly passed an act authorizing a preparatory school and college and petitioned the King for letters patent to raise money. [45] A year later a second petition stated that "for the advancement of learning, promoting piety, and provision of an able and successive ministry in this country, it hath been thought fit that a college of students of the liberal arts and sciences be erected and maintained." [46] Nothing happened. A few years later some wealthy English merchants with business connections in Virginia subscribed £2,500 toward a college. Finally in 1693, through the efforts of Governor Francis Nicholson and Commissary James Blair, the charter was granted. Blair persuaded the government to allow £2,000 out of the quitrents for a building, to give 20,000 acres for an endowment, and to authorize an export tax on tobacco shipped from Virginia and Maryland for the school's support. The founding of the college was largely due to Blair's determination and refusal to be discouraged. On one occasion, when he insisted that a college was needed to train ministers to save Virginian souls, Sir Edward Seymour, Lord of the Treasury, is said to have exclaimed, "Souls! Damn your souls! Make tobacco!" [47] Blair missed no opportunity to raise money for the school. He even worked out a deal whereby three pirates captured in 1688 at the mouth of the James River should be allowed their freedom if they contributed £300 and a fourth of their booty to the projected college. [48]

The charter and the statutes of the College of William and Mary provided for instruction in the liberal arts in the classical tradition, similar in plan and purpose to Harvard except for the differences between Puritan and Anglican theology. It also made an effort to provide for the education of Indians, but its success was no greater than

[44] *Ibid.*, II, 449.
[45] Wright, *First Gentlemen of Virginia*, p. 105.
[46] Knight, *Documentary History*, I, 371.
[47] Wright, *First Gentlemen of Virginia*, p. 106.
[48] Knight, *Documentary History*, I, 372–373, 394–395.

Harvard's. Although for a decade after its founding it remained little more than a grammar school, it gradually came to provide the elements of higher education which Virginians had previously gone without or found only in England. At a celebration in the spring of 1699, college orators emphasized the value of education at home instead of going abroad. This was an issue of genuine importance. The hazards of sending one's children across the Atlantic were not confined to physical dangers. Many boys came home unfitted for plantation life. Gradually the College of William and Mary made it unnecessary to go abroad, and many important figures, one of the most notable being Thomas Jefferson, received their education in Williamsburg.

The availability of an education in Virginia of course did not stop the practice of sending children to school in England. No one can discover from the extant records just how many went overseas during the colonial period, but the number from the southern colonies extended to the hundreds. The records of the colleges at Oxford and Cambridge and the Inns of Court in London list the names of many Southerners.[49]

The third colonial college, Yale, resulted from the dissatisfaction of some of the stricter conservatives with the growing latitudinarianism of Harvard and the contamination of the moral atmosphere of Boston. An election sermon preached by the Reverend Solomon Stoddard of Northampton at Boston in 1703 indicates the worries of the conservatives.

Places of learning [Stoddard asserts] should not be places of riot and pride. Ways of profuseness and prodigality in such a society lay a foundation of a great deal of sorrow. Fond and proud parents should not be suffered to introduce evil customs. 'Tis not worth the while for persons to be sent to the College to learn to compliment men and court women. They should be sent thither to prepare them for public service, and had need to be under the oversight of wise and holy men.[50]

If the professors at Harvard were not sufficiently wise or holy, Stoddard believed that he and his brethren could provide an institution with all of the good qualities that Harvard had possessed in its Puri-

---

[49] *Ibid.,* pp. 553–570.
[50] Quoted from Morison, *Harvard College in the Seventeenth Century,* II, 547.

tan prime—or when Stoddard was an undergraduate there—and be free from the distractions of a city like Boston.

Connecticut folk had long wanted a college, and as early as 1647 John Davenport had started an agitation for one at New Haven. In 1655, £640 was actually subscribed for the purpose, but this plan, like others in the next few years, came to nothing. At last in 1701 the Reverend John Pierpont, pastor of the New Haven church, led a group including Judge Samuel Sewall of Boston in a successful effort to get a charter for what became known as the Collegiate School, which they set up, not in New Haven, but at Saybrook. The historian of Harvard carefully points out that all of the promoters of the new college were Harvard men and that Harvard not only raised no objection but even prayed for the venture.

Cotton Mather, disgruntled at being turned down for the presidency of Harvard, bestirred himself in behalf of the Collegiate School, which in 1716 moved to New Haven. He wrote to a rich East India merchant in London named Elihu Yale, who had been born in New England, suggesting that the college might take his name if Yale would contribute to its welfare. Moved by the letter and pleas from Jeremiah Dummer, agent in London for the colony of Connecticut, Yale sent over three bales of Indian goods, a parcel of books, and a portrait of King George I. The goods brought £500 at a sale and the college was named Yale. Rarely has so small a sum bought so much immortality.

Yale's curriculum naturally followed the traditional pattern. It was not blazing new trails. It merely wanted to restore the best of the old. And all through the eighteenth century Yale remained a stronghold of conservative Congregationalism, a training ground for preachers as well as laymen who were to emphasize the "steady habits of Connecticut."

Zeal for an educated ministry prompted the founding of Princeton and a number of classical academies which preceded it. The Scotch Presbyterians had a profound belief in the value of classical learning, and if they did not actually think a knowledge of Latin, Greek, and Hebrew essential to salvation, at least they preferred ministers who were well versed in these subjects. Since graduates of Edinburgh, Aberdeen, St. Andrews, and Glasgow were not sufficiently numerous among the immigrant ministers to supply all of the colonial pulpits, especially after the revival known as the Great Awakening, candidates for the Presbyterian ministry sometimes studied the classics and divinity under some preacher who conducted a little one-man seminary. "All of these so-called academies," says the official historian of Princeton, "were partly grammar schools and partly colleges. Since they stressed preparation for the ministry, the students devoted their attention to a mixture of Greek, Latin, moral philosophy, and theology." [51] Most famous of the academies was the Log College at Neshaminy, Pennsylvania, run by the Reverend William Tennent. The evangelist George Whitefield was greatly impressed by Tennent's teaching, but the opponents of the evangelical wing of the Presbyterian Church, known as the Old Side, were skeptical and in 1738 attempted to curb Tennent's activities by putting through the synod a requirement that ministers who had no background of a European university or were not graduates of Harvard or Yale should pass an examination set by the synod. The refusal of the New Brunswick presbytery to abide by this decision caused a split in the church between the New Lights and the Old Side and eventually, in 1746, led to the founding of the College of New Jersey, the college that was later named Princeton. The New Lights were determined that the Old Side should never be able to say that their ministers were deficient in learning, either in the classics or in Calvinistic theology. From its beginning, Princeton emphasized both branches of learning.

Princeton's influence in the later years of the eighteenth century and after was enormous. Its classically trained ministers went out to frontier regions and became carriers not only of Calvinistic theology but of classical learning.

The establishment in New York of King's College, later Columbia, was part of a renewed interest in education in the mid-eighteenth century. Plans made in 1753 to set up a college had the support of the powerful De Lancey faction and the Anglicans, but William Livingston and the other political opponents of the De Lanceys fought the proposal. The resulting controversy produced a number of acrimonious pamphlets in which the Presbyterians charged that the Anglicans were trying to gain control of the college.[52] When the charter was finally granted late in 1754, it stipulated that no rule should be made that

[51] Thomas J. Wertenbaker, *Princeton, 1746–1896* (Princeton, N.J., 1946), p. 11.
[52] Beverly McAnear, "American Imprints Concerning King's College," *The Papers of the Bibliographical Society of America,* XLIV (1950), 301–339.

would "exclude any person of any religious denomination whatever from equal liberty and advantage of education, or from any of the degrees, liberties, privileges, benefits, or immunities of the said college on account of his particular tenets in matters of religion." [53] Though the president was required to be of the Church of England, the board of governors included Anglican, Dutch Reformed, Lutheran, and French Huguenot ministers as well as laymen of diverse faiths. Since varied religions were represented, King's College never made any effort to establish a theological faculty. Although political expediency rather than any conviction concerning academic freedom seems to have been responsible for the liberal provisions in the charter, they were nevertheless highly significant of the future development of the institution.[54]

King's College, like the College of William and Mary in its early period, was a feeble institution in the years before 1763. Its first president, however, Dr. Samuel Johnson, a graduate of Yale who went to England and received ordination as a priest of the Church of England, was a man of considerable intellectual attainments. For the first class Johnson served as both president and faculty, but on the admission of a second class in 1755 he added his son William as assistant. A year later Johnson replaced his son with an Englishman, one Leonard Cutting of Cambridge. Johnson had accepted the presidency on condition that "he should be allowed to retire to a place of safety out of town when the smallpox prevailed," [55] a privilege that he invoked in November, 1757. He did not return until March, 1758, and fled from smallpox again in October, 1759. Meanwhile he added another member to the faculty, Daniel Treadwell of Harvard, who unhappily died of consumption in 1760. Despite Dr. Johnson's absences and Mr. Treadwell's ill health, King's College managed to award eight degrees of bachelor of arts on June 21, 1758. Three of them had received their education elsewhere, but for some reason they received the bachelor's degree.[56] Dr. Johnson retired in 1763 and his place was taken by

[53] A History of Columbia University, 1754–1904 (New York, 1904), pp. 16–17.

[54] McAnear, "American Imprints," loc. cit.; Dorothy R. Dillon, The New York Triumvirate: A Study of the Legal and Political Careers of William Livingston, John Morin Scott, William Smith, Jr. (New York, 1949), pp. 31–53. Cf. Richard Hofstadter and Walter P. Metzger, The Development of Academic Freedom in the United States (New York, 1955), passim.

[55] History of Columbia University, pp. 21, 23, 25.

[56] Ibid., p. 23.

Myles Cooper, of Queen's College, Oxford, who had received an appointment as professor of moral philosophy in the previous year. Cooper, a stanch Loyalist, barely escaped from a mob of Patriots on March 10, 1775, by fleeing in his nightshirt over the back fence to the safety of a British ship in the harbor. He sailed for England and never returned.[57]

Though King's College had small opportunity in the years before the Revolution to influence education in New York, it nevertheless gave an impetus to an ideal of higher learning that emphasized secular rather than theological considerations.

Another college strictly secular in its purposes was the College of Philadelphia, later the University of Pennsylvania. The official historian of the university gives 1740 as the date of its founding because that was the date of the creation of the earliest educational trust leading to the university's development.[58] Actually, however, the college did not become a reality until 1755, when the Philadelphia Academy opened under a new charter revised by William Smith and others.

Smith was a forceful personality who had attracted Benjamin Franklin's interest as a result of a pamphlet he had written under the title of *A General Idea of the College of Mirania* (1753). At that time Smith, a Scottish schoolmaster from Aberdeen, was tutoring the sons of a wealthy New Yorker. His tract recommended a practical type of education suitable to conditions that he observed in the colonies. His ideal college was designed to turn out intelligent as well as useful citizens by emphasizing history, religion, and agriculture. On Franklin's invitation he came to Philadelphia and so impressed the group who were promoting a plan for higher education in Philadelphia that in 1755 they made him provost of the college, academy, and charity school. Smith was a great intellectual power in Pennsylvania. Though he became an ordained Anglican minister, he stood for secular control of the college.

The curriculum devised by Smith was remarkable for its day because it marked the greatest divergence shown by any colonial college from the traditional prescription based on the medieval seven liberal arts. In Smith's curriculum one third of the course was devoted to the

[57] *Ibid.*, pp. 48–49.
[58] Edward Potts Cheyney, *History of the University of Pennsylvania, 1740–1940* (Philadelphia, 1940), pp. 47–48.

classics, which included history and related subjects. Another third was devoted to mathematics and the natural sciences, including geometry, trigonometry, physics, chemistry, astronomy, botany, and zoology. The final third was given to logic, ethics, metaphysics, and oratory. The college course lasted three years with three terms each year. Latin and Greek continued through the entire period. The student was expected to cover advanced mathematics, physics, politics, history, economics, and public law in fifteen months while reading classical texts and preparing exercises and orations as he went along. Smith provided an extensive reading list and emphasized that the principal purpose of the college course was to provide a foundation for further study after graduation.[59] Certainly the student who followed conscientiously Smith's curriculum, which prevailed at the College of Philadelphia until the end of the colonial period, could not escape a valuable mental discipline, more modern in its conception than any available elsewhere in the colonies.

Two other colleges were founded before the Revolution: Rhode Island College, later Brown University, in 1764, and Queen's College, later Rutgers, in 1766, but neither became effective in our period.

With the exception of training for the ministry, the opportunities for professional education in the colonies before 1763 were meager indeed. There were of course no law schools. Many of the seventeenth-century lawyers were self-educated and legal training remained throughout the period a matter of apprenticeship to a lawyer as clerk until one learned the mysteries of the profession.[60] A considerable number of colonial Americans received training in one of the Inns of Court in London. In similar fashion, medical education meant going to a university overseas or learning the art through apprenticeship to a practicing physician. The College of Philadelphia established a medical department in 1765 and three years later King's College announced the opening of a medical school, but both were inadequate even by the standards of the eighteenth century.

Higher education in colonial America started out by trying to reproduce English university education, but conditions in the new country brought about changes that were significant for the future.

[59] *Ibid.*, pp. 82–84.
[60] For the history and status of lawyers in the colonies, see Richard B. Morris, *Studies in the History of American Law* (New York, 1930), pp. 42–44, 65–67.

The early colleges were founded under the auspices of religious groups. [61] Harvard, William and Mary, and Yale had their beginnings under the established churches of their regions. At first the colleges had no connection with professional or advanced faculties, were not concentrated in centers of learning, and were not "universities" in the English sense. Perhaps the most important difference was the provision for the control of the colleges by outside boards of trustees instead of their own faculties, as was the practice in the colleges of Oxford and Cambridge. Though the early colleges were under the domination of religious organizations, the hold of religion slowly and gradually relaxed under the influence of eighteenth-century rationalism. If the relaxation was only faintly perceptible in such citadels of orthodoxy as Yale, yet the inroads of science upon theology were nevertheless apparent before the end of the colonial period. Higher education was contributing importantly to the training of many types of leaders in society and was no longer concentrating upon instruction in divinity.

By the end of the colonial period, concern over the improvement in secondary schools was widespread. With the coming of independence, thoughtful men realized that a self-governing republic would not long survive without an intelligent leadership, a leadership ultimately dependent upon a broadly based system of education. Thomas Jefferson's scheme of education, set forth in his "Bill for the More General Diffusion of Knowledge," which he proposed to the Virginia legislature in 1779, was a plan for the education of Virginians in accordance with their talents, with selection of the most talented on each level for further training. [62] Never yet have we had the courage or the good sense to attempt on a state or national basis the theories that Jefferson believed essential to ensure wise leadership in a republic.

[61] Hofstadter and Metzger, *The Development of Academic Freedom,* p. 114.
[62] Roy J. Honeywell, *The Educational Work of Thomas Jefferson* (Cambridge, Mass., 1931), pp. 10–12.

CHAPTER 6

Books, Libraries, and Learning[1]

W HEN prospective colonists, preparing to embark for North
America in the seventeenth century, came to pack their belong-
ings for the long voyage in crowded little ships, the decision as to
what to take and what to eliminate was a matter of such vital importance that it might mean success or failure, life or death. Since
freight was high and even the most elementary essentials of life had
to be transported, the wonder is that the emigrants found room for
such luxuries as books. But the fact is that they did. We can imagine
the bewildered worry of many a pioneer, pondering the relative importance of an extra pair of boots or a stout folio as he chose his
indispensables for the Great Venture. The choice of books brought by
the first settlers, or imported as soon as they had established themselves in the wilderness, provides a significant clue to their conception
of intellectual and social values. Since these values lie at the foundation of American intellectual and literary history, an understanding of
the early colonial attitude toward the purpose of books is necessary
to any study of literary culture in America. Incidentally, the reading
habits of seventeenth-century Americans indicate the continuing influence of Tudor and Stuart writers, and for that reason even those
students who yawn over what they describe as the literary desert of
America will do well to contemplate the vitality of English authors in
the New World.

[1] The portion of this chapter dealing with the seventeenth century in part
is reprinted by permission from an essay entitled "The Purposeful Reading of
Our Colonial Ancestors" in *ELH, A Journal of English Literary History,* IV
(1937), 85–111.

Generalizations about the reading habits of the seventeenth-century colonists are subject to many qualifications. Our evidence is often limited. We cannot be certain that a man read a book because he possessed it, but it is reasonable to suppose that pioneers did not go to the expense and trouble of gathering books merely for show. A large proportion of the inventories do not quote titles but instead make such tantalizing references as "one parcel of old books," or "five great books in folio." Hence it is impossible to say that any author then available was not known in the colonies. For all we know, the unspecified parcels of old books may have contained quartos and folios of Shakespeare. What we can do is to reason from the habits of typical colonists whose records are fairly complete: letters, diaries, wills, and inventories provide the clues that enable us to reconstruct the literary interests of the early settlers. Proof is ample of the presence of books among the possessions of the colonists in the first century of settlement. The ruling classes and even many humbler folk possessed works which they prized as important to their lives and prosperity. The significance of their selection of these books is a problem deserving our attention.

Sectional patriotism and prejudice have produced many facile generalizations about the differences in the literary taste of "Puritan" New England and "Cavalier" Virginia. The facts are that although some significant differences gradually manifest themselves, the similarities between the literary tastes of early Virginians and New Englanders are as striking as their differences. Although one is not surprised to find more theological works in the library of a Puritan preacher of Boston than among the books of a tobacco planter on the Chesapeake, one may be surprised at the large number of titles throughout the seventeenth century common to both sections. This is true even of books of divinity. The intellectual differences between early New Englanders and Virginians were not so great as some of their descendants would have us believe.

Some literary students of the American seventeenth century have been perturbed over the scarcity of belles-lettres in the luggage of the first settlers. They wring their hands because Shakespeare's plays were neglected and other great poets passed over for dull works of divinity. But such critics have rarely taken the trouble to look at the books the colonists actually read, and they forget that these pioneers were more concerned about self-improvement than poetry. Shakespeare had not yet been made "improving" by legions of schoolteachers.

When the colonist began to select books for his five-foot shelf of essential works, he chose items that he proposed to consult. He may have borne in mind the advice of Henry Peacham in *The Compleat Gentleman* (1622), a handbook that some of our ancestors thought necessary to their life in America: "Affect not as some do that bookish ambition," Peacham had warned, "to be stored with books and have well furnished libraries, yet keep their heads empty of knowledge: to desire to have many books and never to use them is like a child that will have a candle burning by him all the while he is sleeping." [2] Prospective Americans could not yet afford libraries for ostentation, nor had they the inclination to burden themselves with useless books. Books that provided guidance in the way of life that the colonists were marking out for themselves predominated therefore in their literary preferences.

A considerable proportion of the books collected by Americans in the seventeenth century were sheer utilitarian works. Since every man was his own doctor, a few books on chirurgery and medicine were essential, and thousands lived—and died—according to the recipes of Philip Barrough's *The Method of Physic* (1583) or William Vaughan's *Directions for Health, Both Natural and Artificial* (1600), the latter work having been written specifically for the benefit of Newfoundland settlers.[3] Likewise, every man had to be his own lawyer and many citizens came equipped with Michael Dalton's *The Country Justice,* Sir Edward Coke's *Reports,* or Sir Thomas Littleton's *Tenures,* works which not only gave them the information and language to represent the sound and fury of the law but also made it possible for laymen to sit as judges in the local courts, to draw up deeds and wills, and to conduct complicated lawsuits in their litigations over land and property. Books of surveying and engineering were of course considered necessary. Miles Standish felt that he needed William Barriffe's *Military Discipline; or, The Young Artilleryman* to aid him in warding off the Indian and Dutch enemies of Plymouth Colony. Planters of Virginia and New England alike brought along Gervase Markham's various books on farming, horsemanship, and sundry country pursuits.

---

[2] Henry Peacham, *The Compleat Gentleman* (London, 1622), p. 52.
[3] Cf. Louis B. Wright, *Middle-Class Culture in Elizabethan England* (Chapel Hill, N.C., 1935), pp. 586 ff.

The foundation of Yankee horsetrading was laid by that popular work of one L. W. C., *A Very Perfect Discourse and Order How to Know the Age of a Horse*. But useful as were these technical works, they can scarcely be called literary assets.

Since the greatest amount of information in the most convenient form is usually to be found in an encyclopedia, the colonists brought along such encyclopedic works as Pierre de La Primaudaye's *The French Academy*, a title found in many inventories in the tobacco colonies and in New England. It was one of the books that Miles Standish read when he was not fighting Indians or quarreling with the saints and sinners who crossed his path. The importance of this work in the informal education of seventeenth-century readers on both sides of the Atlantic has never been fully recognized because few students have bothered to look at it. Indeed, one writer on American colonial culture explains this title, mentioned in a will, as the "publications of the French Academy." La Primaudaye's work in reality is an outline of knowledge with a strong emphasis on the natural sciences, heavily moralized to take away any taint of damnation which meddling with God's mysteries might have suggested.[4] Preachers and laymen, tobacco planters and Boston traders, all found *The French Academy* a useful book in their search for information, cultural, scientific, and godly. Other encyclopedias are found in the lists of colonial libraries, even that wondrous collection of medieval lore, *De Proprietatibus Rerum*, but none so frequently occurs as La Primaudaye's compilation. Home study, or "adult education," in America should regard this book as one of its foundation stones. An important reason for the popularity on both sides of the Atlantic of Du Bartas' versified description of the creation in his *Divine Weeks and Works* was the encyclopedic information it contained. While Anne Bradstreet was absorbing enough poetic inspiration from Du Bartas to make her the Tenth Muse, many a less exalted reader was acquiring from the same source information which he accepted as scientific truth about God's creatures, the stars in the heavens, and even the qualities of the angels themselves. Our ancestors loved "books of knowledge" even as we do, even as had their medieval sires before them.

The zeal to perpetuate learning, to keep alive the desire for knowledge, and to provide the instruments of self-instruction accounts for many volumes of a textbook character. Works whose value had been

[4] *Ibid.*, pp. 555 ff.

first learned in the English grammar schools were brought along to be used by the children of the settlers or to keep the wisdom of the ancients fresh in the minds of adults. Books of rhetoric and logic, collections of aphorisms and the flowers of eloquence, compilations of similes, dictionaries, and other handbooks of learning were common. Many of these books were reliable works that the fathers of the first settlers might have known. Erasmus, for example, remained popular in America throughout the seventeenth century. Schoolboys in Massachusetts and wealthy planters in Virginia had collections of the adages and colloquies of the great humanist. Harvard College students quoted the wisdom of Erasmus in their exercises; [5] and if men like Ralph Wormeley and Richard Lee of Virginia did not quote him in their speeches, they at least owned his works.[6] Books used in the grammar schools were not completely neglected in later life. John Hull, mintmaster and treasurer of the Colony of Massachusetts Bay, must have remembered the concise wisdom of Erasmus or perhaps that in the *Colloquies* of Corderius when he sat down to write out some aphorisms as his own rules of life.[7] Throughout the century, works of aphoristic wisdom were prized. This quality in Bacon's *Essays* no doubt accounts for their popularity.

The humanistic tradition of the Renaissance, with its insistence upon the cultural discipline of Greek and Latin writers, exerted a strong influence upon the choice of books for American libraries throughout the seventeenth century, despite occasional qualms of a Puritan disturbed in his conscience over too much attention to heathen authors. Some of the early settlers in Virginia and New England had a respectable number of classical works, and as libraries became larger and more numerous during the later years of the century, an increasing emphasis was placed upon Greek and Latin writers, both in the originals and in translation. George Sandys, busily translating

[5] Samuel Eliot Morison, *Harvard College in the Seventeenth Century* (Cambridge, Mass., 1936), I, 178.

[6] For an inventory of Ralph Wormeley's library, see *The William and Mary College Quarterly*, II (1893–94), 169–174; for Richard Lee's library, *ibid.*, pp. 247–249. Wormeley's inventory is dated 1701; Lee's, 1715; but both represent collections made in the latter part of the seventeenth century. For identification of Lee's books, see Louis B. Wright, "Richard Lee II, A Belated Elizabethan in Virginia," *The Huntington Library Quarterly*, II (1938), 1–35.

[7] *The Diaries of John Hull, Mint-Master and Treasurer of the Colony of Massachusetts Bay* in *Transactions and Collections of the American Antiquarian Society*, III (1857), 117–118.

Ovid's *Metamorphoses* on the banks of the James in 1622, was not alone in his interest in Latin poetry; and Miles Standish in chilly and pious Plymouth in the 1630's must have derived considerable consolation from his copies of Homer's *Iliad* and Caesar's *Commentaries*. An indication of the classical authors considered necessary to the library of an educated man is found in the inventory of books selected by the Reverend John Goodborne, a minister of the Church of England, who sailed for a plantation in Virginia in 1635.[8] Goodborne, unhappily, died on the voyage, but his library arrived safely to become the subject of a lawsuit which preserved a record of its contents. Destined for a plantation called Merchant's Hope, Goodborne planned to have the benefit there of the works of Homer, Aristotle, Thucydides, Isocrates, Pindar, Seneca, Plautus, Terence, Ovid, Juvenal, Persius, Horace, Cicero, Quintilian, Plutarch, Virgil, Suetonius, Justin, Julius Caesar, Claudius Aelianus, and others. If these were not sufficient to provide ample classical lore, Goodborne made doubly sure by adding Natalis Comes' *Mythologiae*, an anthology much used in the sixteenth and seventeenth centuries. Not all of his classic authors were in their original tongues. Plutarch was represented by a Latin version and North's English translation; Terence was in English; and in addition to a Latin text of Virgil, illustrated with notes and pictures, he had the Elizabethan translation by Thomas Phaer and Thomas Twyne. If this Anglican minister's library seems particularly well supplied with the classics, it is by no means extraordinary in that respect, even for the first half of the century. In New England John Harvard, in the library bequeathed in 1638 to the college that was to bear his name, duplicated many of his Anglican contemporary's classic authors, and added a few others, including Pliny, Sallust, and Lucan.[9] He also had Natalis Comes' *Mythologiae*, a book frequently owned when other works of classic literature were lacking. Like Goodborne he had North's version of Plutarch's *Lives;* in place of Homer in Greek, he had Chapman's translation.

Men of education and culture, brought up in the classical tradition of the English schools and universities, felt that Greek and Latin authors were essential if they were to preserve and transmit the

[8] "A Virginian Minister's Library, 1635," *The American Historical Review,* XI (1905–06), 328–332.

[9] Alfred C. Potter, "Catalogue of John Harvard's Library," *Publications of the Colonial Society of Massachusetts,* XXI (1919), 190–230.

amenities of a cultivated life in New England or Virginia. Literary style was still modeled on Cicero and Quintilian; history was learned from the Greek and Latin historians; much information that passed for science still came from Aristotle, Aelianus, Pliny, and others; the conduct of life was taught by Plutarch, Seneca, Homer, and Virgil; good morality, in some fashion, was extracted from them all, even from Suetonius' *History of the Twelve Caesars.* Since few, even among the sternest Puritans, were willing to deny that the basis of erudition lay in the classics, every colonist who wanted to be learned—or to appear learned—tried to give the impression of an acquaintance with Greek and Latin authors until, at the end of the century, Cotton Mather, himself an inveterate pedant, warned young preachers to stick to the simple style and avoid too much parade of Latin learning. The tradition that Greek and Latin works were essential to a well-rounded library, as to a sound education, persisted; and when the Century of Enlightenment dawned, it found the bookshelves of Boston scholars and Chesapeake planters graced with the classic works that had come to be regarded as the essentials of a gentleman's library.

As the prevalence of Latin historians in the book lists of seventeenth-century America suggests, historical reading was greatly favored, for it was believed to be highly instructive and useful in providing lessons of benefit to both the individual and the commonwealth. History, Richard Brathwaite had assured the readers of *The English Gentleman* (1630), is "the sweetest recreation of the mind," [10] a belief that met with general acceptance. Indeed, the value placed upon historical reading was second only to that accorded works of divinity.[11] When near the end of his life Cotton Mather summed up his advice to young preachers, he urged an acquaintance with history as one of the "most needful and useful accomplishments for a man that would serve God as you propose to do." [12] Whether one proposed to be a preacher in New England or a landed gentleman in Virginia or Maryland, histories were necessary to one's reading.

Some of the historical works of the Elizabethan period maintained their popularity throughout the century. William Camden's *Remains of a Greater Work Concerning Britain,* full of miscellaneous lore and apt moralizations, is listed in many wills and inventories, and even his

[10] Edition of 1630, p. 220.
[11] Wright, *Middle-Class Culture,* pp. 297–338.
[12] Cotton Mather, *Manuductio* (1726), p. 58.

imposing *Britannia,* with its maps and county-by-county descriptions of the British Isles, was frequently owned in the colonies. But the most popular of all histories by an Englishman during the seventeenth century was Sir Walter Raleigh's *History of the World.* Favored by the Puritans because it demonstrated the divine purpose in human events, the book was also well liked by Anglicans. Men like the second Richard Lee, for example, looked upon it as a work of wisdom. Most readers would have agreed with Raleigh's prefatory statement that "we may gather out of history a policy no less wise than eternal by the comparison and application of other men's forepassed miseries with our own like errors and ill deservings." Although it is impossible to measure the influence of Raleigh's *History of the World* upon the political thinking of early American leaders, it is interesting to speculate upon the effect of his digressions on kingship and his skeptical attitude toward the divinity of monarchs. The colonists, like their kindred in England, read Raleigh's *History* not merely as a compendium of facts about the ancient world but also as a source of political and moral truths.

In the later years of the seventeenth century, Bishop Gilbert Burnet's *History of the Reformation* was possessed by many readers, but it never encroached on the popularity of that other source of edification about the era of reform, John Foxe's *Acts and Monuments,* more generally called *The Book of Martyrs.* Many a humble man, whose "library" consisted of the Bible and two or three other books, numbered among them Foxe's great folio volume, which supplied the place of any other works of history or biography. No one can calculate the enormous influence of Foxe's descriptions of persecutions by Catholics in keeping alive hatred of Romanism in the breasts of American Protestants. Even yet traditional stories traceable to Foxe can be heard in the hinterland of American prejudice. The consuming interest of the seventeenth century in religious and Biblical matters gave Thomas Lodge's translation of Josephus' history of the Jews a long life in the colonies.

Current history also made its appeal to colonists, who took an eager interest in events in England and on the Continent. Booksellers in the middle of the century found ready buyers for copies of *The Swedish Intelligencer* with its running narrative of the actions of that doughty champion of Protestantism, Gustavus Adolphus. In the later years of the century, colonial readers who wanted to be informed about recent events in England equipped themselves with John Rushworth's *Historical Collections,* giving an account of parliamentary matters in the stormy years of Puritan dissension, and Bulstrode Whitelocke's *Memorials of the English Affairs . . . from the Beginning of the Reign of King Charles I to King Charles II* (1682). The parliamentary bias of these two works did not keep royalists in the South from reading them.

If historical reading was essential for any Englishman, it was doubly useful to the settlers on the fringe of the vast American wilderness. Through their historical reading they maintained a contact with the past and preserved a sense of their own continuity with the great deeds that had gone before. Out of the Americans' meditation upon their own relation to human events came a notion that later matured in the idea of manifest destiny.

That some of the early colonists were greatly concerned with books on politics and statecraft is what one might expect, for the leaders of the colonial enterprise were convinced that they were going out to found a nation. Though these men were not mere armchair theorizers, they did not neglect books that might contain useful suggestions and lessons. Among the books collected by Elder William Brewster of Plymouth was a copy of Sir Thomas Smith's *The Commonwealth of England and Manner of Government,* the standard Elizabethan work on the subject, which was continually reprinted for nearly a century and is frequently listed in colonial inventories. More remarkable was Brewster's possession of Machiavelli's *Prince* and Richard Knolles' translation from Bodin, *The Six Books of a Commonweal* (1606). Both of these books, however, were fairly common in colonial libraries. Whether Machiavelli influenced the good elder of Plymouth and his fellow settlers in their dealings with the Indians and their neighbors, one cannot say; but it is worth noting that such books were read, as references in sermons, pamphlets, and diaries indicate.

Sir Thomas More's *Utopia,* listed in numerous inventories of seventeenth-century libraries, was a book calculated to excite the interest of theoretical statesmen with a new world before them. If prejudice was still too strong for the tolerance and equality decreed by King Utopus, some at least among More's colonial readers undoubtedly yearned for a peace and prosperity like that of the Utopians. And in a few particulars, Utopia was imitated in the colonies. The banishment of idlers from the commonwealth, the insistence that every man have a calling and labor in it, the distrust of extravagant finery, and similar social attitudes were common to New England and Utopia. Colonists could find in this book passages that confirmed their social views or perhaps suggested ideas that remained dormant but alive in the subconsciousness of Americans.

If More's description of an ideal commonwealth was popular with seventeenth-century Americans, one might naturally suppose that Francis Bacon's *New Atlantis* would also attract attention. It was included at the end of the 1627 edition of Bacon's *Sylva Sylvarum,* a work on natural history recorded in a number of libraries. Bacon, throughout the seventeenth century, was a name to conjure with in America, but his reputation was based primarily on *The Advancement of Learning* and the *Essays.* His influence upon American thought is a theme for a book. In North and South, from the first quarter of the seventeenth century onward, he was regarded as an apostle of the new learning, and his *Advancement of Learning* was read and quoted as an authority by preachers, schoolmasters, and politicians. It was to Bacon that educational theorists looked for wisdom, and it was as a pedagogical expert rather than as a scientific thinker that he was most influential.

The beginning of a scientific spirit, naïve though it may seem, is discernible in the detailed observations of natural phenomena made by a few of the colonists and in their desire for scientific literature. The emphasis upon natural philosophy in *The Advancement of Learning* served to place the stamp of approval of "the great Lord Bacon" upon the normal interest of many educated colonists in things scientific. Although encyclopedic works supplied the ordinary reader with a certain amount of information concerning the world about him, some men wanted more than this, and in the inventories of the period are listed many works dealing with the rarities of the New World, geography, botany, medicine, astronomy, chemistry, and other scientific subjects.

The most influential and, at least until near the end of the century, the largest scientific library in America was that accumulated by John Winthrop, Jr., governor of Connecticut, whose books were freely drawn upon by his neighbors and friends from the time of his arrival in Boston in 1631 until his death in 1676. Jonathan Brewster, for example, was constantly borrowing alchemical books, which served only to confuse a mind already muddled with too much contemplation of esoteric matters. Winthrop's home became a scientific center, stimulating some of his contemporaries to gather books on the subject. Gershom Bulkeley was one of these. His tombstone describes him as being "exquisite in his skill in divinity, physic, and law, and of a most exemplary and Christian life." [13] The last-named virtues did not prevent his probing into God's mysteries and collecting scientific books which he and his Connecticut neighbors read. Scientific interest was undoubtedly stimulated in New England by the dispersal of the library of the Reverend Samuel Lee, who came over in 1686. His library, containing an extraordinary number of scientific books, including works of Newton, was sold in 1693 by Duncan Campbell, the Boston bookseller.[14] Virginians were also curious about natural philosophy, as their libraries indicate. William Fitzhugh, near the end of the century, became greatly interested in mineralogy in the hope of discovering precious metals on his plantation; but his interest did not stop there, for in October, 1690, he was writing to his London factor for a copy of "Cornelius Agrippa's Occult Philosophy in English if it be procured, if not then one in Latin." [15] Science was one of the many interests of William Byrd II of Westover in Virginia, and his library reflects that curiosity.

The theory of conduct and of man's relation with man was a problem of consuming interest to our soul-searching ancestors, whether they were Puritans or adherents of less rigid sects. In this field they were abundantly supplied with books that provided the essentials of instruction in everything from table manners to the means of attaining a heavenly crown. A Renaissance Italian author, who would have felt singularly ill at ease in Plymouth, was the instructor in manners chosen by Elder Brewster to be the Emily Post of the Pilgrims. He was Stefano Guazzo, whose *Civil Conversations* in an Elizabethan translation was prized by Brewster and other colonial Americans. Native English authors on problems of conduct, however, were not overlooked, and, to balance any pagan advice that the Italian might

[13] See C. H. Hoadly's introduction to Gershom Bulkeley's "Will and Doom, Or The Miseries of Connecticut by and under an Usurped and Arbitrary Power," *Connecticut Historical Society Collections,* III (1895), 70–269.

[14] A catalogue of the library was printed by Campbell and distributed prior to the sale. A few photostatic copies of the original catalogue, preserved in the Boston Public Library, have been distributed by the Massachusetts Historical Society. For a comment on Samuel Lee, see Samuel E. Morison, *The Puritan Pronaos* (New York, 1936), pp. 139–141.

[15] *Virginia Magazine of History and Biography,* III (1895–96), 8.

have offered, Brewster had Robert Cleaver's *A Godly Form of Household Government,* a guide in domestic affairs long used in English households. Brewster's neighbor, Governor Bradford, got along without an Italian manners book by sticking to the Reverend William Gouge's treatise, *Of Domestical Duties,* a recent work that united much practical and pious advice. This book and treatises like it commonly found in colonial libraries joined religious authority and bourgeois expediency in emphasizing a standard of conduct as useful to a pioneer society as it was to Gouge's London parishioners.

A determination of colonial leaders to duplicate the best features of the life they had left in England was responsible for a general interest in books concerned with the traditional rationale of conduct. Although the choice of particular books within this type was determined by individual attitudes and points of view, there was widespread agreement on the utility of books with the moral slant of Cleaver and Gouge, but not all the favorite treatises on conduct were necessarily of Puritan origin. John Harvard bequeathed his college a copy of King James's *Basilikon Doron,* doubtless with a hope that future Harvard students would overlook the royal intolerance of Puritans and remember only the excellent advice on the conduct of young men. Nor did the Anglican and royalistic flavor of *The Whole Duty of Man* in the later seventeenth century prevent its acceptance in New England as well as Virginia, though Cotton Mather sneered at the inclusiveness of the title.

While it is true that the older and more pagan Renaissance culture, described by Castiglione in *The Book of the Courtier* and Henry Peacham in *The Compleat Gentleman,* was less at home in the Bay Colony than in Virginia, where men still read these old books, both regions displayed considerable interest in the accomplishments of the gentleman, and bought books of instruction. Elder Brewster had a copy of *A Help to Memory and Discourse,* one of the better-known conversation manuals, and the records of Boston booksellers show frequent importations of a similar book called *The Academy of Compliments.* Colonial Americans were determined that their conversation should not display a provincial rusticity if handbooks could prevent it. The great concern of the colonists, however, was less with the externals of behavior than with deeper problems of conduct that determined reputation and character. When they sought books of guidance in this field, they usually chose highly moralistic works. In the later years of the century they were likely to turn to two of the most edifying books in this genre, *The Whole Duty of Man* and *The Gentleman's Calling*. How far their conduct was patterned on the admonitions of their books we can only guess.

The appetite of the seventeenth century for works of divinity has provoked the scorn of later and more sophisticated generations. Theology, we have been told, was meat and drink to a Puritan, and books of piety were his daily recreation. Of religious controversy, he made a sad-faced sport, and hurled thunderbolts from Calvin, or the Church Fathers, and buried his opponents under deep-piled quotations. We have come to think of the Puritans as a race created in the image of William Prynne, with the literary habits of their prototype. This picture is true only in part, for we are inclined to view it out of perspective and to scoff without understanding. We forget that Puritans had no monopoly of pious reading; that works of divinity and books describing the means of attaining the good life were regarded as essential to every man who pretended to civilized culture. Sectarian beliefs may have influenced the selection of certain books, but readers generally agreed that pious books were essential. For example, Ralph Wormeley, secretary of the colony of Virginia and a most unpuritan gentleman, given to horse racing and lavish hospitality, collected during the last half of the seventeenth century a library of approximately 375 titles, of which more than 120 were books devoted to religion and morals.[16] No one ever accused any of the Carters of excessive piety, yet of the books listed in the inventory made in 1690 of the personal property left by John Carter of Lancaster County, Virginia, nearly a third were religious works, including several titles by Richard Baxter, the sermons of that favorite Jacobean preacher Nicholas Byfield, and the most ubiquitous of all devotional books, Lewis Bayly's *The Practice of Piety*.[17] Few inventories fail to show a considerable proportion of religious books, and if Virginians had more interest in the sermons of Lancelot Andrewes, Jeremy Taylor, and other Anglicans than was displayed by their brethren of the Bay Colony, nevertheless a remark-

[16] Philip A. Bruce, *Institutional History of Virginia in the Seventeenth Century* (New York, 1910), I, 425–426; *The William and Mary College Quarterly*, II (1893–94), 169–174.

[17] Inventory in *The William and Mary College Quarterly*, VIII (1899–1900), 18–19. See Louis B. Wright, "The 'Gentleman's Library' in Early Virginia: The Literate Interests of the First Carters," *The Huntington Library Quarterly*, I (1937), 3–61.

able number of the same sermons and books of devotion are common
to both regions.

Many of the preachers who stirred England in the reigns of Elizabeth, James I, and Charles I, and published sermons to guide their
countrymen, exerted an influence on the American colonists for a century or more. The most widely read of these preachers were perhaps
Richard Greenham, William Perkins, Henry Scudder, John Preston,
Nicholas Byfield, and Richard Sibbes, all men of Puritan leanings.
The works that made them influential, however, were not polemical
fulminations but sane and sensible suggestions for leading a Christian
life. Much of their advice was eminently practical. We are prone to
forget that religion in the seventeenth century was vitally related to
man's daily existence, that a pattern of life that ignored religion was
unthinkable; even reprobates whose personal behavior belied this
belief were not likely to deny the theory. Indeed, the notion that God
prospered his servants and sent afflictions upon sinners was so universal
that many a seventeenth-century settler must have regarded the reading of *The Practice of Piety* or the sermons of a worthy preacher as
a sort of insurance policy.

Seventeenth-century citizens were likely to set themselves up as con-
noisseurs of sermons heard from the pulpit or received from the press.
Hence, even among laymen, there was a semiprofessional interest in
works of divinity of a type read today only by the more scholarly of
our clergymen. A desire to ponder the raw materials of sermon making helps to account for the innumerable commentaries on the Scriptures which circulated in the colonies. Even Anglicans owned and read
Calvin's explanations of the Bible, one of the favorites being his observations on the Book of Job. The struggling colonists were peculiarly
fascinated with the contemplation of Job's sufferings. A work that had
a great vogue in this country in the last three decades of the seventeenth century was Joseph Caryl's *Commentary on the Book of Job,*
first published, 1651–66, in twelve quarto volumes, but brought within
the compass of two great folios in the second edition. This was one of
Samuel Sewall's favorite works, though he usually turned to Calvin in
an emergency. When, for instance, at the turn of the century, Josiah
Willard was risking damnation by wearing a periwig, Sewall prayed
with him and recommended a course of reading in Calvin's *Institutes.*[18]

[18] *Diary of Samuel Sewall* in *Collections of the Massachusetts Historical Society,* 5th Ser., VI (1879), 37.

Sewall's *Diary* provides much useful information about the reading of works of divinity by laymen of New England in the later years of the seventeenth century.

Pious books, good for English readers, were also good for Indians, New Englanders believed. A passage in Mather's *Magnalia,* commenting on John Eliot's translations into Indian of the Bible, the *Practice of Piety,* and Richard Baxter's *Call to the Unconverted,* describes the effect of the last-named work upon a godly young chief who "lay dying of a tedious distemper, and would keep reading of Mr. Baxter's *Call to the Unconverted,* with floods of tears in his eyes, while he had any strength to do it." [19] The works of Richard Baxter were not exclusively reserved to Puritans. In the second half of the seventeenth century, Baxter's various works were common to the libraries of both New England and the southern colonies. Of all the sermons read in the seventeenth century, however, those of William Perkins, the great Elizabethan teacher and preacher of Christ's College, Cambridge, were received with greatest favor by both nonconformists and churchmen.

The main reason for the interest in sermon reading was not theological but devotional and practical: men looked to these divines for wisdom and guidance in both spiritual and temporal affairs, for help in establishing and following a pattern of life fulfilling their ideas of dignity and honor. When readers turned to their favorite sermon writers, they found exhortations and admonitions mingled with common-sense advice on everyday problems. Perkins' writings furnish many examples, but his sermon-essay entitled, *A Treatise of the Vocations,* which first appeared in the 1603 edition of the collected works,[20] is perhaps the most significant. This little treatise epitomizes the gospel of work which became the cornerstone of American economic progress. Long before Poor Richard, Perkins emphasized the prudential qualities of diligence and thrift; he demonstrated that the proper way to live acceptably before God was to fulfill one's worldly duties; and he clearly pointed out that idleness is sin, efficiency a duty, and persistence in one's daily vocation a heavenly virtue, perennial elements in our creed of success. If heaven was the destination of the seventeenth-century citizen, this world was an important way station in which he

[19] Cotton Mather, *Magnalia* (Hartford, Conn., 1853), I, 569.
[20] Wright, *Middle-Class Culture,* pp. 170–185.

could not spend his time in idle whittling. Preachers like Perkins constantly reminded their readers of a mundane as well as a spiritual duty.

A good deal of solemn nonsense about the taste of the American colonists for religious literature has been written by facile critics who have never read more than the titles of the books in colonial libraries. It is sometimes implied that the colonists were devoid of literary taste or aesthetic judgment because they seem to have preferred piety instead of plays, poetry, and romances. If such critics would read the books owned by our ancestors, they would discover that many despised sermons and treatises were written in sinewy, straightforward prose and are full of ideas and good sense. Such books were not the handiwork of half-literate fanatics, as we are sometimes led to believe, but of shrewd and intelligent university men, whose piety did not keep them from being practical social thinkers. From them our ancestors learned to follow closely reasoned and logical argument, to discipline their minds to analytical exposition, to appraise questions raised by their authors. It is not unreasonable to assume that such reading provided as much intellectual nourishment as our forebears would have derived, let us say, from meditating upon the devious plots of contemporary romances and plays. If no pretty poetry, clever drama, and urbane essays graced American literature in the seventeenth century, it is not a sign that our ancestors' minds were stultified with theological reading. We should remember that they were busy establishing a mode of existence and setting patterns that America was to follow in succeeding generations.

Not all seventeenth-century readers confined their interests to solemn treatises, but one should always remember that the prevailing attitude toward literature was so distinctly purposeful that many of our ancestors made themselves believe that they could gain instruction even when reading romances. This fact is important when we come to judge of the quality of belles-lettres in early American libraries. In the seventeenth century few readers admitted even to themselves that they read merely for idle diversion. Idleness was sin, and books—if they were good books—did not encourage this vice. Even at the end of the century, when settled prosperity had relaxed the more rigid life of the earlier period for many Americans, the proportion of trivial books that one finds recorded in inventories and booksellers' lists is small. Though in the later years of the century, especially in Virginia, there is evidence of an increasing interest in polite literature written by modern

or contemporary authors, relatively few trifling or flippant works were
sufficiently prized to get themselves preserved in the records. Some
ballads and sorry pamphlets, it is true, were imported. It was verily a
proof of witchcraft, Cotton Mather thought, that a Boston child in
1688 went into convulsions at the sight of a catechism, but read glibly
from jestbooks and made "cunning descants upon them." [21] But jestbooks, ballads, and idle tales were not characteristic of any colonial
libraries that we know about. If numerous copies of the *History of Dr.
Faustus* were imported by Boston booksellers in the 1680's and nineties,
the reason must be found in the abnormal concern over magic and
witchcraft in those years, not in a sudden shift to light reading. When
colonials bought books, they wanted something substantial, something
worthy and respectable, something to do them good.

George Lyman Kittredge [22] and Samuel Eliot Morison [23] have called
attention to the wide reading, particularly in the English poets, revealed by the commonplace books of three Harvard youths: John
Leverett, later president of Harvard College; Elnathan Chauncy, son
of a Harvard president; and Seaborn Cotton, later a minister. If some
of the passages written down by these boys show a normal interest in
the theme of love and fair ladies, others indicate the age-old tendency
to cull flowers of wisdom for future use. Though some of their contemporaries doubtless disapproved a familiarity with Shakespeare's
Venus and Adonis, or the worldly poetry of Herrick and Cleveland,
few would have questioned the virtue of reading Spenser, whose works
provided Elnathan Chauncy with twenty pages of excerpts. And defi-
nitely improving was an acquaintance with *The Mirror for Magistrates,* Warner's *Albion's England,* Fairfax's version of *Jerusalem
Delivered,* Barclay's romance *Argenis* (which even Michael Wigglesworth did not eschew), and other modern writers. These commonplace books, which have already been adequately described by others,
suggest that Elizabethan and early seventeenth-century poets and prose
writers exerted a strong influence upon some seventeenth-century
Americans. Men still believed that the function of the poet was to
teach and to delight and they did not completely omit recent English
authors in their search for delightful instruction.

[21] Mather, *Magnalia,* II, 462.
[22] George Lyman Kittredge, "A Harvard Salutatory Oration of 1662," *Publications of the Colonial Society of Massachusetts,* XXVIII (1935), 1–24.
[23] Morison, *The Puritan Pronaos,* pp. 46–53.

Probably the most widely read English poet in America in the seventeenth century was George Herbert, though he shared honors with Francis Quarles and other serious poets of the period. Evidence of their influence has been pointed out by Leon Howard in his introduction to Philip Pain's *Daily Meditations*.[24] Puritans especially approved of Herbert's prophetic lines from *The Temple:*

> Religion stands on tiptoe in our land,
> Ready to pass to the American strand.

Michael Drayton, in epistolary verses written to his friend George Sandys, then in Virginia, refers to the possibility of the flight of poetry also to America. But Sandys' translation of Ovid's *Metamorphoses* was the only really literary evidence of this flight for years to come.

One might suppose that John Milton would have appealed to the serious and purposeful colonists, but we should remember that the growth of Milton's reputation as a poet began late in the seventeenth century. His controversial and prose works naturally reached the colonies before his poetry. Records of six or eight copies of *Paradise Lost* in the colonies before 1700 have been preserved,[25] but Milton's great reputation in America was an eighteenth-century development.

The reading of fiction in early America was not entirely unknown, but our ancestors were too busy with the sharpening of their wits, with mundane affairs, or with a serious concern for their souls to have time for much "escape" into the world of romance. A few bold spirits, both male and female, bought old-fashioned romances of the kind Anthony Munday had translated, or the newer and more sugary stories of Scudéry or La Calprenède; booksellers imported a supply of Deloney's narratives for Boston shopkeepers; an occasional library had a copy of *Don Quixote;* but the stories that were best received were those written in an exalted vein. The reputation of Quarles as a divine poet took the curse off his verse romance, *Argalus and Parthenia,* sufficiently to make it fairly popular. Sidney's great name persisted and the *Arcadia* was not wholly unknown even in frontier settlements. John Allyn of Hartford, writing to Fitz-John Winthrop in 1673, alludes playfully to

[24] Philip Pain, *Daily Meditations,* 1668, ed. Leon Howard (San Marino, Calif., 1936).

[25] Leon Howard, "Early American Copies of Milton," *The Huntington Library Bulletin,* No. 7 (1935), 169–179.

incidents in the *Arcadia*.[26] An imitation of the *Arcadia* by Sidney's niece, Lady Mary Wroth, a novel entitled *The Countess of Montgomery's Urania*, enjoyed a considerable vogue. Such stories were capable of a moral interpretation, and they were full of good instruction in the manners and conduct of gentlemen. Our ancestors may have enjoyed them as romance, but we can be sure that those who owned copies considered them improving. Bunyan's *Pilgrim's Progress*, published in Boston in 1681, was undoubtedly regarded as a moral treatise and not as a novel.

No one who has assessed the evidence properly will say that seventeenth-century America was without literary culture; nor can anyone who understands the books gathered by the colonists assert, as some have done, that the Puritans of New England confined their literary interest to theology.[27] The traditional literary heritage of England was transmitted to the New World, and if didactic interpretation, which had always been strong, acquired still greater emphasis, it resulted from the serious purposefulness of the colonists, whether in New England or elsewhere. They regarded their reading as one means of attaining the kind of life that they desired. As the patterns of life in New England and the southern colonies became differentiated, variations in their literary taste developed, but that is another story. A significant fact is that in the seventeenth century, colonists of varied sectarian beliefs drew inspiration and instruction from so many of the same literary sources. Writers of the early Renaissance, of Elizabethan and early seventeenth-century England, continued to influence Englishmen in America. If this literary tradition produced no urbane school of letters in the wilderness, it provided nourishment for a developing intellectual life that came to maturity in the later eighteenth and nineteenth centuries.

By the early years of the eighteenth century, increasing prosperity and urbanity led to the multiplication of private libraries in all the colonies, the beginnings of libraries designed to serve a wider public, and a well-developed book trade in such towns as Boston, New York, Philadelphia, and Charleston. Already in the seventeenth century, private libraries provided reading matter for many more readers than

[26] *Collections of the Massachusetts Historical Society*, 6th Ser., III (1889), 435.

[27] See the protest of C. A. Herrick, "The Early New Englanders: What Did They Read?" *The Library*, 3rd Ser., IX (1918), 1–17.

1. The Hart Room, a second-floor room in the house built by Thomas Hart in 1640 at Ipswich, Massachusetts. All the furniture is of New England origin except the large seventeenth-century gate-leg table from Pennsylvania.

(The Henry Francis du Pont Winterthur Museum)

2. Pine kitchen, showing typical kitchen furnishings and utensils of the eighteenth century.

(The Henry Francis du Pont Winterthur Museum)

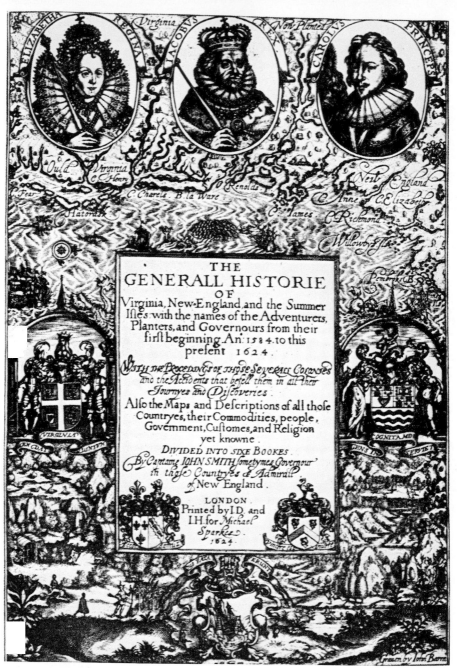

3. The title page of John Smith's *Generall Historie of Virginia, etc.*, one of the earliest compilations describing the colonial settlements.

(The Folger Library)

Grand Rehearsal of the anniversary Ode

4. The "Grand Rehearsal of the Anniversary Ode of the Tuesday Club." Wash drawing attributed to Alexander Hamilton.

(The Johns Hopkins University)

6. The title page of William Barriffe's *Military Discipline* (1635), a manual used by Miles Standish.

And thus farre for drinking of *Tabacco*, which is more vulgarly receiued with vs now than euer, and although it seems that the Indians

5. "Drinking" tobacco. From Anthony Chute, *Tabaco* (1595).

(The Henry E. Huntington Library and Art Gallery)

7. A cottage spinner at work. From Giles Firmin, *Some Proposals for the Imployment of the Poor* (1681).

(The Folger Library)

MILITARY
DISCIPLINE:
OR, THE
YONG ARTILLERY MAN.

Wherein is difcourfed and fhowne the Poftures both of *Musket* and *Pike*: the exacteft way, &c.

Together with the Motions which are to be ufed, in the exercifing of a Foot-company. With divers and feverall formes and figures of Battell; with their reducements; very neceffary for all fuch as are ftudious in the Art Military.

By WILLIAM BARRIFFE.

PSAL. 144. 1.
Bleffed be the Lord my ftrength which teacheth my hands to warre, and my fingers to fight.

LONDON,
Printed by *Thomas Harper*, for *Ralph Mab*, 1635.

Shee layeth her Hand to the Spindle and her hands hold the diftaffe. Pro. 31.

A Short
INTRODUCTION
TO THE
Latin Tongue.
For the Uſe of the Lower Forms in the *Latin School*.

Being the Accidence Abbridg'd and Compiled in that moſt eaſy and accurate Method, wherein the Fa mous Mr. *Ezekiel Cheever* taught; and which he found the moſt advantageous by *Seventy* years experience.

The Third Edition Reviſed & Correcʒed by the Author.
To which are added a Catalogue of Irregular Nouns and of Verbs diſpos'd Alphabetically.

BOSTON in *N. E*
Printed by *B. Green*, for *Benj. Eliot*, at his Shop in King Street. 1 7 2 4.

8. Colonial school texts.

(The Folger Library)

רִקְדּוּק
לִשׁוֹן עֶבְרִית
DICKDOOK LESHON GNEBREET.

A

GRAMMAR
OF THE
Hebrew Tongue,
BEING
An ESSAY
To bring the Hebrew Grammar into Engliſh, to Facilitate the
INSTRUCTION
Of all thoſe who are deſirous of acquiring a clear Idea of this
Primitive Tongue
by their own Studies;
In order to their more diſtinct Acquaintance with the SACRED ORACLES of the Old Teſtament, according to the Original. And Publiſhed more eſpecially for the Uſe of the STUDENTS of *HARVARD-COLLEGE* at *Cambridge*, in NEW-ENGLAND.

נֶחֱבַּר וְהוּגַהּ בְּעִיּוּן נִמְרָץ עַל יְדֵי
יְהוּדָה מוֹנִישׁ

Compoſed and accurately Correcʒed,
By JUDAH MONIS, *M. A.*

BOSTON, N. E.
Printed by JONAS GREEN, and are to be Sold by the AUTHOR at his Houſe in *Cambridge*. MDCCXXXV.

9. Female costume of the early colonial
period. From Wenceslas Hollar, *Ornatus
Muliebris Anglicanus* (1640).

(The Folger Library)

10. A soldier of the early colonial
period. From Jaques de Gheyn,
Maniement d'armes (1608).

(The Folger Library)

11. A colonial tobacco wharf from *The American Atlas* (1776).

(Map Division, The New York Public Library)

12. A view of Charleston, 1739.

(The Phelps Stokes Collection, The New York Public Library)

13. The printing press used by Benjamin Franklin as a journeyman printer in London in 1726.

(The Smithsonian Institution)

14. Valuable commodities of the New World: sassafras and tobacco. From Nicholas Monardes, *Joyfull Newes Out of the Newe Founde Worlde* (1577).
(The Folger Library)

15. Steps in the processing of indigo. From Pomet's *Compleat History of Druggs* (1725).
(The Folger Library)

16. MRS. GABRIEL MANIGAULT, painted by Jeremiah Theus (1757).

(The Metropolitan Museum of Art)

17. Engraving of SIR WILLIAM PEPPERRELL by Peter Pelham (1747) after a painting by John Smibert.

(The Metropolitan Museum of Art)

18. GEORGE WHITEFIELD by Joseph Badger.

(The Fogg Museum of Art, Harvard University)

19. A colonial factory yard, from Du Tertre, *Histoire Generale des Antilles*, II (1667).

(Arents Tobacco Collection, The New York Public Library)

20. Harvard College, engraved by William Burgis (1725-26).

(The Phelps Stokes Collection, The New York Public Library)

21. Colonial craftsmanship: High chest of drawers, mahogany, Chippendale, Philadelphia (1760-75); oak chest of drawers, 1678, Ipswich, Massachusetts, made by Thomas Dennis; sugar box, silver, 1702, made by Edward Winslow of Boston; quart tankard, pewter, 1713-42, made by Simon Edgell of Philadelphia.

(The Henry Francis du Pont Winterthur Museum)

23. The title page of Ovid's *Metamorphoses* (1626), part of which was translated by George Sandys in Virginia.

(The Folger Library)

22. The frontispiece to Dilworth's *New Guide to the English Tongue*, showing boys with their teacher, a dame school, and schoolboys at play.

(The Folger Library)

25. Self-portrait by THOMAS SMITH.
(Worcester Art Museum)

24. ANN POLLARD, painted by an unknown limner.
(Massachusetts Historical Society)

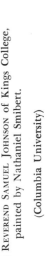

27. EZRA STILES, painted by Nathaniel Smibert.

(Yale University Art Gallery)

26. THE REVEREND SAMUEL JOHNSON of Kings College,
painted by Nathaniel Smibert.

(Columbia University)

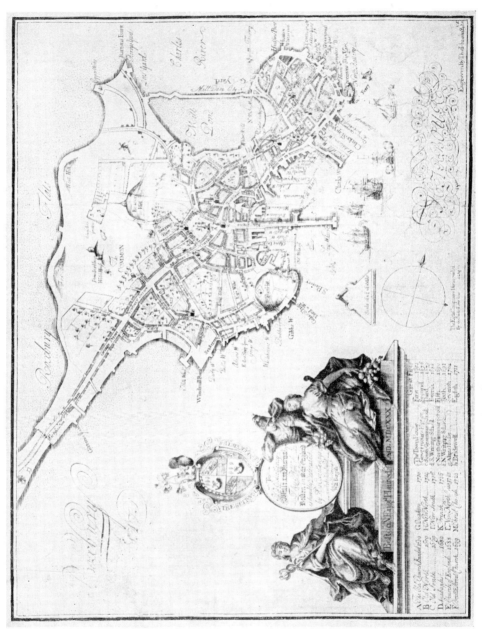

28. A plan of Boston in 1728.

(Metropolitan Museum of Art)

29. The Capitol, Williamsburg, Virginia, reconstructed to its appearance in the early 1700's. (Colonial Williamsburg, Inc.)

30. The Wren Building, College of William and Mary, originally built in 1695-98, from plans said to have been prepared by Sir Christopher Wren. (Colonial Williamsburg, Inc.)

the households of the owners. The failure of neighbors and friends to return borrowed books provoked more than one bitter comment in the correspondence of the day.

Two of the most noteworthy book collectors were Cotton Mather in Boston and William Byrd II of Virginia. Both had the instincts of the bibliophile and loved books for their own sakes. Mather accumulated between 3,000 and 4,000 titles before his death in 1728 [28] and Byrd had a library of more than 3,600 titles at his death in 1744.[29] Their books were varied in subject and included everything from religious tracts to recent books on natural science. Works of history and the Greek and Roman classics were numerous. Despite the difference in social points of view of these two men, their libraries were strikingly similar.

A number of other bibliophiles in the eighteenth century gathered libraries of distinction. Thomas Prince, minister of the Old South Church, collected more than 1,500 volumes, many dealing with civil history. At his death in 1758, his books were stored in the tower of the church. Though many were stolen by British soldiers during the occupation of Boston, a considerable number survived the Revolution and eventually found their way into the Boston Public Library. Thomas Hutchinson, the last royal governor of Massachusetts, had a fine library surpassed in excellence only by the Mathers' collection of books.

James Logan, who came over as secretary to William Penn in 1699, and lived in Pennsylvania until his death in 1751, brought together a library of more than 3,000 volumes, notable especially for classical and scientific works. Great as was Logan's interest in science, he remained always a humanist and looked back to the literature of Greece and Rome for inspiration. In the controversy over the ancients and the moderns, he gave his allegiance to the ancients, but was wise enough to take what suited him from the moderns too.[30] Logan had one of the best scientific libraries in North America, for he himself had a deep

---

[28] Thomas Goddard Wright, *Literary Culture in Early New England, 1620–1730* (New Haven, Conn., 1920), p. 178.

[29] Louis B. Wright, *The First Gentlemen of Virginia* (San Marino, Calif., 1940), p. 333.

[30] Frederick B. Tolles, "Quaker Humanist: James Logan as a Classical Scholar," *The Pennsylvania Magazine of History and Biography,* LXXIX (1955), 415–438.

interest in botany and other aspects of natural science. He kept his books in a small house near his home in Philadelphia and made them available to serious students.

On Logan's death he bequeathed both house and books to the city of Philadelphia for a public library. He stands in the front rank of the founders of practical and useful libraries for the benefit of the public, albeit he was not the first in the colonies to have such an idea. Long before, Robert Keayne, a Boston merchant who died in 1656, left a bequest providing for a library for the town; but though mention is made from time to time of the "public library," it appears to have fallen early into decay and to have disappeared altogether in the fire of 1747.[31] Although New Haven, Concord, and Dorchester had little collections called town libraries in the seventeenth century, they were of no great importance.[32] The establishment of libraries for public use on any considerable scale had to wait until the eighteenth century.

One of the most earnest advocates of libraries as a means of civilizing the colonies was Dr. Thomas Bray, who was responsible for the founding of the Society for Promoting Christian Knowledge (1699), which had as an offshoot the Society for the Propagation of the Gospel in Foreign Parts (1701). Bray himself was a zealous propagandist who labored unceasingly to bring about the official establishment of the Church of England in Maryland, where he personally served for a few months in 1699 as commissary. To improve the status of the clergy, he proposed to provide them with parochial libraries of carefully selected volumes for professional use. Bray sent these parochial libraries to various colonies, but Maryland, as the center of his personal interest, received the largest number. The parochial libraries, composed almost entirely of religious books, were intended for the use of the clergy rather than the public. But Bray also planned provincial libraries for the use of all types of readers. The largest of these was established at Annapolis. In an account dated 1702, Bray listed twenty-nine parochial libraries in Maryland alone, with collections ranging from ten to 314 titles. The provincial library at Annapolis, to which Queen Anne herself had contributed, contained 1,095 volumes.[33]

The care and preservation of the libraries were of concern both to

[31] C. Seymour Thompson, *Evolution of the American Public Library, 1653–1876* (Washington, D.C., 1952), pp. 13–14.

[32] *Ibid.*, pp. 15–18.

[33] Joseph Towne Wheeler, "Thomas Bray and the Maryland Parochial Libraries," *Maryland Historical Magazine*, XXXIV (1939), 246–265.

Bray and the colonial governments. Beginning in 1696, the Maryland Assembly passed several laws designed to prevent dispersal of the Maryland libraries through carelessness. In 1704 Bishop White Kennett wrote earnestly to Thomas Hearne, then a young assistant keeper in the Bodleian Library, urging him to go out to Maryland as a missionary and examiner of the libraries established there. Hearne resisted the offer and was thus saved to antiquarian scholarship.

The provincial library established by Bray at Charleston, South Carolina, in 1698, laid the foundation for library development in that colony. The government itself contributed £225 toward the book fund and in 1700 the Assembly passed a law specifying conditions under which the inhabitants might borrow books from the library. This union of private enterprise and government was a long step toward the concept of a public library for the general benefit of the population.

New York appears to have been less receptive to Bray's efforts to establish a library for general use. The books that he sent over, presumably for a provincial library, remained locked up in Trinity Church and were of no use to any except the clergy. Finally, in 1713, the Reverend John Sharpe, who had served in New York as a chaplain of English troops, gave his books to the Society for the Propagation of the Gospel in Foreign Parts to found a public library in New York. What happened to Sharpe's books is not certain, but in 1739 another parson, John Millington, gave books for an institution called the Corporation Library.[34] These little collections preceded the formation of the New York Society Library in 1754. In North Carolina, in 1723, Edward Moseley, in the hope of establishing a provincial library at Edenton, gave a collection of books to supplement those sent over by Dr. Bray.

Bray's efforts to send books to the British colonies in America may not have had far-reaching results, but they helped to focus interest on the need for books and served a very useful purpose in several colonies, particularly Maryland and North and South Carolina. He was concerned primarily with religion. Even the so-called laymen's libraries that he planned to present to colonial Americans were not really libraries, but were small collections of such books as *The Practice of Piety* and *The Whole Duty of Man* for the religious instruction of individuals who received them.[35]

[34] Thompson, *Evolution of the American Public Library*, pp. 31–32.
[35] *Ibid.*, pp. 28–29.

Before the middle of the eighteenth century, the idea that individuals might pool their resources and set up subscription libraries was beginning to take hold. Like so many other things in eighteenth-century America, the impetus for this came from Benjamin Franklin, who in November, 1731, organized the Library Company of Philadelphia. The first members, belonging to Franklin's discussion club called the Junto, paid forty shillings each for their shares. They took in other members to the number of fifty and later increased the membership to one hundred. The earliest shipment of books, which arrived in October, 1732, indicates the changing nature of American libraries. No longer did religious literature predominate. Of forty-five titles not one concerns dogmatic religion. Here are recent historical works along with English translations of Plutarch's *Lives* and Tacitus' *Annals,* geographies, grammars, dictionaries, Boerhaave's *Chemistry,* Parkinson's *Herbal* and other more recent scientific treatises, books on mathematics, government, politics, agriculture, architecture, and such literary works as *The Spectator, The Tatler,* and *The Guardian.*[36] These were the books that a secular, rationalistic group of ambitious young tradesmen and craftsmen bent upon improving themselves would want to read and study. The Library Company's books are a symbol of a new note in American life, the advance of an independent and forward-looking middle class who saw in self-education the means of raising themselves both economically and socially.

Concerning the Library Company, Franklin wrote with obvious satisfaction in his *Autobiography:* "This was the mother of all the North American subscription libraries, now so numerous. It is become a great thing itself and continually increasing. These libraries have improved the general conversation of Americans, made the common tradesmen and farmers as intelligent as most gentlemen from other countries, and perhaps have contributed in some degree to the stand so generally made throughout the colonies in defence of their privileges." [37]

The Library Company of Philadelphia, first housed in a room in Pewter Platter Alley and later, for more than thirty years after 1740, in the State House, contributed much to the intellectual development

[36] Austin K. Gray, *The First American Library* (Philadelphia, 1936), pp. 11–12.

[37] Max Farrand (ed.), *The Autobiography of Benjamin Franklin* (Berkeley, Calif., 1949), p. 86.

of Philadelphia. The librarian was instructed to let any "civil gentle-man" read the books during the few hours that the library was open each week, but books could be borrowed only by members, with the single exception of James Logan. In deference to his own interest in books—and his encouragement of the enterprise—he was allowed to take books home.

The proprietary library on the model of the Library Company of Philadelphia, or the "social library" as it is sometimes designated, became an important instrument of popular education, as Franklin implies. Two years after the establishment of the Library Company of Philadelphia, a group of citizens of Durham, Connecticut, in 1733 organized the Book Company of Durham, and similar libraries were soon organized at a half-dozen places in Connecticut. Before the Revolution, it is estimated that at least sixty-four subscription libraries had been organized throughout the American colonies.[38] The prob-ability is that there were many more, all records of which are lost.

The Redwood Library of Newport, Rhode Island, founded in 1747, owed its existence to the approval shown by Abraham Redwood, a merchant, of the purposes of the Literary and Philosophical Society of Newport, which was organized "for the promotion of knowledge and virtue." Redwood proposed to some of the men of the Society that they organize a library, which they did, and received from Redwood £500 sterling as a start.[39] When the first catalogue was published in 1764, the Redwood Library had about 700 volumes, with belles-lettres, science, and history predominating. Only about 13 per cent of the collection could be classified as religion and philosophy.[40]

The Charleston Library Society, organized in 1748 by seventeen of the leading citizens of the town, quickly became an important influ-ence in the cultural life of the South Carolina metropolis. Within two years after its founding, it numbered 130 members and had an en-dowment for the purchase not only of books but of scientific apparatus. Its members planned an academy in conjunction with the library and proposed to have a professor of natural philosophy and mathematics to lecture at the library. These grandiose plans failed to develop, but the library itself provided a wide assortment of reading in all fields, especially in science, law, history, and philosophy. Despite lip service

[38] Thompson, *Evolution of the American Public Library,* pp. 54–55.
[39] *Ibid.,* p. 53.
[40] Jesse H. Shera, *Foundations of the Public Library* (Chicago, 1949), p. 39.

to the classics, the literature of Greece and Rome appears to have been neglected in Charleston. When Christopher Gadsden in 1764 resigned because the Library Society rejected his proposal to spend 70 per cent of the annual appropriation for Greek and Latin classics, the librarian pointed out that nobody had called for classical works already on the library shelves.[41]

From an early period, New York was more noted for its commerce than its culture, but in 1754, high-minded citizens succeeded in establishing a proprietary library and King's College. The New York Society Library was apparently planned as a sort of adjunct to the college. The articles of subscription drawn up on April 2, 1754, stated that "a public library would be very useful, as well as ornamental to this city and may be also advantageous to our intended college." [42] Like the college, the library was at first dominated by Church of England influences, much to the disgust of the Presbyterians, one of whom published a letter in the *Mercury* for May 12, 1755, pointing out that "no sooner were the subscriptions complete and a day appointed for the election of trustees than a dirty scheme was concerted for excluding as many English Presbyterians as possible from the trusteeship." [43] Despite the displeasure of the Presbyterians, the New York Society Library became a useful cultural institution. Like the Library Company of Philadelphia, the Redwood Library of Newport, and the Charleston Library Society, the New York Society Library continued to grow through the years and to exert a beneficent influence even to the present day.

Circulating libraries, operated chiefly by booksellers and publishers, which came to have considerable importance in the late eighteenth and early nineteenth centuries, had a beginning in our period. In 1762, William Rind, one of the publishers of the second *Maryland Gazette*, advertised a plan to establish a circulating library which he hoped would be useful in "diffusing a spirit of science through the country." [44] About six months later, a stationer in Charleston named George Wood also advertised a proposal for a circulating library, but neither Rind's nor Wood's ventures flourished, and it was at least a

[41] Frederick P. Bowes, *The Culture of Early Charleston* (Chapel Hill, N.C., 1942), p. 62.

[42] Austin B. Keep, *History of the New York Society Library* (New York, 1908), p. 136.

[43] *Ibid.*, p. 139.

[44] Shera, *Foundations of the Public Library*, p. 132.

decade before circulating libraries began to have much influence on the reading public.

By the middle of the eighteenth century, the libraries of Harvard and Yale were sufficiently large and varied to play a significant part in the cultural development of their students, faculties, and such others as were fortunate enough to have access to the books. A list of Harvard's books in 1723 showed approximately 3,000 volumes in a wide variety of subjects, and Yale's first catalogue in 1742 listed about 2,600 volumes, including a respectable collection of belles-lettres. At both Harvard and Yale one could find works of the chief English classics. Yale's catalogue listed the works of Chaucer, Spenser, Shakespeare, Milton, Dryden, and contemporary authors such as Pope, Gay, Prior, Addison and others.[45]

Both Harvard and Yale benefited from generous benefactors in the first half of the eighteenth century. Beginning with a gift of Milton's poetical works from Thomas Hollis of London in 1722, Harvard received for many years successive gifts of books and money from Hollis and his son and other members of the Hollis family. In 1724 Hollis wrote to the Harvard Corporation a letter that is still timely: "If there happen to be some books not quite orthodox," he warned, "in search after truth with an honest design, don't be afraid of them. A public library ought to be furnished, if it can, with *con* as well as *pro,* that students may read, try, judge; see for themselves, and believe upon argument and just reasonings of the Scriptures. 'Thus saith Aristotle,' 'Thus saith Calvin,' will not now pass for proof in our London disputations."[46] Hollis also showed unusual clairvoyance in anticipating a central repository for little-used books when he wrote to a member of the Harvard Corporation urging him, if necessary to make room for modern books, "to remove the less useful into a more remote place, but not sell any."[47]

The Yale library's most important gift in the first half of the eighteenth century was a donation in 1733 of nearly 1,000 volumes from George Berkeley, Bishop of Cloyne, who took a deep interest in American affairs. He had hoped to found a college in Bermuda and had lived from 1728 to 1731 in Newport, Rhode Island. When he left

[45] E. P. Morris, "A Library of 1742," *The Yale University Library Gazette,* IX (1934), 1–11. *A Catalogue of the Library of Yale College in New Haven* (1742) has been reproduced in facsimile (New Haven, 1931).

[46] Josiah Quincy, *History of Harvard University* (Cambridge, 1840), I, 433.

[47] *Ibid.,* I, 432.

Newport, he donated his ninety-six-acre farm to Yale along with his library, a well-selected collection embracing the major branches of learning.[48] To Harvard he also gave a few books. Thanks to gifts from generous benefactors, the libraries of both Harvard and Yale continued to grow. By the time of the great fire which destroyed the library in 1764, Harvard had a collection of nearly 5,000 books.

The libraries of the other colonial colleges were less important. The College of William and Mary received several small gifts of books from time to time, but it too suffered from fire, and its library probably never totaled as many as 3,000 volumes before the Revolution. Princeton received a gift of several hundred books from Governor Jeremy Belcher and by 1760, when it published a catalogue, it had a library of 1,261 volumes.[49] King's College (later Columbia) received gifts of books from several benefactors before the Revolution, but it could not boast a library of any distinction in our period. The College of Philadelphia had no adequate library in the period before the Revolution.

Bookselling in colonial America was centered chiefly in Boston, New York, Philadelphia, and Charleston, but elsewhere printers and stationers frequently had small stocks of books, and general merchants sometimes advertised schoolbooks and other works of interest to their customers. Between 1669 and 1690, Boston had twenty booksellers, and from this time onward Boston was an important book market.[50] It supplied books to most of New England and frequently shipped them to more distant colonies. The booksellers of Boston were sufficiently numerous in 1724 to found a trade association, and their importations of books multiplied in the eighteenth century until they represented a fair cross section of contemporary publication in England. In 1732 Richard Fry imported 1,200 copies of the Wiltshire poet, Stephen Duck,[51] a fact that may account for the quality of some eighteenth-century American verse. Dr. Alexander Hamilton of Annapolis on a visit to Boston in 1744 attended a book auction and com-

[48] The collection given Yale is listed in Louis Shores, *Origins of the American College Library, 1638–1800* (Nashville, Tenn., 1934), pp. 244–262.

[49] Thomas J. Wertenbaker, *Princeton, 1746–1896* (Princeton, N.J., 1946), p. 106.

[50] Carl Bridenbaugh, *Cities in the Wilderness: The First Century of Urban Life in America, 1625–1742* (New York, 1938), p. 129. Cf. Thomas G. Wright, *Literary Culture in Early New England, 1620–1730* (New Haven, 1920), *passim*.

[51] Bridenbaugh, *Cities in the Wilderness,* p. 452.

mented: "The books that sold best at this auction while I was there were *Pamela, Anti-Pamela, The Fortunate Maid,* Ovid's *Art of Love,* and *The Marrow of Modern Divinity.*" [52]

By the early years of the eighteenth century, New York had at least four booksellers. But in the colonial period, New York never rivaled Boston as a book market. Philadelphia printers and shopkeepers frequently advertised books and by the middle of the eighteenth century the town could boast at least a half-dozen booksellers. Best known was Benjamin Franklin, whose printing shop offered a variety of books on many subjects. After 1731, the newspapers of Charleston carried frequent advertisements of books for sale, an indication that Charleston was a good book market for the colonies of the far South.

The advertisements of eighteenth-century colonial papers indicate a steady market for contemporary English publications and do not suggest that the cultural lag was longer than the time for books to reach the colonies after publication in England. Throughout the colonial period, the interest in books was a vital and growing manifestation of the American genius for self-improvement. Franklin's comment that American tradesmen and farmers were as well read as gentlemen elsewhere was something more than the empty boast of a superpatriot. Americans had learned that books would provide not only inner satisfactions but material rewards as well.

[52] Carl Bridenbaugh (ed.), *Gentleman's Progress: The Itinerarium of Dr. Alexander Hamilton, 1744* (Chapel Hill, N.C., 1948), p. 112.

CHAPTER 7

Literary Production: North and South

LOOKING back from the urban sophistication of the twentieth century, critics have sometimes wondered unnecessarily about the barrenness of literary production in the colonial period and have wasted a deal of ink writing about the sterility of more than a century and a half that produced little worth-while drama, fiction, or imaginative poetry. What they mean is that the characteristic literary productions of the colonial period are no longer in fashion and make no general appeal today. The forms of literature that we cherish today received scant attention from our colonial ancestors. Not until the very end of the period was there anything that can be called American drama or formal fiction, and the verse written before the Revolution is for the most part of interest only to specialists.

But this is not to say that the colonists' imaginations were comatose or that their pens were idle. They left an enormous volume of writings on a wide variety of themes that manifest a vitality and breadth of interest commanding our respect if not always our attention. If too little of the literary production of the seventeenth and eighteenth centuries in America has the capacity to hold our interest, that fact does not indicate a lack of imagination or mental capacity on the part of the writers. They usually had objectives much nearer to their immediate concerns than Milton's noble dream of writing something that the world would not willingly let die. When colonial writers sat down with a goose-quill pen and an inkpot, their minds were usually not focused upon posterity but upon some present problem. Most of them were busy and practical men who wrote, as they read, with a purpose, and that purpose was not to provide entertainment for their descendants.

Polite literature flourishes best, not in a wilderness, but in an urban society where men and women with wit and leisure have time and inclination to exercise their talents. The struggle for existence that occupied the waking hours of colonial Americans gave scarcely more time for the cultivation of letters than for any of the other fine arts. Even when the settlers had passed the first stage of driving out the savages and clearing the woods, they were still too few and too preoccupied with the necessities of existence to give much attention to letters. In the most highly cultivated of societies, the percentage of people who aspire to or achieve success in letters is always infinitesimal; and in a frontier society composed almost entirely of unliterary folk, it would have been a miracle past understanding if belles-lettres had taken root and instantly flourished. Although polite letters had to wait until Americans had acquired maturity and leisure, the more utilitarian forms of writing flourished luxuriantly.

The earliest writers in the thirteen colonies were really transients, explorers, or temporary settlers who came, saw, and wrote down their impressions. Histories of American literature usually begin with Captain John Smith, though his actual residence in America was only a trifle more than two years. Nevertheless, thanks to Smith's capacity for embellishing a good tale, the story of Pocahontas has become a part of our national legend and we forget that Smith the explorer and writer of descriptive geography is an important figure in our early annals. Controversies have raged over his veracity, but modern historiography has come to regard him as a useful narrator of what happened and a valuable reporter of the appearance of the country. Smith's first literary production was *A True Relation of . . . Virginia,* published late in 1608 while the author was still at Jamestown. It is a clear undecorated account of events up to midsummer 1608, when Smith sent back his manuscript containing a description of the Indians and a report of his capture by Powhatan's warriors. Significantly, his only mention of Pocahontas is to describe her as a promising ten-year-old child. After Smith was long since back in England and was putting together another book, *The General History of Virginia* (1624), he inserted the dramatic episode of his rescue by Pocahontas, a piece of heroics characteristically Elizabethan and pleasing to the author's vanity. Another work by Smith which deserves a place in the annals of American literature was *A Description of New England* (1616), a rational account of the potential value of the northern sector of the country. To Smith we owe the name New England, and to Prince Charles (later Charles I), to whom Smith took his map, we owe many place names which still exist. From personal trial on his voyage to New England, Smith learned of the value of fish, and his pamphlet is almost rhapsodical in praise of fish. Fisheries may be worth more than all the gold and jewels of the Spaniards, he asserts, and the Spaniards are less able to pay their debts than the Hollanders who depend chiefly upon "this contemptible trade of fish," which "is their mine, and the sea the source of those silvered streams of all their virtue." [1]

From Smith's time onward, American settlers, both temporary and permanent, turned out a constant stream of travel narratives, promotion pamphlets, geographical descriptions, and summaries of happenings in the several colonies. The promotion pamphlet, a form of literature not often noticed by critics but perhaps of greater significance than poetry or the novel in its influence upon the quality of our civilization, early found skillful practitioners on these shores. The Virginia Company of London encouraged the writing of tracts that would picture the colony at Jamestown in the best light and would encourage investors in the enterprise.

Not every report by eyewitnesses, however, was favorable, and one of the most vivid accounts, William Strachey's *A True Repertory of the Wreck and Redemption of Sir Thomas Gates . . . His Coming to Virginia and the Estate of That Colony,* written in 1610, gives a discouraging picture of Jamestown; but it is significant that it had to wait fifteen years to see print, for the Virginia Company just at that time was subsidizing preachers and others to give glowing descriptions of Virginia and its prospects. [2] Strachey's narrative, sent back to England in the form of a letter to an unknown "noble lady," circulated in manuscript, and its description of the shipwreck on Bermuda provided material for Shakespeare in *The Tempest.* Strachey's later *History of Travel into Virginia Britannia* (1612), which also re-

---

[1] Edward Arber (ed.), *Travels and Works of Captain John Smith* (Edinburgh, 1910), I, 194.

[2] Louis B. Wright and Virginia Freund (eds.), *The Historie of Travell Into Virginia Britania* (1612), by William Strachey, gent., The Hakluyt Society (London, 1953), pp. xxi–xxii. Strachey's *Repertory* first appeared in print in Samuel Purchas, *Hakluytus Posthumus, Or Purchas His Pilgrimes* (1625).

mained in manuscript, to a considerable degree was scissors-and-paste work.

The New England settlers were convinced that God had a particular oversight of their endeavors and that it was their duty to make known his favor to them. This consciousness of being the chosen of God is evident in their reports, journals, diaries, histories, and other writings, and it gives a dignity even to their promotion pamphlets. William Bradford and Edward Winslow jointly were responsible for the earliest narrative of the Plymouth Pilgrims, a report published in London in 1622 as *A Relation or Journal of the Beginning and Proceeding of the English Plantation Settled at Plymouth in New England,* often called "Mourt's Relation" because the preface was signed G. Mourt. This was followed two years later by Winslow's *Good News from New England.* Both tracts emphasize the fruitfulness of the land, the need of honest folk to settle it, and the goodness of God in watching over his people and saving them from danger. A more detailed report, spiced with verse, was William Wood's *New England's Prospect* (1634), which was popular enough to have three editions by 1639. Its appeal lies in the spirited style, the vigor of its Elizabethan metaphors, and the author's keen eye for detail. His interest is primarily in the natural aspects of the country, with descriptions of enough marvels to fascinate English readers. For example, the hummingbird, which continued to arouse the interest of naturalists for the next century, inspires a vivid passage, and a report of lions in New England gains Wood's credence because he had lately heard of one at Cape Ann, "not above six leagues from Boston." One of the purposes of *New England's Prospect* was to refute slanders against the colony and to combat ignorance in England of the virtues of the country and its people.

Some of the best of the reports and narratives never saw print in the colonial period, but in a few instances were used in manuscript by other writers. John Winthrop's *Journal,* for example, was not published in its entirety until 1825–26, though New England chroniclers like Cotton Mather, William Hubbard, and Thomas Prince drew on the document in their own work. Winthrop kept a record of events affecting the Massachusetts Bay group from the time the *Arbella* sailed on March 29, 1630, to January 11, 1649, a record that gravely sets down the special favor of God to his people. No detail is too small to be noted, as, for example, the remarkable instance of the mice that got into a storeroom containing grain and books but touched nothing except a Book of Common Prayer—a work much detested by the Puritans. From that idolatrous book the Puritan mice nibbled every leaf.[3] Winthrop's style is concise and dry, but there is now and then a glint of perhaps unconscious humor, as in his comment on Nathaniel Eaton's taking up residence among the Virginians: "Mr. Nathaniel Eaton . . . being come to Virginia, took upon him to be a minister, but was given up of God to extreme pride and sensuality, being usually drunken, as the custom is there." [4] As literature, the most valuable of all the early narratives was of course William Bradford's account, which he himself simply labeled *Of Plymouth Plantation*. Like Winthrop's *Journal*, it too was not published in full until the nineteenth century, though it was known to all the colonial New England antiquarians. Bradford's chronicle has the simplicity and sincerity of John Bunyan and the dignity of John Milton. As Moses Coit Tyler remarked, "The daily food of his spirit was noble. He uttered himself, without effort, like a free man, a sage, and a Christian." [5] Christian though he was, his report of his fellow Pilgrims is realistic and without effort to disguise the shortcomings of some of them; for despite the exaggerations of a century of orators, not all of the settlers at Plymouth were saints. Interloping sinners were also a trial to Bradford. The most notorious of these disturbers of the peace of Plymouth was Thomas Morton, who set up the famous Maypole at Merrymount and stimulated Bradford to write one of his rare passages of scorn.[6] Not a page of Bradford's narrative is dull or obscure and the account *Of Plymouth Plantation* deserves the high place it has attained in colonial letters.

Morton wrote his own report of the episode which aroused Bradford's dislike and published it in London in 1637 as the *New English Canaan*. Thomas Morton of Merrymount has become a popular hero of folklore, but his own account of his deeds provides little evidence that Bradford was wrong in his estimate.

Far removed from the simple dignity of Bradford but similar in

[3] James K. Hosmer (ed.), *Winthrop's Journal "History of New England"* (New York, 1908), II, 18.

[4] *Ibid.*, II, 20–21.

[5] Moses Coit Tyler, *A History of American Literature During the Colonial Period, 1607–1765* (New York, 1909), I, 126.

[6] Samuel Eliot Morison (ed.), *Of Plymouth Plantation, 1620–1647. By William Bradford, Sometime Governor Thereof* (New York, 1952), p. 205.

purpose was another narrative account, the work of Edward Johnson, published in London in 1654 as *A History of New England,* but better known by the title which the author apparently intended for it, the *Wonder-Working Providence of Sion's Savior in New England*—or, more properly, in Massachusetts Bay. The title page of the first edition makes explicit the matters handled and implies the point of view of the writer, for the work promises an explanation of "the form of their government, civil, military, and ecclesiastic. Their wars with the Indians, their troubles with the Gortonists, and other heretics. Their manner of gathering of churches, the commodities of the country, and description of the principal towns and havens, with the great encouragements to increase trade betwixt them and Old England. With the names of all their governors, magistrates, and eminent ministers. Psalm 107.24: The righteous shall see it and rejoice, and all iniquity shall stop her mouth. Psalm 111.2: The works of the Lord are great, and ought to be sought out of all that have pleasure in them." [7] To make manifest the works of the Lord in establishing Massachusetts Bay as a haven for the saints is patently Johnson's purpose, which he never once lets the reader forget, though he manages to mingle with his piety strong indications that an investment in Massachusetts Bay will have special consideration from the Lord. Unlike Bradford, Johnson is not content with the plain style, for when the afflatus is upon him, he soars into turgid rhetoric or drops into banal verse. Yet his work is significant for the emphasis that it gives to the importance of writing history to record God's particular favor to his people of New England.

This attitude helps to explain the Puritans' zeal for recording every act and deed that concerned them, and it lies behind a succession of histories written during the colonial period. Although the Puritans had no monopoly of the interest in history, for most Englishmen of the seventeenth century regarded historical reading as second only to Holy Writ, nevertheless by training they were peculiarly conditioned to regard themselves as the culmination of a long cycle of history. Like other Protestant Englishmen they had been nourished on John Foxe's *Acts and Monuments,* first published in 1563, a work in which they discerned the working out of God's providences and evidence of the concentration of God's interest upon England and Englishmen.

[7] J. Franklin Jameson (ed.), *Johnson's Wonder-Working Providence, 1628–1651* (New York, 1910), p. 21.

It was natural that they would transfer that focus to themselves and New England. When the Puritan writer sat down at his desk to record God's providences, he thought of himself as performing a duty required as evidence of his gratitude to the Almighty. A great many writers were persuaded that they were called in this fashion to authorship.

Thomas Prince, clergyman, book collector, and author of a *Chronological History of New England,* published in Boston in 1736, reports that he was instructed as a child to read the history of New England as only a little less important than works of sound religious doctrine. And of the preceding histories commended to him, one that had a high contemporary reputation was Nathaniel Morton's *New England's Memorial,* printed in Cambridge in 1669. Morton was Bradford's nephew and the chief virtue of his work lay in his good judgment in printing long passages from his uncle's manuscript *Of Plymouth Plantation* and other passages from unpublished writings of Edward Winslow. His own additions were crabbed and uninspired, but like most of his contemporaries he was intent upon setting forth "the providence of God manifested in the planters of New England." Since Bradford remained unpublished for generations to come, Morton's excerpts served a useful purpose.

The Indians and the Indian wars were themes which New England historians found fascinating for many reasons. Their opinions varied as to whether the red men were children of light or children of the devil, but whatever their views, they set them forth with vigor. Daniel Gookin, a Puritan who tried life in Virginia before migrating to Boston in 1644, shared John Eliot's compassion for the Indians, and wrote two historical narratives dealing with them, neither of which got into print in the colonial period. The first was *An Historical Account of the Doings and Sufferings of the Christian Indians of New England,*[8] which was followed by *Historical Collections of the Indians in New England.*[9] Gookin was reviled by his contemporaries for writing favorably of the Indians at a time when the savages were murdering men and women in outlying settlements during King Philip's War. No such complaint could be made against William Hubbard of Ipswich, who

[8] First published in the *Transactions and Collections of the American Antiquarian Society,* II (1836).

[9] First published in the Massachusetts Historical Society *Collections,* 1st Ser., I (1792).

published in Boston in 1677 *A Narrative of the Troubles with the Indians in New England,* an account which viewed the Indians as murderous heathen richly deserving annihilation. Hubbard later compiled *A General History of New England,* but it remained in manuscript until 1815.[10] The Indian wars could not fail to stir the industrious Mathers to activity. Increase Mather published two treatises on the subject, *A Brief History of the War with the Indians* (1676) and *A Relation of the Troubles Which Have Happened in New England by Reason of the Indians There* (1677), which shared Hubbard's attitude toward the savages. Increase's son Cotton published in 1699 a vivid narrative of atrocities committed in the "sorrowful decade," a term which he used in Latin for his title, *Decennium Luctuosum. An History of Remarkable Occurrences in the Long War Which New England Hath Had with the Indian Savages, from the Year 1688 to the Year 1698.* At one point Mather cries out that only a petrified man could read about the crimes of these hounds of hell without rage. When at last he is finished with the cruelties of the Indians, he turns to an invasion "from another sort of enemies which may with very good reason be cast into the same history with them. If the Indians have chosen to prey upon the frontiers and outskirts of the province, the Quakers have chosen the same frontiers and outskirts for their more spiritual assaults . . . to enchant and poison the souls of poor people." [11] To Cotton Mather, the Quakers were only a little less malignant than the Indians, and all of them he would gladly have exterminated in the name of the Lord.

Cotton Mather has an important place among the New England historians for the views that he exemplified and for his incredible industry, which finally culminated in the *Magnalia Christi Americana, or the Ecclesiastical History of New England,* finished before the end of the seventeenth century and published in London in a huge folio volume in 1702. Into this work he incorporated *Decennium Luctuosum* and many another treatise and tract to make a vast compilation which he imagined would establish him as the John Foxe of the New World. Mather himself referred to his enormous compendium as "my Church history," but it is significant that it covered all manner of activities, even the treasure hunt of Sir William Phips, which was something

[10] First published, *ibid.,* 2nd Ser., V–VI (1815).
[11] Charles H. Lincoln (ed.), *Narratives of the Indian Wars, 1675–1699* (New York, 1913), pp. 277–278.

less than churchly. But in Mather's concept, the history of New England was the history of the church. The two were indistinguishable, and with tedious iteration he asserts and implies that God is working overtime in New England's behalf. Indeed, one gets the impression from Mather that God is so busy with New England and its saints that he has little time for and slight interest in other lands and creatures. No generalization about the *Magnalia* will do it justice. To describe it in a sentence or a paragraph would be impossible. In its endless pages are many varieties of style and subject matter: fantastic and baroque passages of sheer pedantry, crisp paragraphs of vivid description or characterization, maundering effusions of piety, shrewd observations of scientific data; in short, all the odds and ends that packed the singularly learned head of Cotton Mather. The *Magnalia* is a mine of antiquarian lore for the specialist in seventeenth-century New England, but to the modern the assay of the ore is discouragingly low.

A more orderly and more scholarly work but one planned to provide infinite detail was Thomas Prince's *A Chronological History of New England in the Form of Annals,* which began with Adam and included a chronology of world history before launching into the culmination of the cycles of history, the settlement of New England by the Puritan saints. When Prince finally published the first volume in 1736, he stopped with September 7, 1630, because the printer warned him that to include any more would make the book unwieldy. Prince later published as pamphlets the rest of the copy that he had ready, bringing the account down to 1633, but his zeal to discover and include the ultimate fact defeated him and made the completion of the task impossible. Fragment though it is, Prince's *History* is one of the best illustrations of the Puritan concept of history as the working of Providence to reach the grand climax of creation in the commonwealth of the saints.

A far cry from the characteristic Puritan histories was a work produced by William Douglass, a Scottish physician, who took up his residence in Boston in 1718 and published there in 1748–53 his two-volume *Summary, Historical and Political, of . . . the British Settlements in North America,* a work which illustrates the change that eighteenth-century rationalism had made even in Boston; for Douglass announced himself as a rationalist, and he expressed his belief that mankind should regulate its behavior by natural religion. Of John

Eliot, he commented that he respected his goodness but thought it sheer folly for him to have wasted his time translating the Bible for Indians who could not read and would soon be dead. Of all the plagues afflicting New England, he thought the evangelist George Whitefield one of the worst. As one might assume, Douglass was a controversialist who spent such time as he could spare from his medical practice writing pamphlets and tracts to confute his enemies. His *Summary* is a curious work, filled with fascinating digressions that should have pleased the author of *Tristram Shandy*. By calling attention to the *Summary*, Adam Smith gave Douglass something of a European reputation. Modern readers can still find the book amusing.

From the many works dealing with New England one more should be mentioned, Thomas Hutchinson's *History of the Colony of Massachusetts Bay*, the first volume of which was published in Boston in 1764 and in London in 1765, for Hutchinson's history was more secular and therefore more modern in its point of view than its predecessors. Hutchinson was the last royal governor of Massachusetts, an aristocratic merchant himself and a loyalist to the last. The first volume brought the story of Massachusetts down to 1691. Before he had completed the second volume to 1750, a mob of patriots had wrecked his house and scattered his books and papers, but luckily someone picked the manuscript of Volume II from the mud of the street and Hutchinson printed it in 1767. The final volume was completed in England, where the author took refuge, and was published in 1824. Hutchinson displayed the instincts of a scholar and dealt with such matters as the Indian wars with an objectivity not characteristic of his time and place. To Hutchinson the history of New England was important because it was the story of his own land and a good land; and the revelation of the truth about his country was more important than setting forth the manifestation of God's providences toward the most-favored people. Between Edward Johnson and Thomas Hutchinson the difference is infinitely greater than merely the years that separate them.

Something of the same motivation that prompted the writing of histories may have been responsible for the great number of personal journals and diaries kept in New England. The most famous of these is the *Diary of Samuel Sewall, 1674–1729*,[12] a document invaluable

[12] Published in the Massachusetts Historical Society *Collections*, 5th Ser., V–VII (1878–82).

for the light that it throws upon the life and times of one of the leading citizens of Boston. Equally significant though less entertaining is the *Diary of Cotton Mather, 1681–1708*,[13] a document that would prove a treasure trove to any psychoanalyst concerned with the inner consciousness of a man who may be presumed to represent the quintessence of New England Puritanism. Both Sewall and Mather are always conscious of the imminence of God, but Sewall is human with now and then a gleam of grave humor, whereas Mather by reporting his endless supplications and conversations with God manages to convey the impression that he is a junior partner of the Deity's. Though these are the best-known of the New England diaries, diary keeping was a common practice and many others still survive.[14]

New England produced more histories, descriptive narratives, and personal journals than all the rest of British America, but here and there in the other colonies writers turned out similar literary productions. New York, however, displayed an astonishing lack of intellectual interest. The Dutch themselves produced no creditable history of their colony and few writings of any kind.[15] Even after the English occupation, literary activity was limited. Daniel Denton brought out in London in 1670 a promotion tract called *A Brief Description of New York* which asserted that New York was the terrestrial paradise flowing with milk and honey, but New York could boast little that could be called historical writing and not much else of literary effort until the publication in 1727 of the first volume of Cadwallader Colden's *History of the Five Indian Nations*. This work, the author declared, was necessary because Englishmen had been content previously to depend upon French writers, which "seems to throw some reflections on the inhabitants of our province, as if we wanted curiosity to inquire into our own affairs and were willing to rest satisfied with the accounts the French give us of our own Indians." [16] Colden, a man of great breadth of interest, skilled in medicine, mathematics, natural history,

---

[13] Published, *ibid.*, 7th Ser., VII–VIII (1911–12).

[14] Cf. William Matthews, *American Diaries: An Annotated Bibliography of American Diaries Written Prior to the Year 1861* (Berkeley, Calif., 1945), and Harriette M. Forbes, *New England Diaries, 1602–1800* (Topsfield, Mass., 1923).

[15] For a discussion of the cultural state of the Dutch colony, see Ellis L. Raesly, *Portrait of New Netherland* (New York, 1945).

[16] Cadwallader Colden, *The History of the Five Indian Nations* (3rd ed., London, 1755), I, ix, Preface. For facts about Colden's career, see Alice M. Keys, *Cadwallader Colden: A Representative Eighteenth Century Official* (New York, 1906).

and other branches of learning, attempted to give an objective account of the Indians with more attention than previous writers had shown to their qualities of character and personality. In one passage, for example, he quotes a moving speech by a Mohawk orator so that the reader can form "a true notion of the Indian genius." [17]

The only extensive account of New York in the colonial period was William Smith's *History of New York*, published in London in 1757. Smith, a Loyalist who went to England during the Revolution and later moved to Canada, was a politician not above partisanship, but he wrote in the hope of inducing a better understanding of the colony in England. Some of his remarks are barbed with irony, as in his description of Andrew Hamilton's defense of John Peter Zenger, the printer, which impressed Smith as a piece of demagoguery instead of a noble defense of the freedom of the press, the view of later historians. After praising the thrift, neatness, and diligence of New York women, Smith observes that there "is nothing they so generally neglect as reading, and indeed all the arts for the improvement of the mind, in which, I confess, we have set them the example." [18] New Jersey had a chronicler in one Samuel Smith, who wrote *The History of Nova Caesarea or New Jersey*, published in 1765, but it is so tedious that it is of interest only to the specialist.

From the beginning Pennsylvania had a "good press" thanks in part to the skill of William Penn as a publicist and promoter. By the effective use of understatement, Penn's tracts give the impression of complete sincerity and carry conviction to the reader's mind that Pennsylvania really is the earthly paradise. Some of the other writers on Pennsylvania were extravagant in praise of the country. The enthusiasm of one Richard Frame even exploded into verse in 1692 in a pamphlet published in Philadelphia by William Bradford under the title of *A Short Description of Pennsylvania*. A more detailed description in restrained prose was that by Gabriel Thomas, *An Historical and Geographical Account of . . . Pennsylvania and West New Jersey* (London, 1698). Thomas, a Welsh Quaker who had spent fifteen years as a resident of Pennsylvania before returning to England, dedicated his work to William Penn and described it as "a succinct yet complete account of the late improvement and present state of the

---

[17] *Ibid.,* p. 123.
[18] William Smith, *The History . . . of New York* (ed. pub. in *Collections of the New-York Historical Society,* IV–V, 1829–30), I, 278.

noble province and fertile country of Pennsylvania, with the strange things that have been found there, as the salamander-stone, and several others, mentioned in this treatise." [19] Though Thomas called his pamphlet "a plain and pleasant-like piece," its optimistic point of view must have induced many emigrants to set out for Pennsylvania. Somewhat similar descriptive accounts in German by Francis Daniel Pastorius were published in Germany about the turn of the century. Though Philadelphia became a publishing center, the Pennsylvanians did not turn their energies to producing histories of their colony in the manner of the New Englanders.

To the south of Pennsylvania, the colonists of Maryland and Virginia were much too busy in the seventeenth century trying to establish themselves as farmers on the swampy reaches of their bays and rivers to devote much energy to letters. Most of the writing that has survived has to do in some fashion with the promotion of the settlements or the defense of the colonies against traducers. A certain John Hammond wrote a vigorous tract against a ship captain named Roger Heamans who had sided with the rebels against the government of Maryland, and published it in London as *Hammond versus Heamans, or, An Answer to an Audacious Pamphlet Published by an Impudent and Ridiculous Fellow Named Roger Heamans* (1655). Encouraged by his success as author, Hammond a year later published *Leah and Rachel, or, the Two Fruitful Sisters, Virginia and Maryland: Their Present Condition Impartially Stated and Related* (1656). The political dissensions in Maryland had forced Hammond to return to England, he tells us, and he writes in a spirit of homesickness to portray the goodness of the Chesapeake Bay country. A similar motivation inspired George Alsop's *A Character of the Province of Maryland* (1666), in which the author, a former indentured servant, contrasts a life of servitude in Maryland with poverty in England, and concludes that he would rather be in Maryland even as a bond servant.

In Virginia some of the best literary work of the colonial period falls into the general classification of history and personal narrative. In 1697, Henry Hartwell, James Blair, and Edward Chilton prepared a report for the Board of Trade in London entitled *The Present State of Virginia and the College,* which was not published until 1727. The earliest work that attempts a comprehensive description of Virginia is

[19] Albert C. Myers (ed.), *Narratives of Early Pennsylvania, West New Jersey, and Delaware* (New York, 1912), p. 313.

Robert Beverley's *The History and Present State of Virginia,* brought out in London in 1705. Beverley's *History* is significant as one of the earliest literary works that is self-consciously American. The New England historians, it is true, had written of their godly commonwealths as realms of a peculiar people, set apart and watched over by the Protestant Jehovah, but the distinction they made from other men was religious. Beverley, on the contrary, was thoroughly secular and realistic. A fierce loyalty to the new soil burned in Beverley's breast and he did not hesitate to rebuke his fellow Virginians for depending too much, economically and socially, upon the mother country. He adopted a plain style and announced somewhat dramatically that "I am an Indian and don't pretend to be exact in my language." [20] The edition of 1705 contained many sharp comments on his contemporaries which Beverley softened in a second edition of 1722. Perhaps also by Beverley was *An Essay upon the Government of the English Plantations on the Continent of America . . . By an American,* printed in 1701 for Richard Parker, the same stationer who four years later was responsible for Beverley's *History.*[21] This *Essay* is a criticism of the type of royal governor usually sent over and is also a plea for an organic union of the British colonies.

The appearance of the second edition of Beverley's *History* in 1722 may have prompted another Virginian by adoption, the Reverend Hugh Jones, professor of mathematics in the College of William and Mary, to prepare his own version of the history and description of the colony, which he published in London in 1724 as *The Present State of Virginia.* Though Jones is sometimes critical of his fellow Virginians, he is less sarcastic than Beverley, and is convinced that Virginia is the best of the colonies, the "happy retreat of true Britons and true Churchmen." [22] He does not overemphasize the church, however, and his work is secular in its point of view.

Beverley's brother-in-law, William Byrd II of Westover, was the author of the most urbane narrative of the colonial period, the *History*

---

[20] Louis B. Wright (ed.), *The History and Present State of Virginia. By Robert Beverley* (Chapel Hill, N.C., 1947), p. xxi.

[21] Louis B. Wright (ed.), *An Essay upon the Government of the English Plantations on the Continent of America* (1701) (San Marino, Calif., 1945), pp x–xi.

[22] Hugh Jones, *The Present State of Virginia* (1724), p. 48. A new edition edited by Richard L. Morton was published by the University of North Carolina Press in 1956.

of the Dividing Line Run in the Year 1728, which circulated in manuscript in Byrd's own time but was not finally printed until Edmund Ruffin brought out an edition at Petersburg in 1841. Among the writings which Ruffin printed were two shorter descriptive narratives, "A Journey to the Land of Eden," and "A Progress to the Mines." *The History of the Dividing Line* takes the form of a journal and relates episodes of an expedition to survey the boundary between Virginia and North Carolina. Byrd was the leader of the group sent by Virginia and his comment upon his associates and the country is often pungent. The humor and the worldly attitude of the writer stand out in strong contrast to most of the colonial writing that had preceded it. During his adult life Byrd had returned to England on several occasions as agent for Virginia, and his circle of acquaintances was broad. It is understandable that he should write like a gentleman in the age of Queen Anne and George I and not like a rustic provincial. Byrd's diaries, the most extensive known to have been written in the colonial South, provide a matter-of-fact enumeration of the actions in his daily life with little of the introspection characteristic, for example, of Cotton Mather. The only complete work which Byrd printed in his lifetime was an anonymous pamphlet on the plague.

One colonial Virginian who had the same sort of instincts for the antiquarian recovery of the past as had motivated Thomas Prince in Massachusetts was William Stith, a B.A. of Oxford, third president of the College of William and Mary, and chaplain of the House of Burgesses. In his spare time Stith worked at his research in the records of the colony and in 1747 he published at Williamsburg his *History of the First Discovery and Settlement of Virginia,* which brought the narrative down to the dissolution of the Virginia Company in 1624. Stith hoped to complete a definitive history of the colony, but detailed research took so long that the first volume proved the last. Jefferson found Stith's work too prolix, as he found Beverley's too brief, but Stith's detailed discussion was widely used by later historians, and his documented defense of the Virginia Company against King James has colored most interpretations of that episode in the colony's development. His use of John Smith's work was not so undiscriminating as earlier critics thought, for he admitted that Smith's history was confused, but he recognized its value for the period when Smith himself was a resident of Jamestown.

The most colorful narrative of the colony of North Carolina was an account of explorations and adventures among the Indians written by John Lawson and published in London in 1709 as *A New Voyage to Carolina, Containing the Exact Description and Natural History of That Country.* So readable was this narrative that it had new editions in 1714 and 1718, and the proprietors of the colony were instrumental in having it published in two German editions in 1712 and 1722. Lawson wrote with vigor and it is unfortunate that his literary career was cut short when the Indians in 1711 burned him at the stake. Dr. John Brickell of Edenton, who in 1737 published *The Natural History of North Carolina* in Dublin, borrowed extensively from Lawson but added valuable new material of his own.

A considerable amount of the world's history has been written out of irritation, and the best piece of writing to come out of the new colony of Georgia resulted from the disgruntlement of a composite group of authors who brought out in 1741 *A True and Historical Narrative of the Colony of Georgia* signed by "Pat. Tailfer, M.D., Hugh Anderson, M.A., David Douglas, and Others," who declared themselves fugitives in South Carolina from the wrath of General James Oglethorpe's agents. The little book is an excellent satire which, with elaborate mock deference, criticizes Oglethorpe's administration of the colony.

That descriptions of the country and historical narratives of its settlement should have occupied so large a place in the literary production of the colonies was logical and natural, for these were purposeful people, eager to promote their undertakings and induce others to share their enterprises. Nevertheless, a few of them found time for other forms of writing, even occasionally for efforts at belles-lettres. Occasionally a man of letters found himself an adventurer in the American wilderness and in a few rare instances he demonstrated a continuing interest in literature. Such a one was George Sandys, who came to Virginia in 1621 and remained there seven years. During his stay he translated part of Ovid's *Metamorphoses,* in which some imagery from the New World may be discerned.[23]

The muse of poetry, however, did not feel at home in Virginia, or in any of the other colonies for that matter, though a considerable quantity of verse found its way to the printers, some in thin little

---

[23] See Richard B. Davis, *George Sandys, Poet-Adventurer* (London, 1955), and "America in George Sandys' 'Ovid,' " *The William and Mary Quarterly,* 3rd Ser., IV (1947), 297–304. Cf. also Chapter VI.

volumes, some in the columns of the colonial newspapers. A little of the best poetry of the period remained in manuscript and did not see print until modern times. One of the most vivid pieces of verse in the southern colonies is an anonymous elegy entitled "Bacon's Epitaph, Made by His Man," which pays tribute to the rebel of 1676, Nathaniel Bacon. Fifty years later, William Parks, the printer, who established presses at both Annapolis and Williamsburg, undertook to encourage poets by publishing some of their efforts. The most pretentious volume of poetry published by Parks at Annapolis was a translation by an Annapolis schoolmaster, Richard Lewis, of Edward Holdsworth's Latin poem *Muscipula,* a satire on the Welsh, which Lewis entitled *The Mouse-Trap, or the Battle of the Cambrians and Mice* (1728). In the first year of Parks' press at Williamsburg he printed, appropriately enough, a volume of poetry by J. Markland, *Typographia, an Ode on Printing* (1730).

As in every other form of writing, the New England Puritans produced more verse than the other colonists because their poetry like their prose was dedicated to serious matters and was an instrument in their purposeful pursuit of the Christian life. If poetry in the concept of the ancients had a dual function to instruct and to delight, most of the Puritans seem to have been content to emphasize the first and forget the latter, though there were a few exceptions where the emotional content of the verse and the skill of composition transcend the didactic. As in all the colonies, much of the verse was either printed in the ephemeral pages of newspapers or remained in manuscript.

The first piece of poetic printing was of course the so-called "Bay Psalm Book," *The Whole Book of Psalms,* published at the new Cambridge press in 1640. The faithful in Massachusetts wanted a literal version of the Psalms which they could sing in their church services, a version better in their estimation than the one in use. Accordingly, a committee of ministers, Richard Mather, John Eliot, and Thomas Welde, prepared and published a work that is a landmark in the history of American printing, a work that served its purpose, which was to teach God's word in song, and not to titillate the ears with sweet rhythms.

The first "best-seller" in America was not a work of prose but a phenomenally successful volume of poetry, Michael Wigglesworth's *Day of Doom,* first printed at Cambridge in 1662 and reprinted at least ten times in the colonial period. No more than the Bay Psalm

Book was its purpose to provide sweet music; rather it sought by versifying Puritan theology and Biblical teachings to make them easy to learn and to remember. For a century after its first publication, children memorized the *Day of Doom's* ballad stanzas and shivered at the prospect of death and damnation. How much religious hysteria Wigglesworth's grim poem may have stimulated is a speculation for psychiatrists, but its baleful influence must have been enormous.

Almost as religious as Wigglesworth's but more humane were the poems of Anne Bradstreet, whose volume, *The Tenth Muse Lately Sprung Up in America,* was printed in London in 1650. It was popular enough to have a second edition, in Boston in 1678. Writing under the influence of the contemporary metaphysical school of poetry, Mrs. Bradstreet's best verse at times compares favorably with lines in George Herbert or John Donne; but like other New England poets, the obsession to instruct, even to instruct in such subjects as natural history, keeps her poetic spirit closely tethered.

In recent years, a hitherto unknown New England poet, Edward Taylor, has been exhumed in the Yale Library and his works made available.[24] Taylor, an Englishman of twenty-three, came to New England in 1668, entered Harvard, graduated in 1671, and forthwith became a minister at Westfield, Massachusetts, where he remained for the rest of his life. He enjoined his heirs never to publish the volume of verse that he left at death, but a grandson, Ezra Stiles, president of Yale College, presented it to the college library where it remained unknown until 1937. Like Anne Bradstreet, Taylor wrote under the old-fashioned influence of the metaphysical poets, but he did it better than Mrs. Bradstreet and at times his verse is almost sensuous in the richness of its imagery, a quality that probably led him to suppress it. Rediscovered at a time when the cult of neo-metaphysical poetry was in high favor among academic critics, Taylor's work received extravagant praise. He clearly merits, however, the considered opinion of one of the ablest literary scholars that he is the "greatest poet of New England before the nineteenth century." [25]

Throughout the colonial period, New England preachers turned out a quantity of rhymed lamentations on the death of some hopeful youth

[24] Taylor's poems were rediscovered by Thomas H. Johnson while working in the Yale College library in 1937 and edited by him as *The Poetical Works of Edward Taylor* (New York, 1939).

[25] Kenneth Murdock, "Writers of New England," in *Literary History of the United States* (New York, 1938), I, 65.

lent by the Lord for a little while to this earth, but not much of it qualifies for the most tolerant of anthologies. As the eighteenth century wore on, however, the fog of religious gloom lifted slightly, and versifiers, even among the clergy, began to write with more urbanity. John Adams, a Congregational minister, who gained a reputation in Cambridge for eloquence and literary skill, was the author of *Poems on Several Occasions* (1745) which contained passages that sound like James Thomson. A glimmer of humor appeared amongst the poets in 1733 when Joseph Green, a Boston distiller, wrote a parody of the Reverend Mather Byles' "Hymn to Be Sung at Sea," and Byles replied with a "Parody of Green's Parody."

In the newspapers and almanacs, secular verse gradually came to occupy a place of prominence. Nathaniel Ames, who compiled one of the most widely read of the New England almanacs, added verse and humorous aphorisms. In his almanac for 1741, for example, he included in verse "An Essay upon the Microscope."

Without the spur of religious purpose to urge them on, poets to the south of New England were less prolific, but even in unliterary New York, some writers felt the urge to give expression in rhyming numbers. For example, William Livingston, who became a prominent political figure in the Revolutionary period, at the age of twenty-four published *Philosophic Solitude, or The Choice of a Rural Life* (1747) as by "a gentleman educated at Yale College." If Livingston's education at Yale did not provide him with an acquaintance with good eighteenth-century English poets, his own library supplied that want, for *Philosophic Solitude* shows considerable skill in its use of the heroic couplet. Encouraged by this taste of authorship, Livingston next published in London in prose *A Review of the Military Operations in North America* (1756).

As Philadelphia developed into a city of size and importance in the eighteenth century, its literary activities increased and its newspapers and presses at intervals published the poetic efforts of such of its citizens as were moved to express themselves in this fashion. The almanacs were vehicles for a considerable body of versification, some but not all of it humorous in intent. Franklin in his *Autobiography* mentions a few of the hopeful writers of Philadelphia when he first came to that city, and later in *Poor Richard's Almanac* he printed some of the verse, humorous, satirical, and serious. In *Titan's Almanac* for 1730, an unknown versemaker foresees Philadelphia's pre-eminence as a literary center:

> 'Tis here Apollo does erect his throne;
> This his Parnassus, this his Helicon.
> Here solid sense does every bosom warm;
> Here noise and nonsense have forgot to charm,
> Thy seers how cautious, and how gravely wise!
> Thy hopeful youth in emulation rise;
> Who, if the wishing muse inspired does sing,
> Shall liberal art to such perfection bring,
> Europe shall mourn her ancient fame declined,
> And Philadelphia be the Athens of mankind.[26]

Philadelphia was only one of many reincarnations of Athens that optimistic writers were to see in America, but it had to wait beyond 1730 for fulfillment. Some of the verse produced by Philadelphians in this period did have an urbanity that smacked of London if not of Athens. Joseph Shippen, for example, produced graceful poetry, and his poem, "The Glooms of Ligonier," enjoyed a long popularity. One Philadelphian who gave promise of making a reputation for belles-lettres was Thomas Godfrey the younger. Before his untimely death in 1763 he had composed a play in blank verse, *The Prince of Parthia*, and had written sundry poems, which another Philadelphia poet, Nathaniel Evans, brought together and published as *Juvenile Poems on Various Subjects, with The Prince of Parthia* (1765). The play was produced in Philadelphia in 1767. This tragedy, on an Oriental theme, is the first full-length verse play by an American to be acted professionally in this country, and as such is a landmark in the history of the drama.

The early establishment of presses in Cambridge and Boston gave that region an advantage over colonies that lacked printing facilities and had to depend upon London printers. Gradually, however, as printing developed elsewhere, particularly in Philadelphia, New England's pre-eminence in literary production was approached or equaled. By the end of the colonial period, Philadelphia in variety and breadth of its literary interest surpassed all the other colonial cities. New England, however, had one statistical advantage in the prolific pens of the tribe of Mather. Increase Mather and his son Cotton were diligent

[26] Quoted by Moses Coit Tyler, *History of American Literature*, II, 239.

writers and Cotton Mather alone poured out a flood of titles on every conceivable subject—religion, science, history, witchcraft, and anything else that popped out of his well-crammed head—an incredible list of 444 known titles, enough for an army of writers.[27] The writings of the Mathers, highly intelligent men that they were, preserve for posterity an enormous amount of information about the attitudes and ideas of New England Puritanism, but unhappily not much of their great output can be read today for any other purpose. Perhaps the best remembered of the works of Increase Mather is *An Essay for the Recording of Illustrious Providences* (1684) and Cotton Mather's best-known work of course is the *Magnalia*.

Works in some fashion concerned with religious interests were the predominant type of publication in New England in the seventeenth century and the first third of the eighteenth century. Even with the growing secularization of the press by the mid-eighteenth century, New England's printers continued to turn out an incredible number of sermons, tracts, and controversial pamphlets. Students of literature and science in a later day have lamented that Jonathan Edwards, possessed of one of the clearest and most acute minds in colonial America, should have devoted his intellectual talents to what appears to them an outworn theology. He was the author of a number of sermons, the most famous being *Sinners in the Hands of an Angry God* (1741). By the mid-century he was setting forth in print some of the philosophic speculations and arguments that sought to justify the ways of Calvin to man. Though several of his tracts in this period discuss the problem, the one for which Edwards is best known is *A Careful and Strict Enquiry into . . . That Freedom of Will* (1754), a monument of logical argument in defense of Calvinism. Edwards could write with vividness and clarity and had he turned his pen to something other than the dry bones of theology, his fame as a man of letters might have been higher.

The secularization of literary production from the mid-eighteenth century onward may be symbolized in the person and publications of Benjamin Franklin, a great figure in any century. Brought up in Boston under the influence of Puritanism, where he learned the craft of

[27] Cf. T. J. Holmes, *Increase Mather, A Bibliography of His Works* (2 vols., Cleveland, Ohio, 1931); *Cotton Mather, A Bibliography of His Works* (3 vols., Cambridge, Mass., 1940); and *Minor Mathers, A List of Their Works* (Cambridge, Mass., 1940).

printing, Franklin as a youth of seventeen removed in 1723 to Philadelphia. By diligence and the application of the principles that he explains in his *Autobiography,* he established himself as a prosperous businessman and went from there to success in many fields. As a man of letters, he first achieved fame for the compilation of his almanacs filled with aphorisms attributed to Poor Richard. In ephemeral pieces, Franklin gained experience as an essayist and pamphleteer which he put to good use in the period of the Revolution. Interested in everything pertaining to the world around him, Franklin turned his pen to the discussion of all sorts of problems, social, political, and scientific. His published essays included such matters as *A Proposal for Promoting Useful Knowledge* (1743), *Advice to a Young Man on Choosing a Mistress* (1745), *Reflections on Courtship and Marriage* (1746), *Proposals Relating to the Education of Youth in Pennsylvania* (1749), *Some Account of the Pennsylvania Hospital* (1754), *Observations Concerning the Increase of Mankind* (1755), and *Advice to a Young Tradesman* (1762). In his own writings Franklin demonstrated that one could be both purposeful and readable, serious without being solemn, and humorous without being trivial. That classic of personal writing known to us as the *Autobiography* was set down by Franklin after the period we are discussing, but it gives a remarkable portrayal, not only of the man himself, but of the intellectual milieu of mid-eighteenth-century Philadelphia. Franklin as a man of letters was an exemplification of the Age of Enlightenment. But Franklin was only one of many eighteenth-century Americans who had practiced the art of writing and were ready to take up their pens in behalf of the embattled colonies in the controversies that raged after 1765. The long apprenticeship of colonial authors in purposeful writing had its effect when they applied their talents to building up public opinion for the break with England and the creation of a new nation.

CHAPTER 8

Drama, Music, and Other Diversions

MONG THE first settlers who landed at Jamestown in 1607 were some who undoubtedly had frequented the London theaters, for many of the adventurers, to Captain John Smith's sorrow, were gentlemen and gallants, inveterate playgoers in that day. Though theaters were regarded by the pious as the devil's schoolhouses, playgoing was a popular diversion in London during the first decade of the seventeenth century. Most of Shakespeare's great plays had already appeared on the London stage. *King Lear* and *Macbeth* were the most recent plays that the Virginia voyagers might have seen before their departure. In the year of Jamestown's settlement, the ship's company of an East India vessel lying off Sierra Leone had performed *Hamlet* and *Richard II*. Dramatic entertainment had already enjoyed a long history in England, and it was no monopoly of any group. Everybody from the sailor and the butcher's apprentice to the silken-coated nobleman might go to the theater and enjoy the afternoon's comedy or tragedy. One might suppose that the first settlers would have brought with them an inherited taste for the drama and would have whiled away tedious hours, as did the sailors on the East Indiaman, with amateur plays. But if they did, no record of it has survived.

The reasons for the early neglect of the drama are easy to understand. The incredible hardships of the early years of settlement left no time or desire for dramatic entertainment. The settlers found drama enough in their fight for survival, and the weary laborers in the desperate little colony needed no play acting to distract them from the tasks of ensuring their continued existence. The earliest settlers were also without women, and not even song and dance enlivened their days, though it is recorded that Indian maidens, Pocahontas among them, turned handsprings in the nude before the marveling eyes of gallants.

Drama should have appealed to the coterie around Sir William Berkeley, who became royal governor of Virginia in 1642, the very year that the Puritans closed the theaters in London, for Sir William, a former fellow of Merton College, Oxford, had already written a play called *The Lost Lady*. But the governor himself was soon involved in a quarrel with the Puritans in Virginia, and presently an Indian war caused a further distraction. Virginia had other things to think about besides stage plays. The earliest play known to have been produced in Virginia—or anywhere else in the English-speaking colonies, for that matter—might not have been remembered today if a puritanic spectator had not felt that such a manifestation of wickedness deserved the condemnation of the law; for one Edward Martin reported to the authorities that on August 27, 1665, on Accomac peninsula on the Eastern Shore, "a play commonly called the Bear and the Cub" had been acted by Cornelius Watkinson, Philip Howard, and William Darby. The author of the piece was not named. In November the accused actors underwent an examination in Accomac County Court and were ordered to return at the December session "in the habiliments which they had acted in," and repeat the play in open court. It is cheering to note that the court found nothing corrosive of society in the play and that the informer, Edward Martin, was required to pay all court costs.[1] But this legal victory does not appear to have stimulated any further dramatic activity.

Opposition to stage plays, as expressed in Edward Martin's information against the performers of *The Bear and the Cub*, was not a new attitude among Englishmen. Traditionally in England actors had borne a low reputation, and the statutes against vagrants had enumerated "rogues, vagabonds, stage-players, and sturdy beggars" as deserving jail or hard labor. The Puritans particularly railed against plays as immoral, indecent, and ungodly. London tradesmen and merchants had also looked askance at the theaters because they lured apprentices from work and wasted precious time. The Quakers likewise regarded stage plays as vain and wasteful luxuries unworthy of serious men.

[1] Mary Newton Stanard, *Colonial Virginia: Its People and Customs* (Philadelphia, 1917), pp. 229–230.

All of this opposition to theatrical entertainment was transmitted to the English colonies and helps to explain the long refusal of Boston, Philadelphia, New York, and other towns to permit the erection of playhouses or to countenance even amateur acting. But the primary reason that drama did not flourish in seventeenth-century America was the simple fact that no towns were large enough to support theatrical entertainment. Stage plays, concerts, opera, and all such formal and sophisticated entertainment require a settled and urban life to support them. Later in America, it is true, actors often took to the road and entertained frontier towns, but they had a history of city experience and support behind them, and they invariably returned to the big towns after a foray into the hinterland. In the seventeenth century, however, there were no big towns, and in such towns as existed there was more hostility than favor toward dramatic entertainment. Theaters had to wait for society to become settled and reasonably sophisticated.

The very rumor of stage plays was enough to stir some communities to concern for the salvation of their citizens' souls. Judge Samuel Sewall was scandalized, he indicates in his *Diary* for November 12, 1685, because a dancing master, complained of by the ministers of Boston, had boasted that "by one play he could teach more divinity than Mr. Willard or the Old Testament." [2] Not that anyone yet dared propose a play in Boston, but the very mention was lewd. Unhappily for the ministers, however, Boston was getting rich from trade, and a wealthy town eventually will have relaxation and amusements. Mixed dancing and dancing schools were an entering wedge for the devil. Since the early days when Thomas Morton had scandalized William Bradford and his brethren by setting up a Maypole at Merrymount and by dancing around it with available Indian squaws, New England had tried to keep out all bacchanalian revels—not with absolute success, to be sure, but with sufficient effectiveness at least to discourage professional stage players from trying to crack Boston's defenses.

Nevertheless there were disturbing signs. In 1687 John Wing, a tavern keeper of Boston, fitted up a room with seats where he proposed to allow a magician to perform his tricks. Judge Sewall was a member of a committee of four who waited upon Wing on Sunday evening,

[2] *Diary of Samuel Sewall* in *Collections of the Massachusetts Historical Society*, 5th Ser., V (1877), 103–104. Also cited by George C. Odell, *Annals of the New York Stage* (New York, 1927), I, 4.

December 4, and pointed out his errors. "He saith," Sewall notes, "seeing 'tis offensive, he will remedy it. It seems the room is fitted with seats. I read what Dr. Ames saith of callings, and spake as I could, from this principle, that the man's practice was unlawful, and therefore Capt. Wing could not lawfully give him an accommodation for it." [3] Worse things were to follow. On March 2, 1714, Sewall wrote in great perturbation to Isaac Addington that "there is a rumor, as if some designed to have a play acted in the Council-Chamber next Monday; which much surprises me: And as much as in me lies, I do forbid it. . . . Let it not be abused with dances, or other scenical divertisements. . . . Ovid himself offers invincible arguments against public plays. . . . Let not Christian Boston go beyond heathen Rome in the practice of shameful vanities." [4]

In the meantime, Pennsylvania had been frightened lest a play might desecrate that Quaker haven. In 1700 the Pennsylvania Assembly prohibited by statute "stage-plays, masks, revels" as well as "rude and riotous sports." [5] This prohibition was only one of many which the Pennsylvania Assembly tried to enact during the next half-century, only to have them vetoed by the English government. Though year after year the Assembly found its laws against plays overruled by the home government, the Yearly Meeting of the Friends in Philadelphia warned the faithful against "plays, games, lotteries, music, and dancing." [6] Evidently the imminence of plays and other amusements was sufficient to worry the pious.

Strolling players made their appearance in New York and at other points in the colonies at the beginning of the eighteenth century. Sometime between 1699 and 1702, one Richard Hunter petitioned the governor of New York for permission for himself and a company of players to perform in New York.[7] About 1703 Anthony Aston, an Englishman who described himself as "gentleman, lawyer, poet, actor, soldier, sailor, exciseman, [and] publican," arrived in Charleston "full of lice, shame, poverty, nakedness, and hunger." To relieve his distress, he reports that he "turned player and poet, and wrote one play on the

[3] Sewall, *Diary*, p. 196.
[4] *Letter Book of Samuel Sewall* in *Collections of the Massachusetts Historical Society*, 6th Ser., II (1888), 29–30.
[5] Thomas Clark Pollock, *The Philadelphia Theatre in the Eighteenth Century* (Philadelphia, 1933), p. 4.
[6] *Ibid.*, p. 4.
[7] G. C. Odell, *Annals of the New York Stage* (New York, 1927), I, 5.

subject of the country." [8] He took ship for New York and, after acting there, made his way to Virginia, where he also displayed his dramatic talents before sailing for home in the tobacco fleet.

The first theater in the colonies of which there is a record was built on lots bordering the Palace Green in Williamsburg, Virginia, between 1716 and 1718. The promoters of this enterprise were William Levingston, a merchant, surgeon, and tavern keeper; Charles Stagg, a dancing master; and Mary Stagg, his wife and dancing partner. On July 11, 1716, they entered into a partnership to put on plays and to teach dancing. Earlier in the year, Levingston had petitioned the Board of Visitors of the College of William and Mary for permission to teach "the scholars and others to dance until his own dancing school in Williamsburg be finished." [9] The theater of course also served as a dancing school, and the Staggs were the principal performers in both, though Levingston sent to England for other players and musicians.

Levingston unhappily made no money on his theatrical venture and was constantly in litigation over his finances. About 1723 he left Williamsburg and a few years later died in Spotsylvania County. The Staggs, because of their varied skills, were more successful. When Charles Stagg died in 1736, he left a comfortable estate. Mrs. Stagg continued to run a dancing school, and to give public balls and assemblies, a fairly lucrative business, as evidenced by the keen rivalry of Mrs. Barbara de Graffenreidt during 1737 and 1738, when each was constrained to hold expensive raffles to outdo the other. The theater building itself fell into decay sometime before 1745, when Williamsburg petitioned the "gentlemen subscribers for the play house" to bestow the building upon the town to be used for a town hall. This was done, but the building had to be completely renovated, for it had not been used for several years. Williamsburg, however, was not to be permanently without a theater. By 1752 it had a second playhouse, which enjoyed a greater success than Levingston's.

The taste for dramatic entertainment in Virginia was well developed, and the repertories of the professional and amateur players were varied. After William Parks started printing the *Virginia Gazette* in 1736, we have frequent allusions to plays. For example, on Septem-

[8] *Ibid.,* p. 7. Odell quotes from *The Fool's Opera,* an undated work by Aston himself which prefixes "A Sketch of the Author's Life."
[9] Robert H. Land, "The First Williamsburg Theater," *The William and Mary Quarterly,* 3rd Ser., V (1948), 359–374.

ber 10, 1736, Parks announced: "This evening will be performed at the theatre, by the young gentlemen of the college, *The Tragedy of Cato:* And, on Monday, Wednesday, and Friday next, will be acted the following comedies, by the gentlemen and ladies of this country, viz., *The Busy-Body, The Recruiting-Officer,* and *The Beaux' Strata- gem.*" [10] The gentlemen and ladies of the country appear to have favored plays by Mrs. Centlivre and Farquhar, but the college boys, probably with prompting from their instructors, stuck to Addison. A week after Parks' first announcement they were acting Addison's *The Drummer; or, the Haunted House.*

By the fourth decade of the eighteenth century, opposition to theaters was slowly breaking down as theatrical entertainment became more frequent. The theater at Williamsburg was not the only spot where plays might be seen. Some sort of playhouse existed in New York in 1732 in a building owned by Rip Van Dam, where, on December 6, New Yorkers had a chance to see Farquhar's *The Re- cruiting Officer* with the leading role acted by the governor's barber.[11] Theatricals gradually came to occupy a more important place in the entertainment of such centers as Charleston, Williamsburg, Philadel- phia, and New York. Charleston showed such favor to the drama that officials of the city permitted the use of the Court House for the per- formance of plays in the 1730's before the opening of its first theater, in Dock Street, in 1736.[12] Charlestonians had the opportunity of see- ing during the season of 1736 Farquhar's *The Recruiting Officer,* Otway's *The Orphan,* Lillo's *The London Merchant,* Addison's *Cato,* and Colley Cibber's little opera, *Flora or Hob in the Well,* given as an afterpiece. The two plays repeated most often were *Cato* and *The Recruiting Officer.*

The identity of strolling players who entertained the colonies be- tween 1736 and 1749 is unknown, but in the latter year a group headed by Thomas Kean and Walter Murray came to Philadelphia and pro- duced among other pieces Addison's *Cato.* After trouble with the authorities in Philadelphia, the troupe proceeded to New York, where they had considerable success with plays by Shakespeare, Congreve, Dryden, Lillo, Addison, and Farquhar. It was this same company that

[10] Quoted by Land, *ibid.,* pp. 372–373.
[11] Odell, *Annals,* I, 11.
[12] Eola Willis, *The Charleston Stage in the Eighteenth Century* (Columbia, .S.C., 1924), pp. 8–9, 16, 33.

played in Williamsburg, Annapolis, and other points in Virginia and Maryland in 1751 and 1752.

The second professional company of which there is definite information was headed by Lewis Hallam, brother of William Hallam, a London actor-manager. Lewis Hallam and his actress wife, with a company of ten actors, arrived at Yorktown, Virginia, in June, 1752, in a vessel auspiciously named *The Charming Sally*. On September 15, they began a series of performances in Williamsburg, which lasted until the following summer. For their first performance they chose Shakespeare's *Merchant of Venice*. Their repertory included Lillo's *The London Merchant*, Moore's *The Gamester*, Farquhar's *The Beaux' Stratagem*, Cibber's *The Careless Husband*, Gay's *The Beggar's Opera*, and a half-dozen other Restoration and eighteenth-century favorites, but their most popular author was Shakespeare. In addition to *The Merchant of Venice* they gave *Othello, King Lear, Richard III, Hamlet*, and *Romeo and Juliet*. As was customary on the English stage in the eighteenth century, the Hallams usually included a farce along with the main comedy or tragedy to vary the dramatic fare.

By July, 1753, the Hallam company had moved on to New York and were toying with the idea of trying their luck in Philadelphia, where Quaker opposition to the theater was still strong. Even in New York they encountered opposition which caused them to publish a letter in the New York *Mercury* on July 2, 1753, appealing for public support. By September they had ironed out their difficulties and were successfully performing plays three times a week in a theater which they had built. To convince doubting New Yorkers that drama was not harmful, they opened with the highly moralized play by Richard Steele, *The Conscious Lovers*. The reputation of Addison and Steele for good morality was so great that any work of theirs would take the taint off theatrical entertainment and lull the audience into accepting less-edifying plays of the Restoration. Shakespeare also had a good reputation, which may account for the frequency with which the early companies advertised the performance of his plays.

Although the Quakers of Philadelphia continued obstinately to fight against an invasion by stage players, they lost the battle and in the spring of 1754 Hallam and his company received permission from the governor of Pennsylvania to open a theater in Philadelphia and to perform a repertory of twenty-four plays with their usual farces, after-pieces, and dances provided that "they offered nothing indecent and immoral." [13] The New Theater in Water Street, which they opened on April 15 with a performance of Nicholas Rowe's *The Fair Penitent* followed by a farce of David Garrick's, *Miss in Her Teens,* was in William Plumsted's warehouse, where in 1749–50 the company of Murray and Kean had performed before the authorities had discouraged them.

When Hallam's company had exhausted their repertory of twenty-four plays in Philadelphia, they took ship for South Carolina. On October 7, they began a three months' season in Charleston with Rowe's *The Fair Penitent.* The next week they offered Mrs. Centlivre's *A Bold Stroke for a Wife* supplemented with Fielding's farce, *The Mock Doctor,* and followed this with Otway's *The Orphan,* Lillo's *The London Merchant,* Addison's *Cato,* Farquhar's *The Recruiting Officer,* Philips' *The Distressed Mother,* and Dodsley's farce, *The King and the Miller of Mansfield.* The winter of 1754–55 in Charleston was an entertaining period, with both stage plays and the preaching of George Whitefield to provide excitement, as the diary of Mrs. Gabriel Manigault makes manifest.[14] At the close of the season in Charleston the Hallam company sailed for Jamaica, where Lewis Hallam died shortly thereafter.

The death of Hallam, however, did not mean the end of his family's connection with the stage in the North American colonies. His widow married another actor, David Douglass, who reorganized the company with Lewis Hallam, Jr., as a leading man, and with sundry other young Hallams in the cast. Hallams and descendants of Hallams were to appear on the American stage for years to come. The new troupe, known as the American Company, set sail for New York, where on December 28, 1758, they made their debut with Rowe's *Jane Shore.* Douglass had built a theater near the modern location of the Wall Street ferry, but he was soon in such difficulties with the town officials that he announced in the *Mercury* that he would give over acting and open an academy of histrionic art, probably a subterfuge for the presentation of illustrations of that art. At length he made his peace and had a successful season, the forerunner of many more. The company's repertory included familiar plays by Shakespeare, Farquhar, Dryden, Otway, Rowe, Garrick, Fielding, Addison, and Cibber.

[13] T. C. Pollock, *Philadelphia Theatre,* p. 8.
[14] Quoted by Willis, *The Charleston Stage,* pp. 40–41.

In the spring of 1759 the American Company under Douglass went to Philadelphia and received permission of the governor to establish a theater on Society Hill, just outside the city limits. There, despite the opposition of religious groups in Pennsylvania, they played from June 25 to December 28, when they closed with a performance of *Hamlet* On the previous evening they gave a benefit performance of *The London Merchant* "towards the raising a fund for purchasing an organ to the college-hall in this city and instructing the charity children in psalmody," [15] a work of grace in view of the bitter opposition led by the Quakers, Lutherans, Presbyterians, and Baptists which finally resulted in a law suppressing stage plays. Though this law was vetoed by the English authorities in the autumn of 1760, it had the effect of discouraging the company and sending it on a tour which took it to Annapolis and other points in Maryland, and finally to Williamsburg, Virginia, where it played during the winter season of 1760–61.

An actor-manager in the eighteenth century had to be a man of determination undismayed by persistent opposition. Such was Douglass' courage that after the close of his season in Williamsburg, he decided to try his luck in the summer of 1761 in New England. The decision was not so foolhardy as it may seem, for he picked Newport, Rhode Island, as his target, and Newport was already a summer resort where indulgent Southerners came to escape the heat and sickness of their own climates. To testify to the virtue of his company, Douglass received from the governor of Virginia a certificate declaring that the actors behaved "with prudence and discretion" and were "capable of entertaining a sensible and polite audience."[16] By advertising his plays as "moral dialogues" Douglass evaded the law against theatrical performances. For example, *Othello* was described as "Moral Dialogues in Five Parts, Depicting the evil effects of jealousy and other bad passions, and proving that happiness can only spring from the pursuit of virtue." Certainly this was sufficient to warrant the Newport *Mercury's* assertion that the players had merited the Virginia governor's testimonial of good character.

During the winter of 1761, Douglass took his company for a two

[15] George O. Seilhamer, *History of the American Theatre before the Revolution* (Philadelphia, 1888), p. 111.
[16] Charles Blake, *An Historical Account of the Providence Stage* (Providence, 1868), p. 19.

months' season in New York. To his distress he continued to encounter opposition from religious folk as well as from merchants who thought that players took too much money out of the town. Later, in 1762, the company returned to Newport and then went on to Providence, where Douglass announced the opening of a "Histrionic Academy," a euphemism for a theater. This effrontery aroused religious groups in the community to such a frenzy of hostility that they were restrained from attacking the theater only by the quick action of John Brown, a prominent citizen, who pointed a cannon at the mob and threatened to shoot if they molested the players.[17]

Though Douglass had made a little money playing in New York, persistent hostility both in Rhode Island and New York induced him to look for a more favorable climate. The company stopped for a time in Williamsburg in the early autumn of 1763 but soon were again headed south. On November 5, 1763, the *South Carolina Gazette* announced that a "company of comedians arrived here last Monday from Virginia who are called the American Company." [18] During the next six months Mrs. Manigault noted in her diary frequent visits to the Charleston theater, where she saw, among other plays, *Romeo and Juliet* and *King Lear*. In Charleston, the players found a milieu both hospitable and profitable and made that town their principal base until the spring of 1766, when Douglass went to England. On his return in the autumn of that year, he once more braved the Philadelphia Quakers and Presbyterians and erected there a building of brick and wood called the Southwark Theater, the most substantial theatrical structure yet erected in the American colonies. Previous theaters had been adapted from halls and rooms in warehouses and similar buildings. From this time until the approach of the Revolution in 1775, Douglass and his company acted in the principal towns of the Atlantic seaboard from Charleston to New York. The drama was now well established as part of the formal diversion of Americans, though Boston still held out strongly against stage plays. The British occupation of Boston was made doubly humiliating by the performance of General John Burgoyne's own play, *The Blockade of Boston*.[19]

Not all of the theatrical entertainment in colonial America came

[17] *Ibid.*, p. 35.
[18] Willis, *The Charleston Stage*, p. 43.
[19] William W. Clapp, Jr., *A Record of the Boston Stage* (Boston, 1853), pp. 3–4.

from the repertory of the strolling players. Amateurs occasionally put on plays, but records are scanty and we have no way of knowing how often groups tried their skill at play acting. In September 1754, Ezra Stiles reported after a visit to the little college at Newark, New Jersey (which was to become Princeton), that he "went to prayers, after which 2 young gent. of the college acted *Tamerlane and Bajazet,* &c." [20] These were Presbyterian youths under the tutelage of their pious president, Aaron Burr. The play was Nicholas Rowe's *Tamerlane* with high-flown rhetoric sufficient to give scope to young men eager to practice dramatic speeches. Addison's *Cato* was so filled with rhetorical moralizations that it too was useful for amateurs. A musical drama by David Mallet and James Thomson called *The Masque of Alfred* was performed at the College of Philadelphia during the Christmas and New Year's holidays of 1756–57. Provost William Smith adapted the piece and in an introduction asserted that the young men of the college had "from time to time delivered proper speeches and acted parts of our best dramatic pieces, before large audiences with great applause." [21] Clearly the drama was not completely neglected in colonial colleges, even though it might be dragged in merely to provide training in oratory.

Colonial America was not productive of original drama. Who wrote the mysterious play *The Bear and the Cub* we do not know. The earliest extant play written and printed in America bears the title of *Androboros, A Bibliographical Farce in Three Acts.* It is a political satire attributed to Robert Hunter, governor of New York between 1710 and 1719. It was never acted and the only copy known is in the Huntington Library. Hunter was an Englishman. The earliest play to be produced from the pen of a native-born American was Thomas Godfrey's *Prince of Parthia,* acted in Philadelphia in the spring of 1767.

The variety of entertainment offered in the earlier years of the colonial period increased during the eighteenth century. Punch and Judy shows, waxworks, clockwork performances, an occasional lion, elephant, or camel, and trapeze artists traveled up and down the

[20] Ezra Stiles, "Extracts from the Travel Diary . . . on a Journey . . . from New Haven to Philadelphia . . .," *Proceedings of the Massachusetts Historical Society,* 2nd Ser., VII (1801–92), 340.

[21] Quoted by Arthur H. Quinn, *A History of the American Drama from the Beginning to the Civil War* (2nd ed., New York, 1943), p. 18.

country. By 1724 a rope dancer and a traditional clown called "Pickle Herring" were advertising in Philadelphia and performing in something called "the New Booth on Society Hill" outside the official limits of the town. The New York newspapers in 1749 advertised a waxworks show of the royal family and Peg Woffington the actress, a puppet show displaying the cruelties of Queen Mary Tudor and Bishop Gardiner against the Protestants, and various scientific displays, including a curious optical machine and an ingenious rapid-firing piece of ordnance.[22] The scientific show became increasingly popular in the eighteenth century. The *Virginia Gazette* on September 5, 1755 advertised to be seen at the Exchange Tavern in Norfolk "That elaborate and celebrated piece of mechanism, called the microcosm . . . built in the form of a Roman temple . . . by the late ingenious Mr. Henry Bridges of London." This was a sort of planetarium with variations, including the appearance of the "Nine Muses playing in concert on divers musical instruments, as the harp, hautboy, bass viol, &c." and other mechanical marvels even more wondrous. This show reached Williamsburg on October 12, and doubtless was seen in many other towns and villages of the Atlantic seaboard. The *South Carolina Gazette* on March 2, 1752, announced "To be exhibited at Mr. Doughty's dancing room, in Meeting Street, Charles-Town. A course of natural philosophy, and mechanics illustrated by experiments by Lewis Evans." From the description that followed Mr. Evans gave an exciting depiction of some of the wonders of astronomy, chemistry, and physics, with a demonstration of "electrical fluid." From this time forward to the days of the Redpath Chautauqua, the popularizer of science would grow in favor.

Though theaters were slow to develop in the colonies, that does not mean that the colonists were lacking in entertainment, some of it histrionic. In the modern world, we forget the sheer entertainment value of the church—where, indeed, the drama had its European birth. In the Puritan colonies particularly, the sermon on Sunday and the sermon on "Lecture Day"—usually Thursday—provided an interest that we find hard to imagine. The eloquence of some of the preachers was moving, and many a congregation felt some of the catharsis of pity and fear provided by an Aristotelian tragedy as the minister pictured the progress of sinful man from the cradle to the grave and thence to Divine judgment. In some communities the interest in sermons resulted

[22] Odell, *Annals*, I, 28–29.

in an excessive attendance at "lectures" in addition to the regular church service on Sunday. New England of course had no monopoly of sermons as social occasions. In the South churchgoing also had a high social value as entertainment.

Festivals and holidays provided amusements which in a measure took the place of theatrical entertainment. Although the colonists had various feast days to celebrate, the holidays that we prize most— Christmas and Thanksgiving—played only a small part in seventeenth- and eighteenth-century life in this country. Despite the legend of the first Thanksgiving by the Pilgrims, the celebration of a fixed annual day of Thanksgiving was not universal in the colonies, even in New England.[23] By proclamation of the governor or of some other official, a colony or town might declare a day of thanksgiving in gratitude for good crops, for an escape from yellow fever, or for some other favor of the Almighty. Many days of thanksgiving were celebrated, sometimes with fasting and prayer, sometimes as feast days. Christmas was a day of quiet feasting but little else anywhere in the colonies. Though Samuel Sewall bitterly opposed the observance of Christmas in Boston and rejoiced to see shops open and business as usual on December 25, some of the less puritanical celebrated it as a holiday, fired muskets, visited friends, and ate big dinners. But even in Virginia William Byrd makes no mention of any particular celebration at Christmas beyond going to church and having a special dinner. Other days were more convivial. Election days, muster days, commencement days at Harvard, William and Mary, Yale, and other colonial colleges were the occasions of celebrations and merriment. New Year's Day in New York traditionally was the time for the exchange of visits. That colony also had another period of celebration following Whitsunday, or the day of Pentecost, which they called "Pinkster Day" after the Dutch word for Pentecost.[24] By custom the Negro slaves in New York had particular license during the week after Whitsunday, and the festivities were sometimes riotous. Guy Fawkes Day on November 5 gave an opportunity in most of the colonies for the firing of guns, burning a "Guy" in effigy, and maligning Catholics for the

[23] For an interesting discussion of New England thanksgiving days, see Alice Morse Earle, *Customs and Fashions of Old New England* (New York, 1898), pp. 214–233.

[24] Alice Morse Earle, *Colonial Days in Old New York* (New York, 1899), pp. 195 ff.

"horrid Gun-Powder" Plot. Shrove Tuesday was sometimes observed in the traditional manner of Old England. On February 15, 1687, Samuel Sewall records his disapproval because on Shrove Tuesday "Jos. Maylem carries a cock at his back, with a bell in his hand, in the Main Street; several follow him blindfold, and under pretence of striking him or his cock, with great cart-whips strike passengers, and make great disturbance." [25] This was a variation of "cock-skailing," which had been a common practice on Shrove Tuesday for many generations in England.

Cockfighting was a popular sport throughout the colonies and on occasion even the clergy attended. By the mid-eighteenth century in New York, Shrove Tuesday had become a special occasion for cocking mains, but cockfights were not confined to any particular time. The Reverend John Sharpe, an Anglican minister in New York between 1710 and 1713, kept a journal in which he enumerates many occasions when he attended cockfights, sometimes after his prayer service.[26] Cockfighting was especially popular in the southern colonies throughout the colonial period.

Many of the sports of Old England were adapted to new conditions in America. Shooting, hunting, and fishing were often a means of providing necessary food as well as sport. In the seventeenth century, hunters frequently put out bait and shot as vermin the wolves and foxes which it attracted. Fox hunting with horses and hounds became a sport that Virginians and Marylanders particularly enjoyed, but never in the colonial period did it acquire the status of the conventionalized social activity of later times. Bears, wolves, and sometimes bulls were baited with hounds. The cruelty of such sports apparently did not oppress the colonists, who had inherited a taste for these activities from their ancestors in England.

Horse racing was popular from an early date throughout the colonies. Bostonians enjoyed racing, which they justified as a means of improving the breed of horses. In Rhode Island, which had a plantation economy similar to that in the South, races, run for a silver tankard or some other prize, were frequent. Virginians were so addicted to racing that even humble planters wasted their time and substance in the sport. Hugh Jones in 1724 observed that the lesser Virginia planters "don't much admire labor, or any manly exercise, except horse-racing,

[25] Sewall, *Diary, Col. Mass. Hist. Soc.*, 5th Ser., V, 167.
[26] Odell, *Annals*, I, 8.

nor diversion, except cock-fighting, in which some greatly delight." [27] Anybody could race his horse, of course, but Virginians quickly developed a social snobbery about their races. In 1674 in York County, a tailor named Bullock scandalized the community and was fined for entering his horse in a race against a mare owned by a "gentleman," Dr. Matthew Slader. But when it was discovered that Slader had connived with the tailor to "fix" the race, he too was punished by being set in the stocks.[28] So many wild horses bred in the swamps and woods of Virginia that Robert Beverley in 1705, after mentioning methods of hunting, fowling, and fishing, comments: "There is yet another kind of sport, which the young people take great delight in, and that is, the hunting of wild horses; which they pursue sometimes with dogs and sometimes without." [29]

Dancing was so prevalent in colonial America that neither Puritans nor Quakers were able to suppress this form of entertainment. The Puritans were greatly troubled over dancing. There was scriptural authority for it, and the example of David was mentioned by the advocates of this accomplishment. Nevertheless, dancing was clearly an inducement to sin, and the catechism compiled by the Westminster Assembly expressly condemned "lascivious dancing." Whether all mixed dancing between men and women was lascivious was a matter of controversy never satisfactorily resolved, but the stricter Puritans had no hesitancy in condemning it as wanton and unseemly. Despite their objections, the devil and the dancing master found harborage in New England. In 1714 Edward Enstone, the Anglican organist of King's Chapel, Boston, applied for permission to open a school of music and dancing, but the selectmen refused. Yet, with or without their approval, he advertised two years later that he would teach both music and dancing and in 1720 he was still advertising his services as dancing master and music teacher.[30] The Quakers in Pennsylvania opposed dancing as frivolous and idolatrous, but Philadelphia also had its dancing schools. In the areas where the Anglican faith prevailed,

[27] Hugh Jones, *The Present State of Virginia* (1724), ed. Joseph Sabin (New York, 1865), p. 48. See also Louis B. Wright, *The First Gentlemen of Virginia* (San Marino, Calif., 1940), pp. 86–88.

[28] Wright, *The First Gentlemen*, p. 59.

[29] Robert Beverley, *The History and Present State of Virginia* (1705), ed. Louis B. Wright (Chapel Hill, N.C., 1947), p. 312.

[30] Percy A. Scholes, *The Puritans and Music in England and New England* (Oxford, 1934), p. 74.

dancing was a part of the social routine on all levels of society and was sometimes carried to excess. The Virginia records, for example, show a number of instances of fines being levied for dancing on Sunday, which even Virginia Anglicans regarded as pushing a good thing too far.[31] To South Carolinians, Virginians, and Marylanders of the upper class, life without balls and "assemblies" would have been regarded as barren and uncivilized. The Reverend Hugh Jones even recommended that the College of William and Mary provide for dancing lessons, along with fencing and music.

Dancing of course implied appropriate music, of which there appears to have been no dearth. English men and women of the sixteenth and seventeenth centuries were probably much more musical than their descendants today. In Shakespeare's day, a lute was commonly found in barber shops, and both men and women reveled in music and song. Much nonsense has been written about the Puritan opposition to music and their addiction to psalm singing through their noses as their only musical manifestation. Evidence abounds that the Puritans on either side of the Atlantic had no abhorrence of music provided it was not "lascivious." They did rail against the singing of "bawdy ballads" and other profane songs, and they objected to organs in the church, but they did not condemn music in general as so many writers have assumed.[32]

That is not to say that the citizens of Massachusetts Bay, for example, were a nest of singing birds, but they often took pleasure in secular songs and in the music of lutes, violins, drums, trumpets, flutes, the virginals, and other instruments. Jew's-harps they imported and used as trading goods with the Indians, and presumably the traders demonstrated their use. When Josiah Flynt, a freshman at Harvard, wrote in 1661 to a clergyman uncle in London for a fiddle, the good man replied that attention to music would be more proper for his sisters than for him. If he did not apply himself sufficiently to become skillful, music would be worth nothing at all, and he could not afford the time to become proficient, "unless you intend to take upon you the trade of fiddling," a frivolity unthinkable.[33]

Among the Puritans, church music consisted of psalm singing, a

[31] Wright, *The First Gentlemen,* pp. 81–83.
[32] Scholes, *The Puritans and Music, passim.*
[33] Quoted by John Tasker Howard, *Our American Music* (3rd edition, New York, 1946), p. 21.

skill not confined to Puritans alone, for Drake's sailors on the coast of California in 1579 had delighted the Indians with the singing of psalms. Several different versions of the psalms were used by the English. Henry Ainsworth published in Amsterdam in 1612 *The Book of Psalms* in prose and verse, a book popular with the Separatists, and regarded as musically superior to any English Psalter then in print. The Psalter first used by the settlers in New England was that prepared by English Protestant exiles in Geneva, Thomas Sternhold, John Hopkins, and others, and published in countless editions. Because this version was not sufficiently faithful to the original Hebrew to suit the scholarly divines in Massachusetts Bay, in 1640 they brought out a new version, *The Whole Book of Psalms Faithfully Translated into English Metre.* This is the famous "Bay Psalm Book," which had frequent editions until late in the eighteenth century. Since this book had no printed music with the psalms, the tune had to be "set" by one of the congregation. Samuel Sewall, for example, was conscientious in his duty of setting the tune in his church. A custom also prevailed of "lining out" or reading the psalm line by line for the congregation to follow. This practice continued until modern times in rural districts where books were scarce or many of the congregation could not read. Congregational psalm singing did not reach a high degree of musical perfection, but it did provide an emotional outlet for the pious.

During the late seventeenth and early eighteenth centuries, the improvement in psalm singing occupied the attention of reformers in New England. John Tufts of Harvard published a little book about 1714 called *A Very Plain and Easy Introduction to the Singing of Psalm Tunes* which was popular enough to have eleven editions. Tufts and a number of others including Cotton Mather sought to regularize the singing of psalms. They called their reformed method "regular singing" or "singing by note," and they opposed the "common way of singing." [34] This showed a growing interest in more sophisticated music in the churches.

Elsewhere in the colonies hymn singing was an important element in the musical experience of the people, though in the seventeenth century the singing of hymns hardly surpassed in quality the psalm

[34] For a discussion of the technical differences between the methods of singing psalms and the agitation for "regular" singing, see Gilbert Chase, *America's Music from the Pilgrims to the Present* (New York, 1955), pp. 25–40.

singing for which their enemies ridiculed the Puritans. Early in the eighteenth century, however, Isaac Watts' hymns and adaptations of the psalms gained an enormous popularity in both Great Britain and the colonies, and in many areas Watts' versions revolutionized church music. His *Hymns,* first published in 1707, and his *Psalms of David* (1719) gave new variety and range to religious music—and, incidentally, precipitated a controversy which lasted into the nineteenth century, when one faction of the Presbyterians still refused to approve either Watts' hymns or his versions of the psalms, singable though they were, because they departed too far from literal translation.[35]

Probably the earliest organ used in a church service was one that a group of German Pietists brought to the Philadelphia region at the beginning of the eighteenth century. The Gloria Dei Church in Philadelphia, built by Swedish Lutherans, borrowed it in 1703. An English craftsman, Christopher Witt, a few years later was building organs in Philadelphia, and is supposed to have built one for Christ Church in 1728.[36] Thomas Brattle brought the first organ to Boston and willed it to the Brattle Street Church when he died in 1713. Because Brattle's Congregational brethren were not yet prepared for so revolutionary a development, his executors gave the organ to the less squeamish Anglicans of King's Chapel. Bruton Church in Williamsburg also had an organ.

With the increasing urbanity of the eighteenth century, religious and secular music alike showed a marked development throughout the colonies. There is evidence of a "concert of music" performed in 1735 in the Sun Tavern in Boston, followed a few months afterward by a concert in Charleston, South Carolina. In January, 1736, Karl Theodor Pachelbel, distant relative of Johann Sebastian Bach, gave a concert in New York. Pachelbel played the harpsichord and was supported by other musicians playing violins and German flutes. Pachelbel moved on to South Carolina and for several years lived in Charleston. From this time onward, the colonial newspapers recount fairly frequent appearances of musicians and singers, and there are numerous advertisements of the sale of musical instruments.

[35] The most popular and original native contributor to American religious music in the late eighteenth century was William Billings of Boston, whose activities fall outside the scope of the present study. At the age of twenty-four he published *The New England Psalm Singer, or American Chorister* (Boston, 1770). See Chase, *America's Music,* pp. 139–145.

[36] Howard, *Our American Music,* p. 18.

Charleston, South Carolina, was always hospitable to musicians and dancing masters. Frequent newspaper notices from the mid-eighteenth century onward record the appearance of musicians in instrumental and vocal concerts. In 1762 a group of Charleston citizens organized the St. Cecilia Society, the earliest musical group in British America to support a paid orchestra. As the historian of early concert life in America has commented, "when and where the first public concert took place in what are today the United States . . . would be difficult and useless to answer." [37] But certainly concerts had been frequent, from Boston to Charleston, in the generation preceding the founding of the St. Cecilia Society. The concerts sponsored by the St. Cecilia Society were an important contribution to musical development in the colonies in the years just prior to the Revolution.

Some of the German religious groups greatly emphasized music as an integral part of their worship. A group of Pietists under the leadership of Johannes Kelpius, himself a musician and hymn writer, settled in 1694 on the Wissahickon, near Philadelphia. At the ordination of Justus Falckner in Gloria Dei Church in 1703, Kelpius' group provided music which included viols, hautboys, trumpets, and kettle-drums.[38] Falckner himself believed that music would have an effect in soothing and civilizing the Indians. The Seventh-Day Baptists who established themselves at Ephrata in Lancaster County in the 1730's had as one of their leaders Johann Conrad Beissel, a musician of distinction. He wrote a treatise on harmony, composed hymns, organized a religious choral society, and was perhaps the earliest composer in the colonies to publish his works.[39] Benjamin Franklin brought out a series of hymnbooks prepared by Beissel. The Moravians who settled at Bethlehem in the Lehigh Valley in 1741 also emphasized music. By 1743 they had organized an orchestra and a year later a musical group for the performance of chamber music and symphonies. This group kept up with the musical developments in Europe and performed compositions by Mozart, Haydn, Johann Christian Bach, and others of that day.[40] One group of Moravians went to Salem, North Carolina,

---

[37] O. G. Sonneck, *Early Concert-Life in America (1731–1800)*, photographic reproduction of edition of 1906 (New York, 1949), p. 10. See also Frederick P. Bowes, *The Culture of Early Charleston* (Chapel Hill, N.C., 1942), p. 106.

[38] Chase, *America's Music*, p. 55.

[39] *Ibid.*, p. 57; Howard, *Our American Music*, p. 26.

[40] Chase, *America's Music*, pp. 58–61. The Moravian colony at Bethlehem developed a group of composers after the period covered in the present study.

and established there a tradition of instrumental and choral music that has persisted down to the present. German craftsmen, especially German organ builders, helped to provide musical instruments which gradually improved music throughout the colonies. By the decade preceding the Revolution organs could be found in many churches throughout the colonies.

With the growing pre-eminence of Philadelphia as a cosmopolitan center, music and the arts received a new stimulation. A talented young poet and musician, Francis Hopkinson, gathered about him a group of musicians who frequently met to play a variety of instruments. Hopkinson himself was a harpsichordist and to him is given credit for some of the earliest original musical compositions in this country.[41]

Peter Kalm, the Swedish botanist, in Philadelphia on Christmas Day, 1750, was impressed by the music heard in the Roman Catholic church there, but he adds: "It must be emphasized that of all the churches in Philadelphia only the Swedish and the Catholic possessed organs. There had formerly been one in the English temple, but it had later become useless, and there had not yet been any measures taken to procure a new one." [42] Kalm observed that the officiating priest, a Jesuit, played the violin, and had assembled a competent group of violinists to assist him.

With the attainment of relative stability after the second half of the eighteenth century, music both religious and secular had become much more important in colonial lives. Nearly every community could boast a fiddler, or some other musician, and the variety of music ranged from jigs and ballads played and sung in country cabins to concerts by the carefully selected orchestra brought together by the St. Cecilia Society in Charleston.

Though the opportunities in colonial America for formal entertainment and amusement were barren indeed by modern standards, the men and women of that age had about as many diversions as their scanty leisure would accommodate.

The most notable among them was probably John Frederick Peter, who came to this country in 1770.

[41] Howard, *Our American Music*, p. 39.

[42] Adolph B. Benson (ed.), *The America of 1750. Peter Kalm's Travels in North America* (New York, 1937), II, 675.

CHAPTER 9

Architecture and the Decorative Arts

SETTLERS on a new frontier, if they are wise, utilize to their best advantage the materials and the physical protection afforded by the country. Even when the terrain is barren and inhospitable, resourceful men contrive to find some refuge from wind and weather in the land itself. Although the earliest settlers in English America were inexperienced as woodsmen and in the arts of survival in the forests, they knew enough about simple construction to adapt to their uses the materials at hand. Most of them had come from towns and country villages where they had observed the erection of dwellings of simple construction that had been traditional since medieval times.[1] It took little knowledge of architecture and no extraordinary skill to put together a hut of wattles and mud similar to ones that seventeenth-century Englishmen might have seen in many parts of their country. The new land afforded ample materials waiting only for the labor of men to shape them into houses.

The first shelters were of course the rudest of huts. Because Captain John Smith and his company landed at Jamestown at the beginning of warm weather, they had to worry only about rain and the arrows of the Indians. A tent of rotten sailcloth, which served as their first

[1] Traditional architectural design in colonial dwelling houses, described as Gothic or medieval, is discussed with illustrative drawings and pictures in Hugh Morrison, *Early American Architecture from the First Colonial Settlements to the National Period* (New York, 1952), pp. 3–48. See also Henry C. Forman, *The Architecture of the Old South: The Medieval Style, 1585–1850* (Cambridge, Mass., 1948), pp. 3–46.

church, was also their main protection from foul weather. But they did not take long to learn how to make fairly tight huts of boughs, bark, sod, and thatch. In time axmen and sawyers produced hewn timbers and clapboards for frame houses. They also made brick very early at Jamestown. At Plymouth and in Massachusetts Bay, the first arrivals lived in huts much like those at Jamestown, but the severity of the weather was an inducement to hasten the erection of more substantial houses. Soon the Pilgrims were building small frame houses with walls of mud plaster. Frequently the builders used grass as a binder for the mud. But since such walls were not sufficient protection against the cold, whenever they could New Englanders covered the outside walls with clapboards.

So far as the existing evidence shows, the early English settlers did not build log cabins, but the myth that they lived in log houses like Daniel Boone's has long been popular—probably as a result of the romantic association of log cabins with democratic origins in America. A few years ago a book by Harold R. Shurtleff entitled *The Log Cabin Myth* summed up evidence which architectural historians like Fiske Kimball and others had long been accumulating to show that Englishmen in America built huts and houses like the traditional structures they had known in England. And the log dwelling, built pen fashion of notched logs, was unknown to them. Those Europeans from heavily forested countries—the Swedes who came to Delaware and the Germans who came to Pennsylvania—had known pen constructed log houses at home, and they reproduced them in America. But culturally conservative Englishmen required several generations and much hard labor with handsaws before they discerned the merits of notching logs and building a pen to live in. The Scotch-Irish, who filtered through German settlements on their way to more remote frontiers early in the eighteenth century, adopted the log cabin and made it their own. The only log houses built by Englishmen along the Atlantic seaboard in the seventeenth century seem to have a few forts and blockhouses, erected at great effort, for purposes of defense.[2]

[2] Harold R. Shurtleff, *The Log Cabin Myth* (Cambridge, Mass., 1939), pp. 55–56 *et passim*. See also Morrison, *Early American Architecture*, pp. 12–13, for further evidence of the unwillingness of the English to adopt the log house even in the eighteenth century; only a few scattered instances of Englishmen building log cabins in the colonial period have come to light. One of the rare instances is recounted in "Lancashire Emigrants Helped to Build America," *Lancashire Life*, IV (1956), p. 55, which relates the construction in 1723 by

The early frame houses of the Chesapeake Bay region and New England were much alike in construction. Their size depended upon the necessities—and the means—of the owners. A returned official of the Virginia colony wrote in 1615 that Jamestown had "two fair rows of houses all of framed timber, two stories and an upper garret, or corn loft, high." [3] If more than two or three rooms were required, it was economical to build a two-story house. Under the pitched roof was a windowless garret which could be used for the storage of supplies or as sleeping space for excess children. As more room was needed, a lean-to or ells could be added. A chimney in the center was sufficient for a moderate-sized house, but larger houses might have chimneys at each end. The first chimneys were crude stacks made of sticks and lined with clay—certainly a hazardous form of construction, but the best available until the settlers could burn brick.

Rudimentary sawmills and brickkilns were among the earliest industries in the various settlements. A simple frame of hewn logs above a pit provided a place where two men, one below and one above, could split a log into planks with the long thin handsaws of the day. Water power was used in some localities, for water-powered sawmills were known in the seventeenth century. [4] Brickmaking requires no unusual skill and clay was abundant. As early as 1612 a report from Virginia mentions houses at Henrico, "the first story all of bricks." [5] Jamestown's brick church, a portion of which still stands, dates from the 1640's. Only a few houses were built of brick in the early seventeenth century, but local kilns furnished enough brick for foundations and chimneys, and by the end of the century brick houses were fairly common in colonial towns. A legend that many colonial houses still standing were built "with brick brought from England" is often heard and is almost pure myth. According to one historian of architecture only a few thousand brick are known with certainty to have been imported from England, though the Dutch brought some brick to New Amsterdam as ballast. [6] The reason is clear. Space for goods in ships

---

a Lancashireman of a house made of oak logs, notched at the corners, with the interstices filled with mortar.

[3] Shurtleff, *The Log Cabin Myth*, p. 145, quoting Ralph Hamer, *True Discourse of the Present Estate of Virginia* (1615).

[4] Shurtleff, *The Log Cabin Myth*, pp. 45, 156.

[5] *Ibid.*, p. 146, quoting Robert Johnson, *The New Life of Virginia* (1612).

[6] Fiske Kimball, *Domestic Architecture of the American Colonies and the Early Republic* (New York, 1927), pp. 38–39.

to the English colonies was precious and rates were high; most ships could use heavy casks and other freight in lieu of brick ballast.

Little stone was used in the construction of seventeenth-century houses. Tidewater Virginia and Maryland had little or no building stone; New England had plenty of rock, but lime was scarce and mortar of mud will not hold field stone in place. Stone was used in foundations and occasionally in chimneys. A few Pennsylvanians roofed their houses with slate, and in the other colonies, especially in New Amsterdam, builders occasionally used tiles. But riven shingles covered most roofs, whether the houses were of wood or masonry.

In the early period, the interior walls of rooms were sometimes lime-plastered, sometimes ceiled with boards. Not until fairly late in the century could many houses boast much wall decoration. Windows in the earliest houses were mere wooden shutters, and immigrants were sometimes advised to bring oiled paper for their windows. A few who could afford the cost brought or imported glass panes. Although small-paned glass windows became standard equipment in the better houses as the century wore on, many of the poor throughout the colonial period had to be content with shutters. No one for nearly two centuries to come would dream of screens to keep out flies.

Seventeenth-century houses, whether in the southern colonies, Pennsylvania, New York with its Dutch heritage, or New England, were primarily functional and carried over traditional designs which went back in details to the Middle Ages. The Dutch houses built in New Netherland with their high gabled ends facing the street were the most distinctive domestic buildings on the Atlantic seaboard. At the time of the English occupation of New Amsterdam in 1664 that little city had many of the characteristics which a visitor to Leiden or Delft might have observed. Dutch styles of construction continued to influence buildings in New York long after the English had occupied the country.

Although most houses in the colonies were simple structures often retaining traditional medieval features, houses during the first half of the eighteenth century began to show a new elegance. As wealth increased, more and more Americans were able to build fine houses. Professional architects were unknown, but master carpenters had the benefit of a variety of architectural manuals being published in England and imported into America.[7] Inventories of colonial libraries

[7] *Ibid.,* p. 60. For examples of the skill of master carpenters, such as Richard

show an astonishing number of these handbooks for builders, and the houses erected during the eighteenth century show their influence.

Buildings, both private and public, display a growing acceptance of classical design and use of classical ornament and decoration. Inigo Jones, the famous Jacobean architect, had popularized in England a style that owed its modern adaptation to the sixteenth-century Italian architect Andrea Palladio. Palladio in turn derived much of his own inspiration from the Roman architect and engineer Vitruvius. Book I of Palladio's works in pocket size was first published in English in 1663 and went through twelve editions by 1733. Under the influence of the Earl of Burlington, a powerful advocate of classical design, Giacomo Leoni published in 1715 a complete Palladio in English. Isaac Ware published a new translation of Palladio in 1738. Burlington also encouraged William Kent in 1727 to edit and publish the designs of Inigo Jones. Dozens of other books describing and illustrating the new taste in architecture appeared in this period and influenced building on both sides of the Atlantic.[8]

Since architecture was not yet a specialized profession, the design of buildings was left either to gentleman amateurs or to carpenters who undertook to interpret the manuals in accordance with the desires of their customers. Although an over-all classical influence is apparent, most colonial domestic architecture of the first three-quarters of the eighteenth century displays a wide divergence of taste and freedom of application of any rules that may have been laid down in the books.

Sometimes the effort to adopt new fashions and still not depart too far from the old resulted in the creation of a monstrosity, as in the plantation house of "Mulberry," Goose Creek, South Carolina, built in 1714, which grouped four Jacobean-style turrets around a central building with a hipped roof and classic dormer windows.

Nevertheless, increasing wealth and growing sophistication throughout the colonies resulted in houses of improved symmetry and design, whether the material was wood, stone, or brick. New England still favored wood, though brick houses became common in Boston and in

Munday at Newport, see Antoinette F. Downing and Vincent J. Scully, *The Architectural Heritage of Newport, Rhode Island, 1640–1915* (Cambridge, Mass., 1952), pp. 43–71.

[8] Kimball, *Domestic Architecture of the American Colonies*, p. 58. See also the excellent summary of the influence of architectural books in Carl Bridenbaugh, *Peter Harrison, First American Architect* (Chapel Hill. N.C., 1949), pp. 38–44.

other towns, where the danger of fire gave an impetus to the use of more durable material. A few houses in New England were built of stone, but only in Pennsylvania and adjacent areas was stone widely used in dwellings. An increased use of brick in dwelling houses and outbuildings is noticeable in Virginia and Maryland, but wood remained the most popular material even in houses built by the wealthier planters. Since more brick than wooden houses have survived, a popular but erroneous notion has gained currency that most eighteenth-century planters had brick houses. In the Carolinas, even in closely packed Charleston, wooden houses were much more common than brick.

Eighteenth-century houses showed great interior improvements over their predecessors. Since houses no longer were regarded as fortresses, windows could be made larger and shutters removed. Large, clear panes replaced the small leaded glass of the seventeenth century. Doorways were larger and more decorative, sometimes showing cornices and friezes. Fireplaces, no longer mere smoke-blackened caverns, became decorative features of rooms; the opening was usually framed with a mitered molding designed like the classical architrave. In houses built before 1765, the fireplace frequently had no mantel shelf, but fireplaces with a cornice, which served as a shelf, and a carved frieze were not unknown. Walls were made of plaster or wood, sometimes elaborately paneled. White paint began to take the place of blues, yellows, greens, and lead colors, which had been popular for walls in the earlier years. After about 1730, advertisements of wallpaper in scenic patterns began to appear in colonial newspapers.

Public buildings of substantial construction and dignified design multiplied rapidly in the larger towns. Even in the agrarian South, simple but well-proportioned brick courthouses, some of which are still to be seen in Virginia, began to replace earlier wooden buildings. The majority of the more imposing public buildings followed traditional designs based on the building manuals current in the day and are now loosely described as "Georgian." The State House in Philadelphia, erected between 1733 and 1741, is an excellent example of the adaptation of classical design without subservience to a rigid "school" of architecture. Philadelphia had the benefit of an influential guild of builders, the Carpenters' Company, which published a manual of its own—and a book of prices. During the second half of the eighteenth century, the Carpenters' Company had a great influence upon building throughout the region. Elsewhere virtuosi in architecture were consulting books of designs and planning better buildings. John Smibert, the painter, drew up plans for Faneuil Hall (1741), which differed somewhat from the rebuilt structure as it exists today. The Old State House (1728) in Boston is another example of early Georgian public building, inspired by the builders' manuals.

Buildings at Harvard, Yale, William and Mary, Princeton, and other colonial colleges followed the same trend. A credible tradition has it that the old college building at William and Mary was designed by Sir Christopher Wren. The Capitol at Williamsburg, built from designs approved in 1669, and the Governor's Palace, erected a few years after the completion of the Capitol, are examples of the solidity and dignity that colonial builders achieved in masonry. The Capitol with its round towers suggests an old European influence combined with newer classic details of the Renaissance style. The Governor's Palace conforms more closely to the Georgian type.

Throughout the colonies, the members of various sects and creeds built churches in keeping with their faiths—and their increasing prosperity. Eighteenth-century engravings of Boston, New York, Philadelphia, or Charleston show a skyline marked by church spires. By theological prescription, Puritan churches and Quaker meetinghouses remained simple and austere, but the quality of materials and construction improved. Anglican churches were more concerned with architectural richness, and a few achieved imposing dignity. St. Michael's (1752) in Charleston, South Carolina, Christ Church (1727) in Philadelphia, King's Chapel (1749) in Boston, and St. Paul's Church (1756) in New York were among the finest examples of classically inspired church buildings. The white interior columns in these churches illustrated the Greek orders, and their classic porticoes gave promise of the Greek temple type of construction which in a later generation would characterize not only many churches but other public buildings.

The mid-eighteenth century saw the emergency of a significant architect, Peter Harrison of Newport, Rhode Island. A ship captain who married a well-to-do Newport girl and settled down to become a substantial citizen of that town, Harrison was an ingenious man. The master of various crafts, including navigation, military engineering, cartography, surveying, drafting, and shipbuilding, he was most interested in architecture. He brought together an excellent library on this subject and his own designs show the influence of books in his collection. Though Harrison's skill was sufficient for him to be described as an architect, he never practiced this profession for profit and he remained a gentleman amateur though far from a dilettante. When Abraham Redwood in 1747 founded the Redwood Library at Newport, Harrison drew the plans for the building—a Palladian temple with portico, a design which future generations would repeat in countless banks and churches, those twin bulwarks of American society.[9] Harrison's work, described by his most recent biographer as "the supreme achievement in American colonial architecture,"[10] included the Jewish synagogue, the Freemason's Hall, the Brick Market, all in Newport, and Christ Church in Cambridge. These classical buildings were designed in 1759–60. Evidence points to his hand also in the design of St. Michael's in Charleston.[11]

As wealth increased in the colonies, the amenities that go with an improved social status multiplied. In settled and well-ordered communities, men took thought for comforts and luxuries. Few of mankind genuinely relish the Spartan life which frontier conditions impose, and most put aside austerity as soon as their milieu and their pocketbooks permit. By the first third of the eighteenth century, the older towns on the seaboard were beginning to acquire a little of the patina of age, and leading citizens were showing a concern for the evidences of good living, cultivation—and occasionally even of leisure, though the worship of leisure was never a characteristic of colonial life. The physical surroundings in the homes of eighteenth-century Americans illustrated the upward trend in prosperity and a growing sense of stability. Eighteenth-century homes were vastly different from the sparsely furnished houses of preceding generations. Immigrants can rarely transport heavy household goods, and our seventeenth-century ancestors brought with them very little furniture. A few chests, bedding, cooking utensils, farming implements, and a cradle were sufficient for the establishment of a household in the New World. Some immigrants had even less. Benches, stools, tables, and crude bedsteads they could fashion from timber to be found everywhere. Not even the services of a trained carpenter were required for these things.[12] The

[9] A discussion of the inspiration for the Redwood Library will be found in Carl Bridenbaugh, *Peter Harrison,* pp. 47–50.

[10] *Ibid.,* p. 98.

[11] *Ibid.,* pp. 63–67.

[12] Cf. Scott G. Williamson, *The American Craftsman* (New York, 1940),

forests furnished a variety of native woods—oak, walnut, ash, hickory, maple, birch, and cherry—which could be easily worked. Much of the simple furniture of the seventeenth century—and of later periods on the frontier—was homemade.

The development of more advanced cabinetmaking varied with conditions in the different regions. New England and Pennsylvania, for instance, had many more skilled craftsmen and produced more furniture than the tobacco colonies, where individual planters with money from the production of tobacco and direct communication with London and Bristol preferred to import most of their household articles. "Nay, they are such abominable ill-husbands," complained Robert Beverley, the historian of Virginia, in 1705, "that though their country be over-run with wood, yet they have all their wooden ware from England; their cabinets, chairs, tables, stools, chests, boxes, cart-wheels, and all other things, even so much as their bowls, and birchen brooms, to the eternal reproach of their laziness." [13] To set an example to Virginians, Beverley supplied himself with furniture made on his own plantation, and his example was followed by later planters.

Many examples of the work of New England, New York, and Pennsylvania cabinetmakers have survived, and are prized by collectors today. Solid oak chairs, tables, and chests of the seventeenth century show traditional English or Dutch characteristics. Occasionally craftsmen developed artistic qualities peculiar to a locality, as in the "Hadley" chests, so called from the Massachusetts town in the region where they were produced. Though carved chests were among the earliest pieces of decorative furniture produced in the colonies, the evolution of desks, lowboys, and highboys was an easy step. Such furniture was

---

pp. 3–4, where he quotes a North Carolina parson, John Urmstone, writing in 1711 that settlers had to be jacks of all trades: "Men are generally carpenters, joiners, wheelwrights, coopers, butchers, tanners, shoemakers, tallow-chandlers, watermen, and what not; women soap-makers, starch-makers, dyers, etc. He or she who cannot do all these things . . . over and above all the common occupations of both sexes will have but a bad time of it; for help is not to be had at any rate, everyone having business enough of his own." City dwellers of the present day will find it hard to comprehend the enforced versatility of the colonial pioneer, but any farmer will understand it. Conditions in the colonial towns, of course, were somewhat different, and the person with money in his pocket could depend upon the services of specialized craftsmen: carpenters, cabinetmakers, joiners, and all the others who contributed to a division of labor unknown on the frontier, whether in the seventeenth or the nineteenth centuries.

[13] Robert Beverley, *The History and Present State of Virginia* (1705), ed. Louis B. Wright (Chapel Hill, N.C., 1947), p. 295.

produced in considerable quantity by craftsmen in Philadelphia. About 1730, Philadelphia cabinetmakers began supplying Windsor chairs, which were adaptations of models currently popular in England. An advertisement in the *South Carolina Gazette* for June 23, 1766, announced the arrival from Philadelphia of a "large and neat assortment of Windsor chairs, made in the best and neatest manner, and well painted, high backed, low backed, and settees or double seated." [14]

During the period from 1730 to the Revolution, craftsmen in the colonies showed notable advances in the making of furniture, particularly in their freedom of line, their sense of fitness in ornamentation, and their simplicity of design. Though English cabinetmakers, who were in great demand in the colonies and could command high wages, brought in their heads memories of fashionable design and in their equipment pattern books in which customers could pick out designs that suited them, in America craftsmen felt free to vary designs to suit local taste and conditions. The appearance in 1754 of Thomas Chippendale's *The Gentleman and Cabinet-Maker's Director*, however, provided a handbook that was influential on both sides of the Atlantic for many years. Even in the southern colonies, especially in such centers of fashion as Charleston, South Carolina, cabinetmakers turned out creditable work. In the second half of the eighteenth century Philadelphia became a notable center for crafts of all sorts, and its cabinetmakers were especially noted. Men like Thomas Affleck, James Gillingham, Jonathan Gostelowe, Benjamin Randolph, William Savery, and Thomas Tuffts produced a quantity of well-designed and well-made furniture.[15] Many craftsmen went from Philadelphia to other localities to ply their trades, and so well known was that city for the quality of its workmanship that Philadelphia artisans found it profitable to advertise their origins. For example, the *South Carolina Gazette* for March 22, 1740, announced that Josiah Claypoole "from

[14] Alfred Coxe Prime, *The Arts and Crafts in Philadelphia, Maryland, and South Carolina, 1721–1785. Gleanings from Newspapers* (Topsfield, Mass., 1929), p. 189.
[15] Carl Bridenbaugh, *The Colonial Craftsman* (New York, 1950), p. 79. For details of the American craftsman's art, see Joseph Downs, *American Furniture. Queen Anne and Chippendale Periods in the Henry Francis du Pont Winterthur Museum* (New York, 1952), *passim*. Some attention is given American craftsmen in Richard B. Morris, *Government and Labor in Early America* (New York, 1946), pp. 33–35.

Philadelphia" was prepared to supply desks, chests, sideboards, tea tables, marble tables, and a variety of other objects, including coffins, at his shop near Market Square.[16] John Biggard, lately arrived from Philadelphia, advertised in the *South Carolina Gazette* for March 24, 1767, that he would make Windsor and garden chairs "cheaper than can be imported." [17]

Newport, Rhode Island, also had excellent cabinetmakers, one of the most famous being John Goddard, whose secretaries and kneehole desks are highly prized by collectors today. Boston, New York, Annapolis, and almost every other city and town of the seaboard could boast carpenters, joiners, and cabinetmakers who were producing furniture that was noteworthy for its functional design as well as for its aesthetic appeal.

Both workmanship and material showed marked changes during the eighteenth century. Oak, which had been the favorite wood of the seventeenth century, gave way to mahogany imported from the West Indies and sometimes from Central America. Native black walnut, however, was almost as popular as mahogany, and New Englanders continued to make chairs and beds from maple, hickory, ash, and birch. Occasionally other more unusual woods were used, as evidenced by an advertisement in the Boston *News-Letter* for December 5, 1728, of a "fine red new cedar desk." [18] Well-made furniture, of local manufacture or imported, found its way into the houses even of the less well-to-do.

The mania for things Chinese, which the East India Company stimulated with its imports of exotic wares along with its tea, exerted an influence upon furniture design as local craftsmen imitated the japanned work of Oriental artisans. Oriental designs and techniques further added to the variety of colonial furniture and household decorations.[19]

If frontiersmen have neither the time nor patience for "art" as such, they—or their womenfolk—rarely leave behind all sense of artistic decoration. Captain John Smith's rabble of men made no effort to

[16] Prime, *The Arts and Crafts in Philadelphia*, p. 163.

[17] *Ibid.*, p. 160.

[18] George Francis Dow, *The Arts and Crafts in New England, 1704–1775. Gleanings from Boston Newspapers* (Topsfield, Mass., 1927), p. 108. See also Downs, *American Furniture*, opposite Pl. 76.

[19] Downs, *American Furniture*, pp. 187–188.

beautify their habitations, but as soon as they had wives their homes began to improve. A little needlework on the coverlet of a bed, a bit of embroidered hanging, a painted cloth which served to keep out the draft and decorate a wall, helped to brighten their houses. Virginians and New Englanders were not very different in their household decorations. Much nonsense has been written about the alleged Puritan distaste for art. The Puritans, to be sure, had no patience with the paintings of saints and other religious subjects, which they believed relics of popery, but they showed about as much interest in the arts as any other colonials, except the New Netherlanders. Indeed, if New Englanders would have no traffic with art in their churches, they showed a morbid interest in mortuary designs and lavished upon tombstones some of the macabre artistry that we commonly associate with funeral monuments in medieval churches.

Indigenous art, however, made slow progress. Men and women were too busy in the early years of settlement to spend their time in artistic pursuits. John White, the governor of Raleigh's ill-fated colony, it is true, took time to paint in water colors excellent pictures of Indians—pictures which are preserved to this day in the British Museum—but his work was intended as a scientific report on the natives, not as art for the sake of art.

But vanity in time caught up with more elementary urges. Having attained a little prosperity and time to think about the future, men began to want their likenesses painted. By the 1670's a few stiff portraits of prominent citizens were hanging in American houses. The identification of the painters of these early portraits is a matter for argument among the historians of art. Obviously they were craftsmen who did not depend upon portrait painting for a livelihood but combined such work with other skills. John Foster, for example, who set up the first printing shop in Boston and died in 1681, was not the sour Puritan of legend, for he played the fiddle and is believed to have painted the likenesses of some of his contemporaries, John Davenport and Richard Mather, among others. At any rate he excised a likeness of Mather on a wood block and printed an engraving of that worthy, Bible in hand.[20] An unknown limner, to use the term generally applied to these journeymen painters, in 1674 was plying his trade in the neighborhood of Boston. Among the surviving pictures from his hand

[20] James Thomas Flexner, *American Painting: First Flowers of Our Wilderness* (Boston, 1947), pp. 14–16.

are Elizabeth Freake and Baby Mary,[21] the child being as flat and stiff as a wooden doll. Similar pictures from the hands of this limner and other journeymen painters survive from this period. About 1680, one Thomas Smith, a sea captain turned artist, painted with considerable skill a portrait of his black-haired, full-bosomed daughter Maria, and another of himself, revealing a ruddy, shrewd-faced man holding a skull.[22]

As prosperity increased in the colonies, portraits of members of the more substantial families—men, women, and children—multiplied. The number of craftsmen who turned out these pictures must have been greater than we are likely to imagine, for the surviving primitives are fairly numerous. The limners, like even the more sophisticated painters later in the eighteenth century, eked out their existence by painting tavern and shop signs, crests on coaches, and house painting.[23] In general, the early artists showed more skill in painting men than women. The unknown itinerant craftsmen who painted most of the early portraits either did not take the trouble or were unable to portray the mystery that is woman. A few exceptions have survived, notably the portrait of Ann Pollard, a tavern keeper, who claimed to have jumped ashore in Boston ahead of John Winthrop and to have been a hundred years old when her picture was painted in 1721.[24]

Dutch painters in New Netherland showed more skill and variety, as one might expect; an urban people for the most part, the Dutch had inherited a greater interest in art than the English. The burghers who came to New Amsterdam brought with them many pictures, tapestries, and other objects of art which were common in Holland. One resident owned at least sixty-one pictures portraying a wide variety of subjects, religious as well as secular.[25] The craftsmen who set out to paint pictures in New Amsterdam had something to imitate and a tradition of art behind them. Near the end of the Dutch regime, an unknown artist painted a picture of Christ at Emmaus,[26] which would not have been tolerated by the Boston Puritans who still associated such subjects with a religion they detested, but the Dutch Cal-

---

[21] Illustrated in Alan Burroughs, *Limners and Likenesses: Three Centuries of American Painting* (Cambridge, Mass., 1936), Fig. 8.

[22] Illustrated in Flexner, *American Painting*, p. 18.

[23] Virgil Barker, *American Painting* (New York, 1950), p. 97.

[24] Flexner, *American Painting*, p. 48.

[25] *Ibid.*, p. 53.

[26] *Ibid.*, p. 56.

vinists were accustomed to their own school of religious art. A picture of New Amsterdam in water color, dating from about 1650 and done by Laurens Block, shows a characteristic Dutch interest in landscape. In portraiture, the Dutch painters, if not precisely Rembrandts and Hals, displayed more skill than most other limners. One of them painted a picture of Peter Stuyvesant [27] which revealed the old governor in all of his strength and ugliness. While New England limners were struggling to paint their subjects in courtly respectability, the Dutch were displaying a commendable effort at realistic characterization. As elsewhere, painters could not make a living as artists but combined their avocations with other trades. Evert Duyckinck, for example, and his son Gerret, combined the crafts of glazier, painter, and limner. As painters and limners, they could paint and decorate a customer's house and then do a portrait of him and his wife for the parlor wall. A dynasty of Duyckincks carried on the family crafts until late in the eighteenth century; one of them advertised in 1746 that he was prepared to do "limning, painting, varnishing, japanning, gilding, glazing, and silvering looking glasses . . . He also will teach young gentlemen all sorts of drawing and painting on glass " [28]—an indication that at this time men did not regard such avocations as suitable merely for young ladies.

In the southern colonies, from the mid-seventeenth century onward, portraits were common, but most of them were painted in England. As a recent historian of art has commented satirically of Virginia portraits, "eventually they will all be attributed to Kneller." [29] Actually most Virginians were painted by English artists, now unknown, sometimes merely from written descriptions. A requirement which transcended the achievement of a likeness was that the subject should appear as a courtly aristocrat.

William Byrd II, a remarkable social climber, commissioned the painting of sundry British noblemen with whom he curried favor; he brought home the pictures to hang at Westover, where he could dazzle less fortunate planters by pointing out a roomful of noble friends. Byrd took much pleasure in his pictures and his diary frequently alludes to them. On April 3, 1711, he comments that he "carried Mrs. Russell into the billiard table and to the library and

[27] *Ibid.*, p. 58.
[28] *Ibid.*, p. 61.
[29] *Ibid.*, p. 90.

showed her some prints" [30]—an interest that may not have been strictly in art. Byrd did make a considerable collection of prints and engravings, and up to the end of his life he enjoyed looking at them and showing them to others. Portraits of members of his own family were painted by Charles Bridges, an Englishman who in 1735, when an old man, came to Williamsburg.[31] The portait of Byrd's second wife, Maria Taylor, was probably painted about 1724, before Bridges left England.

Charleston, South Carolina, boasted a lady artist, one Henrietta Johnston, who was active there from about 1708 to 1729. Probably trained in England, she did pastels of fashionable Charlestonians and succeeded in giving William Rhett, conqueror of pirates, the look of Joan of Arc in a periwig.[32] Other South Carolinians, like the Virginians, had their portraits painted in England and bought other pictures abroad.

A highly competent craftsman was Jeremiah Theus, a Swiss, who came to Charleston in 1735 and made a living by painting and teaching art there until his death in 1774. An advertisement in the *South Carolina Gazette* for September 6, 1740, indicates the variety of his work: "Notice is hereby given that Jeremiah Theus, limner, is removed into the Market Square near Mr. John Laurens, sadler, where all gentlemen and ladies may have their pictures drawn, likewise landskips of all sizes, crests and coats of arms for coaches or chaises. Likewise for the conveniency of those who live in the country, he is willing to wait on them at their respective plantations." [33] Four years later he was advertising an evening school for "all young gentlemen and ladies inclinable to be taught the art of drawing." Theus was a careful though unoriginal craftsman who contrived to make all his subjects look like the aristocrats they wanted to be.

Maryland and Pennsylvania, thanks to German craftsmen, had a more vigorous art. Justus Englehardt Kühn, who flourished at Annapolis between the years 1708 and 1717, painted Maryland planters with such elegance that he quickly became the favorite of such aristocrats as Charles Carroll. A more significant painter, however, was

[30] *The Secret Diary of William Byrd of Westover, 1709–1712,* ed. Louis B. Wright and Marion Tinling (Richmond, Va., 1941), p. 324.

[31] *Another Secret Diary of William Byrd of Westover, 1739–1741,* ed. Maude H. Woodfin and Marion Tinling (Richmond, Va., 1942), p. 9.

[32] Illustrated in Flexner, *American Painting,* p. 92.

[33] Prime, *Arts and Crafts,* pp. 10–11. The notice of the art school is dated Oct. 22, 1744.

Gustavus Hesselius, a Swede, kinsman of the mystic Emanuel Swedenborg, who arrived at what is now Wilmington, Delaware, in 1712.
Hesselius painted portraits of planters, religious pictures, classical
myths, landscapes, and Indians. For more than forty years, he ranged
up and down Maryland, Delaware, and Pennsylvania, and set an example for native painters to follow. His son, John, who married a
well-to-do girl and lived on the Eastern Shore of Maryland, was a
fashionable painter during the later colonial period.

American art reached a new level of competence with the arrival
of John Smibert, one of a group of idealists whom George Berkeley
brought to Newport in 1729 when he was projecting a university for
the Indians in Bermuda. Berkeley intended to make Smibert professor
of fine arts. This Utopian scheme collapsed for lack of funds, but
Smibert had the practical judgment to marry an heiress and settle in
Boston, where he brought a new sense of realism to painting. Not for
nothing had he been Hogarth's companion in a London art school. In
Boston, Smibert was closely associated with Peter Pelham, an English
engraver and painter, who engraved six of Smibert's best portraits.[34]
Smibert's influence on painting was important. He helped popularize
art by holding an exhibition in Boston in 1730, and he maintained an
art shop where he sold painting materials, engravings, and prints—
which were much sought after. Many a household which could not
afford paintings had framed engravings to hang on the walls. More
important, however, was Smibert's influence on later—and greater—
American artists.

Another artist who achieved a reputation in the mid-eighteenth
century was Robert Feke, described in his death notice in 1767 as a
"mariner." Little is known of his life. He was a resident of Newport,
and is recorded as painting at various times there, in Philadelphia,
and in Boston. Less perceptive of character in his subjects than Smibert, he nevertheless displayed a high degree of craftsmanship, a keen
sense of color, and a vigor which he may have learned from some
English master. Many surviving portraits, including one of Benjamin
Franklin, are attributed to him. But portrait painters were growing
numerous in this period and even the shrewdest art historians have
difficulty distinguishing their work. Traveling artists from England
and Scotland were finding it profitable to visit the colonies and paint
prosperous merchants, parsons, and planters. Itinerant painters, both

[34] Henry W. Foote, *John Smibert, Painter* (Cambridge, Mass., 1950), p. 26.

native and foreign, skillful and primitive, made their way even to the back country and sold portraits—and occasionally "landskips"—to those Americans able to pay for them. One of the most industrious of these was Joseph Blackburn, a British painter of considerable grace, who traveled through the colonies from 1755 to 1761. Native artists, most of them imitating English contemporaries, plied their crafts with new diligence. Boston attracted more artists than other cities, even Philadelphia. Joseph Badger of Boston, who died in 1765 after a long career, was somewhat naïve and rigid in style, but he pleased Boston and a large number of his portraits survive. His work is occasionally confused with that of John Greenwood, who gave up Boston for Surinam in 1752.

Two American artists who attained international reputations emerged in the 1760's, but most of their work comes after our period, and their reputations were achieved in England. They are John Singleton Copley, born in Boston in 1738, and Benjamin West, born the same year at a country inn a few miles from Philadelphia. Copley's stepfather was Peter Pelham, the engraver. When West as a child began to draw birds and flowers, his father took him to the Philadelphia studio of a professional painter, William Williams, who showed an interest in the boy. Both Copley and West were boy prodigies and attained professional status before they were of age. By the time they were fifteen both had painted acceptable portraits. Copley's exhibition of his *Boy with the Squirrel* in London in 1766 helped to give him a reputation in England. West, who had combined portrait and sign painting, sailed from New York for Italy in 1760 and in 1763 took up his permanent residence in England. Copley went to England in 1774 and never came back. Like Henry James and the expatriates of the late nineteenth century, West and Copley felt that America was too barren of aesthetic interest and artistic examples for the full development of their talents. Their examples, however, profoundly influenced later American artists and stimulated the development of a more vigorous and versatile art in this country.

The painting that influenced the great majority of colonial people was not great art, nor even good art. All during the eighteenth century, journeymen painters supplied pictures of various sorts, at prices within the range of modest incomes. Itinerant craftsmen bearing canvases with figures ready-painted and the heads blank peddled portraits in the towns and among the plantations; they would hurriedly paint faces that resembled their subjects sufficiently to be salable. Much of the art work was done by house painters.

A certain B. Roberts advertised in Charleston in 1735 "to give notice to all gentlemen and others, that portrait painting and engraving, heraldry and house painting are undertaken and performed expeditiously in good manner, and at the lowest rates by B. Roberts." Two years later the same craftsman advertised "land-scapes for chimney pieces of all sizes," and in 1740 Mary Roberts recommended her own "face painting, well performed." [35] In Maryland, which had more Catholics than the other colonies, one A. Pooley in 1752 announced his readiness to do anything "in the limning way, history, altar pieces for churches, landscapes, views of . . . houses and estates, signs, or any other way of painting and also gilding." [36] Religious themes were not unknown even in Boston, at least in needlework for the home, as evidenced by an advertisement in the Boston *Gazette* for May 23, 1757, of a "chimney piece imitating Adam and Eve in Paradise, wrought with a needle after the best manner." [37] Prints and small pictures were common. John Welch of Hanover Street, Boston, "purposing to go for England in a short time," advertised household goods in the *Gazette* for April 24, 1758. Among the objects advertised were "A number of metzitinto prints, large and small pictures suitable for a stair-case." [38]

Even that portion of the population who could not buy prints and small pictures for the stairway were not devoid of artistic interest. Indeed, folk art and craftsmanship frequently managed to combine the useful and the aesthetically pleasing. Everyone had to have dishes, pottery or pewter, which often showed skill in design and workmanship. Those who could afford silver could find expert silversmiths in the towns. German potters in Pennsylvania brought the traditional patterns of the Rhineland, but gradually developed originality as they painted their ware with birds, beasts, and flowers typical of the New World. These potters also carried their skills to other regions, notably North Carolina.

Although large quantities of pewter and glass came from England,

[35] Prime, *Arts and Crafts,* p. 8.
[36] *Ibid.,* p. 7.
[37] Dow, *Arts and Crafts,* p. 115.
[38] *Ibid.,* p. 117.

some of it was made in this country. From the 1720's onward, local pewterers were advertising their wares in the newspapers, and much old pewter has survived to this day. A large amount of silver was fabricated in the colonies; silversmiths could be found in most towns, and a few were very ingenious artists. John Hull of Boston was a skilled silversmith who was authorized by the colony to mint coins.[39] John Coney and Jeremiah Dummer were early New England silversmiths of note.[40] Best remembered today of the Boston silversmiths, however, is Paul Revere, a versatile craftsman who, like some other silversmiths, combined that art with dentistry and advertised false teeth "that looks as well as the natural and answers the end of speaking."[41] Revere was also a skillful engraver.[42] Silversmiths in New York, Philadelphia, Newport, Annapolis, Charleston, and other towns developed distinctive styles and made American silver almost as popular as that imported from London. Much of it displayed originality and grace of design. A remarkable artist was Myer Myers of New York,[43] and some of the Philadelphia silversmiths like the famous Richardsons showed unusual artistry and versatility.[44] In their skill in working silver, the best American artists were the equal of any.

Glass was one of the first commodities manufactured in this country. Because of the fuel required in the making of glass, the promoters of colonization thought they might produce it cheaply in the New World, and they sent Italian glassmakers to Jamestown. The experiment failed and the making of glass never became a very profitable enterprise. But from time to time in various colonies, hopeful craftsmen opened "glasshouses" where they produced bottles, dishes, pitchers, goblets, windowpanes, and occasionally beads for use in the Indian trade. The most famous of the colonial glassmakers was Henry William Stiegel, who began operating a glassworks in Pennsylvania in 1763, and in the next year opened a factory at Mannheim near Lancaster. There for a

[39] Herman F. Clarke, *John Hull, a Builder of the Bay Colony* (Portland, Me., 1940), *passim.*

[40] See Frederick Clarke, *John Coney, Silversmith, 1655-1722* (Boston, 1932), and Frederick Clarke and Henry W. Foote, *Jeremiah Dummer, Colonial Craftsman and Merchant, 1645-1718* (Boston, 1935).

[41] Dow, *Arts and Crafts,* p. 55.

[42] Clarence S. Brigham, *Paul Revere's Engravings* (Worcester, Mass., 1954).

[43] Jeannette W. Rosenbaum, *Myer Myers, Goldsmith, 1723-1795* (Philadelphia, 1954).

[44] See the catalogue of an exhibition of Philadelphia silver, *Philadelphia Silver, 1682-1800,* published by the Philadelphia Museum of Art, 1956.

time Stiegel produced glass of a quality and design rarely seen before in America.

Painting on glass was a popular form of "art" that attracted the interest of both professionals and amateurs. Many homes displayed painted glass dishes, or paintings on clock faces and the heads of mirrors. Other household objects sometimes show the effort of an amateur with a paintbrush: chests, fire screens, and wooden panels to cover fireplaces in summer.

Ornamental metalwork flourished in certain areas, particularly among the Germans of Pennsylvania. These German craftsmen also made the famous squirrel rifles, beloved of the frontiersmen, guns which reached such perfection of workmanship that they deserve mention in any discussion of folk art. Weaving, quilting, and ornamental needlework were skills enjoyed by women in all regions. Certain localities were noted for their individual styles, but women everywhere were familiar with these basic household arts.

Busy as were colonial Americans, hard as was their lot on the successive frontiers of settlement, our ancestors made a great effort to improve the amenities of life. They were not "arty," but they managed to attain artistic excellence in many of the ordinary things of life. They achieved dignity in architecture, and they filled their houses with interior furnishings that combined the highest utility with aesthetic satisfaction. The inventories of their estates reveal a surprising number of objects, including many musical instruments,[45] that were intended to satisfy their aesthetic yearnings.

From the earliest times Americans demonstrated inventiveness, ingenuity, and skill in adapting older designs to the necessities of life in a new country. In their household equipment, furniture, utensils, and implements, the tendency was usually toward simplification in the direction of utility, but that simplification resulted in clarity of design and frequently achieved an aesthetic effect more appealing to modern taste than the elaboration of detail in sophisticated European styles. Colonial Americans bequeathed to later generations a tradition that has had an important influence in the artistic development of the nation.

[45] The advertisements of musical instruments were numerous. Cf. Dow, *Arts and Crafts,* p. 297, and Hennig Cohen, *The South Carolina Gazette, 1732–1775* (Columbia, S.C., 1953), pp. 100–106.

CHAPTER 10

Scientific Interest and Observation

THE DISCOVERY of the New World served as a stimulus to scientific observation and speculation. By the time of the English settlement at Jamestown, most of Europe had heard of the wonders of the countries overseas and were ready to believe anything. Curiosity about the flora and fauna of America was keen. The inhabitants of this world, their origin, their religion, and their relation to the rest of mankind were subjects that aroused endless discussion. Already in the accounts of travelers one could find indications of an incipient doctrine of the noble savage, or of the contradictory belief in the degradation of nature which more than two centuries later Buffon would publicize and Jefferson would refute. The mineralogy, botany, zoology, anthropology, and climatology of America were themes that excited the interest of explorers and settlers as well as stay-at-home Europeans. The earliest manifestation of scientific investigation in the New World quite logically centered upon natural history.

Because the scientific interest of Americans today is prevailingly utilitarian in motivation, it is worthy of note that utilitarianism predominated from the beginning. Next after geography and navigation, the science that most concerned the early explorers was mineralogy, if one may so describe sixteenth- and seventeenth-century methods of detecting precious metals. Human cupidity made the assayer of gold and silver a valued specialist. But precious metals were not the only resources sought by scientific investigators. Europeans quickly came to believe that America would provide many natural products of untold value to mankind. Who knew but that America might have medicines to heal all of man's ills? A belief in the efficacy of American herbs, minerals, and animal products stirred the curiosity of doctors and laymen who set out to discover the secrets of nature, particularly any mysteries that the Indians might possess. Still lingering in backward areas today is a faith in the recipes of "Indian doctors," snake oil, medicinal herbs, and other folk remedies popular since colonial days.

The contemplation of the curative powers of American products stirred a spirit of optimism in gouty and scrofulous Europeans. When John Frampton, an English merchant trading in Spain, wanted to give an enticing title to a translation of Nicholas Monardes' medicinal treatise, he called it *Joyful News out of the New Found World Wherein Is Declared the Rare and Singular Virtues of Diverse and Sundry Herbs, Trees, Oils, Plants, and Stones, with Their Applications, as well for Physic as Chirurgery, the Said Being Well Applied Bringeth Such Present Remedy for All Diseases, as May Seem Altogether Incredible* (1577). This book, widely read by Elizabethans, stimulated an interest in collecting American products that persisted until the end of the colonial period. Among other advice, Monardes commended tobacco as a cure-all for every ailment from worms to toothache and prescribed sassafras tea as an elixir of wonderful potency.

A book of general science by José de Acosta, inspired by experiences in the New World, was translated by Edward Grimston in 1604 as *The Natural and Moral History of the East and West Indies.* Grimston's translation popularized the learned Jesuit's systematic natural history and was influential in stimulating observations by English explorers and scientific-minded folk in the colonies.[1] Acosta's inclusive work was characteristic of many later treatises. He attempted to reconcile religion and new scientific observations, to explain obvious discrepancies in the works of Aristotle and other ancients, and to clarify apparent errors in the Church Fathers. Everything, from comment on the heavens as seen from the southern continent to a description of the tricks of monkeys and the virtues of the bezoar stone in the treatment of disease, found its way into this compendium, which started many

[1] Theodore Hornberger, "Acosta's *Historia Natural Y Moral De Las Indias:* A Guide to the Source and the Growth of the American Scientific Tradition," *University of Texas Studies in English* (Austin, Tex., 1939), pp. 139–162.

a seventeenth-century Englishman on his way to the acquisition of scientific knowledge.[2]

When Raleigh was projecting the colony that he settled on Roanoke Island in 1585, he included among the planters an artist, John White —who painted an extraordinary lot of water colors of the Indians— and a mathematician and scientist, Thomas Hariot, who wrote the first original English description of the country, *A Brief and True Report of the New Found Land of Virginia* (1588). Bibliographical interest in this rare book has been so great that we have sometimes forgotten that it provides personal observations by one of the best scientific minds of the day. Hariot's description, as his title promised, has the brevity and clarity of a good report. For example, in one short paragraph he gives a clear and vivid account of the Indians' method of planting corn, of how "beginning in one corner of the plot, with a pecker they make a hole wherein they put four grains with that care they touch not one another, (about an inch asunder) and cover them with the mold again: and so through out the whole plot, making such holes and using them after such manner: but with this regard that they be made in ranks . . ."[3] Hariot's botanical and zoological information shows the eye of an accurate man careful to distinguish between what he had seen himself and what was merely hearsay.

In the seventeenth century, specialization had not rigidly separated scientific knowledge into compartments. Natural philosophy covered the whole area of what today we would describe as the facts and theories of the natural sciences. Furthermore, every literate man felt that he could encompass natural philosophy in its various branches if he turned his mind to reading a few good books on the subject, beginning with Aristotle, Pliny, and Ptolemy, and coming on down through some up-to-date discussion of the curiosities of the New World. Scientific information of this kind was common among the better-educated pioneers who settled in the English colonies. They realized that a knowledge of botany, zoology, mineralogy, climatology, and medicine might mean the difference between success and failure of their ventures, and they often brought along the necessary books to supply such information.

Knowledge of the medical theories and practice of the day was widespread. Although the promoters of colonization tried to send along professional doctors and surgeons whenever they could, trained physicians were so scarce in the colonies that laymen often practiced the healing arts. Most colonial libraries had a book or two on medicine, surgery, and the compounding of drugs. Colonial men and women studied the books, listened to old wives' tales, picked up folk remedies, and prescribed for their families and friends. Occasionally a layman became so proficient that he assumed the title—and the emoluments— of a doctor of medicine and enjoyed considerable reputation for his medical learning. Sometimes a doctor came to the colonies boasting a degree from Leiden or Padua, but most of those calling themselves physicians or surgeons had assumed their titles after an apprenticeship to some doctor who imparted such knowledge as he possessed. Medical education was relatively informal and there were few legal impediments to hinder anyone who wished to dose his neighbors or set a broken bone. In 1729 the Virginia Council freed a Negro slave belonging to Mrs. Francis Littlepage of New Kent County in compensation for his revelation of medical secrets useful in the cure of diseases and the expelling of poisons.[4]

Several of the early settlers in Virginia are described in the records as physicians or surgeons. Captain John Smith thought he owed his life to Dr. Walter Russell, who applied a "precious oil" to a swelling caused by a sting ray. The injury had scared Smith so badly that he picked out a spot for his burial.[5] Smith prized his own medical knowledge. When an Indian was severely burned, Smith brought him back to life, to the astonishment of the victim's fellow tribesmen, by giving him a heavy dose of brandy. Dr. Lawrence Bohun, who came with Lord Delaware in 1610, appears to have been the first experimental scientist at Jamestown. He collected specimens, tested the medical value of native plants and mineral substances, and recommended sassafras so successfully that returning ships carried cargoes of the aromatic shrub to England. Bohun's successor, Dr. John Pott, was a

[4] *Virginia Magazine of History and Biography,* XXXIV (1926), 103–104, 408.

[5] Wyndham B. Blanton, *Medicine in Virginia in the Seventeenth Century* (Richmond, Va., 1930), p. 9.

more colorful if less laudable figure. He was responsible, it was charged, with trying to solve the Indian problem by poisoning a great number who came to Jamestown. He was also a bibulous soul whose interest in Indian corn as a source for an alcholic beverage transcended objective science.

The founding of Harvard College in 1636 paved the way for the organized study of scientific subjects. The curriculum set up by President Henry Dunster in the 1640's provided courses in arithmetic, geometry, physics, astronomy, and botany.[6] By modern standards, science occupied only a modest place in the curriculum, but the significant fact is that here in a new country the first college was making possible the study of scientific subjects and devoting about the same proportion of time to these topics as did Oxford and Cambridge.

With the caution characteristic of academic institutions everywhere, Harvard retained Aristotelian physics and Ptolemaic astronomy until the 1670's. To be on the safe side, the college gradually introduced newer theories parallel with the older systems. In 1671 students rebelled against lectures out of the scholastic texts of Johannes Magirus and were pacified with Adrian Heereboord's *Parallelismus Aristoteliscae et Cartesianae Philosophiae Naturalis* (1643) and other works with a more up-to-date point of view.[7] The teachings of Peter Ramus, Descartes, Gassendi, and other moderns slowly eroded Aristotelianism and made Harvard a center for the promulgation of Copernican and presently Newtonian science.

Although many learned men of the seventeenth century, in the colonies as elsewhere, lived and died in Ptolemaic orthodoxy, as early as 1659 a young Harvard graduate, Zechariah Brigden, published an almanac that expounded Copernican astronomy. President Chauncy of Harvard and Governor John Winthrop, Jr., of Connecticut were greatly pleased with this evidence of scientific thinking, but a few diehards thought it too advanced. Brigden's almanac was only one indication of the acceptance of the new astronomy. Other compilers of almanacs and writers on natural science followed the new theories.

An important influence in the dissemination of modern scientific ideas came in 1686 with the adoption at Harvard of Charles Morton's

[6] Theodore Hornberger, *Scientific Thought in the American Colleges, 1638–1800* (Austin, Tex., 1945), pp. 22–24. For a detailed discussion of the scientific curriculum at Harvard, see Samuel Eliot Morison, *Harvard College in the Seventeenth Century* (Cambridge, Mass., 1936), I, 208–251, 281–284.

[7] *Ibid.*, p. 233.

Compendium Physicae, a textbook on natural science prepared by the learned headmaster of Newington Green Academy, who emigrated to Massachusetts in the expectation of being elected president of Harvard. Morton's book, in the words of the historian of Harvard, "was the principal agent for spreading in New England the scientific discoveries of the 'century of genius,' and preparing people for the 'century of enlightenment.' His book was the first to inculcate among Harvard students that observing and curious attitude toward the physical world which, in modern times, marks the educated man." [8]

The "observing and curious attitude" was demonstrated by many colonials in the later seventeenth century, both North and South. The Royal Society, founded in 1662 for the purpose of collecting and studying scientific information from all the world, greatly stimulated scientific interest among Americans by enlisting correspondents in this country and by electing some of the most distinguished colonials as fellows of the Society. At least twenty-five colonial Americans, if one includes royal governors, were fellows of the Royal Society.[9] The insatiable curiosity of the Royal Society about the natural history of the New World prompted a constant stream of inquiries from its members, who solicited information and specimens from correspondents overseas and in turn supplied books, data, and sometimes instruments valuable to colonials. Some of the American fellows demonstrated as much scientific ability as their brethren in London.

The first fellow to be chosen from the colonies was John Winthrop, Jr., son of the governor of Massachusetts Bay and himself the perennial governor of Connecticut. Elected a fellow in 1663, Winthrop took a great interest in the Royal Society and was in frequent communication with its members, including Robert Boyle, Robert Hooke, and Isaac Newton. A student of alchemy, chemistry, metallurgy, astronomy, botany, and medicine, Winthrop, like most of his generation, was concerned with the practical application of his knowledge to the improvement of man's estate. In one letter to William Brereton, he even

[8] *Ibid.,* p. 249. Theodore Hornberger has edited Morton's *Compendium Physicae* in the *Publications of the Colonial Society of Massachusetts, Collections,* XXXIII (Boston, 1940).

[9] Raymond Phineas Stearns, "Colonial Fellows of the Royal Society of London, 1661–1788," *The William and Mary Quarterly,* 3rd Ser., III (1946), 208–268. An earlier article by Frederick E. Brasch, "The Royal Society of London and Its Influence upon Scientific Thought in the American Colonies," *The Scientific Monthly,* XXXIII (1931), 336–355, 448–469, is also useful.

suggests that the Royal Society might use its influence in helping him with "some proposals concerning a way of trade and bank without money." [10] His knowledge of metallurgy enabled him to establish iron mines and a foundry, and he also had a license for working lead, copper, tin, antimony, vitriol, alum, salt, and saltpeter. His skill in medicine brought inquiries from patients far afield, some of whom begged for a secret powder called "rubila" which Winthrop compounded. This prescription, believed to be a sovereign remedy for a variety of ailments, enjoyed a long fame. Years after Winthrop's death, Increase Mather wrote to his grandson asking for some of the magic medicine for the people of Boston. "I had the honor to be intimately acquainted with your honorable father and grandfather," Mather wrote. "They designed that excellent powder they called rubila should be a public benefit. . . . It is a principle of charity to my neighbors that has induced me to write these lines." [11]

Winthrop's personal influence and his library helped to disseminate scientific information. Many neighbors and friends borrowed books from him, and he was constantly writing to impart information to some distant acquaintance. John Alcock, physician of Roxbury, wrote in 1660 to thank Winthrop for the loan of a book, which had so stirred his interest that he was "willing to employ both money and friends to gain the skill and knowledge of it." [12] Winthrop's correspondence shows a persistent interest in the newest books on scientific subjects and a generosity in lending those books to kindred spirits. Cotton Mather was so impressed with his influence that he wrote in the *Magnalia* that "a blessed land was New England, when there was over part of it a governor who was not only a Christian and a gentleman, but also an eminent philosopher [i.e., scientist]. . . . But it was not unto New England alone that the respects of this accomplished philosopher were confined." [13]

Winthrop's example was followed by others. Gershom Bulkeley, for instance, a preacher, gave up his clerical vocation when his voice failed, settled at Glastonbury, Connecticut, about 1667, and took up the practice of medicine. Like Winthrop he brought together an ex-

---

[10] *Collections of the Massachusetts Historical Society,* 5th Ser., VIII (1882), 86–88.

[11] *Ibid.,* 6th Ser., V (1892), 380–381.

[12] *Ibid.,* 5th Ser., I (1871), 390.

[13] Cotton Mather, *Magnalia Christi Americana* (Hartford, Conn., 1853), I, 159.

cellent collection of scientific books which were available to his friends. His chemical apparatus also fascinated visitors to his laboratory.[14]

In the South William Byrd II displayed a scientific curiosity and purpose not unlike Winthrop's, and before the end of the seventeenth century he too became a member of the Royal Society and began the acquisition of scientific books for his excellent library at Westover. Like Winthrop he was interested in the practical application of science. Fancying himself something of a physician, he liked to prescribe for his neighbors and servants and was convinced that the herb ginseng was a wonderful cure-all. Author of *A Discourse Concerning the Plague, With some Preservatives Against it*—printed in London in 1721 as "By a Lover of Mankind"—Byrd used his medical learning to "extol the singular virtue of tobacco, in checking the contagion of the plague." [15] The most blatant advertisers of cigarettes in our time could go no further than Byrd in promoting the sale of Virginia tobacco by recommending it as a preservative of health and life.

Byrd began his career as a member of the Royal Society by contributing in 1697 "An Account of a Negro Boy That is Dappled in Several Places of His Body with White Spots" and for the rest of his life was in communication with members of the Society. In 1741, three years before his death, he wrote to Sir Hans Sloane protesting because his name had been left off the yearly list of the Royal Society, "of which I have the honor to be one of its ancientest members." [16] For more than thirty years Byrd had corresponded with Sloane and other distinguished scientists and had supplied information as well as animal, vegetable, and mineral specimens.

Scientific interest increased and matured as the seventeenth century drew to a close, and by the early years of the eighteenth century the colonies had a respectable number of "philosophers"—as scientists were then described—who could discourse learnedly about physics, chemistry, astronomy, medicine, and related subjects. An ancient heresy that the Puritans were opposed to experimental science and the new science generally is not borne out by the facts. The Puritans, it is

[14] W. R. Steiner, "Gershom Bulkeley," in C. E. Perry, *Founders and Leaders of Connecticut, 1633–1738* (Boston, 1934), pp. 128 ff.

[15] *Another Secret Diary of William Byrd of Westover, 1739–41. With Letters and Literary Exercises, 1696–1726*, ed. Maude H. Woodfin and Marion Tinling (Richmond, Va., 1942), p. 440.

[16] Louis B. Wright, *The First Gentlemen of Virginia* (San Marino, Calif., 1940), p. 332.

true, sought to demonstrate the handiwork of God in the wonders of nature, but they were not alone in this endeavor. William Byrd, for example, in his tract on the plague devoted considerable effort to showing the manifestation of God's will in the visitations of pestilence. The Puritans proved receptive to both Copernican astronomy and Newtonian physics. A suggestion that Puritans favored Copernican astronomy partly because they believed Catholics opposed it is found in a statement by Charles Morton accepting Galileo's confirmation of the new theories. "Only Papists were tender of declaring their mind too plainly in this matter," Morton asserted, "because the Pope (forsooth out of a private peck to Galilaeus) had from St. Peter's Chair condemned the opinion." [17] In Newton's assertion of the laws of nature, Puritans discovered proof of God's revelation of His immutable laws. Although some did not miss the mechanistic and materialistic implications of Newton, which were to disturb religious ideas throughout the century, Puritan casuistry enabled men like Cotton Mather, and later Jonathan Edwards, to turn Newton to their own philosophic purposes.[18]

During the first decades of the eighteenth century, American colleges began to pay more attention to scientific subjects. The first chair of science in an American college was established at the College of William and Mary in 1711 with the appointment of a certain Mr. LeFevre as professor of natural philosophy and mathematics. Unhappily LeFevre did little to advance knowledge because he soon fell victim to "an idle hussy" and strong drink, twin hazards which an academic man even in tolerant Williamsburg could not survive. Six years later William and Mary appointed the Reverend Hugh Jones, a man of probity, to teach courses in mathematics and natural philosophy. Since the students at William and Mary, the sons of Virginia planters, were directly concerned with the application of mathematics and scientific knowledge to the problems of existence, Jones emphasized arithmetic, algebra, geometry, surveying, and navigation.

A genuine advance in scientific instruction resulted from the establishment at Harvard in 1727 of an endowed chair of mathematics and natural philosophy through the generosity of Thomas Hollis of Lon-

---

[17] Morison, *Harvard College in the Seventeenth Century*, I, p. 219.
[18] Frederick E. Brasch, "Newtonian Epoch in the American Colonies (1680–1783)," *Proceedings of the American Antiquarian Society*, New Ser., LXIX (1939), 314–332; Theodore Hornberger, "The Effect of the New Science upon the Thought of Jonathan Edwards," *American Literature*, IX (1937), 196–207.

don. The first incumbent of the Hollis professorship was Isaac Greenwood, a Harvard graduate, who had gone to England to study divinity but wound up listening to lectures on mathematics and physics by disciples of Newton. Greenwood introduced new courses in mathematics at Harvard, published a textbook in arithmetic, and prepared a manuscript text in algebra. He also gave his students an indoctrination in Newtonian physics. But like LeFevre at William and Mary, Greenwood too was overtaken in drink and dismissed from his professorship.

Greenwood's successor was John Winthrop IV, who held the Hollis professorship from 1738 until his death in 1779. His course in natural philosophy provided the most advanced scientific instruction in North America in its time, and Winthrop was honored for his learning. One of his first steps after receiving the appointment was to procure a copy of Newton's *Principia,* which became his guide. Friends in England sent Winthrop books and "philosophical apparatus," including a telescope which had belonged to Edmund Halley, after whom a spectacular comet was named. Said to have been the first in America to teach Newton's fluxions (calculus), Winthrop stimulated a fresh interest in mathematics, theoretical speculation, and investigation. He gave an impetus to theoretical studies, or what today we would call "pure science," as distinguished from the mere practical application of knowledge. His astronomical observations attracted widespread attention. During his long career he published six pamphlets and contributed eleven papers to the Royal Society.[19] In recognition of his scientific contributions the University of Edinburgh conferred upon him the honorary degree of doctor of laws. With the progress made by Winthrop at Harvard academic training in science came of age in this country.

Other institutions made slower progress. Yale, more conservative than Harvard, held on to Aristotelian theories until well into the eighteenth century. An intellectual explosion, however, was set off by the arrival in New Haven of a shipment of books collected in England by Jeremiah Dummer, who had persuaded Newton, Halley, and other distinguished members of the Royal Society to contribute some of their own works. From these books, students and faculty alike gained a new vision of science and speculative philosophy. One of those affected was

[19] Brasch, "The Royal Society of London and Its Influence," *loc. cit.* See also I. Bernard Cohen, *Some Early Tools of American Science* (Cambridge, Mass., 1950).

Samuel Johnson, later to be president of King's College (Columbia), a member of the class of 1714. Between 1716 and 1719, Johnson, a tutor at Yale, undertook to revise mathematical instruction and introduced the study of algebra. From this time forward, scientific instruction improved at Yale.[20] One may also conjecture that the reading of Dummer's books helped persuade Johnson and others of his college generation to join the Anglican Church, an event that vastly disturbed Yale's orthodox Congregationalists.

Scientific speculation and experiment, however, were not such an exclusive academic monopoly in the seventeenth and eighteenth centuries as they are in our age. Individuals throughout the colonies developed their special interests, ordered books and apparatus from London, and communicated with like-minded people. Urban centers naturally offered the best opportunities for scientific discussion and the meeting of kindred spirits. Boston, Newport, New York, Philadelphia, and Charleston, South Carolina, were notable for the scientific interests of some of their citizens. At the turn of the century, the Cambridge-Boston region had a greater concentration of natural philosophers than any other part of the country, but by 1750 Philadelphia had taken the lead.

The concentration of learned clergymen in New England helps to explain the early and widespread interest in science in that region, for the clergy adapted science to their own pious purposes, not always realizing where their investigations might ultimately lead them. The most advanced scientific thinker among them was probably Cotton Mather,[21] son of Increase Mather, who also displayed keen interest in natural phenomena. Cotton Mather, for all his learning, exhibited a

[20] See Louis W. McKeehan, *Yale Science: The First Hundred Years 1701–1801* (New York, 1947). For evidence of Samuel Johnson's interest in science, see Herbert and Carol Schneider (eds.), *Samuel Johnson, President of King's College: His Career and Writings* (4 vols., New York, 1929), *passim;* and Theodore Hornberger, "Samuel Johnson of Yale and King's College: A Note on the Relation of Science and Religion in Provincial America," *New England Quarterly,* VIII (1935), 378–397.

[21] Cotton Mather's interest was wide-ranging and his observations were often acute. For his contributions to an understanding of plant genetics, see Conway Zirkle, *The Beginnings of Plant Hybridization* (Philadelphia, 1935), pp. 103–107. Mather's contributions to medical thinking are enumerated in Otho T. Beall, Jr., and Richard H. Shryock, *Cotton Mather, First Significant Figure in American Medicine* (Baltimore, 1954).

curious mixture of rationalism and superstitious credulity, as evidenced in his espousal of the witchcraft delusion in 1692.

The impact of the new science had produced a number of treatises in England by pious natural philosophers who sought to prove that science could be the handmaiden of religion. Robert Boyle's *Usefulness of Experimental Natural Philosophy* (1663) was typical of the school of natural theology, to which Cotton Mather in 1720 contributed *The Christian Philosopher*, a tract summarizing his own scientific beliefs and setting forth the thesis that science was an incentive to rather than an enemy of religion.[22]

Mather sent to the Royal Society a manuscript containing observations on rainbows, rattlesnakes, plants, and variations in the magnetic needle, along with a letter hinting that he would welcome election. So impressed were the members with his data that they elected him a fellow in 1713, and Mather characteristically became one of their most prolific contributors.

He also advanced his own scientific thinking by reading the papers of the Royal Society. Two months after publication of reports on the success of inoculation for smallpox, Mather was advocating the new technique in the Boston epidemic of 1721. Convinced by Mather's evidence, Dr. Zabdiel Boylston successfully inoculated his own son and two Negro servants. Although nearly three hundred Bostonians received inoculation during the year and only six died, the public outcry against Mather and Boylston was excessive and resulted in attempts at bodily violence. Nevertheless they stood their ground and continued to recommend and practice inoculation as a method of combating one of the most terrifying diseases of the day. Although the controversy that started in Boston broke out in other localities throughout the colonies where inoculation was tried, time eventually justified Mather's enlightened views.

If Cotton Mather was the most learned of the New Englanders, others were only a little behind him. Thomas Brattle, a wealthy Boston merchant, made such careful observations of Halley's comet in 1680 that Newton cited his data in the *Principia*. During the witchcraft hysteria at Salem, Brattle displayed an enlightened point of view, in

22 Theodore Hornberger, "The Date, Source, and the Significance of Cotton Mather's Interest in Science," *American Literature*, VI (1935), 413–420; and the same author's "Notes on the Christian Philosopher," in Thomas J. Holmes, *Cotton Mather, A Bibliography of His Works* (Cambridge, Mass., 1940), I, 133–138.

contrast to Mather's; his reasoned and calm plea for justice to the accused persons had the urbanity and rational approach characteristic of a scientific mind in the next century.[23] Brattle's brother William was elected to the Royal Society in 1713. Paul Dudley, a lawyer, sent to the Royal Society papers on a variety of subjects including the preparation of maple sugar; plant breeding of pumpkins, Indian corn, and squash; the habits and value of whales; and an account of New England's earthquakes, including the most recent, which occurred on October 29, 1727. In the latter paper Dudley explained the rhythmic motion of the earthquake as movements in the earth's crust—a far cry from the less enlightened notion that it merely represented God's angry shaking up of sinners. About a quarter of a century later Professor John Winthrop of Harvard further advanced thinking on the subject of earthquakes by comparing the waves of motion in the earth to musical vibrations.

During the first half of the eighteenth century, the rapid growth of Philadelphia, its broad tolerance, and the diversity of its citizens' background gave that city an intellectual vitality not equaled elsewhere in the colonies. James Logan, whose own interests in mathematics and physics had led him to import some of the latest books on these subjects, including Newton's *Principia,* opened his library to any intelligent reader and encouraged talented young men to pursue mathematical and scientific studies. Such an atmosphere was conducive to the development of a spirit of free inquiry, and it was no accident that a group of alert craftsmen under the leadership of Benjamin Franklin should establish in 1727 a society called the Junto whose purpose was discussion and intellectual stimulation. As Philadelphia grew into the greatest port in the colonies, its commercial ties with the outer world increased and the contacts of its merchants with businessmen abroad helped to open channels for the communication of ideas.

One of the most important of these intellectual intermediaries was Peter Collinson, a London merchant, who had been brought up a Quaker. Himself a member of the Royal Society and keenly interested in natural philosophy, Collinson served as agent for English virtuosos who wanted specimens from the New World. Through his business connections, he established contacts with American collectors and observers and assisted them in procuring books, materials, and instru-

[23] "Mr. Brattle's Account of the Witchcraft in the County of Essex, 1692," *Collections of the Massachusetts Historical Society,* V (1798), 61–80.

ments. About 1730, through the good offices of Joseph Breintnal, one of Franklin's Junto, Collinson learned about a promising young naturalist, John Bartram, a Philadelphia Quaker, who had been inspired to pursue botanical studies by James Logan, a botanist of some attainments himself. Collinson's correspondence with Bartram, which lasted until the former's death in 1768, proved mutually helpful. The extant letters provide an insight into the curiosity of Europeans about American natural history and the devotion of men like Bartram to the study of the world about them. Collinson, the Duke of Richmond, and Lord Petre each subscribed ten guineas a year for specimens which Bartram collected and sent them. In 1765 George III appointed Bartram botanist to the King at fifty pounds per year; the royal horticultural gardens were soon filled with plants, shrubs, and trees sent over by the indefatigable Quaker, who traveled at various times from the Great Lakes to Florida on collecting expeditions.

The letters exchanged between Collinson and Bartram are filled with acute scientific observations, as well as much of human interest. On one occasion Collinson urges his Quaker friend to be neat and careful of his dress on a journey into Virginia "and not appear to disgrace thyself or me; for . . . these Virginians are a very gentle, well-dressed people, and look, perhaps, more at a man's outside than his inside." [24] On another occasion Collinson banteringly reproves Bartram for having given away an old cap which he had sent him because it had a hole or two in it. At least the lining was new, and if Bartram had returned it, it would have "served me two or three years, to have worn in the country, in rainy weather." [25]

Bartram established a botanical garden on the Schuylkill River three miles from Philadelphia where he could cultivate and study specimens collected on his journeys. Scholarly in his approach, he learned Latin in order to read the works of the Swedish scientist, Linnaeus, the greatest botanist of the age. The fame of Bartram's knowledge of botany and other phases of natural history spread abroad. His reports to Collinson, his journals, and the specimens which he sent to Europe made his name familiar in scientific circles everywhere. Linnaeus called him the greatest contemporary "natural botanist" and sent his favorite student, Peter Kalm, to visit his garden and talk with him.

[24] William Darlington (ed.), *Memorials of John Bartram and Humphry Marshall* (Philadelphia, 1849), p. 89. Letter dated Feb. 17, 1737.
[25] *Ibid.*, p. 114. Undated letter of 1738.

Franklin had great respect for his knowledge and transmitted to Jefferson a suggestion made by Bartram for exploring the western portion of the continent, a suggestion that may have influenced Jefferson's plans for the Lewis and Clark expedition. Bartram's son William followed in his father's footsteps and became a naturalist of some note.

Bartram and his garden near Philadelphia served as a focus for a great deal of American interest in botany and related subjects. Most of the American naturalists were in communication with him, and he supplied them with information as well as materials.

Of all the colonial naturalists, Bartram is best remembered today, but others were not far behind him in contemporary fame. John Banister, of Charles City County, Virginia, an Anglican parson by profession, devoted himself to botany, zoology, and entomology, but his career was cut short in 1692 when a companion on an expedition to the Roanoke River accidentally shot him. He was in communication with John Ray, the English botanist, and supplied Ray and others with accurate descriptions of Virginia plants and animals. John Clayton, who was appointed attorney general for Virginia in 1705, planted a botanical garden and spent much time in the collection and study of plants. Specimens, drawings, and information which he supplied enabled John Frederick Gronovius of Leiden to prepare his *Flora Virginica* (1739–1743). Dr. John Mitchell, of Urbanna, Virginia, fellow of the Royal Society, wrote on botany, zoology, and medicine; he corresponded with Linnaeus, Gronovius, Collinson, and other Europeans interested in natural history. Dr. Cadwallader Colden, physician, merchant, scientist, and finally lieutenant governor of New York, supplied Linnaeus with descriptions of the flora of New York for publication in the transactions of the Royal Society of Upsala. His broad scientific interests also included medicine, mathematics, physics, and anthropology. Colden wrote on yellow fever, cancer, the "throat distemper" (diphtheria), the virtues of tar water, light, color, gravitation, and a variety of other topics, including *The History of the Five Indian Nations,* first published in 1727.

The career of Dr. Alexander Garden of Charleston, South Carolina, who gave his name to the gardenia, illustrates the community of interest of these eighteenth-century naturalists. A Scottish physician who settled in South Carolina shortly after he received a medical degree from Aberdeen in 1753, Garden was soon avidly studying the natural history of his adopted country. On a visit to New York in 1754 he met

Cadwallader Colden and saw in his library some of the latest works of Linnaeus. On the journey south from New York he visited John Bartram in Philadelphia and began a correspondence with Colden, Bartram, and John Clayton of Virginia. Soon he was also corresponding with the leading naturalists of Europe: Linnaeus, Gronovius, Collinson, and others. In 1763 he was elected a member of the Royal Society of Upsala and ten years later a fellow of the Royal Society of London. A Tory at the onset of the Revolution, he left South Carolina to die in London. Garden's observations of plants and animals were unusually accurate and many of his deductions were scientifically ahead of his time.

The community of interest displayed by the naturalists is indicative of the intellectual climate that induced Benjamin Franklin to propose in 1743 the establishment of the American Philosophical Society. Franklin had already been in communication with scientists throughout the colonies. Well acquainted with Bartram and his group, he had also been in correspondence with Collinson and other scientists in England and on the Continent. From his own experience and his knowledge of the amount of scientific interest dispersed through the colonies, Franklin realized that a society where information could be pooled and ideas exchanged would have immense benefits for the whole country. As he conceived his plan, the Society, centered in Philadelphia, would devote itself to the "promotion of useful knowledge." Although it was primarily designed to be utilitarian, mathematics and the more abstract sciences would have a place. Franklin thought that the Society could best serve mankind by collecting data on useful plants, animals, and minerals and by encouraging needed inventions. Kindred spirits agreed with Franklin, and by 1744 he had organized the American Philosophical Society with himself as secretary. Franklin was disappointed because some of the members were "very idle gentlemen," [26] but in 1769 the Philosophical Society united with the American Society, which had grown out of Franklin's old Junto, and henceforth became a more active and mature scientific organization.

On a trip to Boston in 1746, Franklin met a visiting Scot named Dr. Spence who had recently brought over an "electrical bottle," an early type of condenser, soon to be known as a Leyden jar. Excited by Spence's demonstrations, Franklin returned to Philadelphia and devoted himself with such zeal to electrical studies that within a few

[26] Carl Van Doren, *Benjamin Franklin* (New York, 1938), p. 141.

years he was known throughout the world as the first scientist in the American colonies.

Franklin set up a laboratory in his house and made improvements in the condensers and crude batteries then known. Retiring from his printing business in 1748, he now had leisure for study and experimentation which he turned to good advantage. He soon came to the conclusion that electricity generated in the laboratory and lightning from the clouds had the same properties. His letters to Collinson on the subject attracted the attention of other members of the Royal Society. In one of these letters, which Collinson had printed in the *Gentleman's Magazine* for May, 1750, Franklin characteristically made a suggestion for the practical application of the knowledge that he had accumulated through experimentation. This letter first suggested the use of lightning rods.[27]

Other letters to Collinson detailed Franklin's views on the identity of electricity and lightning, a proposed method of testing this theory, and observations made in his various experiments. These Collinson had printed in London in 1751 as *Experiments and Observations on Electricity, Made at Philadelphia in America, by Mr. Benjamin Franklin*. A reprint of this volume with additions came out in 1753 and again in 1760–62. It was translated almost immediately into French, and later into German and Italian. Franklin found himself famous overnight. Honors came fast. Harvard, Yale, and William and Mary made him honorary Master of Arts. The Royal Society awarded him the Copley Medal. In 1759 the University of St. Andrews conferred upon him the degree of doctor of laws and henceforth he was known as "Dr. Franklin," a title that pleased him immensely. In 1762 Oxford gave him the degree of doctor of civil law.

The test of Franklin's proposed method of drawing electricity from a cloud was first made in France, and Franklin himself in the summer of 1752 made his famous experiment with the kite.[28] Throughout the learned world, the excitement over electricity spread Franklin's fame. Many repeated his experiments, and at least one scientist, a Swede, lost his life drawing lightning from the clouds by Franklin's methods.

[27] *Ibid.*, pp. 159–160. See also I. Bernard Cohen, *Benjamin Franklin's Experiments* (Cambridge, Mass., 1941).

[28] See Van Doren, *Benjamin Franklin,* pp. 164–170, where the confusion in the chronology of Franklin's kite experiment, which has led some to doubt whether he performed it, is discussed in detail.

In the meantime, Franklin himself was busy persuading his fellow citizens that his studies would prove useful to any who cared to protect their houses and barns by the erection of lightning rods.

Electricity was not Franklin's only scientific interest. Throughout the rest of his life, even in the midst of political activity of great importance, he never forgot his "philosophical" studies, which included subjects as various as the habits of ants, the organisms in sea water, wind currents, eclipses, the causes of storm, and a hundred other matters which stirred his fertile imagination. A biographer appraising Franklin's experiments has observed that his contribution resulted from "a fundamental mind, which almost at once mastered the general problem as it then existed and went deeper into it than any observer had yet gone. He found electricity a curiosity and left it a science." [29] Although Franklin got amusement and entertainment out of his scientific studies, his activities went beyond the sort of thing relished by the virtuosos to something that we can dignify as scientific thinking. Always he expressed himself with admirable clarity, precision, and a disdain of learned humbuggery. "If my hypothesis is not the truth," he observed of himself, "it is at least as naked. For I have not with some of our learned moderns disguised my nonsense in Greek, clothed it in algebra, or adorned it with fluxions. You have it *in purus naturalibus*." [30]

Benjamin Franklin was not the only one of Philadelphia's craftsmen who acquired skill in scientific matters. Thomas Godfrey, a glazier and one of the original Junto, was befriended by his employer, James Logan, who encouraged him in mathematical and astronomical studies. Although Godfrey had little education, he showed a natural genius for these subjects. His chief accomplishment was the invention in 1730 of an improved mariner's quadrant for the determination of latitude. This is the quadrant named after John Hadley, who perfected one about the same time, possibly after hearing about Godfrey's instrument.

More distinguished than Godfrey was David Rittenhouse, a Philadelphia clock and instrument maker, who became an astronomer and mathematician of distinction. He was also interested in optics and in 1756 constructed a telescope which excited the admiration of his contemporaries. In 1767 he built an orrery—an instrument to show the relations of the various bodies in the solar system—which caused Jef-

[29] *Ibid.,* p. 171.
[30] *Ibid.,* p. 175.

ferson to comment that he had approached nearer to the Almighty "than any man who has lived from the creation to this day." [31] Rittenhouse's instruments as well as his theoretical knowledge helped to advance physical sciences and astronomy in the colonies and later in the new nation.

A combination of the practical and the theoretical characterized most scientific thinking in America in the eighteenth century. Jared Eliot of Connecticut was typical of his generation. Clergyman and physician, he also interested himself in experimental agriculture and mineralogy. His *Essay on Field Husbandry in New England,* published in six parts from 1748 to 1759, had considerable influence on farming. He and Ezra Stiles, later president of Yale, who also had many scientific interests, attempted to introduce silk culture in Connecticut. Eliot's *Essay on the Invention, or Art of Making Very Good, If Not the Best Iron, from Black Sea Sand* (1762) won a medal from the Royal Society. That Eliot was not merely a theoretician and a projector may be indicated by his own prosperity, which enabled him to endow a book fund at Yale.

Although colonial colleges gradually increased their emphasis on mathematics and natural philosophy as the eighteenth century wore on, scientific progress continued to center in nonacademic groups and in individuals like Bartram, Franklin, and Rittenhouse. Preachers, physicians, and lawyers as the most learned of society showed the greatest proficiency in scientific knowledge. From the mid-eighteenth century onward nearly every town of consequence had a few natural philosophers capable of performing an experiment with a Leyden jar, classifying the flora of the neighborhood according to Linnaeus, or giving an opinion on the cause of earthquakes or epidemics.

The vogue of natural philosophy was such that preachers even in their pulpits sometimes expounded God's wonders in the manner of a professor. Dr. Alexander Hamilton, physician of Annapolis, on a visit to Boston in July, 1744, found such a sermon at King's Chapel an annoyance. "He [the minister] gave us rather a philosophical lecture than a sermon . . ." Hamilton observes. "We had a load of impertinence from him about the specific gravity of air and water, the exhalation of vapours, the expansion and condensation of clouds, the operation of distillation, and the chemistry of nature. In fine it was

[31] Hornberger, *Scientific Thought in the American Colleges,* p. 67.

but a very puerile physical lecture and no sermon at all." [32] In the same year an anonymous poet published an "Epistle from Cambridge" in *The American Magazine and Historical Chronicle* lamenting that poets had been superseded in college by science:

> Now algebra, geometry,
> Arithmetic, astronomy,
> Optics, chronology, and statics,
> All tiresome parts of mathematics,
> With twenty harder names than these
> Disturb my brains, and break my peace.
> We're told how planets roll on high,
> How large their orbits, and how nigh;
> I hope in little time to know,
> Whether the moon's a cheese, or no.[33]

Itinerant lecturers with a few pieces of philosophical apparatus went up and down the land explaining their marvels to open-mouthed audiences. The day of popular science had dawned, and the interest in natural wonders would increase from that time until our own.

Physicians occupied an increasingly important place in the scientific advances of the eighteenth century. Philadelphia developed a distinguished group of doctors interested in medical research. Partly as a result of the humanitarianism of the Quakers, partly because of the intelligence of a group of physicians, the first modern hospital in the North American colonies was erected in Philadelphia in 1755. This hospital attracted medical students and served as a training school until the opening of the school of medicine at the College of Philadelphia (later the University of Pennsylvania) in 1765.

The new medical school got off to a good start under the direction of two Philadelphians who had received their medical degrees at the University of Edinburgh, Dr. John Morgan and Dr. William Shippen. A part of the commencement exercises at the College of Philadelphia in May, 1765, was *A Discourse Upon the Institution of Medical Schools in America* delivered by Dr. Morgan. This address paved the way for the establishment of the school. That fall the college announced lectures in anatomy and surgery by Dr. Shippen and lectures

[32] Carl Bridenbaugh (ed.), *Gentleman's Progress: The Itinerarium of Dr. Alexander Hamilton, 1744* (Chapel Hill, N.C., 1948), p. 110.
[33] Quoted by Hornberger, *Scientific Thought in American Colleges*, pp. 68–69.

in materia medica by Dr. Morgan. The first class of physicians graduated in 1768. The next year Dr. Benjamin Rush became professor of chemistry.[34] The first medical school in North America was launched on a career destined to be long and distinguished. Three years after the medical school opened in Philadelphia, King's College (later Columbia) established a medical school with six of the ablest physicians in New York as a faculty.

Medical instruction helped to disseminate scientific knowledge, not merely among the profession, but among laymen as well, for lectures and demonstrations were frequently open to the public—for a fee. Dr. Shippen, for example, sold tickets to his lectures in anatomy at five shillings per meeting and did his best to enlist popular interest in other medical subjects as well.[35] This he regarded as useful public education. Other physicians also welcomed lay auditors. Medical knowledge was regarded as a desirable addition to any eighteenth-century gentleman's training.

The zeal for lectures on all phases of natural philosophy increased as its wonders became more widely known. One of the most active lecturers was Ebenezer Kinnersley, a Pennsylvania Baptist preacher, who set out early in the 1750's to popularize Franklin's experiments in electricity. For the next thirty years Kinnersley lectured so constantly in various cities that in the popular consciousness he became a scientist better known than Franklin himself. During the 1760's and seventies in Philadelphia, lectures on popular science excited almost as much interest as the growing political controversies.[36]

The reorganization in 1769 of the American Philosophical Society Held at Philadelphia for Promoting Useful Knowledge gave that body an intercolonial status and increased the scope of its activities. In that year the *American Magazine or General Repository* published serially some of the Society's more important papers. The reception of the learned contributions was so encouraging that in 1771 the Society began publishing its *Transactions*. These papers attracted attention among learned men throughout the colonies and won the acclaim of European scientists. Rittenhouse's report on the transit of Venus was singled out for particular praise for the accuracy of its observations.

[34] Francis R. Packard, *History of Medicine in the United States* (New York, 1931), I, 341–362.
[35] Carl and Jessica Bridenbaugh, *Rebels and Gentlemen: Philadelphia in the Age of Franklin* (New York, 1942), pp. 280–281.
[36] *Ibid.*, p. 355.

As the political controversies with the mother country multiplied, the need for improving scientific knowledge and applying technological skills became even more apparent. As always, war would create necessities that would have to be met by the best scientific talent available. The foundation for self-sustaining technological developments had already been laid in the broad scientific interests of the American people. As the membership of the American Philosophical Society illustrated, scientific knowledge and skill were not confined to any group or class. Aristocrats, farmers, craftsmen, and artisans of all kinds shared the secrets of natural philosophy.

CHAPTER 11

The Press and Communications[1]

TO AN AGE accustomed as we are to daily newspapers, radio, and television, to overnight air flights between continents, and to instantaneous trans-world conversations, the inadequacy of communications in the early days of the American colonies is well-nigh incomprehensible. But our ancestors did not suffer from the same sense of urgency to know the latest happening. Perforce they were content to wait for a report from a chance traveler or a ship captain, a newsletter from abroad, or a budget of pamphlets sent by a bookseller who might be no nearer than London.

The spread of printing in the colonies was necessarily slow. A few people struggling to establish themselves in widely separated frontier communities do not constitute a profitable market for the output of the printing press. Demand was limited and distribution was difficult when even the most rudimentary postal service was lacking.

Nevertheless, the settlers who established their homes along the coastal fringe of North America were not oblivious to the importance of communications. As Englishmen established the nucleus of a new civilization they looked back to the mother country and hoped to keep open their lines of communication. At first they lacked both the material resources and the knowledge required to survive in the wilderness. For many years they continued to think of themselves as Englishmen and they maintained their contacts with relatives at home as best

[1] Various aspects of these topics are treated in other volumes in the series. The limitations of space forbid more than a brief summary here.

they could. Many of them sampled the New World and returned to live out their lives in England and to tell tall stories of their adventures beyond the seas.[2] The traveler who had seen something of North America or the West Indies and was eager to report his observations was a well-known character from the seventeenth century onward. He was a source of information on both sides of the Atlantic, and though his stories might be exaggerated and erroneous, they rarely failed to stimulate interest. The long tradition of English observations on America began with Thomas Hariot and has continued to the present day. Throughout the colonial period, explorers, speculators, businessmen, government officials, soldiers, sailors, preachers, missionaries, peddlers, adventurers, and rogues were constantly crossing the Atlantic and roaming about in the English colonies. All of them, even the rascals, helped to maintain the liaison between the colonies and the mother country.

The Atlantic Ocean was such a formidable barrier that it is a wonder that so many travelers willingly risked their lives to seek adventures overseas. A westward crossing of six to eight weeks was considered good, though occasionally the trip might be made in a month. The eastbound crossing usually took somewhat longer because of the prevalence of head winds. Unfavorable winds or periods of calm might delay ships for weeks or months. Even when a ship had made a quick crossing of the Atlantic, it might have to lie offshore for as long or longer than the overseas passage for a wind that would bring it into port. One ship reported a delay of twelve weeks off the Virginia capes while it battled westerly winds that prevented its making port.[3] During the first half of the seventeenth century, the route most favored was roughly the one Columbus followed: southward past the Canaries, across to the West Indies, and up the Atlantic coast, past Cape Hatteras—a very long way to Virginia, but one believed to insure favorable northeast trade winds. This was the route that Captain Christopher Newport took in the expedition that settled Jamestown in 1607, a voyage that required from late December to mid-May. By the end of the century, however, ship captains bound for either Virginia or New England for the most part had abandoned the long southern route and

[2] See, for example, William L. Sachse, "The Migrations of New Englanders to England, 1640–1660," *The American Historical Review*, LIII (1948), 251–278.

[3] Arthur P. Middleton, *Tobacco Coast: A Maritime History of Chesapeake Bay in the Colonial Period* (Newport News, Va., 1953), p. 6.

were following the northern track now used by transatlantic liners from New York to Southampton. The average time for this crossing was six to eight weeks.

As trade developed between the North American ports, the West Indies, and the rest of the world, ships carrying American sailors abroad and bringing foreign sailors to American ports were constantly on the increase. Boston, New York, Philadelphia, and Charleston became busy centers of commerce with the activities and distractions common to port towns. Though the colonial ports were not precisely centers of cosmopolitan culture, their communications with the rest of the world represented a broadening if not invariably an edifying experience.

The correspondence between colonials and their relatives overseas, between planters and merchants and their agents abroad, helped to keep Americans informed about the state of the world beyond their own shores. Individuals in the early years of the seventeenth century had to make such arrangements for the transport of letters as could be worked out with ship captains, but eventually a rudimentary postal system developed. The first organized effort for the transport of letters between New England and the mother country came in 1639, when Richard Fairbank, tavern keeper of Boston, agreed to accept responsibility for delivering letters from overseas left in his care.[4]

Since New England in the seventeenth century had more trade across the seas than the other colonies, it had the fastest mail service. Lord Cornbury, governor of New York, in 1702 complained of the slowness of the post between England and New York because of scanty sailings. To ensure speed, New York at this time had to send its overseas mail to Boston or Philadelphia, both of which had better service. Service from England to Virginia and Maryland was also slow and seasonal, depending upon the arrival of the tobacco fleets. Because of the dangers from pirates and privateers, the valuable tobacco ships were generally convoyed by men-of-war. That meant that the majority of the ships arrived at one time, normally in the autumn, and sailed together again for England in the spring or early summer.[5] A tobacco planter might write to his factor by a ship sailing in June and receive a reply, if lucky, by the returning tobacco fleet in November. Ships

[4] William Smith, *The History of the Post Office in British North America, 1639–1870* (Cambridge, 1920), p. 3.
[5] Middleton, *Tobacco Coast,* pp. 289–309.

other than those in the convoyed fleet occasionally called in the Chesapeake Bay region. These included coastal vessels and ships in the West
Indian trade, but most of the mail between the Chesapeake Bay
colonies and England was carried in the tobacco fleet. Mail service to
the Carolinas, and later to Georgia, made more use of ships in the
West Indian trade.

For most of the seventeenth century, postal service between the
various regions along the Atlantic seaboard was wholly inadequate, and
communication between Virginia and London was easier than between
Virginia and Boston or New York. An intercolonial postal system was
slow to develop, partly because during the early years of colonial settlement the several colonies had less reason to communicate with each
other than with England. Finally in 1691, Thomas Neale, Master of
the Mint in London, received a patent for twenty-one years to establish
post offices in the principal ports of British America. To serve as
deputy in the colonies, Neale appointed Andrew Hamilton, an energetic Scottish merchant of Edinburgh who in 1692 became governor of
New Jersey. Hamilton succeeded in establishing a reasonably effective
mail service in the northern colonies, but neither Maryland nor Virginia would agree to his terms and little was done to improve facilities
for letter delivery south of Philadelphia.

So little concern was felt by Virginia and Maryland over the need
for communicating with the colonies to the north that Andrew Hamilton in 1699 reported that an extension southward of the postal service,
already operating at a deficit, would result in further loss, for the
number of letters carried to and from Virginia and Maryland would
not amount to one hundred a year.[6] An amendment of the post-office
act in 1717 provided, among other things, for the establishment of a
post office in Virginia and made illegal the delivery of mail by ship
captains to the planters' own wharves, as had long been the practice.
Finding ways to evade the post-office act, Virginia made no consistent
effort to improve postal communications with the rest of the colonies
until after the middle of the eighteenth century.

The greatest advance in the postal service came about with the
appointment in 1753 of Benjamin Franklin and William Hunter of
Virginia as joint deputy postmaster generals. Franklin had already
served for fifteen years as postmaster at Philadelphia and the improve-

[6] Smith, *History of the Post Office,* p. 22.

ments in the postal service in the following twenty-one years of his tenure are attributed to his experience and acumen. Franklin improved facilities and cut down the time of mail delivery so much that a Philadelphia merchant might mail a letter to New York on one day and receive a reply the next. Mail to distant points, of course, was slower, but Franklin advertised that his post riders traveled by night as well as by day, and he reduced the time for delivery and reply between Philadelphia and Boston from three weeks to six days. There still remained the problem of mail to the southern colonies, and though this was less pressing, some improvements were made in the facilities.

Efforts were made during the various wars of the eighteenth century to ensure the safety of transatlantic mails and to improve their speed by establishing lines of fast, armed packet ships which would carry only mail. The first packet vessels plied between England and the West Indies; but when Braddock's defeat in 1755 convinced the British government that more rapid communication with North America was imperative, it established a packet line between England and New York which attempted to provide a monthly mail service.

The far South remained a problem. What to do about mails to South Carolina, for example, perplexed even Franklin. The packet line to the West Indies extended its service to Charleston in 1764, but so slow was this service that the British government in the same year provided a special service direct to Charleston. There were thus three packet services between England and the colonies: to New York, to Charleston, and to the West Indies. Mail sent from New York to Charleston via England often made better time than when sent by post riders south through Virginia. To the end of the colonial period, mail service between the far North and the far South remained a slow procedure. Fortunately—or unfortunately—the demand was not great.

The development of the earliest colonial newspapers was related to the growth of the postal system. The first successful paper, the *News-Letter,* was founded in 1704 by John Campbell, postmaster at Boston.[7] With a few interruptions it ran until the Revolution. Campbell's successor, William Brooker, in 1719 started the Boston *Gazette,* which was edited by the next four postmasters after Brooker. The postmaster

[7] The first newspaper, Benjamin Harris' *Public Occurrences,* which appeared in Boston on September 25, 1690, died with the initial issue because Harris had failed to get a government license. For an account of the early newspapers, see Frank Luther Mott, *American Journalism* (New York, 1949), pp. 3–64.

had the privilege of using the post for the distribution of his paper, a privilege that made postmaster-editors very cautious about criticizing the constituted authorities.

Toward the end of the colonial period, when a break with England appeared inevitable, many Americans became greatly concerned because the principal vehicle of communication was under the control of a government agency that might refuse to convey material containing comment unfavorable to the government. In effect this might mean a censorship of newspapers; for although newspapers in the colonies, as in England, were not regarded as mail, one of the perquisites of the deputy postmaster generals was the privilege of making contracts with publishers for the conveyance of newspapers by the post riders.

Not all of the colonial newspapers, of course, were in the hands of the postmasters and not all were so timid that they stayed out of trouble. Colonial printers frequently found it to their advantage to publish newspapers,[8] some of which were outspoken. One of the most courageous of the Boston printers in the early eighteenth century was James Franklin, half-brother of Benjamin, who learned the rudiments of his craft in James' shop. Spurred by a group opposed to the reigning authorities in Church and State, James Franklin in 1721 began publication of the *New England Courant*. He set out to entertain Boston with the publication of satirical commentary on local events and personalities and to engage in sensational controversies. He avoided stale foreign news and solicited sprightly contributions. Nothing like Franklin's paper had been seen previously in the colonies. When satirical comment on the royal government for tenderness to-

---

[8] See Lawrence C. Wroth, *The Colonial Printer* (1st ed., New York, 1931; 2nd ed., Portland, Me., 1938), and Wroth's section of *The Book in America* (New York, 1939). For very nearly contemporary accounts of the early presses, Isaiah Thomas, *The History of Printing in America* (1st ed., Worcester, Mass., 1810; rev. ed., Albany, N.Y., 1874), is still useful.

The colonial printers frequently combined the business of publishing and bookselling with the functions of what we would today call job printing. Pious works, schoolbooks, laws, tracts, and a variety of utilitarian books including almanacs made up the bulk of the publications issued by the American printers, though occasionally they ventured into belles-lettres. The volume of their work is attested by Charles Evans, *American Bibliography: A Chronological Dictionary of All Books, Pamphlets, and Periodical Publications Printed in the United States of America from the Genesis of Printing in 1639 Down to and Including the Year 1820 with Bibliographical and Biographical Notes* (12 vols., Chicago, 1903–34). Volume 12 brings the account only to 1799.

ward pirates finally landed James Franklin in jail, young Ben got out the paper alone. Franklin finally ceased publication of the Boston *Gazette* in 1726 and moved to Newport, Rhode Island, where in 1732 he founded the *Rhode Island Gazette,* which ran for only eight months. His son James, however, established the Newport *Mercury,* which lasted until long after the colonial period. James Franklin made a major contribution to American journalism by popularizing the familiar essay type of commentary which had already gained wide currency in both England and America through the *Tatler* and *Spectator* papers. A part of Ben Franklin's apprenticeship consisted in imitating Addison's essays.

Among other important Boston papers were Samuel Kneeland's *New England Weekly Journal* (1727–41), which enlisted the services of some of the intellectuals whom Franklin had offended, and Thomas Fleet's *Evening Post* (1735–75), one of the liveliest journals of the day.[9]

Philadelphia's first newspaper was established in 1719 by William Bradford, progenitor of a dynasty of printers, under the title of *The American Weekly Mercury.* It ran for thirty years and served as a medium for criticizing the conservative government dominated by the Quakers. A rival to Bradford's *Mercury* was founded in 1728 by Samuel Keimer, a religious enthusiast, with the impossible title of *The Universal Instructor in All Arts and Sciences and Pennsylvania Gazette.* To provide the instruction Keimer began reprinting serially Ephraim Chambers' *Cyclopaedia* and Defoe's *Religious Courtship.* Bradford would have had no cause to worry about competition if Benjamin Franklin had not bought out Keimer the following year.

Franklin had modern ideas about journalism. He threw out the encyclopedia and Defoe, and cut the title to the *Pennsylvania Gazette.* Then with fresh type and a new make-up, he set out to entertain as well as to instruct his readers. So successful was the *Gazette* that it ran until 1815. Franklin's prosperity as a printer helped to spread that craft, for apprentices trained in his shop scattered abroad to set up print shops and newspapers. In some instances Franklin helped finance them. The most distant—and one of the best—of the papers of this sort was the *South Carolina Gazette,* established in Charleston in 1732

[9] The essential facts about every newspaper published in the colonies can be found in the monumental work of Clarence Brigham, *History and Bibliography of American Newspapers, 1690–1820* (2 vols., Worcester, Mass., 1947).

by one of Franklin's printers, Thomas Whitmarsh. When Whitmarsh died the next year, Franklin sent another of his workmen, Louis Timothée, to succeed him. Though South Carolina had at least three other colonial papers, the *South Carolina Gazette* was the most successful and lasted until 1775.[10]

William Bradford, who had learned caution from frequent encounters with the Quakers of Philadelphia, founded New York's first newspaper, the New York *Gazette* (1725–44), a journal that played safe and remained dull for the whole of its tedious existence. More sprightly and provocative was John Peter Zenger's *Weekly Journal,* established in 1733. Zenger boldly meddled in politics and took sides against unpopular Governor William Cosby. When Zenger's attacks became too violent, the authorities in November, 1734, threw him into jail, but allowed him to continue to edit his paper for the next nine months. His trial, which began on August 4, 1735, has been interpreted as a landmark in the history of the freedom of the American press, but its influence was less extensive than we have been led to believe. Actually publishers and printers in New York and elsewhere continued to struggle with official censorship long after the Zenger trial.[11] Zenger was defended by a famous lawyer, Andrew Hamilton of Philadelphia, who argued that the jury had the right to decide whether the sense of Zenger's articles constituted seditious libel. After listening to a moving address, the jury returned a verdict of "Not guilty" and Zenger went free amidst the cheers of the spectators.

Among several other papers that flourished in New York, the liveliest was the result of a partnership between Benjamin Franklin and James Parker. In 1743 Parker brought out the first issue of the New York *Weekly Post-Boy,* changed four years later to the New York *Gazette or Weekly Post-Boy,* under which designation it lasted until 1773. Parker expanded beyond New York and founded the *Connecticut Gazette* at New Haven in 1755 and the *Constitutional Courant* in 1765 at Woodbridge, New Jersey. The *Courant* published the famous device of the snake with the motto "Join or die."

[10] For a very useful discussion of this paper, and sidelights on colonial journalism, see Hennig Cohen, *The South Carolina Gazette, 1732–1775* (Columbia, S.C., 1953).

[11] The latest and best-balanced discussion of the Zenger trial will be found in Richard B. Morris, *Fair Trial* (New York, 1952), pp. 69–95. See also Livingston Rowe Schuyler, *The Liberty of the Press in the American Colonies before the Revolution* (New York, 1905).

The agrarian colonies on Chesapeake Bay were slow to acquire either printing presses or newspapers. The first successful printer was William Parks, who in 1726 established a press at Annapolis and began publishing the *Maryland Gazette*, and in 1730 founded the *Virginia Gazette*. After a somewhat halting start, the *Maryland Gazette* was taken over in 1745 by Jonas Green and lasted until the nineteenth century. The *Virginia Gazette* under a succession of editors flourished until 1778.

The only foreign-language periodicals in the colonies to survive for any considerable period were German papers published in Pennsylvania. Christopher Sauer in 1739 began a quarterly journal, later to become a monthly, and finally a weekly, the *Germantowner Zeitung*, which continued until 1777. Heinrich Müller published *Der Wochentliche Philadelphische Staatsbote* (1762–79), which reflected the religious and pacifist views of a majority of the Pennsylvania Germans.

Although Benjamin Franklin, William Bradford, and others tried to found magazines, the colonies were not yet ready to support such periodicals. The one having the longest life was *The American Magazine and Historical Chronicle*, edited in Boston from 1743 to 1746 by Jeremiah Gridley, a literary lawyer. Although Gridley found some local contributions, he was forced to fill out his pages with material reprinted from English journals. The newspapers of the day provided such opportunity as was needed by would-be authors of essays and verse.

Before the end of the colonial period every region had local newspapers which supplied some outlet for popular expression and provided a means of informing the public about what was going on in the world beyond their own towns and villages. The political controversies between the colonies and the mother country, which culminated in the Stamp Act of 1765, had a profound effect upon the press, and the press in turn played an important part in fanning the fires of revolt. If the government of George III had deliberately set out to offend the most vocal portion of the American public, it could not have succeeded better than by a placing a stamp tax on paper and legal documents, thus offending both publishers and lawyers.[12]

[12] A discussion of the role of the newspapers in the coming of the Revolution is outside the scope of the present volume. It is worth noting, however, that between 1763 and 1775 the number of newspapers in the colonies doubled in

Intercolonial travel and communication greatly increased during the eighteenth century. The colonial wars caused militiamen to forget for a moment provincial boundaries and to venture beyond their own borders. In periods of peace, peddlers, traders, and miscellaneous travelers made their way along the trails and tracks of the Atlantic seaboard. With the accumulation of wealth, the prosperous began to look for resorts where they could experience a change of climate and refresh their spirits with gossip and social activities. As early as the 1730's, Southerners discovered that Newport, Rhode Island, was a desirable refuge from the ague and fever of their own torrid summers. A summer migration by ship regularly set out from Charleston, South Carolina, and summer visitors to Newport also came from other towns along the coast, and from the West Indies.[13] By the beginning of the second half of the eighteenth century, colonial Americans were beginning to know one another in a way that had not existed in earlier periods.

The eager pioneer was also probing the unknown country beyond the mountain barriers. Traders and explorers were bringing back tales of good land to be had for the taking, tales that stirred men's blood and set them on their travels toward the romantic dream of a better world somewhere beyond the village or clearing where the present found a daring colonist. News of the opportunities in the back country needed no newspaper or penny post. It was reported around camp fires, in taverns, at church, and wherever men and women gathered. In the study of communications in the colonial period one should not

response to the need for expression during the controversies. See Philip David, *Propaganda and the American Revolution, 1763–1783* (Chapel Hill, N.C., 1941), p. 225 *et passim*.

The growing acuteness of the controversies between Great Britain and her colonies at the very end of the colonial period made speedy communication between all of the colonies essential. In the year 1774 the colonies began an agitation to abrogate postal arrangements made by the British government and to establish an independent intercolonial system; in the following year the Continental Congress passed a resolution recommending the establishment of a new postal system. Benjamin Franklin naturally was chosen postmaster general and at once set about creating a system that would make intelligence between the colonies more effective. The reformed postal system of course influenced the circulation of newspapers.

[13] For details of the popularity of Newport, see Carl Bridenbaugh, "Colonial Newport as a Summer Resort," Rhode Island Historical Society, *Collections*, XXVI (1933), 1–23. See also "Baths and Watering Places of Colonial America," *The William and Mary Quarterly*, 3rd Ser., III (1946), 151–181.

overlook the importance of grapevine news, for it had a great importance in stimulating the travel toward the West.

The news of western lands affected the speculator and the real-estate promoter, who first came into his own in the eighteenth century and has been a potent force in American life ever since. He amplified the news and spread it further, and hoped to reap a profit from the public interest.

The gregariousness of Americans has been a noticeable quality since the beginning, and various agencies catered to their need to get together. The church of course has always been a great factor in American social life in addition to its purely religious function. For generations after the colonial period, the country church continued to be the one place where members of a rural community could meet and exchange information. Other agencies in the colonial period were also important. The taverns were informal clubs and gathering places for men. They served as a focal point for all comers and frequently were the places of meeting for civic bodies, committees, and councils of one kind and another.[14] On muster days, the militia converged on the nearest tavern, and on election days the tavern was the busiest spot in the community. Its influence as a source of information and communication can hardly be overestimated. Before the middle of the eighteenth century, coffeehouses were flourishing in the principal towns, as in London, and were the resorts of merchants, businessmen, politicians, and others who had use for a convenient meeting place. The coffeehouse was also a popular place for auctions, real-estate sales and transfers, and a variety of other business transactions.[15]

The improvements in the roads during the eighteenth century made travel between the colonies much easier than in the earlier days when Indian trails were the only semblance of overland roadways. By 1744, when Dr. Alexander Hamilton made a journey from Annapolis to the North, through New York to Albany, then from New York to York, Maine, and eventually back home to Annapolis, he found roads that often surpassed the highways of Great Britain, which he had experienced before coming to America. The country was far from primitive,

[14] See Elise Lathrop, *Early American Inns and Taverns* (New York, 1926); Alice Morse Earle, *Stage-Coach and Tavern Days* (New York, 1935); and Edward Field, *The Colonial Tavern* (Providence, R.I., 1897).

[15] Carl Bridenbaugh, *Cities in the Wilderness* (New York, 1938) and *Cities in Revolt* (New York, 1955), *passim*.

and although he reports both good and bad roads, and facilities for entertaining the traveler as ranging from comfortable to meager, the amazing thing about his narrative is the revelation of the network of communications in all of the regions traversed: roads, ferries, and bridges that made communication between the principal towns easy by the standards of that day. The roads in summer were dusty, and in winter they were deep in mud, a condition that made the Pennsylvanians take pride in the rockiness of their own roads;[16] but nevertheless, it was now possible for a traveler to make a tour, as Hamilton did, merely for his health and pleasure. Hamilton made the trip on horseback, but most of the roads could be traversed by carts, wagons, chaises, and coaches. One of Hamilton's friends, whose doctor would not let him ride horseback, joined him in Philadelphia, making the journey from Annapolis partly by water and partly by chaise.[17] By Hamilton's time, there was also available to the traveler a precursor of the highway guides of today, published in 1732 as *The Vade Mecum for America: or, A Companion for Traders and Travellers,* a little volume that provided information about roads, gave the names of taverns, and listed tables of distances.

Although coaches were used in the colonies in the later years of the seventeenth century, they did not become common until the eighteenth century, and then only the well-to-do could afford them. Indeed, the ownership of wheeled vehicles for pleasure was regarded as evidence of conspicuous wealth. By the mid-eighteenth century, coaches, chariots, chaises, chairs, and various types of two-wheeled vehicles were in fairly common use. Coaches for hire were obtainable in the principal towns. "Stage wagons" rather than stagecoaches appear to have been the earliest form of public vehicular transportation between towns,[18] but by the 1750's stagecoach lines were being developed, especially in New England, and connections between stagecoaches and packet-boat lines made communication between the principal towns easier than ever before.[19]

The development of the interior had at first depended upon accessibility by water, but gradually other forms of transportation made

[16] *Gentleman's Progress. The Itinerarium of Dr. Alexander Hamilton, 1744,* ed. Carl Bridenbaugh (Chapel Hill, N.C., 1948), p. 15.
[17] *Ibid.,* p. 3.
[18] Earle, *Stage-Coach and Tavern Days,* p. 265.
[19] Bridenbaugh, *Cities in Revolt,* pp. 55–57, 289–290.

trade with the back country profitable. Traders like William Byrd I sent pack trains far into the Indian country to exchange pots, pans, guns, and rum for furs and hides. From Charleston, South Carolina, a little later, pack trains went deep into the Cherokee territory beyond the mountains to trade for deerskins. When the Germans and the Scotch-Irish began to settle the interior regions of Pennsylvania, Maryland, and Virginia, some means of getting the products of the soil to market became imperative. The Germans particularly were skillful farmers, and their corn, wheat, cured meats, cattle, and other farm products were in great demand in Philadelphia for the export trade. To give an outlet for the wealth of produce grown by these thrifty farmers, Pennsylvanians built the Great Philadelphia Wagon Road, which after the mid-eighteenth century, according to Professor Bridenbaugh, was the "most important and heavily thronged highway in all America . . . running west to Lancaster, then turning southward to York, winding on into the Valley of Virginia, and finally debouching through a gap onto the Carolina Piedmont." [20] The Germans developed the covered wagon, known as the "Conestoga wagon" because apparently farmer-craftsmen along Conestoga Creek first made them. This roomy, high-wheeled vehicle, pulled by stout horses, could carry a heavy load of produce over the roughest roads. For a century after its creation, the Conestoga wagon would help to transform the face of America. By 1765 it was estimated that Pennsylvania had at least twenty thousand wagons, and Philadelphia on market days was choked with them.[21] The Conestoga wagon or its equivalent came into use in other parts of the country, and by the end of the period wagon trains were making their way from Philadelphia through the Valley of Virginia to the Carolina back country. From the Carolina highlands wagons took produce to the seaport of Charleston, until by 1770 three thousand wagons were engaged in this traffic. No longer was transportation confined to the waterways. Men were building roads and opening up the country for wagon and coach traffic.

By the middle of the eighteenth century, contacts had multiplied, not merely between the separate colonies, but with Europe as well. A variety of agencies contributed to the broadening of American horizons. These included the growing number of American students who were going to England and Scotland for their education, the exchange

[20] *Ibid.,* p. 57.
[21] *Ibid.,* p. 265.

of letters and information between European and American scientists, the activities of religious groups, the communications established between English and American printers, and the boom in business which brought English and Scottish merchants to this country and increased the ramifications of American overseas trade. All of the urban portions of America had some contacts with the great world beyond the seas, and towns like Boston, New York, Philadelphia, and Charleston were becoming quite cosmopolitan in their interests.[22]

Travelers from Europe were on the increase. Between 1700 and the outbreak of the Revolution, more than eight hundred of these visitors wrote down accounts of their impressions, which, remarks Michael Kraus, "mixed the veracious with the fallacious in proportions familiar to travellers since Herodotus." [23] The great proportion of these visitors were British, but a large number of Germans and Frenchmen also came to visit a country which had provided a refuge for many of their countrymen. The accounts of some of these visitors provide valuable information about conditions that they observed. For example, Peter Kalm, who came as an emissary of the Royal Swedish Academy of Sciences, kept a detailed journal that illustrates the interest of a trained scientific observer. Many of the travelers were missionaries and agents of religious bodies. The Quakers and Lutherans were particularly zealous in keeping up with their brethren in the colonies. Perhaps the greatest influence conducive to travel was the peace established in 1763, which, for the time at least, promised greater safety on the seas and greater opportunities on land. The end of the colonial period saw a country very different from the thinly settled strip of disconnected British territories that even by the last years of the seventeenth century still seemed to have a precarious hold on the American continent. By 1763, these territories were stronger, more unified, and in relatively close contact with one another and with Europe. They were less remote in mind and spirit from the rest of the world than were some of the more isolated counties of England.

[22] For detailed treatment of the growing contacts between Europe and the colonies see Michael Kraus, *The Atlantic Civilization: Eighteenth Century Origins* (Ithaca, N.Y., 1949), *passim.*
[23] *Ibid.,* p. 37.

Bibliography[1]

Chapter 1

Much has been written about the social structure of the southern colonies. One of the best of the older studies is that by Ulrich B. Phillips, *Life and Labor in the Old South* (Boston, 1929). A more recent study is Thomas J. Wertenbaker, *The Old South: The Founding of American Civilization* (New York, 1949). Suggestive chapters are to be found in Leonard W. Labaree, *Conservatism in Early American History* (New York, 1948). The background of Virginia society is studied in Thomas J. Wertenbaker, *Patrician and Plebeian in Virginia* (Charlottesville, Va., 1910), and *The Planters of Colonial Virginia* (Princeton, N.J., 1922); Philip A. Bruce, *Social Life of Virginia in the Seventeenth Century* (2nd ed., Lynchburg, Va., 1927); and Louis B. Wright, *The First Gentlemen of Virginia: Intellectual Qualities of the Early Colonial Ruling Class* (San Marino, Calif., 1940). Useful sidelights will be found in Arthur P. Middleton, *Tobacco Coast: A Maritime History of Chesapeake Bay in the Colonial Era* (Newport News, 1953).

Contemporary revelations of upper-class life in Virginia may be found in Robert Beverley, *The History and Present State of Virginia,* ed. Louis B. Wright (Chapel Hill, N.C., 1947); *The Secret Diary of William Byrd of Westover, 1709–1712,* ed. Louis B. Wright and Marion Tinling (Richmond, Va., 1941); *Another Secret Diary of William Byrd of Westover, 1739–1741,* ed. Maude H. Woodfin and Marion Tinling (Richmond, Va., 1942); *Letters of Robert Carter, 1720–1727,* ed. Louis B. Wright (San Marino, Calif., 1940); *Journals and Letters of Philip Vickers Fithian, 1773–1774,* ed. Hunter D. Farish (Williamsburg, Va., 1943); Hugh Jones, *The Present State of Virginia,* ed. Richard L. Morton (Chapel Hill, N.C., 1956); and Louis Morton, *Robert Carter of Nomini Hall: A Virginia Tobacco Planter of the Eighteenth Century* (Williamsburg, Va., 1941).

For life in Maryland in the eighteenth century, an excellent treatise is Charles A. Barker, *The Background of the Revolution in Maryland* (New

[1] Further references will be found in footnotes to the individual chapters. To save space, some items previously mentioned are not repeated in the bibliography.

Haven, Conn., 1940), which provides bibliographical information about original source material. Suggestive also is *Gentleman's Progress. The Itinerarium of Dr. Alexander Hamilton, 1744,* ed. Carl Bridenbaugh (Chapel Hill, N.C., 1948).

For South Carolina, useful material may be found in the early chapters of David D. Wallace, *South Carolina: A Short History, 1520–1948* (Chapel Hill, N.C., 1951), and Mrs. St. Julien Ravenal, *Charleston: The Place and the People* (New York, 1927). Frederick P. Bowes, *The Culture of Early Charleston* (Chapel Hill, N.C., 1942), is brief but valuable.

The best account in print of an aristocratic landholder in New York is Dixon Ryan Fox, *Caleb Heathcote, Gentleman Colonist: The Story of a Career in the Province of New York, 1692–1721* (New York, 1926). Useful for the areas covered are Aubrey C. Land, *The Dulanys of Maryland* (Baltimore, 1955); Marion Buckley Cox, *Glimpse of Glory: George Mason of Gunston Hall* (Richmond, Va., 1954); and Ella Lonn, *The Colonial Agents of the Southern Colonies* (Chapel Hill, N.C., 1945).

Chapter 2

Documentary material on the rise of New England families may be found in the various historical and antiquarian publications. Most important are the *Collections* and *Proceedings* of the Massachusetts Historical Society, the *Proceedings* of the American Antiquarian Society, the Essex Institute *Historical Collections,* the *Publications* of the Colonial Society of Massachusetts, the *New England Historical and Genealogical Register,* and the *New England Quarterly.* The best documented and most useful work dealing with general conditions affecting the artisan and craftsmen groups is Richard B. Morris, *Government and Labor in Early America* (New York, 1946). The scope of this book is wider than the title would indicate and the references in the copious footnotes are invaluable. More specialized is Abbot E. Smith, *Colonists in Bondage: White Servitude and Convict Labor in America, 1607–1776* (Chapel Hill, N.C., 1947). Marcus W. Jernegan, *Laboring and Dependent Classes in Colonial America, 1607–1783* (Chicago, 1931), is still a useful guide. See also Carl Bridenbaugh, *The Colonial Craftsman* (New York, 1950). Valuable for the light it throws on attitudes toward business and trade is Samuel E. Morison, *Builders of the Bay Colony* (Boston, 1930). The chapter on "The Colonial Background," in his *The Maritime History of Massachusetts, 1783–1860* (Boston, 1921), is also helpful.

Several histories of merchant families provide insights into general conditions of trade and commerce: James B. Hedges, *The Browns of Providence Plantations: Colonial Years* (Cambridge, 1952); William T. Baxter, *The House of Hancock: Business in Boston, 1724–1775* (Cambridge, Mass., 1945);

and James D. Phillips, *The Life and Times of Richard Derby, Merchant of Salem, 1712 to 1783* (Cambridge, Mass., 1929).

Bernard Bailyn, *The New England Merchants in the Seventeenth Century* (Cambridge, Mass., 1955), provides a brief bibliography. Frederick B. Tolles, *Meeting House and Counting House: The Quaker Merchants of Colonial Philadelphia, 1682–1763* (Chapel Hill, N.C., 1948), emphasizes the cultural interests of the great Philadelphia merchants. Information about the mercantile societies in Boston, New York, Newport, Philadelphia, and Charleston may be found in Carl Bridenbaugh, *Cities in the Wilderness, 1625–1742* (New York, 1938) and *Cities in Revolt, 1743–1776* (New York, 1955). Among many special studies of the rise of merchant families, the following may be mentioned: Margaret E. Martin, *Merchants and Trade of the Connecticut River Valley, 1750–1820,* Smith College *Studies in History,* XXIV, Nos. 1–4 (1938–39); Virginia D. Harrington, *The New York Merchant on the Eve of the Revolution* (New York, 1935); Mary A. Hanna, *Trade of the Delaware District before the Revolution,* Smith College *Studies in History,* II, No. 4 (1917); Margaret S. Morriss, *Colonial Trade of Maryland, 1689–1715* (Baltimore, 1914); Arthur P. Middleton, *Tobacco Coast: A Maritime History of Chesapeake Bay in the Colonial Era* (Newport News, Va., 1953); and Harold C. Syrett, "Private Enterprise in New Amsterdam," *The William and Mary Quarterly,* 3rd Ser., XI (1954), 536–550. Further references may be found in Merrill Jensen, *English Historical Documents: American Colonial Documents to 1776* (London, 1955), in the bibliographical introductions to the relevant sections, especially pp. 315–321. Information on the English background of certain of the ideas and attitudes of the merchant class may be found in Louis B. Wright, *Middle-Class Culture in Elizabethan England* (Chapel Hill, N.C., 1935) and *Religion and Empire: The Alliance Between Piety and Commerce in English Expansion, 1558–1625* (Chapel Hill, N.C., 1943).

Chapter 3

The most significant attempt yet made to determine the national origins of the American white population at the end of the eighteenth century is the *American Council of Learned Societies Report of the Committee on Linguistic and National Stocks in the Population of the United States* (1927), published in the *Annual Report of the American Historical Association for the Year 1931* (Washington, 1932). This study, which analyzed the first census of 1790 on the basis of the linguistic evidence in proper names, concluded that previous estimates of the English element in the population were too high. This work supersedes conclusions in William S. Rossiter, *A Century of Population Growth . . . 1790–1900* (Washington, 1909). The *ACLS Report* also has a useful bibliography of works dealing with national origins in the period before 1790, pp. 325–359.

Books and articles on the various racial and national groups who have peopled America are legion. Many of them are written with more enthusiasm than objectivity. One of the best books on foreign immigration, with a useful bibliography, is Marcus L. Hansen, *The Atlantic Migration, 1607–1860* (Cambridge, Mass., 1940). Thomas J. Wertenbaker, *The Founding of American Civilization: The Middle Colonies* (New York, 1949), devotes more space to non-British influences than is usually found in general histories, particularly to the evidence in architecture and domestic arts.

For the various nationalities treated in this chapter, the following titles will be found useful. The French: Gilbert Chinard, *Les Réfugiés Huguenots en Amérique* (Paris, 1925); Lucian J. Fosdick, *French Blood in America* (New York, 1906); Charles W. Baird, *History of the Huguenot Emigration to America* (New York, 1885); J. B. Laux, *The Huguenot Element in Pennsylvania* (New York, 1896); Arthur H. Hirsch, *The Huguenots of Colonial South Carolina* (Durham, N.C., 1928); Howard M. Jones, *America and French Culture* (Chapel Hill, N.C., 1927); *Transactions of the Huguenot Society of South Carolina* (1889 to date); Arthur G. Doughty, *The Acadian Exiles* (Toronto, 1916); and Oscar W. Winzerling, *Acadian Odyssey* (Baton Rouge, La., 1955). Dutch: Maud Wilder Goodwin, *Dutch and English on the Hudson* (New Haven, 1919); Alexander C. Flick (ed.), *History of the State of New York* (New York, 1933), Vol. I; Ellis L. Raesly, *Portrait of New Netherland* (New York, 1945); Edmund B. O'Callaghan, *History of New Netherland* (2 vols., New York, 1846–48). Swedes and Finns: A. B. Benson and M. Hedin (eds.), *Swedes in America, 1638–1938* (New York, 1938); Amandus Johnson, *The Swedish Settlements on the Delaware . . . 1638–1664* (2 vols., Philadelphia and New York, 1911); *The Swedes and Finns in New Jersey*, American Guide Series (Bayonne, N.J., 1938); Evert A. Louhi, *The Delaware Finns, or, the First Permanent Settlements in Pennsylvania, Delaware, and Western New Jersey* (New York, 1925); John H. Wuorinen, *The Finns on the Delaware, 1638–1655* (New York, 1938). The Germans: Albert B. Faust, *The German Element in the United States* (2 vols., New York, 1927); Ralph Wood (ed.), *The Pennsylvania Germans* (Princeton, N.J., 1942); Harry M. and Margaret B. Tinkcom and Grant M. Simon, *Historic Germantown*, American Philosophical Society, *Memoirs*, No. 39 (Philadelphia, 1955); Frank R. Diffenderffer, *German Immigration into Pennsylvania through the Port of Philadelphia* (Lancaster, Pa., 1900); Charles Henry Smith, *Mennonite Immigration into Pennsylvania* (Norristown, Pa., 1929); Paul A. Wallace, *The Muhlenbergs of Pennsylvania* (Philadelphia, 1950); Levi Oscar Kuhns, *The German and Swiss Settlements of Colonial Pennsylvania* (New York, 1914); W. A. Knittle, *Early Eighteenth Century*

Palatine Emigration (Philadelphia, 1937); Ada L. F. Snell, *Palatines along the Mohawk and Their Church in the Wilderness* (South Hadley, Mass., 1948); Hermann Schuricht, *History of the German Element in Virginia* (Baltimore, 1900); G. D. Bernheim, *History of the German Settlements and the Lutheran Church in North and South Carolina* (Philadelphia, 1872); Carl Hammer, *Rhinelanders on the Yadkin; The Story of the Pennsylvania Germans in Rowan and Cabarrus* (Salisbury, N.C., 1943); Adelaide L. Fries (ed.), *Records of the Moravians in North Carolina* (Raleigh, N.C., 1922); Adelaide L. Fries, *The Moravians in Georgia, 1735–1740* (Raleigh, N.C., 1905); Dieter Cunz, *The Maryland Germans, A History* (Princeton, N.J., 1948). There is also an extensive literature on the colonial Germans in the various historical periodicals, particularly the Pennsylvania German Society *Proceedings*. Both Faust and Dieter Cunz have detailed bibliographies that are helpful. The Jews: Lee Max Friedman, *Pilgrims in a New Land* (Philadelphia, 1948), contains a valuable bibliography of the subject, on which there is an extensive literature; Lee Max Friedman, *Early American Jews* (Cambridge, Mass., 1934); Peter Wiernik, *History of the Jews in America from the Period of the Discovery of the New World to the Present Time* (New York, 1931); Anita L. Lebeson, *Jewish Pioneers in America, 1492–1848* (New York, 1931). Useful and concise information with a discriminating bibliography is supplied by Abram V. Goodman, *American Overture: Jewish Rights in Colonial Times* (Philadelphia, 1947).

Patriotic and filial zeal has produced a vast literature concerned with the Scots who settled in America. Much of it is written *con amore* and must be used with care. An excellent book is Wayland F. Dunaway, *The Scotch-Irish of Colonial Pennsylvania* (Chapel Hill, N.C., 1944), which throws light on the other colonies, and contains a discriminating bibliography. Highly useful are the articles in a special issue of *The William and Mary Quarterly*, 3rd Ser., XI (April, 1954), under the general title of "Scotland and America," particularly George Shepperson, "Writings in Scottish-American History: A Brief Survey," and Jacob M. Price, "The Rise of Glasgow in the Chesapeake Tobacco Trade, 1707–1775."

Among older books, Henry J. Ford, *The Scotch-Irish in America* (Princeton, N.J., 1915), is one of the best. Charles A. Hanna, *The Scotch-Irish or The Scot in North Britain, North Ireland, and North America* (2 vols., New York, 1902), is a compendium of information. Concise and helpful is George F. Black, *Scotland's Mark on America* (New York, 1921). Lyman H. Butterfield, *John Witherspoon Comes to America* (Princeton, N.J., 1953), is both instructive and entertaining.

Chapter 4

The most complete bibliography of American religious history is that by

Peter G. Mode, *Sourcebook and Bibliographical Guide for American Church History* (Menasha, Wis., 1921). William Warren Sweet, *Religion in Colonial America* (New York, 1949), provides a succinct account and a bibliography. The religious motivations behind the early colonial ventures are discussed in Louis B. Wright, *Religion and Empire: Piety and Commerce in English Expansion, 1558–1625* (Chapel Hill, N.C., 1943). Useful for the background of English Puritanism are William Haller, *The Rise of Puritanism . . . 1570–1643* (New York, 1938) and *Liberty and Reformation in the Puritan Revolution* (New York, 1955); Marshall M. Knappen, *Tudor Puritanism* (Chicago, 1939); and W. K. Jordan, *The Development of Religious Toleration in England* (4 vols., Cambridge, Mass., 1932–41). Other background information is available in Louis B. Wright, *Middle-Class Culture in Elizabethan England* (Chapel Hill, N.C., 1935), and Thomas Cuming Hall, *The Religious Background of American Culture* (Boston, 1930).

The literature on the various religious groups is so extensive that only a selection can be given. Particularly helpful are Elizabeth H. Davidson, *The Establishment of the English Church in Continental American Colonies* (Durham, N.C., 1936); William W. Manross, *A History of the American Episcopal Church* (New York, 1935); William S. Perry (ed.), *Papers Relating to the History of the Church in Virginia, A.D. 1650–1776* (privately printed, 1870) and *Historical Collections Relating to the American Colonial Church* (5 vols., Hartford, Conn., 1870–1873); George M. Brydon, *Virginia's Mother Church* (Richmond, Va., 1947); Stephen B. Weeks, *The Religious Development in the Province of North Carolina*, Johns Hopkins University Studies, 10th Series, V–VI (Baltimore, 1892); Reba C. Strickland, *Religion and the State in Georgia in the Eighteenth Century* (New York, 1939); Sister Mary Augustina Ray, *American Opinion of Roman Catholicism in the Eighteenth Century* (New York, 1936); E. E. Beardsley, *The History of the Episcopal Church in Connecticut* (New York, 1865); and Frank J. Klingberg, *Anglican Humanitarianism in Colonial New York* (Philadelphia, 1940).

Information about Dr. Thomas Bray's activities will be found in a series of articles by Samuel C. McCulloch in the *Historical Magazine of the Protestant Episcopal Church* (1945–46).

The literature concerning the New England Puritans is voluminous and repetitious. A short essay by Charles M. Andrews, "Historic Doubts," *Publications of the Colonial Society of Massachusetts, Transactions,* 1930–33, XXVIII (1935), 280–294, is a salutary introduction to the Puritan tradition. Of the older works, the following are among the most useful: Henry M. Dexter, *Congregationalism of the Last Three Hundred Years, As Seen in its Literature* (London, 1879); Williston Walker (ed.), *Creeds and Platforms of Congregationalism* (New York, 1893), *A History of the Congregational Churches in the United States* (New York, 1894), and *Ten New England*

Leaders (New York, 1891); and, for the Antinomian controversy, Charles Francis Adams, *Three Episodes in Massachusetts History* (Boston, 1892). Much incidental information on the religious attitudes of the Puritan colonies will be found in Samuel E. Morison, *The Founding of Harvard College* (Cambridge, Mass., 1935) and *Harvard College in the Seventeenth Century* (Cambridge, Mass., 1936). Puritan theology is treated in minute detail in Perry Miller, *Orthodoxy in Massachusetts, 1630–1650: A Genetic Study* (Cambridge, Mass., 1933); *The New England Mind* (New York, 1939); and *The New England Mind: From Colony to Province* (Cambridge, Mass., 1953). A brief and more general work is Herbert W. Schneider, *The Puritan Mind* (New York, 1930). Also useful are Joseph Haroutunian, *Piety versus Moralism: The Passing of the New England Theology* (New York, 1932); Babette May Levy, *Preaching in the First Half Century of New England History* (Hartford, Conn., 1945); and Kenneth Murdock, *Increase Mather, the Foremost American Puritan* (Cambridge, Mass., 1925), which gives a compendium of information about the whole Mather group. A list of the Mathers' publications will be found in Thomas J. Holmes, *Increase Mather, a Bibliography of His Works* (2 vols., Cleveland, 1931) and *Cotton Mather: a Bibliography of His Works* (3 vols., Cambridge, Mass., 1940). Roland G. Usher, *The Pilgrims and Their History* (New York, 1918), is a standard work.

The best account of the Puritans is to be derived from their writings. A convenient anthology is Perry Miller and Thomas H. Johnson (eds.), *The Puritans* (New York, 1938). Cotton Mather, *Magnalia Christi Americana* (London, 1702), ed. Thomas Robins (2 vols., Hartford, Conn., 1853–55), is a quarry of information. Cotton Mather's Diary in the *Collections of the Massachusetts Historical Society*, 7th Series, VII–VIII (1911–12), gives an amazing insight into the mind of a Puritan clergyman. The documents in the *Winthrop Papers*, which the Massachusetts Historical Society began publishing in *extenso* in 1929, furnish diverse and valuable information. Samuel Eliot Morison (ed.), *Of Plymouth Plantation, 1620–1747. By William Bradford, Sometime Governor Thereof* (New York, 1952), is the latest and best edition.

For Roger Williams and religious developments in Rhode Island, Samuel H. Brockunier, *The Irrepressible Democrat: Roger Williams* (New York, 1940), is a good factual treatment. Perry Miller, *Roger Williams: His Contribution to the American Tradition* (Indianapolis, 1953), includes excerpts from Williams' own writings, which have also been printed in the *Publications of the Narragansett Club*, I–VI (1866–74).

The religious history of New York is discussed in the appropriate sections of the *History of the State of New York*, ed. Alexander C. Flick (10 vols.,

New York, 1933–37). Frederick J. Zwierlein, *Religion in New Netherland . . . 1623–1664* (Rochester, N.Y., 1910), is a useful account.

The best discussion of the Quakers is Rufus M. Jones, *The Quakers in the American Colonies* (London, 1911). Wayland F. Dunaway, *The Scotch-Irish of Colonial Pennsylvania* (Chapel Hill, N.C., 1944), provides a comprehensive bibliography of the early Presbyterians on the expanding frontier. German religionists in Pennsylvania and in other colonies are discussed in the first ten chapters of Albert B. Faust, *The German Element in the United States* (2 vols., New York, 1927). Dieter Cunz, *The Maryland Germans* (Princeton, N.J., 1948), supplies a useful bibliography. The histories of the various German sects compose a large literature. Among the most useful are Julius F. Sachse, *The German Sectarians of Pennsylvania, 1708–1742: A Critical and Legendary History of the Ephrata Cloister and the Dunkers* (Philadelphia, 1899), and C. H. Smith, *The Mennonite Immigration to Pennsylvania in the Eighteenth Century* (Norristown, Pa., 1939).

Significant interpretation and new information on the Presbyterians will be found in Leonard J. Trinterud, *The Forming of an American Tradition: A Re-Examination of Colonial Presbyterianism* (Philadelphia, 1949). See also Guy Soulliard Klett, *Presbyterians in Colonial Pennsylvania* (Philadelphia, 1937). John M. Mecklin, *The Story of American Dissent* (New York, 1934), gives a good account of early Baptists as well as other dissenting sects.

The most convenient discussion of Roman Catholics in the colonies is that by John G. Shea, *The Catholic Church in Colonial Days* (New York, 1886). See also Thomas O'Gorman, *A History of the Roman Catholic Church in the United States* (New York, 1895), and John T. Ellis, *A Select Bibliography of the History of the Catholic Church in the United States* (New York, 1947). Treatments of early American Jewish history are found in Lee M. Friedman, *Early American Jews* (Cambridge, Mass., 1934), which provides a bibliography; and Jacob R. Marcus, *Early American Jewry: The Jews of New York, New England and Canada, 1649–1794* (2 vols., Philadelphia, 1951).

Early American revivalism is treated in several specialized treatises. Charles H. Maxson, *The Great Awakening in the Middle Colonies* (Chicago, 1920), has a useful bibliography. Wesley M. Gewehr, *The Great Awakening in Virginia, 1740–1790* (Durham, N.C., 1930), is a well-documented monograph with a bibliography. Ola Elizabeth Winslow, *Jonathan Edwards, 1703–1758: A Biography* (New York, 1930), is a useful factual biography with three chapters on the Great Awakening. A recent study by Perry Miller, *Jonathan Edwards* (New York, 1949), concentrates on Edwards' ideas and theology. The commentary by Clarence H. Faust and Thomas H. Johnson in *Jonathan Edwards: Representative Selections,* American Writers Series (New York, 1935), is succinct and accurate.

For the special topics indicated, the following volumes are useful: Evarts B. Greene, *Religion and the State: the Making and Testing of an American Tradition* (New York, 1941); Arthur L. Cross, *The Anglican Episcopate and the American Colonies* (New York, 1902); H. J. Eckenrode, *Separation of Church and State in Virginia: a Study in the Development of the Revolution* (Richmond, Va., 1910); and Alice M. Baldwin, *The New England Clergy and the American Revolution* (Durham, N.C., 1928).

Chapter 5

Most of the general histories of education give scanty attention to the colonial period. Perhaps the best of these is Paul Monroe, *Founding of the American Public School System; a History of Education in the United States, from the Early Settlements to the Close of the Civil War Period* (New York, 1940). Highly useful for its concise information about education in the colonial period and the European background are the earlier portions of Richard Hofstadter and Walter P. Metzger, *The Development of Academic Freedom in the United States* (New York, 1955).

The best approach to education in the southern colonies is to be found in Edgar W. Knight (ed.), *A Documentary History of Education in the South before 1860* (Chapel Hill, N.C., 1949), Vol. I, and *Public Education in the South* (Boston, 1922). The most thorough study of seventeenth-century education is Samuel Eliot Morison, *The Founding of Harvard College* (Cambridge, Mass., 1935) and *Harvard College in the Seventeenth Century* (2 vols., Cambridge, Mass., 1936). Despite Morison's major concern with Harvard, and with higher education, these volumes are indispensable for an understanding of educational theory and practice on various levels in the colonial period. For divergent interpretations, see Winthrop S. Hudson, "The Morison Myth Concerning the Founding of Harvard College," *Church History,* VIII (1939), 148–159; and James J. Walsh, *Education of the Founding Fathers of the Republic; Scholasticism in the Colonial Colleges; a Neglected Chapter in the History of American Education* (New York, 1935). Useful for the light that it throws on early secondary education is Pauline Holmes, *A Tercentenary History of the Boston Public Latin School, 1635–1935* (Cambridge, Mass., 1935). See also Walter H. Small, *Early New England Schools* (Boston, 1914); Elmer E. Brown, *The Making of Our Middle Schools* (New York, 1903); and Clifford K. Shipton, "Secondary Education in the Puritan Colonies," *The New England Quarterly,* VII (1934), 646–661. Lists of schools and schoolmasters without much interpretation may be found in Robert F. Seybolt, *The Public Schools of Colonial Boston, 1635–1775* (Cambridge, Mass., 1935), and *The Private Schools of Colonial Boston* (Cambridge, Mass., 1935). Seybolt's *Apprenticeship and Apprentice Education in Colonial New York and New England* (New York, 1917) is criticized by

Marcus W. Jernegan in *Laboring and Dependent Classes in Colonial America, 1607–1783* (Chicago, 1931), p. 235, note 36, for inaccuracy and failure to consult colonial codes of law.

Still useful for information about the educational beginnings in the separate colonies are the pamphlets issued more than half a century ago by the United States Bureau of Education as "Circulars of Information." Among the best are Bernard C. Steiner, *History of Education in Connecticut* (Washington, 1893) and *History of Education in Maryland* (Washington, 1894); Lyman P. Powell, *The History of Education in Delaware* (Washington, 1893); David Murray, *History of Education in New Jersey* (Washington, 1899); William H. Tolman, *History of Higher Education in Rhode Island* (Washington, 1894); and Herbert B. Adams, *The College of William and Mary* (Washington, 1887). Similar in purpose and scope is Edward McCrady, Jr., "Education in South Carolina Prior to and during the Revolution," *South Carolina Historical Society Collections,* IV (1887), 7–15. For education in New York, succinct treatments may be found in the appropriate chapters in Alexander C. Flick (ed.), *History of the State of New York* (10 vols., New York, 1933–37), Vols. II and III. Still helpful is Daniel J. Pratt, *Annals of Public Education in the State of New York from 1626 to 1746* (Albany, N.Y., 1872). For Rhode Island, see Thomas B. Stockwell, *History of Public Education in Rhode Island, from 1636 to 1876* (Providence, 1876). For Pennsylvania, the most comprehensive study is James Mulhern, *A History of Secondary Education in Pennsylvania* (Philadelphia, 1933). See also appropriate chapters in *Historic Philadelphia . . . Papers Dealing with Its People and Buildings,* issued as Part I, Vol. 43, of the *Transactions of the American Philosophical Society* (Philadelphia, 1953). Information about the academies preceding the founding of Princeton, as well as the early years of the college, is to be found in Thomas J. Wertenbaker, *Princeton, 1746–1896* (Princeton, 1946). The beginnings of Yale are related in Rollin G. Osterweis, *Three Centuries of New Haven, 1638–1938* (New Haven, 1953). Detailed but poorly organized is Edwin Oviatt's *The Beginnings of Yale (1701–1726)* (New Haven, 1916). The best history of the University of Pennsylvania is Edward P. Cheyney, *History of the University of Pennsylvania, 1740–1940* (Philadelphia, 1940). Much detail for the early period is to be found in Thomas H. Montgomery, *A History of the University of Pennsylvania from Its Foundations to A.D. 1700* (Philadelphia, 1900). The most recent and detailed history of Columbia University is Dwight C. Miner, *Two Centuries of Columbia University* (2 vols., New York, 1954).

From a vast literature dealing with special topics in the field of education, the following will be found useful: Edmund G. Goebel, *A Study of Catholic Secondary Education during the Colonial Period* (New York, 1937); Colyer Meriwether, *Our Colonial Curriculum, 1607–1776* (Washington, 1907);

George E. Littlefield, *Early Schools and School-Books of New England* (Boston, 1904); Elizabeth P. Gould, *Ezekiel Cheever, Schoolmaster* (Boston, 1904); Arthur W. Brayley, *Schools and Schoolboys of Old Boston* (Boston, 1894); W. W. Kemp, *The Support of Schools in Colonial New York* (New York, 1913); J. P. Corry, "Education in Colonial Georgia," *Georgia Historical Quarterly*, XVI (1932), 136–145; H. P. Thompson, *Thomas Bray* (London, 1954); Frank J. Klingberg, *Carolina Chronicle: The Papers of Commissary Gideon Johnston, 1707–1716* (Berkeley, 1946); David D. Oliver, *The Society for the Propagation of the Gospel in the Province of North Carolina*, James Sprunt Historical Publications, IX, No. 1 (Chapel Hill, N.C., 1910); Albert F. Gegenheimer, *William Smith, Educator and Churchman, 1727–1803* (Philadelphia, 1943); Wyndham B. Blanton, *Medicine in Virginia in the Eighteenth Century* (Richmond, Va., 1931); Archibald Malloch, *Medical Interchange between the British Isles and America before 1801* (London, 1946); Whitfield Bell, Jr., "Philadelphia Medical Students in Europe, 1750–1800," *Pennsylvania Magazine of History and Biography*, LXVII (1943), 1–29; Richard B. Morris, *Studies in the History of American Law with Special References to the Seventeenth and Eighteenth Centuries* (New York, 1930); Marcus W. Jernegan, *Laboring and Dependent Classes in Colonial America, 1607–1783* (Chicago, 1931); Richard B. Morris, *Government and Labor in Early America* (New York, 1946); Abbot Emerson Smith, *Colonists in Bondage: White Servitude and Convict Labor in America, 1607–1776* (Chapel Hill, N.C., 1947).

Chapter 6

The historical and antiquarian journals are filled with articles dealing with records of the ownership of books and libraries in colonial America. The library journals also contain a considerable number of historical articles of varying quality.

An excellent introduction to the literary learning of New Englanders is Thomas Goddard Wright, *Literary Culture in Early New England, 1620–1730* (New Haven, 1920). The literary culture of early Virginia is treated by Louis B. Wright, *The First Gentlemen of Virginia* (San Marino, Calif., 1940). For the identification of books read by Virginians, see also the same writer's "The 'Gentleman's Library' in Early Virginia: The Literary Interests of the First Carters," *The Huntington Library Quarterly*, I (1937), 3–61; and "Richard Lee II, A Belated Elizabethan in Virginia," *ibid.*, II (1938), 1–35. For the literary interests of Maryland, see Joseph T. Wheeler, "Booksellers and Circulating Libraries in Colonial Maryland," *Maryland Historical Magazine*, XXXIV (1939), 111–137; "Thomas Bray and the Maryland Parochial Libraries," *ibid.*, 246–265; "Reading and Other Recreations of Marylanders, 1700–1776," *ibid.*, XXXVIII (1943), 37–55, 167–180.

For a further discussion of Dr. Thomas Bray's work, see Samuel C. McCullough, "Dr. Thomas Bray's Commissary Work in London, 1696–1697," *The William and Mary Quarterly*, 3rd Ser., II (1945), 333–348; "The Importance of Dr. Thomas Bray's *Bibliotheca Parochialis*," *Historical Magazine of the Protestant Episcopal Church*, XV (1946), 50–59; Bernard Steiner, "Rev. Thomas Bray and His American Libraries," *The American Historical Review*, II (1896), 59–75; and H. P. Thompson, *Thomas Bray* (London, 1954). Material on early libraries in America will be found in C. Seymour Thompson, *Evolution of the American Public Library, 1653–1876* (Washington, 1952), and in Jesse H. Shera, *Foundations of the Public Library* (Chicago, 1949), which has a selected bibliography.

The following books and articles are useful: Austin K. Gray, *The First American Library: A Short Account of the Library Company of Philadelphia 1731–1931* (Philadelphia, 1936); Austin B. Keep, *History of the New York Society Library* (New York, 1908); Louis Shores, *Origins of the American College Library, 1638–1800* (Nashville, Tenn., 1934); Henry W. Boynton, *Annals of American Bookselling, 1638–1850* (New York, 1932); Worthington C. Ford, *The Boston Book Market, 1679–1700* (Boston, 1917); Charles K. Bolton, *American Library History* (Chicago, 1919) and *Proprietary and Subscription Libraries* (Chicago, 1917); George C. Mason, *Annals of the Redwood Library and Athenaeum* (Newport, R.I., 1891); Lawrence C. Wroth, "Book Production and Distribution from the Beginning to the War between the States," in Hellmut Lehman-Haupt, *The Book in America* (New York, 1939), pp. 1–111; Henry J. Cadbury, "John Harvard's Library," Colonial Society of Massachusetts, *Transactions*, XXXIV (1937–42), 353–377; Anne King Gregorie, "The First Decade of the Charleston Library Society," *Proceedings of the South Carolina Historical Association*, 5 (1935), 3–10; Edgar Legare Pennington, "The Beginnings of the Library in Charles Town, South Carolina," *Proceedings of the American Antiquarian Society*, New Ser., XLIV (1934), 159–187; Frances L. Spain, "Libraries of South Carolina: Their Origins and Early History, 1700–1830," *The Library Quarterly*, XVI (1947), 28–42; Stephen B. Weeks, "Libraries and Literature in North Carolina in the Eighteenth Century," *American Historical Association Annual Report for 1895* (Washington, 1896), 171–267; Caroline Robbins, "Library of Liberty— Assembled for Harvard College by Thomas Hollis of Lincoln's Inn," *Harvard Library Bulletin*, V (1951), 5–23, 181–196; William D. Houlette, "Books of the Virginia Dynasty," *The Library Quarterly*, XXIV (1954), 226–239; Julia Cherry Spruill, "The Southern Lady's Library, 1700–1776," *The South Atlantic Quarterly*, XXXIV (1935), 23–41; and Frederick B. Tolles, "Quaker Humanist: James Logan as a Classical Scholar," *The Pennsylvania Magazine of History and Biography*, LXXIX (1955), 415–438.

Chapter 7

Bibliographical references pertinent to this chapter will be found in the bibliographies for Chapters IV, VI, VII, VIII, IX, XI, and XII. Charles Evans, *American Bibliography: A Chronological Dictionary of All Books, Pamphlets, and Periodical Publications Printed in the United States of America from the Genesis of Printing in 1639 Down to and Including the Year 1820, with Bibliographical and Biographical Notes* (12 vols., Chicago, 1903–34), supplies an index to colonial publication. More extensive is Joseph Sabin, *A Dictionary of Books Relating to America from Its Discovery to the Present Time* (29 vols., New York, 1868–1936). Begun by Sabin, this bibliography was carried on by Wilberforce Eames and completed by R. W. G. Vail. A convenient and valuable bibliography of early American narratives and comment is R. W. G. Vail, *The Voice of the Old Frontier* (Philadelphia, 1949). Bibliographies of individual writers, themes, and topics dealing with colonial literature will be found in Vol. III of the *Literary History of the United States,* ed. Robert E. Spiller, Willard Thorp, and Thomas E. Johnson (3 vols., New York, 1948). The preliminary chapters of the *Literary History* deal with colonial literature and represent the most recent synthesis of scholarship on the subject.

Though much new information has come to light since it was written, Moses Coit Tyler, *A History of American Literature During the Colonial Period, 1607–1765* (2 vols., New York, 1878), has not yet been surpassed in information and wisdom. For the period of controversial pamphleteering that began about 1763, Tyler's *The Literary History of the American Revolution, 1763–1783* (2 vols., New York, 1897) is still the best guide. A brief but penetrating discussion is Kenneth B. Murdock, *Literature and Theology in Colonial New England* (Cambridge, Mass., 1949). The latest and most complete treatment of literature in the South will be found in Jay B. Hubbell, *The South in American Literature, 1607–1900* (Durham, N.C., 1954), which has valuable bibliographies.

Useful for its anthology, commentary, and bibliographical notes is Perry Miller and Thomas H. Johnson (eds.), *The Puritans* (New York, 1938). The most convenient excerpts from the early travel accounts may be found in the volumes of the *Original Narratives of Early American History* (18 vols., New York, 1906–30). A useful guide to the literary aspects of a colonial newspaper is Hennig Cohen, *The South Carolina Gazette, 1732–1775* (Columbia, S.C., 1953). A provocative essay on Virginia is Howard M. Jones, *The Literature of Virginia in the Seventeenth Century,* Memoirs of the American Academy of Arts and Sciences (Boston, 1946); but a review by Virginia H. Adair, *The William and Mary Quarterly,* 3rd Ser., IV (1947), 373–375, calls attention to inconsistencies in this essay. See also an essay by Howard M. Jones,

"Desiderata in Colonial Literary History," in his *Ideas in America* (Cambridge, Mass., 1944).

Chapter 8

The most recent general history of the American drama, Arthur H. Quinn, *A History of the American Drama* (2nd ed., New York, 1943), Vol. I, provides a good summary of theatrical history in the colonies, with a bibliography. George C. D. Odell, *Annals of the New York Stage* (New York, 1927), Vol. I, is discursive but informative about the early stage not only in New York but elsewhere. Other histories of the theater in particular areas are useful, especially Thomas Clark Pollock, *The Philadelphia Theatre in the Eighteenth Century* (Philadelphia, 1933); Eola Willis, *The Charleston Stage in the Eighteenth Century* (Columbia, S.C., 1924); and Robert H. Land, "The First Williamsburg Theatre," *The William and Mary Quarterly*, 3rd Ser., V (1948), 359–74. The early chapters of Charles Blake, *An Historical Account of the Providence Stage* (Providence, R.I., 1868), and William W. Clapp, *A Record of the Boston Stage* (Boston, 1853), throw some light on conditions in New England. Among the older books, the most useful is George O. Seilhamer, *History of the American Theatre Before the Revolution* (Philadelphia, 1888). William Dunlap, *History of the American Theatre* (New York, 1832), contains a considerable amount of source material, but both Dunlap and Seilhamer have to be checked for accuracy by more modern works. For the periods covered, the best contemporary sources are the newspapers, especially the *South Carolina Gazette*, founded in 1732; the *Virginia Gazette*, founded in 1736; and the *Pennsylvania Gazette*, founded in 1728. Robert L. Shurter, "Shakespearean Performances in Pre-Revolutionary America," *South Atlantic Quarterly*, XXXVI (1937), 53–58, throws an interesting sidelight on colonial taste in plays.

The best treatise on formal music in the colonial period is O. G. Sonneck, *Early Concert-Life in America, 1731–1800* (1st ed., 1906; photographic reproduction, New York, 1949). Also helpful are John Tasker Howard, *Our American Music* (3rd ed., New York, 1946), and Gilbert Chase, *America's Music from the Pilgrims to the Present* (New York, 1955). *Ex parte* but useful is Percy Scholes, *The Puritans and Music in England and New England* (Oxford, 1934). Valuable information is provided in F. P. Bowes, *The Culture of Early Charleston* (Chapel Hill, N.C., 1942); Thomas W. Balch, *The Philadelphia Assemblies* (Philadelphia, 1916); Hennig Cohen, *The South Carolina Gazette, 1732–1775* (Columbia, S.C., 1953); Richard Moody, *America Takes the Stage* (Bloomington, Ind., 1955); and Henry Wilder Foote, *Musical Life in Boston in the Eighteenth Century* (Boston, 1940).

Information on amusements may be found in the various books by Alice Morse Earle, especially *Colonial Days in Old New York* (New York, 1899);

Philip A. Bruce, *Social Life of Virginia in the Seventeenth Century* (2nd ed., Lynchburg, Va., 1927); William B. Weeden, *Economic and Social History of New England, 1620–1789* (2 vols., Boston, 1890); and Foster R. Dulles, *America Learns to Play: A History of Popular Recreation, 1607–1940* (New York, 1940).

Chapter 9

The literature on architecture and the arts in colonial America is enormous. Many books on local antiquities are uncritical and almost useless as sources of accurate historical information, but some show meticulous care in assembling data concerning buildings, arts, and crafts. A helpful guide through this mass of material is Frank J. Roos, *Writings on Early American Architecture: An Annotated List . . .* (Columbus, Ohio, 1943). The standard treatment of domestic architecture is Fiske Kimball, *Domestic Architecture of the American Colonies and the Early Republic* (New York, 1927). Brief but useful is Talbot F. Hamlin, *The American Spirit in Architecture* (New Haven, 1926). Also valuable are Thomas T. Waterman, *The Dwellings of Colonial America* (Chapel Hill, N.C., 1950); Hugh Morrison, *Early American Architecture From the First Colonial Settlements to the National Period* (New York, 1952); Talbot F. Hamlin, *Greek Revival Architecture in America* (New York, 1944); and Harold Eberlein and Cortlandt Van Dyke, *American Georgian Architecture* (Bloomington, Ind., 1952). A study of the earliest housing is Harold R. Shurtleff, *The Log Cabin Myth* (Cambridge, Mass., 1939). Edward F. Rines, *Old Historic Churches of America* (New York, 1936), provides a brief account of ecclesiastical architecture, with a bibliography and illustrations. See also Stephen D. Dorsey, *Early English Churches in America, 1607–1807* (New York, 1952). Among the most useful of the treatments of the architecture of special regions are Frank Cousins and Philip M. Riley, *Colonial Architecture of Salem* (Boston, 1919), and the same authors' *The Colonial Architecture of Philadelphia* (Boston, 1920); John Frederick Kelly, *Early Domestic Architecture of Connecticut* (New Haven, 1924), and various other books on the same subject by this author; Anthony Garvan, *Architecture and Town Planning in Colonial Connecticut* (New Haven, 1951); Isaac N. P. Stokes, *Iconography of Manhattan Island* (6 vols., New York, 1915–28); Thomas T. Waterman and John A. Barrows, *Domestic Colonial Architecture of Tidewater Virginia* (New York, 1932); Thomas T. Waterman, *Mansions of Virginia, 1706–1776* (Chapel Hill, N.C., 1946); Henry I. Brock, *Colonial Churches in Virginia* (Richmond, Va., 1930); Edith Tunis Sale, *Interiors of Virginia Houses of Colonial Times, from the Beginnings of Virginia to the Revolution* (Richmond, Va., 1927) and *Manors of Virginia in Colonial Times* (Philadelphia, 1909); Harriette K. Leiding, *Historic Houses of South Carolina* (Philadelphia,

1921); Samuel G. Stoney, *Plantations of the Carolina Low Country* (Charleston, S.C., 1938); Frances B. Johnston and Thomas T. Waterman, *The Early Architecture of North Carolina* (Chapel Hill, N.C., 1941); Samuel Chamberlain, *Salem Interiors. Two Centuries of New England Taste and Decoration* (New York, 1950); Lewis Coffin and Arthur C. Holden, *Brick Architecture of the Colonial Period in Maryland and Virginia* (New York, 1919); Henry C. Forman, *Early Manor and Plantation Houses of Maryland* (Easton, Md., 1934); Helen Reynolds, *Dutch Houses in the Hudson Valley before 1776* (New York, 1929); Harold D. Eberlein, *The Manors and Historic Houses of the Hudson Valley* (Philadelphia, 1924); Henry C. Forman, *The Architecture of the Old South: The Medieval Style, 1585–1850* (Cambridge, Mass., 1948); and Antoinette F. Downing and Vincent J. Scully, Jr., *The Architectural Heritage of Newport, Rhode Island, 1640–1915* (Cambridge, Mass., 1952). A revealing book is Carl Bridenbaugh, *Peter Harrison, First American Architect* (Chapel Hill, N.C., 1949).

For the history of painting, the following are useful: Virgil Barker, *American Painting: History and Interpretation* (New York, 1950); James T. Flexner, *American Painting: First Flowers of Our Wilderness* (Boston, 1947); Alan Burroughs, *Limners and Likenesses* (Cambridge, Mass., 1936); Oliver W. Larkin, *Art and Life in America* (New York, 1949); Louisa Dresser (ed.), *Seventeenth Century Painting in New England, a Catalogue of an Exhibition* (Worcester, Mass., 1935); Oskar F. L. Hagen, *The Birth of the American Tradition in Art* (New York, 1941); Margaret Simons Middleton, *Jeremiah Theus, Colonial Artist of Charles Town* (Columbia, S.C., 1953); Henry Wilder Foote, *John Smibert, Painter: With a Descriptive Catalogue of Portraits, and Notes on the Work of Nathaniel Smibert* (Cambridge, Mass., 1950), and the same author's *Robert Feke, Colonial Portrait Painter* (Cambridge, Mass., 1930).

The best introduction to the decorative arts in early America is not to be found in books but in the carefully arranged exhibits of the Henry Francis du Pont Winterthur Museum at Wilmington, Delaware. There the visitor can see the most significant collection ever brought together of furniture and other household equipment from early America in contemporary settings. Both the selection of material and the settings have been made with a high degree of scholarly accuracy, and the whole museum is designed to serve the ends of scholars and students of social history. Of great value is Joseph Downs, *American Furniture: Queen Anne and Chippendale Periods in the Henry Francis du Pont Winterthur Museum* (New York, 1952).

A vast amount of information about the arts, culled from newspapers, has been compiled in the following volumes: George F. Dow, *The Arts and Crafts in New England, 1704–1775* (Topsfield, Mass., 1927); Alfred C. Prime, *The Arts and Crafts in Philadelphia, Maryland, and South Carolina,*

1721–1785 (Topsfield, Mass., 1929); and Rita S. Gottesman, *The Arts and Crafts in New York, 1726–1776* (New York, 1938). An invaluable guide to the decorative arts is R. T. H. Halsey and Charles O. Cornelius, *A Handbook of the American Wing* [of the Metropolitan Museum] (7th ed., rev. by Joseph Downs, New York, 1942). For furniture and decoration, see Edwin J. Hipkiss, *Eighteenth Century American Arts* (Cambridge, Mass., 1941); Charles Nagel, *American Furniture, 1650–1850: A Brief Background and an Illustrated History* (New York, 1949); Nina F. Little, *American Decorative Wall Painting, 1700–1850* (Sturbridge, Mass., 1952); Edgar G. Miller, *American Antique Furniture* (New York, 1927); Russell H. Kettell, *The Pine Furniture of Early New England* (New York, 1929); Luke Vincent Lockwood, *Colonial Furniture in America* (2 vols., New York, 1926); Holger Cahill, *American Folk Art: the Art of the Common Man in America, 1750–1900* (New York, 1933); and Erwin O. Christensen, *Early American Wood Carving* (Cleveland, Ohio, 1950). A valuable guide to material in this category is Erwin O. Christensen, *The Index of American Design* (New York, 1950). For glass: Helen and George S. Kearin, *American Glass* (New York, 1941), and the same authors' *Two Hundred Years of American Blown Glass* (New York, 1950). For pottery: Arthur W. Clement, *Notes on Early American Porcelain, 1738–1838* (New York, 1946), *Notes on American Ceramics, 1607–1943* (Brooklyn, 1944), and *Our Pioneer Potters* (New York, 1947); John Ramsay, *American Potters and Pottery* (New York, 1947); and Lura W. Watkins, *Early New England Potters and Their Wares* (Cambridge, Mass., 1950). For pewter: Leslie I. Laughlin, *Pewter in America, Its Makers and Their Marks* (Boston, 1940). For silver: John Marshall Phillips, *American Silver* (New York, 1949), and Louise Avery, *Early American Silver* (New York, 1930). For wallpaper: Nancy McClelland, *Historic Wall-Papers from Their Inception to the Introduction of Machinery* (Philadelphia, 1924). The mortuary art of New England is discussed in H. M. Forbes, *Gravestones of Early New England and the Men Who Made Them, 1653–1800* (Boston, 1927). Scores of articles on individual artists and craftsmen are to be found in the magazine *Antiques*.

Chapter 10

The best bibliography of writings on colonial science is to be found in Whitfield J. Bell, Jr., *Early American Science: Needs and Opportunities for Study* (Williamsburg, Va., 1955). Brooke Hindle, *The Pursuit of Science in Revolutionary America, 1735–1789* (Chapel Hill, N.C., 1956), provides information about the interest in science in the colonial period. Frederick B. Tolles, "Philadelphia's First Scientist: James Logan," *Isis*, XLVII (1956), 20–30, deals with James Logan and other early scientists. See also Tolles, *Meeting House and Counting House* (Chapel Hill, N.C., 1948), and Brooke

Hindle, "The Quaker Background of Science in Colonial Philadelphia," *Isis*, XLVI (1955), 243–250.

An introduction to the history and bibliography of botany in eighteenth-century America is Earl G. Swem, "Brothers of the Spade: Correspondence of Peter Collinson of London and John Custis of Williamsburg, Virginia, 1734–1746," American Antiquarian Society, *Proceedings*, LXVIII (1948), 17–201. See also Ernest Earnest, *John and William Bartram* (Philadelphia, 1940); William Darlington (ed.), *Memorials of John Bartram and Humphry Marshall* (Philadelphia, 1849); and Margaret Denny, "Linnaeus and His Disciple in Carolina, Alexander Garden," *Isis*, XXXVIII (1948), 161–174. Valuable as a source for the history of science, particularly botany, are the letters of Cadwallader Colden in the *Collections* of the New-York Historical Society, Vols. IX and X (1876–77), L–LVI (1917–23), and LXVII–LXVIII (1934–35). See also Alice M. Keys, *Cadwallader Colden* (New York, 1906). John W. Harshberger, *The Botanists of Philadelphia* (Philadelphia, 1899), is helpful though not always accurate.

A discussion of scientific interest in New England will be found in Samuel Eliot Morison, *Harvard College in the Seventeenth Century* (2 vols., Cambridge, Mass., 1936) and *The Puritan Pronaos* (New York, 1936). The relevant chapters in Merle Curti, *The Growth of American Thought* (New York, 1943), and Michael Kraus, *The Atlantic Civilization* (Ithaca, N.Y., 1949), are provocative and contain further bibliographical suggestions. Especially valuable are monographs and articles by Theodore Hornberger: *Scientific Thought in the American Colleges, 1638–1800* (Austin, Tex., 1945); "The Date, the Source, and the Significance of Cotton Mather's Interest in Science," *American Literature*, VI (1935), 411–420; "The Effect of the New Science upon the Thought of Jonathan Edwards," *ibid.*, IX (1937), 196–207; and "Acosta's *Historia Natural Y Moral De Las Indias:* A Guide to the Source and the Growth of the American Scientific Tradition," *University of Texas Studies in English* (Austin, Tex., 1939); "Samuel Johnson of Yale and King's College: A Note on the Relation of Science and Religion in Provincial America," *New England Quarterly*, VIII (1935), 378–397; "The Science of Thomas Prince," *ibid.*, IX (1936), 20–42; "Puritanism and Science: The Relationship Revealed in the Writings of John Cotton," *ibid.*, X (1937), 503–515; and "The Scientific Ideas of John Mitchell," *The Huntington Library Quarterly*, X (1946–47), 277–296. Raymond P. Stearns, "Colonial Fellows of the Royal Society of London, 1661–1788," *The William and Mary Quarterly*, 3rd Ser., III (1946), 208–268; and Frederick E. Brasch, "The Royal Society of London and Its Influence upon Scientific Thought in the American Colonies," *The Scientific Monthly*, XXXIII (1931), 336–355, 448–469, throw light on the contributions of the leading colonial scientists. Also useful is Brasch's "The Newtonian Epoch in the American Colonies, 1680–1783,"

American Antiquarian Society, *Proceedings,* New Ser., LXIX (1939), 314–332.

For colonial medicine, information may be found in Francis R. Packard, *History of Medicine in the United States* (2 vols., New York, 1931); Wyndham B. Blanton, *Medicine in Virginia in the Seventeenth Century* (Richmond, Va., 1931) and *Medicine in Virginia in the Eighteenth Century* (Richmond, Va., 1931); Stephen Wickes, *History of Medicine in New Jersey and Its Medical Men* (Newark, N.J., 1879); Henry R. Viets, *Brief History of Medicine in Massachusetts* (Boston, 1930); and Richard H. Shryock, *The Development of Modern Medicine* (New York, 1936). The best book on natural history is William M. and Mabel S. C. Smallwood, *Natural History and the American Mind* (New York, 1941). See also G. Brown Goode, "The Beginnings of Natural History in America," *Proceedings of the Biological Society of Washington,* III (1884–1886), 35–105. Pertinent chapters on science and medicine in Carl and Jessica Bridenbaugh, *Rebels and Gentlemen: Philadelphia in the Age of Franklin* (New York, 1932), are useful. Franklin's contributions to science are given adequate treatment in Carl Van Doren, *Benjamin Franklin* (New York, 1938), and I. Bernard Cohen, *Benjamin Franklin's Experiments* (Cambridge, Mass., 1941).

For reasons suggested by their titles, the following will be found useful: Lyman Butterfield (ed.), "A Sketch of the Revolutions and Improvements in Science, Arts, and Literature in America, Reprinted from Samuel Miller's *Brief Retrospect of the Eighteenth Century* (1803)," *The William and Mary Quarterly,* 3rd Ser., X (1953), 578–627; Frederick G. Kilgour, "The Rise of Scientific Activity in Colonial New England," *Yale Journal of Biology and Medicine,* XXII (1949), 123–138; Louis W. McKeehan, *Yale Science: The First Hundred Years 1701–1801* (New York, 1947; E. B. Krumbhaar, "The State of Pathology in the British Colonies of North America," *Yale Journal of Biology and Medicine,* XIX (1947), 801–815; I. Bernard Cohen, *Some Early Tools of American Science* (Cambridge, Mass., 1950); Howard N. Eavenson, *Map Makers and Indian Traders* (Pittsburgh, Pa., 1949); David E. Smith and Jekuthiel Ginsburg, *History of Mathematics in America before 1900* (Chicago, 1934); Philip Shorr, *Science and Superstition in the Eighteenth Century* (New York, 1932); Dirk J. Struik, *Yankee Science in the Making* (Boston, 1948); Sarah Augusta Dickson, *Panacea or Precious Bane: Tobacco in Sixteenth Century Literature* (New York, 1954); and Otho T. Beall, Jr., and Richard H. Shryock, *Cotton Mather, First Significant Figure in American Medicine* (Baltimore, 1954).

Chapter 11

The earliest full account of American printing—and still valuable—was Isaiah Thomas, *The History of Printing in America. With a Biography of*

Printers and an Account of Newspapers (2 vols., Worcester, Mass., 1810). A revised edition was brought out under the auspices of the American Antiquarian Society and published at Albany, N.Y., in 1874. One of the most accurate of modern histories is Lawrence C. Wroth, *The Colonial Printer* (New York, 1931; 2nd ed., Portland, Me., 1938). Also highly useful is Wroth's section of *The Book in America* (New York, 1939). Both contain useful bibliographies. Some new material is to be found in Douglas C. McMurtrie, *A History of Printing in the United States . . . Vol. II. Middle and South Atlantic States* (New York, 1936), the only volume printed of a projected four-volume work, which includes material previously published in periodicals and privately printed in pamphlets. McMurtrie's work does not achieve the high degree of accuracy attained by Wroth. Among the best accounts of regional printing presses are Lawrence C. Wroth, *History of Printing in Colonial Maryland, 1686–1776* (Baltimore, 1922) and *William Parks, Printer and Journalist of England and Colonial America* (Richmond, 1926); Charles R. Hildeburn, *Sketches of Printers and Printing in Colonial New York* (New York, 1895) and *A Century of Printing. The Issues of the Press in Pennsylvania, 1685–1784* (2 vols., Philadelphia, 1885–86); Stephen B. Weeks, *The Press of North Carolina in the Eighteenth Century* (New York, 1891); A. S. Salley, "The First Presses of South Carolina," Bibliographical Society of America, *Proceedings and Papers,* II (1907–8), 26–69; Hennig Cohen, *The South Carolina Gazette, 1732–1775* (Columbia, S.C., 1953); G. E. Littlefield, *The Early Massachusetts Press, 1638–1711* (2 vols., Boston, 1907); J. H. Trumbull, *List of Books Printed in Connecticut, 1709–1800* (Hartford, Conn., 1904; *Supplement,* 1938); R. F. Roden, *The Cambridge Press, 1638–1692* (New York, 1905); and George P. Winship, *The Cambridge Press, 1638–1692* (Philadelphia, 1945). Benjamin Franklin's career as a printer is treated in John Clyde Oswald, *Benjamin Franklin, Printer* (Garden City, N.Y., 1917).

The most succinct accounts of colonial newspapers and magazines are by Frank Luther Mott, *American Journalism* (New York, 1941; new ed., 1949) and *A History of American Magazines, 1741–1850* (New York, 1930; 2nd ed., 1938). See also Lyon N. Richardson, *A History of Early American Magazines* (New York, 1931); James Wood Playsted, *Magazines in the United States* (New York, 1949); and Elizabeth C. Cook, *Literary Influences in Colonial Newspapers, 1704–1750* (New York, 1912). Indispensable is the work of Clarence S. Brigham, *History and Bibliography of American Newspapers, 1690–1820* (2 vols., Worcester, Mass., 1947). Brigham lists every newspaper published in his period under place of publication and gives facts about each. A discussion of censorship in the colonial period and of the struggle for the freedom of the press is given by Livingston Rowe Schuyler, *The Liberty of the Press in the American Colonies before the Revolutionary*

War (New York, 1905). See also Clyde A. Duniway, *The Development of the Freedom of the Press in Massachusetts*, Harvard Historical Studies, XII (New York, 1906), and Livingston Rutherfurd, *John Peter Zenger, His Press, His Trial, and a Bibliography of Zenger Imprints* (New York, 1904).

An account of the influence of the newspapers and printing presses in the controversies leading up to the Revolution is provided by Philip Davidson, *Propaganda and the American Revolution, 1763–1783* (Chapel Hill, N.C., 1941). Also useful is an article by A. M. Schlesinger, "Colonial Newspapers and the Stamp Act," *New England Quarterly*, VIII (1935), 63–83.

Additional references that will be helpful are Sidney Kobre, *The Development of the Colonial Newspaper* (Pittsburgh, Pa., 1944); C. M. Christian (ed.), *Two Hundred Years with the Maryland Gazette, 1727–1927* (Annapolis, Md., 1927); Edward W. Hocker, *The Sower Printing House of Colonial Times* (Norristown, Pa., 1948); J. Eugene Smith, *One Hundred Years of Hartford's Courant; from Colonial Times Through the Civil War* (New Haven, Conn., 1949); Paul Leicester Ford (ed.), *The Journals of Hugh Gaine, Printer, 1726–1807* (New York, 1902); Samuel A. Green, *John Foster: the Earliest American Engraver and the First Boston Printer* (Boston, 1909); Jarvis M. Morse, *Connecticut Newspapers in the Eighteenth Century* (New Haven, Conn., 1935); Anna J. DeArmond, *Andrew Bradford, Colonial Journalist* (Newark, Del., 1949); Lawrence C. Wroth, *Typographic Heritage: Selected Essays by Lawrence C. Wroth* (New York, 1949); Clarence S. Brigham, *Journals and Journeymen* (Philadelphia, 1950).

Valuable for factual information about communications and related subjects are two volumes by Carl Bridenbaugh, *Cities in the Wilderness* (New York, 1938) and *Cities in Revolt* (New York, 1955). Michael Kraus, *The Atlantic Civilization: Eighteenth Century Origins* (Ithaca, N.Y., 1949), provides a great deal of material on the contacts between the colonies and Europe. See also his *Intercolonial Aspects of American Culture on the Eve of the Revolution, With Special Reference to the Northern Towns* (New York, 1928). William L. Sachse, *The Colonial American in Britain* (Madison, Wis., 1956), is also useful. Much information about early sea communications will be found in Arthur P. Middleton, *Tobacco Coast: A Maritime History of Chesapeake Bay in the Colonial Period* (Newport News, Va., 1953). An adequate discussion of the colonial postal service is William Smith, *The History of the Post Office in British North America, 1639–1870* (Cambridge, 1920). A chapter on "Colonial Travel" in Charles M. Andrews, *Colonial Folkways* (New Haven, 1919), is suggestive. See also Alice Morse Earle, *Stage-Coach and Tavern Days* (New York, 1935); Elise Lathrop, *Early American Inns and Taverns* (New York, 1926); Edward Field, *The Colonial Tavern* (Providence, R.I., 1897); John Duffy, "The Passage to the Colonies," *The Mississippi Valley Historical Review*, XXXVIII (1951), 21–38; Wheaton

J. Lane, *From Indian Trail to Iron Horse. Travel and Transportation in New Jersey, 1620–1860* (Princeton, 1939); William B. Weeden, *Economic and Social History of New England, 1620–1789* (2 vols., Cambridge, Mass., 1890); and Philip A. Bruce, *Economic History of Virginia in the Seventeenth Century* (2 vols., New York, 1907). Newton D. Mereness (ed.), *Travels in the American Colonies* (New York, 1916), provides a compendium of early narratives. Contemporary diaries and journals throw light on the means of communication. See particularly *The Private Journal of Sarah Kemble Knight, Being the Record of a Journey from Boston to New York in the Year 1704* (Norwich, Conn., 1901); *Gentleman's Progress. The Itinerarium of Dr. Alexander Hamilton, 1744,* ed. Carl Bridenbaugh (Chapel Hill, N.C., 1948); *The Diary of Samuel Sewall, 1674–1729* in the *Collections of the Massachusetts Historical Society,* 5th Ser., V–VII (1874–82); *The Secret Diary of William Byrd of Westover, 1709–1712,* ed. Louis B. Wright and Marion Tinling (Richmond, Va., 1941); *Another Secret Diary of William Byrd of Westover, 1739–1741,* ed. Maude H. Woodfin and Marion Tinling (Richmond, Va., 1942); Peter Kalm, *The America of 1750: Peter Kalm's Travels in North America,* ed. Adolph B. Benson (2 vols., New York, 1937); *Some Cursory Remarks Made by James Birket* (New Haven, Conn., 1916); "Diary of Hannah Callender, 1758–1762," *Pennsylvania Magazine of History and Biography,* XII (.1888), 432–456; "Diary of Daniel Fisher," *Pennsylvania Magazine of History and Biography,* XVII (1893), 263–278; "Travel Diary of William Black," *Pennsylvania Magazine of History and Biography,* I (1877), 117–132, 233–249, 404–419; II (1878), 40–49. Information on the problem of communications between colonial planters and their factors in England may be found in *Letters of Robert Carter 1720–1727: The Commercial Interests of a Virginia Gentleman,* ed. Louis B. Wright (San Marino, Calif., 1940).

Index

Abbeville (S.C.), 53
Academy of Compliments, 137
Acadians, 35, 52, 54
Accomac (Va.), 177
Acosta, José de, *Natural and Moral History of* . . . *Indies*, 217
Act of Union, 69
Adams, James, quoted, 114
Adams, John, *Poems on Several Occasions*, 172
Adams, Samuel, 97
Addington, Isaac, 178
Addison, Joseph, 151, 182, 244; *The Drummer*, 181; *The Spectator*, 148, 244; *Tragedy of Cato*, 181, 183, 186
Aelianus, Claudius, works, 132
Affleck, Thomas, 205
Africa, *see* Slave trade
Agriculture, 4, 21, 28–29; importance in colonial culture, 1, 2; experiments of Robert Carter, 12; in Maryland, 16; in S.C., 17; German skill in, 58, 62
Agrippa, Cornelius, "Occult Philosophy," 136
Ainsworth, Henry, *Book of Psalms*, 192
Albany (N.Y.), 48, 49, 86
Albemarle, Duke of, 37
Alcock, John, 222
Alison, Francis, 109
Alkmaar, 48
Allaire family, 57
Allestree, Richard, *Gentleman's Calling*, 138; *Whole Duty of Man*, 137, 138, 147

Alloway Town (N.J.), 63
Allyn, John, 143
Alsop, George, *Character of the Province of Maryland*, 166
America, melting pot of nationalities, 45; religious motive for colonization, 73–74; stimulus to scientific observation, 216–217
American Company, 183–185
ACLS study of population distribution, 46
American Magazine and Historical Chronicle, 235
American Magazine or General Repository, 236
American Philosophical Society, 231, 236, 237
American Weekly Mercury, 241
Ames, Nathaniel, 172
Amsterdam, 86, 87
Ancient and Honorable Artillery Company, 35, 36
Anderson, Hugh, 169
Andrewes, Bishop Lancelot, sermons, 138
Androborus, A Biographical Farce, 186
Andros, Governor Edmund, 83
Anglicans, *see* Church of England
Annapolis (Md.), 3, 14, 15, 16, 18, 110, 146, 170, 182, 184, 206, 210, 214, 246, 249
Anne, queen of England, 37, 146
Anti-Pamela, 153
Antinomianism, 82
Arbella, 157
Architecture, amateur design, 200,

201; Dutch influence, 48, 199; early domestic, 196–199; influence of classical design, 200–201, 203; log cabin, 51, 197; public buildings, 201–203

Argyle, Duke of, 8

Aristocracy, New England, 30–40

Aristocracy, New York, 40–42

Aristocracy, Philadelphia, 42–43

Aristocracy, Southern, 21, 30; imitators of English gentry, 3, 4, 5, 6, 19; land and social status, 2, 4, 10, 17–18; literary interests, 11–12, 13, 15, 127–135, 136–144; respect for trade, 7, 17, 44

Aristotle, 131, 132, 217, 218, 220, 225

Arminianism, 93

Art, 207–215; see also Drawing, Painting

Ashley River, 5

Assemblies, see Balls

Associates of Dr. Bray, 115

Aston, Anthony, 179–180

Austin, Ann, 82

Bach, Johann Sebastian, 193, 194

Bacon, Francis, Essays, 130; other works, 135

Bacon, Nathaniel, "Epitaph," 170

Bacon, Reverend Thomas, 111

Badger, Joseph, 212

Bahamas, 37

Balls, 180, 191

Baltimore, Cecil Calvert, 2nd Lord, 77

Baltimore, George Calvert, 1st Lord, 77

Baltimore (Md.), 13, 16

Baltimore Iron Works, 13

Banister, John, 230

Baptists, 59, 84, 88, 90, 184, 194

Barbados, 17, 32, 33, 42, 82

Barclay, William, Argenis, 142

Barriffe, William, Military Discipline, 128

Barrough, Philip, Method of Physic, 128

Bartram, John, 229–230, 231, 234

Bartram, William, 230

Battle of the Boyne, 65

Baxter, Richard, 138; Call to the Unconverted, 140

"Bay Psalm Book," 170, 192

Bayly, Lewis, Practice of Piety, 138, 139, 140, 147

Beacon Hill, 40

Bean, "Judge," 21

"Bear and the Cub, The," 177, 186

Beissel, Johann Conrad, 194

Belcher, Governor Jonathan, 36, 152

Belfast (Ire.), 66

Bennetts, Maryland landholders, 14

Berkeley, George, Bishop of Cloyne, 152, 211

Berkeley, Sir William, 177

Bermuda, 74, 151, 211

Bethesda Orphan House, 91, 115

Bethlehem (Pa.), 61, 194

Beverley, Robert, 12, 168; Essay upon . . . English Plantations, 167; History and Present State of Virginia, 167, quoted, 54, 55, 75, 190, 204

Biggard, John, 206

Blackamore, Reverend Arthur, 10

Blackburn, Joseph, 212

Blair, Dr. James, 96, 118, 166

Blair, Mrs. James, 10

Blair, Reverend John, 88

Block, Laurens, 209

Bodin, Jean, Six Books of a Commonwealth, 134

Bodleian Library, 147

Boerhaave, Herman, Chemistry, 148

Bogardus, Reverend Everardus, 86

Bohemians in New Amsterdam, 47

Bohun, Dr. Lawrence, 219

Books, printed at Germantown, 62; read and collected by colonists, 8, 11, 43, 127–144; written by colonists, 154–175; see also Libraries, Literature

Booksellers, 132, 133, 136, 142, 143, 152–153

Boone, Daniel, 197

Boston (Mass.), 16, 25, 31, 32, 33, 34, 35, 36, 37, 38, 42, 50, 57, 93, 97, 104, 105, 106, 119, 120, 132, 144, 145, 146, 152, 153, 160, 161, 162, 171, 173, 178, 179, 185, 188, 189, 190, 193, 194, 200, 202, 206, 207, 208, 212, 213, 214, 222, 226, 234, 240, 241, 242, 243, 244, 246, 251

Boston Common, 1

Boston Evening-Post, 244

Boston Gazette, 213, 242, 244

Boston Latin School, 102
Boston *News-Letter*, 206, 242
Boston Public Library, 145
Boudinot family, 56
Bowdoin family, 57
Boyle, Robert, 117, 221; *Usefulness of Experimental Philosophy*, 227
Boylston, Dr. Zabdiel, 227
Braddock's defeat, 242
Bradford, William, 77, 137, 157, 160; *Of Plymouth Plantation*, 158, 159, 160
Bradford, William (printer), 165, 244, 245, 246
Bradstreet, Anne, 129; *The Tenth Muse*, 171
Brathwaite, Richard, *English Gentleman* quoted, 132
Brattle, Thomas, 193, 227–228
Brattle, William, 228
Brattle Street Church, 193
Bray, Margery, 36
Bray, Commissary Thomas, 146–147
Breintnal, Joseph, 229
Brend, William, 82
Brereton, William, 221
Brewster, Jonathan, 135
Brewster, William, 134, 136, 137
Brick, importation to colonies, 198–199; manufacture in colonies, 197, 198
Brickell, John, *Natural History of North Carolina*, 169
Bridenbaugh, Carl, quoted, 250
Bridges, Charles, 210
Bridges, Henry, 187
Brigden, Zechariah, 220
Bristol (Eng.), 2, 3, 39, 69
British Museum, 207
Bronck, Jonas, 47
Bronx, the, 47
Brooker, William, 242
Brown, James, 38–39
Brown, John, 39, 185
Brown, Joseph, 39
Brown, Moses, 39
Brown, Nicholas, 39
Brown, Obadiah, 39
Brown University, 124
Browne, Chad, 38
Browne, William, 38
Browne's Folly, 38

Browns of Providence, 38–39
Bruton Church, 10, 193
Buffalo breeding attempted by French settlers, 55
Buffon, George Louis Leclerc, Comte de, 216
Bulkeley, Gershom, 136, 222–223
Bunyan, John, *Pilgrim's Progress*, 144
Burgoyne, General John, *Blockade of Boston*, 185
Burlington, Earl of, 200
Burlington (N.J.), 42
Burnet, Bishop Gilbert, *History of the Reformation*, 133
Burr, Aaron, president of College of New Jersey, 186
Burrill, George, 35
Burrill, John, 35
Burrill, Theophilus, 35
Burrill, "Royal Family of Lynn," 35
Byfield, Nicholas, 138, 139
Byles, Reverend Mather, "Hymn to be Sung at Sea," 172
Byrd, Maria Taylor, 210
Byrd, William (I), 6, 55, 111, 250
Byrd, William (II), 7–10, 11, 12, 60, 61, 111, 136, 188, 209–210; quoted, 88; diary, 7, 9; library, 8, 145, 223; scientific interest, 223–224; writings, 167–168, 223

C., L. W., *A Very Perfect Discourse*, 128
Caesar, Julius, works, 131
Calverts of Maryland, 13, 16; *see also* Baltimore, Cecil Calvert, etc.
Calvin, John, 138, 139
Calvinism, 87–88, 174; and capitalism, 24; of Dutch settlers, 85, 87; of Puritans, 78–79; preached by revivalists, 93, 94; training in, at Princeton, 121
Cambridge (Mass.), 40, 82, 160, 170, 173, 226
Cambridge University, 117, 119, 122, 125, 220
Camden, William, *Britannia*, 133; *Remains*, 132
Campbell, Duncan, 136
Campbell, John, 242
Candle manufacture from spermaceti, 39, 64

Cape Fear, 20
Carnegie, Andrew, 44
Carpenter, Samuel, 42
Carpenters' Company of Phila., 201
Carroll, Charles, 13, 15, 210
Carroll family, 16
Carter, Charles, 7
Carter, John, 138
Carter, Robert (of Corotoman), 76, 111
Carter, Robert (of Nomini Hall), 12, 13, 112
Carver, John, 77
Caryl, Joseph, *Commentary on the Book of Job*, 139
Castiglione, Baldassare, *Book of the Courtier*, 137
Castile soap manufacture, 64
Catholics in colonies, 16, 52, 54, 65, 73, 74, 76, 77, 90, 109–110, 195
Censorship of the press, 243, 245
Centlivre, Susanna, *Bold Stroke for a Wife*, 183; *Busy-Body*, 181
Central America, 206
Cervantes, Miguel Saavedra de, *Don Quixote*, 143
Chambers, Ephraim, *Cyclopedia*, 244
Charles I, 31, 78, 96, 156
Charles II, 37
Charleston (S.C.), 1, 3, 5, 16–19, 29, 39, 40, 44, 52, 53, 54, 60, 64, 65, 67, 69, 91, 113, 144, 147, 149–150, 152, 153, 179, 181, 183, 185, 187, 193, 194, 195, 201, 202, 205, 210, 213, 214, 226, 231, 240, 242, 244, 247, 250, 251
Charleston Library Society, 149–150
Charlestown (Mass.), 35
Charming Sally, The, 182
Chaucer, Geoffrey, works, 151
Chauncy, President Charles, 220
Chauncy, Elnathan, 142
Cheever, Ezekiel, 25, 102
Cherokee Indians, 69
Chesapeake Bay area, 2, 3, 69, 198, 241, 246
Chesterfield, Lord, cited re George Whitefield, 94
Chestertown (Md.), school, 110
Chilton, Edward, *Present State of Virginia,* 166

Chippendale, Thomas, *Gentleman and Cabinet-Maker's Director,* 205
Chiswell, Mrs., 9
Chocolate, importation, 39
Christ Church (Cambridge), 203
Christ Church (Phila.), 193, 202
Church of England, 10, 11, 49, 53, 54, 73, 74, 75, 79, 81, 90, 95–97, 113, 115, 131, 137, 138, 150, 190, 191, 193, 202, 226; aristocratic faith, 16, 19; in Maryland, 16, 110, 146; in New England, 83–84; in New York, 87, 121–122; in North Carolina, 88, 114; in Virginia, 74–76, 96
Churches, 2, 70, 71, 75, 76, 193, 194, 195, 202, 203; *see also* Religion
Cibber, Colley, 183; *Careless Husband,* 182; *Flora or Hob in the Well,* 181
Cicero, works, 131, 132
Classical learning in the colonies, 8, 11, 13, 70, 105, 108, 116, 117, 118, 120, 121, 124, 130–132, 145, 150
Claypoole, Josiah, 205
Clayton, John, 230, 231
Cleaver, Robert, *Godly Form of Household Government,* 137
Cleveland, John, 142
Cockfighting, 189, 190
Cock-scaling, 189
Codfish, 32
Coffeehouses, 248
Coke, Sir Edward, *Reports,* 128
Colden, Dr. Cadwallader, *History of the Five Indian Nations,* 164–165, 230; scientific interest, 230, 231
College of New Jersey, 70, 121, 186
College of Philadelphia, 123–124, 152, 186, 235, 236
College of William and Mary, 10, 118–119, 122, 124, 152, 168, 180, 188, 191, 202, 224, 225, 232
Colleges and universities, 70, 99, 116–124
Collegiate School, 106
Collinson, Peter, 228–229, 230, 231, 232
Columbia University, 121–123, 124, 150, 152, 226, 236
Columbus, Christopher, 239
Comenius, 11

Comes, Natalis, *Mythologiae*, 131
Communications, 2, 3, 238–251; inter-
colonial, 240–243, 247, 248–250;
transatlantic, 238–240, 250–251;
see also Transportation, Newspapers
Concord (Mass.), 146
Conestoga wagons, 62, 250
Coney, John, 214
Congregationalism, 90, 97; of Puri-
tans, 79, 83, 84, 85, 193; at Yale,
120, 226; weakened by revival
movement, 94–95
Congreve, William, 8, 182
Connecticut, colony of, 26, 84, 97, 99,
103, 117, 120, 135, 136, 149, 221,
222, 234
Connecticut *Gazette*, 245
Constitutional Courant, 245
Cooper, Myles, 123
Cooper River, 5
Copernicus, 220, 224
Copley, John Singleton, 212
Corderius, *Colloquies*, 130
Cornbury, Governor Edward, 87, 106,
240
Corporation Library, 147
Cosby, Governor William, 245
Cotton, Seaborn, 142
Cotton production, attempted by
Robert Carter, 12
Covenant theology, 79, 80, 81
Crafts, cabinetmaking, 203–206; glass,
214–215; pewterers, 213–214;
silversmithing, 213, 214
Crashaw, William, 74
Crefeld (Germany), 58
Crèvecoeur, Hector St. John de, cited,
45
Cromwell, Oliver, 35
Crouch, Ralph, 109–110
Curtius, Alexander Carolus, 106
Custis, John, 9
Cutting, Leonard, 122

Dalton, Michael, *Country Justice*, 128
Dancing, 104, 109, 110, 178, 180, 187,
190, 191
Dancing masters, 178, 194
Danes in New Amsterdam, 47
Davenport, John, 120, 207
De Proprietatibus Rerum, 129
Declaration of Independence, 40

Defoe, Daniel, *Religious Courtship*, 244
de Forest family, 56
de Graffenreidt, Barbara, 180
de Graffenried, Baron Christopher, 60
DeLancey family, 21, 41, 121
Delaware, Lord, 219
Delaware, colony of, 50–51, 89, 197,
211
Delaware River, 50, 51, 59
Delft, 199
Dellius, Godfrey, 20
Deloney, Thomas, 143
Denton, Daniel, *Brief Description*, 164
Derby, Richard, 40, 44
Derby family, 40
de Richbourg, Reverend C.P., 55
Descartes, René, 220
DeVeaux, Andrew, 53
Dickinson, Jonathan, 42, 43; quoted,
59–60
Digges, Colonel Dudley, 9
Doctors, 219–220, 222, 227, 230, 235,
236
Dodsley, Robert, *The King and the
Miller of Mansfield*, 183
Donne, John, 73, 171
Dorchester (Mass.), 84, 102, 146
Dorchester (S.C.), 84
Doughty, Mr., 187
Douglas, David, 169
Douglas, John, 113
Douglass, David, 183–185
Douglass, William, *Summary, His-
torical and Political*, 162–163
Dove, 33
Downing family, 30
Drake, Francis, 192
Drama, 15, 19, 89, 173, 176–186; see
also Theaters
Drawing, 209–210
Drayton, Michael, 143
Dryden, John, plays performed, 182,
183; works, 151
Du Bartas, Guillaume Salluste, *Divine
Weeks and Works*, 129
Dublin, University of, 14
Duck, Stephen, 152
Dudley, Joseph, 37
Dudley, Paul, 228
Dudley family, 30
Dueling in the South, 6
Dulany, Daniel, 14

Dulanys of Maryland, 14
Dummer, Jeremiah, 12, 214, 225, 226
Dunaway, Wayland, quoted on Ulster Scots, 66–67
Dunkers, 59, 90
Dunster, Henry, 117, 220
Du Puy family, 57
Durand, Monsieur, 54
Durham (Conn.) Book Company, 149
Dutch in New York, 20, 35, 46–50, 63, 85–87, 105–106, 198, 199, 207; in census of 1790, 46
Dutch Reformed Church, 49, 85, 86, 87, 91–92, 105, 106
Dutch West India Company, 47, 73, 85, 87, 105, 106
Duyckinck, Evert, 209
Duyckinck, Gerret, 209
Duyckinck family, 209
Dyer, Mary, 83

East India Company, 206
Eaton, Nathaniel, 158
Eaton, Thomas, 100
Eaton Free School, 100
Edict of Nantes, 52
Edinburgh, University of, 225, 235
Education, 30, 98, 102, 106, 110, 118, 120, 121, 122; abroad, 8, 11, 15, 18, 19, 111, 112, 113, 119, 124, 251; legal, 124; medical, 124, 235–236; of girls, 103, 104, 109; of indigents, 99, 107, 111, 114, 115, 116; of Indians, 99, 115, 117; of Negroes, 111, 115; private tutoring, 100, 111, 112, 113, 114–115, 123; provided for in wills, 100–101; scientific, 220–221, 224–226; sought in books of instruction, 128–130; vocational, 103, 104, 105, 108, 109, 115
Edwards, Jonathan, 92–93; writings, 174, 224
Eliot, Jared, 234
Eliot, John, 160, 163, 170; Indian Bible, 117, 140
Endecott, Judge John, 83
Enfield (Conn.), 93
England, 8, 31, 35, 38, 51, 52, 73, 74, 77, 78, 95, 96, 117, 122, 123, 133, 134, 137, 140, 155, 156, 157, 165, 166, 168, 175, 180, 185, 189, 198, 199, 200, 209, 210, 211, 212, 213, 219, 225, 239, 240, 243, 244; communications with colonies, 238–240, 250–251; education of colonials in, 8, 11, 18, 19, 111, 112, 113, 119, 124, 250; influence on colonies: architectural, 196–197; ethics of middle class, 25 ff., 104, 177; literary, 9–10, 42, 126 ff., 144, 151, 153; social (of country gentry), 3, 4, 5, 6, 19; language of, predominant in colonies, 49, 51; numerical superiority of settlers from, 45–56; political differences with colonies, 69–70, 90, 95, 96–97, 246; "Scotch-Irish" policy, 65–66, 90; trade with colonies, 2, 3, 4, 5, 6, 7, 12, 32, 33, 69, 159, 204
Enstone, Edward, 190
Entail, 4 fn.
Ephrata Choral society, 194
"Epistle from Cambridge," 235
Erasmus, 130
Evans, Lewis, 187
Evans, Nathaniel, *Juvenile Poems,* 173
Exchange Tavern, 187

Fairbank, Richard, 240
Fairfax, Edward, *Jerusalem Delivered,* 142
Falckner, Justus, 194
Faneuil, Peter, 44
Faneuil family, 57
Faneuil Hall, 202
Farnefold, Reverend John, 100
Farquhar, George, *Beaux Stratagem,* 181, 182; *Recruiting-Officer,* 181, 183
Feke, Robert, 211
Fielding, Henry, plays, 183
Finns, in New Amsterdam, 47; on the Delaware, 50–51
Fisher, Mary, 82
Fithian, Philip Vickers, diary cited, 13, 70, 112–113
Fitzhugh, William, 7, 12, 54, 111, 136
Flax production, attempted by Robert Carter, 12
Fleet, Thomas, 244
Flemings in New York state, 56
Fletcher, Governor of New York, quoted, 21

Flynt, Josiah, 191
Foreign language instruction in private schools, 109
Fort Orange (N.Y.), 48
Fortunate Maid, 153
Foster, John, 207
Fox, George, 84
Foxe, John, *Acts and Monuments,* 133, 159, 161
Fox-hunting, 189
Frame, Richard, *Short Description of Pennsylvania,* 165
Frampton, John, 217
Frampton, William, 42
Frankfurt (Germany), 58, 89
Franklin, Benjamin, 33, 42, 53, 62, 123, 148, 153, 194, 211, 228, 230, 236, 243; *Autobiography,* 28, 94, 148, 172, 175; improves postal service, 241–242; other writings, 175; *Poor Richard's Almanac,* 23–24, 140, 172, 175; printer, 174–175, 244–245, 246; scientific activities, 231–233, 234
Franklin, James, 243–244
Franklin, James (II), 244
Freke, Elizabeth, 208
Frelinghuysen, Theodorus J., 91–92
French Catholics, 35, 52, 54
French settlers, 18, 41, 44, 47, 52–58, 85, 87–89; in census of 1790, 46, 57; influence disproportionate to numbers, 51, 53, 57; skilled craftsmen, 15, 17, 20, 52, 53, 56, 57
French threat to English colonies, 47
Friends Public School, 108
Friendship, 33
Fry, Richard, 152
Fur trade, 44, 69
Furniture, 48, 63, 69, 203–206

Gadsden, Christopher, 150
Galileo, 224
Gallaudet family, 56
Garden, Dr. Alexander, 230–231
Garrick, David, cited re George Whitefield, 93–94; plays, 183
Gassendi, 220
Gates, Sir Thomas, 74
Gay, John, *Beggar's Opera,* 182; works, 151

Gentleman's Magazine, 232
George III, 68, 229, 246
Georgia, 61, 62, 63, 68, 90–91, 93, 115, 169, 241
German Palatines, 58, 59–60
German Reformed Church, 59, 89, 108
German settlers, 16, 19, 20, 46, 47, 51, 55, 63, 89–90, 193, 194, 195, 197, 246, 250; in census of 1790, 46; neglect of education, 108; skilled farmers and craftsmen, 58–62, 210, 212, 215
Germanna (Va.), 63
Germantown (Pa.), 58, 59, 62, 108
Germantowner Zeitung, 246
Gilbert, Humphrey, 73
Gildersleeve, Basil Lanneau, 54
Gillingham, James, 205
Girard family, 56
Glasgow (Scotland), 69
Glass manufacture in colonies, 62–63, 214–215
Gloria Dei Church, 193, 194
Goddard, John, 206
Godfrey, Thomas, 233
Godfrey, Thomas (II), *Prince of Parthia,* 173, 186
Goedwater, John Ernst, 86
Goodborne, Reverend John, 131
Gookin, Daniel, *An Historical Account,* 160
Gordon, William, quoted, 114–115
Gortonists, 159
Gostelowe, Jonathan, 205
Gouge, Reverend William, *Of Domestical Duties,* 137
Great Awakening, 91, 92, 94–95, 120
Great Philadelphia Wagon Road, 250
Great Plantation, 65
Great Rebellion of 1641, 66
Green, Jonas, 20
Green, Joseph, 172, 246
Greenham, Richard, 139
Greenwood, Isaac, 225
Greenwood, John, 212
Gridley, Jeremy, 246
Griffin, Mr., 114, 115
Grimston, Edward, 217
Gronovius, John Frederick, 230–231
Guardian, The, 148

282

INDEX

Guazzo, Stefano, *Civil Conversations*, 136
Gustavus Adolphus, King of Sweden, 133
Guy Fawkes Day, 188

Haarlem, 48
Hadley, John, 233
Hadley chests, 204
Haiti, 37, 54
Hakluyt, Richard, 73
Half-Way Covenant, 81
Hallam, Lewis, 182, 183
Hallam, Lewis, Jr., 183
Hallam, Mrs. Lewis, 182, 183
Hallam, William, 182
Halley, Edmund, 225
Halley's comet, 225, 227
Hals, Franz, 209
Hamilton, Dr. Alexander, *Itinerarium*, cited, 15, 153, 234–235, 248–249
Hamilton, Andrew, 165, 245
Hamilton, Andrew, Deputy Postmaster, 241
Hammond, John, writings, 166
Hampton Academy, 100
Hancock, John, 40
Hancock, John (II), 40
Hancock, Nathaniel, 40
Hancock, Thomas, 40, 44
Hancocks of Boston, 39–40
Hariot, Thomas, 239; *Brief and True Report*, 218
Harrison, Nathaniel, 7
Harrison, Peter, 63, 202–203
Hartwell, Henry, *Present State of Virginia*, 166
Harvard, John, 116, 131, 137
Harvard College, 25, 35, 38, 40, 64, 94, 96, 116–118, 119, 120, 121, 122, 124, 130, 131, 137, 142, 151–152, 171, 188, 191, 192, 202, 219, 220, 224, 225, 232; Indian College, 117
Hawley, Joseph, 92
Haydn, Josef, 194
Heamans, Roger, 166
Hearne, Thomas, 147
Heathcote, Anne, 41
Heathcote, Caleb, 20–21, 41
Hebrew grammar, 64
Heereboord, Adrian, *Parallelismus Aristotelicae*, 220

Help to Memory and Discourse, 137
Hemp production, attempted by Robert Carter, 12
Henrico (Va.), proposed university, 99, 198
Henry, Patrick, 68
Herbert, George, 143; *The Temple* quoted, 171
Herrick, Robert, 142
Hesselius, Gustavus, 211
Hesselius, John, 211
Hill, Richard, 42
Hill, Valentine, 34
Hillegas family, 56
Hirst, Mary, 36
History of Dr. Faustus, 142
Hobby, Charles, 36, 37
Hogarth, William, 211
Holdsworth, Edward, *Muscipula*, 170
Holland, 8, 47, 48, 51, 63
Hollis, Thomas, 96–97, 151, 224
Holyoke, Reverend Edward, 35
Homer, *Iliad* and other works, 131, 132
Hooke, Robert, 221
Hopewell, 33
Hopkey, Sophia, 90–91
Hopkins, John, *Whole Book of Psalms*, 192
Hopkinson, Francis, 195
Horace, works, 131
Horse-racing, 15, 189–190
Horses, as an article of commerce, 32, 33
Housewares, 48, 57n, 63, 203, 204, 207, 213–215
Howard, Leon, 143
Hubbard, William, 157; *General History*, 161; *Narrative of the Troubles*, 161
Huber, Johann, 63
Hudson River, 35, 49
Hudson Valley, 47, 49
Hughes, Lewis, *Letter . . . from the Summer Islands*, 74
Hull, Hannah, 34
Hull, John, 31–34, 37, 130, 214
Hunter, Richard, 179
Hunter, Governor Robert, 186
Hunter, William, 241
Huntington Library, 186

Hutchinson, Anne, 82
Hutchinson, Thomas, 145; *History of the Colony of Mass. Bay,* 163

Indentured servants, 4, 14, 60, 101, 166
Indians, 61, 67, 74, 81, 160, 161, 163, 164, 165, 169, 207, 217, 218
Indigo culture in colonies, 17, 44, 53
Inner Temple, 18
Inns of Court, 119, 124
Ipswich (Mass.), 160
Ireland, 33, 65, 66
Irish settlers, 65; in census of 1790, 46
Ironworks, 13, 63
Isocrates, works, 131
Italians, in early Jamestown, 46, 214; in New Amsterdam, 47

Jamaica, 36, 42
James I, 65, 99, 168
James II, 37
James, Henry, 212
James, Margaret, quoted on Eng. poor relief, 26
James River, 5, 8
Jamestown (Va.), 1, 2, 46, 63, 74, 99, 155, 156, 168, 176, 196, 197, 198, 214, 216, 219, 220, 239
Jefferson, Thomas, 119, 125, 168, 216, 230, 233–234
Jenner, Samuel, *Neu-gefundenes Eden,* 61
Jews, 47, 63–65, 84, 87, 90
Johnson, Edward, *History of New England,* 159, 163
Johnson, Samuel, president of King's College, 122, 226
Johnson, William, 122
Johnson family, 30
Johnston, Henrietta, 210
Jones, Hugh, 191, 224; *Present State of Virginia,* 167, quoted, 189–190
Jones, Inigo, 200
Josephus, *History of the Jews,* 133
Junto, 148, 228, 229, 231, 233
Justin, works, 131
Juvenal, works, 131

Kalm, Peter, 229, 251; cited on Dutch New York, 48, 49–50; on

church music in Phila., 195; on Jews in New York, 64–65; on Swedes, 51
Kean, Thomas, 181, 183
Keayne, Robert, 146
Keimer, Samuel, *Universal Instructor,* 244
Kelpius, Johannes, 194
Kennett, Bishop White, 147
Kent, William, 200
Kent County (Md.), school, 110
Kieft Willem, 86
Kimball, Fiske, 197
King Philip's War, 35, 160
King William's School, 110
King's Chapel, 83, 190, 193, 202
King's College, 121–123, 124, 150, 152, 226, 236
Kinnersley, Ebenezer, 236
Kittery (Me.), 36
Kittredge, George L., 142
Kneeland, Samuel, 244
Kneller, Sir Godfrey, 209
Knolles, Richard, 134
Kraus, Michael, quoted, 251
Kühn, Justus Englehardt, 210

La Calprenède, Gaultier de Coste, seigneur de, stories, 143
Labor, competition between white and slave, 28–29; scarce and costly, 23, 27, 29, 33
Lamb, Andrew, 109
Lancaster (Pa.), 59, 62, 63, 90
Land speculation, 8, 14, 16
Lanneau family, 54
Latin language in school curricula, 101, 102, 103, 106, 107, 108, 110, 111, 112, 113, 117, 124
Laud, William, Archbishop of Canterbury, 78, 79, 96
Laurens, Henry, 44
Laurens, John, 210
Law, apprenticeship training, 124; learned from books, 15, 36, 128; studied abroad, 8, 15, 18, 119, 124
Lawson, John, *New Voyage to Carolina,* 169
Lectures on science, 187, 235, 236
Lee, Francis, 111
Lee, Richard (II), 12, 130, 133
Lee, Reverend Samuel, 136

Le Fevre, Professor, 224, 225
Leiden, 199, 219, 230
Leoni, Giacomo, 200
Leverett, Captain John, 35, 142
Levingston, William, 180
Lewis, Richard, trans. of *Muscipula*, 170
Lewis and Clark expedition, 230
Leyden jar, 231, 234
Libraries, circulating, 150–151; college, 151–152; established by SPG, 115, 146–147; private, 8, 11, 15, 40, 43, 130–146, 152, 222, 223; public, 146, 147; *see also* Books
Library Company of Philadelphia, 148–149, 150
Lillo, George, *London Merchant,* 181, 182, 183, 184
Linnaeus, 229, 230, 231, 234
Literary and Philosophical Society of Newport, 149
Literature, belles-lettres, 127, 155; English tradition, 9–10, 42, 126, 144, 151, 153; histories and narratives, 155–169; poetry, 169–173; utilitarian emphasis, 127 ff.; writings of B. Franklin, 178; writings of Mathers, 161–162, 173–174; *see also* Books, Libraries, Classical Learning
Lititz (Pa.), 61
Littlepage, Mrs. Francis, 219
Littleton, Sir Thomas, *Tenures,* 128
Livingston, Philip, 41
Livingston, Robert, 20, 21, 41
Livingston, William, 21–22, 121; writings, 172
Livingston family, 41
Lloyds of Maryland, 14
Locke, John, 17; *Essay on Toleration,* 94
Lodge, Thomas, 133
Log College, 92, 108, 121
Logan, James, 43, 149, 229, 233; library, 145–146, 228
Lombrail, Thomas, 55
London, Bishop of, 75, 95, 110
London merchants, 3, 31, 39; agents for colonial businessmen 5, 11, 40, 204
London (Eng.), 2, 3, 5, 19, 39, 40, 69, 97, 158, 159, 164, 165, 166, 167, 173, 176, 177, 187, 204, 211, 214, 226, 232, 238, 241, 248
Londonderry, 66
Long Island (N.Y.), 20, 49, 85
Long rifle, 62, 67, 215
Lopez, Aaron, 64
Louisburg expedition, 36
Louisiana, 52, 54
Lucan, 131
Lucas, Eliza, 53
Lucena, James, 64
Lutheran Church, 51, 58, 59, 61, 86, 89, 90, 108, 184, 193, 195, 251
Luyck, Aegidius, 106
Lynn (Mass.), 35, 102

Machiavelli, Niccolo, *Prince,* 134
Mackemie, Reverend Francis, 87
Madeira Islands, 32, 33
Magirus, Johannes, 220
Maine, 28, 34, 36, 60
Malaga grapes, imported, 32
Mallet, David, *Masque of Alfred,* 186
Manakin Town (Va.), 54, 55, 56
Manexit (French) River, 56
Manhattan Island, 49, 50
Manigault, Gabriel, 18
Maniguault, Gabriel (II), 18
Manigault, Mrs. Gabriel, 183, 185
Maniguault, Judith (Giton), 18
Manigault, Peter, 18
Manigault, Pierre, 18
Manigault family, 53
Mannheim (Pa.) glassworks, 63, 214
Manorial system, in Maryland, 13; in New York, 20–21
Markham, Gervase, 128
Markland, J., *Typographia,* 170
Marrow of Modern Divinity, 153
Martin, Edward, 177
Martinique, 38
Maryland, colony of, 2, 3, 5, 13–16, 18, 19, 34, 42, 58, 59, 60, 62, 67, 69, 118, 146, 147, 199, 201, 210, 211, 213, 240, 241, 250; drama and other recreations, 15, 182, 184, 189, 191; education, 99, 100, 101, 109–111; literary efforts, 15, 166; literary taste, 15, 132; religion, 16, 73, 76–77, 97, 146
Maryland *Gazette,* 15, 150, 246
Mason, George, 10

Massachusetts Bay Colony, 26, 31, 35, 37, 56, 73, 77, 78, 79, 80, 81, 82, 83, 84, 96, 99, 101–105, 108, 118, 130, 137, 138, 157, 158, 159, 163, 191–192, 197, 204, 221; see also Puritans

Massachusetts General Court, 80, 82, 102

Massacre of St. Bartholomew, 51

Mather, Cotton, 25, 44, 83, 84, 120, 132, 137, 142, 157, 168, 192, 222; Decennium Luctuosum, 161; Diary, 164; Magnalia, 38, 140, 160–162, 174, 222; other writings, 173–174; scientific interest, 224, 226–227

Mather, Increase, 37, 83, 222, 226; writings, 161, 173, 174

Mather, Richard, 170, 207

Maude, David, 102

Mayflower, 77

Mayhew, Reverend Jonathan, quoted, 97

Medicine, from New World plants, 216–217, 222; practiced by laymen, 219–220, 223; see also Education

Megapolensis, Reverend Johannes, 86

Mennonites, 58, 59, 89, 90

Merrymount maypole, 158, 178

Methodism, 90–91

Michaëlius, Domine Jonas, 85–86

Middle Temple, 8, 15

Miller, John, quoted, 40–41

Millington, John, 147

Milton, John, 151, 154, 158; Paradise Lost, 143

Minuit, Peter, 50, 86

Mirror for Magistrates, 142

Mitchell, Dr. John, 230

Molasses as part of "triangular trade," 36, 38, 39

Molasses Act, 39

Monardes, Nicholas, Joyful News Out of the New Found World, 217

Monis, Jonah, 64

Monte Christi (Hispaniola), 39

Moore, Edward, The Gamester, 182

Moravians, 61, 90, 91, 108, 194

More, Sir Thomas, Utopia, 134–135

Morgan, Dr. John, 235, 236

Morison, Samuel E., cited, 31, 32, 101, 116, 142

Morrey, Humphrey, 42

Morris, Anthony, 42

Morris, Richard B., quoted, 27, 28

Morton, Charles, 224, Compendium Physicae, 220–221

Morton, Nathaniel, New England's Memorial, 160

Morton, Thomas, 158, 178; New English Canaan, 158

Moseley, Edward, 147

"Mourt's Relation," 157

Mozart, Wolfgang Amadeus, 194

"Mulberry" plantation house, 200

Müller, Heinrich, 246

Munday, Anthony, 143

Murray, Walter, 181, 183

Music, 19; concerts, 193–195; in churches, 191–193, 195; instruction in private schools, 104, 109, 190–191; of Moravians, 61

Musical instruments, 191, 193, 194, 195

Myers, Myer, 64, 214

Navigation Acts, 40, 43

Nazareth (Pa.), 61

Neale, Thomas, 241

Neshaminy (Pa.), 92, 108, 121

Neuse River, 55

New Amsterdam, 46, 47, 48, 50, 63, 85, 86, 106, 198, 199, 208–209; see also New York

New Bern (N.C.), 60

New Bordeaux (S.C.), 52

New Brunswick (N.J.), 92, 121

New England, 26–27, 106, 156, 197, 198, 199, 200, 201, 204, 207, 209, 221, 222, 224, 225, 226, 227, 228, 239, 240, 249; drama and other recreations, 177–179, 187–193; educational system, 29–30, 99, 101–105, 116–118; literary output, 157–164, 170–172, 173–174; literary taste, 127–124; merchants, 30–40; religion, 77–85, 92–93, 94, 95, 96

New England coasting ships, 7

New England Courant, 243–244

New-England Weekly Journal, 244

New England's First Fruits, quoted, 116

New Hampshire, 118

New Haven (Conn.), 84, 102, 104, 120, 146, 245

New Jersey, 27, 49, 67, 88, 91–92, 165, 241
New Light Presbyterians, 71, 94–95, 121
New London (N.J.), 109
New Mooners, 59
New Netherland, 20, 46, 63, 85, 86, 87, 105, 199, 208; see also New York
New Paltz (N.Y.), 56
New Rochelle (N.Y.)56, 57n.
New Theatre in Water Street, 183
New World, propaganda for settlement, 2; stimulus to science, 216–218
New York, colony of, 13, 20, 21, 22, 40–42, 46–50, 52, 56, 64–65, 85–87, 96, 97, 106–107, 164–165, 172, 188, 189, 204, 208–209, 230, 240, 245
New York (N.Y.), 21–22, 30, 40–42, 49, 50, 56, 64, 65, 106, 121–123, 144, 147, 150, 152, 153, 164–165, 172, 178, 179, 180, 181, 182, 183, 185, 187, 188, 189, 193, 198, 202, 206, 208–209, 214, 226, 230, 231, 240, 241–242, 245, 251
New York Gazette, 243
New York Gazette, or Weekly Post Boy, 245
New York Mercury, 182, 183
New York Society Library, 147, 150
New York Weekly Journal, 245
New York Weekly Post-Boy, 245
Newark (N.J.), 186
Newington Green Academy, 221
Newport, Capt. Christopher, 239
Newport (R.I.), 30, 32, 39, 40, 63, 64, 84, 103, 149, 152, 153, 184, 185, 202–203, 206, 211, 214, 226, 244, 247; a summer resort, 184, 247
Newport Mercury, 184, 244
Newspaper advertisements, artists, 210, 213; books, 153; entertainments, 187; furniture, 205, 206; musical performances, 193, 194; plays, 180, 181, 182, 183, 184, 185; schools, 104, 105, 113
Newspapers, 62, 169, 242–246, 246–247, fn. 12

Newton, Sir Isaac, 136, 220, 221, 225; Principia, 225, 227, 228
Nicholson, Governor Francis, 110, 118
Nomini Hall, 12, 70
Norfolk (Va.), 187
Norris, Isaac, 42, 43
North Carolina, 20, 55, 60, 61, 67, 68, 87, 88, 109, 114–115, 147, 158, 168–169, 201, 213, 241
Northampton (Mass.), 92, 93
Norwegians in New Amsterdam, 47

Oglethorpe, General James, 169
Old Side Presbyterians, 71, 94, 121
Old South Meeting House, 83, 145
Old State House (Boston), 202
Organs, 62, 193, 195
Orrery, Earl of, 8
Otway, Thomas, The Orphan, 181, 183
Ovid, cited by Samuel Sewall, 179; Art of Love, 131, 153; Metamorphoses, 131, 169
Oxford University, 117, 119, 123, 125, 168, 177, 220, 232

Pachelbel, Karl Theodor, 193
Padua, 219
Pain, Philip, Daily Meditations, 143
Painting, of colonial artists, 207–213; private instruction in, 209, 210
Palladio, Andrea, 200, 203
Paper Mill, established on the Wissahickon, 59
Parke, Daniel, 10
Parker, James, 245
Parkinson, John, Herbal, 148
Parks, William, 15, 170, 180–181, 246
Pastorius, Francis Daniel, 58, 59, 89, 108, 166
Patroon system, 20
Patuxent River, 5
Peacham, Henry, Compleat Gentleman, 137, quoted, 128
Peale, Charles, 111
Peale, Charles Willson, 111
Pelham, Peter, 211, 212
Penn, William, 58, 88, 107, 145, 165; Charter School, 108
Pennsylvania, 19, 20, 97, 145–146, 165–166, 179, 182–183, 197, 199, 201, 204, 210, 211, 213, 215, 246,

250; education, 104, 107–109, 123–124; non-British elements, 52, 55–56, 58–62, 63, 65, 67, 68; religious diversity, 58–61, 73, 88–90, 193
Pennsylvania Assembly, 179
Pennsylvania *Gazette*, 244
Pennsylvania, University of, 123–124, 235, 236
Pepperrell, William, 36
Pepperrell, William (II), 36
Pepperrell family, 36
Periodicals, *see* Newspapers
Perkins, William, *Cloud of Faithful Witnesses*, 34; sermons, 139, 140–141; *Treatise of the Vocations*, 104, 140
Perry & Lane, 8
Persius, works, 131
Petersburg (Va.), 168
Petre, Lord, 229
Phaer, Thomas, 131
Philadelphia (Pa.), 16, 55, 56, 58, 60, 64, 65, 70, 93, 108, 109, 123, 124, 144, 145, 146, 148–149, 152, 153, 165, 166, 172–173, 175, 178, 181, 182, 183, 184, 185, 187, 190, 193, 194, 195, 202, 205, 206, 211, 214, 226, 228, 229, 231, 232, 235, 236, 240, 241, 242, 244, 249, 250, 251; merchants, 1, 30, 42, 43; port of entry for immigrants, 42, 67, 88–89, 90
Philadelphia Academy, 123
Philipps, Caleb, 105
Philips, Ambrose, *The Distressed Mother*, 183
Philipse, Frederick, 20
Phillips, Ulrich B., quoted, 18–19
Phips, Lady, 37
Phips, Sir William, 37, 38, 44, 161
"Pickle Herring," 187
Pierpont, Reverend John, 120
Pietists, 58, 59, 61, 89–90, 193, 194
Pilgrims, 77, 157, 188, 197
Pindar, works, 131
Pinetree shillings, 33
"Pinkster Day" in New York, 188
Plater, Colonel George, 14
Plautus, works, 131
Plays, 176–186
Pliny, 131, 132, 218
Plumsted, William, 183

Plutarch, works, 131, 132, 148
Plymouth colony, 77, 78, 81, 118, 128, 157, 158, 197
Pocahontas, 2, 155, 177
Poles, at Jamestown, 46; in New Amsterdam, 47
Pollard, Ann, 208
Pooley, A., 213
Poor relief, 25, 26, 27
Pope, Alexander, works, 151
Population by national groups in colonies, 46
Pormort, Philemon, 101–102
Portuguese in New Amsterdam, 47
Postal service in the colonies, 240–243
Potomac River, 5
Pott, Dr. John, 219–220
Powhatan, 155
Presbyterian Latin Grammar School, 109
Presbyterians, 16, 43, 72, 75, 87, 88, 89, 97, 109, 120, 121, 150, 184, 185, 193; belief in learned ministry, 108, 121–122; split by revival movement, 92, 94–95
Preston, John, sermons, 139
Preston, Samuel, 42
Primaudaye, Pierre de la, *French Academy*, 129
Primogeniture, 4
Prince, Thomas, 145, 157, 168; *Chronological History*, 160, 162
Princeton University, 70, 71, 94, 112, 120, 121, 152, 186, 202
Printers, 62, 165, 170, 172, 173, 174, 207, 238, 242, 243, 244, 245, 246; *see also* Newspapers
Prior, Matthew, works, 151
Protestantism, 73, 77, 79, 117; and capitalism, 24, 25; specified for New Netherland, 47; strengthened in colonies by "Book of Martyrs," 133
Providence (R.I.), 38, 39, 84, 85, 185
Prynne, William, 138
Psalm-singing, 191–193
Ptolemy, 218, 220
Puritan Revolution, 26, 32
Puritans, 50, 53, 74, 76, 85, 99, 104, 158, 159, 160, 162, 164, 170–172, 174, 177, 187, 202, 208; and art,

207; and drama, 177, 178; and literature, 127–145; and music and dancing, 190–194; and science, 223–224, 226; theology, 77–84
Purry, Jean Pierre, 54, 60

Quakers, 20, 58, 59, 68, 73, 88, 97, 109, 161, 190, 202, 244, 245, 251; cultural interests, 43; dislike of drama, 87, 177, 179, 182, 184, 185; emphasis on prudential virtues, 23, 24, 42, 104, 107–108; scientific interest, 228–229; unpopularity, 82–83, 84, 86, 87, 114, 115
Quarles, Francis, *Argalus and Parthenia*, 143
Queen's College, 124
Quintilian, works, 131, 132

Raleigh, Walter, 73, 207, 218; *History of the World*, 133
Ramus, Peter, 220
Randolph, Benjamin, 205
Rappahannock River, 5
Ray, John, 230
Recreation, holidays and other celebrations, 3, 9, 15, 50, 188–189; non-dramatic shows, 186–188; social clubs, 15, 114; sports, 189–190
Red Bluff (Ga.), 90
Redwood, Abraham, 149, 203
Redwood Library, 149, 150, 203
Relation or Journal . . . Plymouth, 157
Religion, 72, 86; church in social life, 248; Great Awakening, 91, 93–95; in Carolinas, 87–88; in Georgia, 90–91; in New Netherland, 85–87; in Pennsylvania, 89–90; in Virginia, 75–76; motive for colonization, 73–74; of Maryland planters, 76–77; pervasive influence in New England, 77–85; revival movement, 91–92, 94–95
Rembrandt, 209
Renaissance culture, 130, 137
Rensselaerswyck, 20
Revere, Paul, 57, 214
Rhett, William, 210
Rhode Island, 38, 39, 63, 64, 65, 84–85, 99, 103, 118, 184–185, 189, 202–203, 206

Rhode Island College, 124
Rhode Island *Gazette,* 244
Ribou, Pierre, 55
Rice culture in S.C., 17, 44
Richardson, Samuel, *Pamela,* 153
Richardson, Samuel, merchant, 42
Richardsons, silversmiths, 214
Richmond, Duke of, 229
Richmond (Va.), 8, 54
Rind, William, 150
Rittenhouse, David, 233–234, 236
River Brethren, 59
Rivera, Jacob, 64
Roanoke Island, 207, 218
Roberts, B., 213
Roberts, Mary, 213
Robinson, William, 83
Rockefeller, John D., 44
Roelantsen, Adam, 105
Rolfe, John, 2
Rowe, Nicholas, plays, 183, 186
Roxbury (Mass.), 31, 222
Royal Society of London, 8, 221, 222, 223, 225, 227, 228, 230, 232, 234
Royal Society of Upsala, 230, 231
Royal Swedish Academy of Sciences, 251
Ruffin, Edmund, 168
Rum, 32, 33
Rush, Dr. Benjamin, 236
Rushworth, John, *Historical Collections,* 134
Russell, Richard, 100
Russell, Dr. Walter, 219
Rutgers University, 124
Ruttinghausen, Wilhelm, Claus & Gerhard, establish paper mill, 59

Sable Island (Me.), 36
St. Andrews, University of, 232
St. Cecilia Society, 194, 195
St. Michael's Church, 202, 203
St. Paul's Church, 202
Salem (Mass.), 31, 38, 40, 81, 102
Salem (N.C.), 194–195
Sallust, 131
Saltonstall family, 30
Sanderson, Robert, 33
Sandys, George, quoted, 46; translates Ovid, 130–131, 143, 169
Sauer, Christopher, 62, 246
Savannah (Ga.), 90, 91, 115

Savannah River, 52, 90
Savery, William, 205
Saybrook (Conn.), 120
Scarsdale (N.Y.), 20
Schools, 2, 30, 56, 61, 69, 70, 71, 98, 99, 100, 101, 102, 103, 104, 105, 106, 107, 108, 109, 110, 111, 113, 114; dame, 102, 103–104; free, 98, 100, 102, 108, 110, 113, 114; evening, 105, 109, 210; private, 103, 104, 105, 107, 109, 111, 112, 210; public, 101, 102, 104, 105, 106, 107, 108, 109, 110
Schuyler, Peter, 20
Science, interest of educated colonists, 135–136, 218–234; utilitarian emphasis of colonial interest, 216 ff.; *see also* Education, Medicine
Scotch-Irish, defined, 65; numbers in census of 1790, 46; *see also* Scots
Scots in colonies, 19, 20, 69, 197, 250; hostility to Great Britain, 90, 97; in census of 1790, 46; Presbyterian faith, 16, 65–68, 89, 92; respect for learning, 70, 71, 108–109, 120–121
Scott, Dr. John, *Christian Life*, 12
Scott, Sir Walter, 6
Scottish Highlanders, 65, 67
Scudder, Reverend Henry, sermons, 139
Scudéry, Madaleine de, 143
Sea-Flower, 36
Seaflower, 33
Sedgwick, Robert, 35–36
Seneca, works, 131, 132
Sermons, as entertainment, 187; as popular reading, 9, 12, 138, 139
Seven Years' War, 39
Seville oranges imported, 32
Sewall, Samuel, 34, 36, 37, 120, 139, 178, 179, 188, 189, 192; *Diary*, 140, 163–164
Seymour, Sir Edward, 118
Shakespeare, William, works, 127, 128, 142, 151, 156, 176, 181, 182, 183, 184, 185, 191
Sharpe, Reverend John, 147, 189; quoted, 106–107
Shenandoah Valley, 60
Shepard, Thomas, 25
Shipbuilding in New England, 32, 37

Shippen, Edward, 42
Shippen, Joseph, "Glooms of Ligonier," 173
Shippen, Dr. William, 235, 236
Ships' stores, 17, 32
Shorthand instruction in private schools, 105
Shurtleff, Harold R., *Log Cabin Myth*, 197
Sibbes, Richard, sermons, 139
Sidney, Sir Philip, *Arcadia*, 143, 144
Sigourney family, 57
Silk production hoped for in colonies, 46, 53, 234
Silversmiths, 57, 64, 213, 214
Slader, Dr. Matthew, 190
Slave trade, 7, 8, 17, 32, 33, 36, 44, 69
Slavery, 5, 12, 14, 28, 29
Sloane, Sir Hans, 223
Smallpox inoculation in the colonies, 227
Smibert, John, 202, 211
Smith, Adam, 163
Smith, Captain John, 176, 196, 206, 219; writings, 155–156
Smith, Maria, 208
Smith, Rebecca, 14
Smith, Samuel, *History of Nova Caesarea*, 165
Smith, Thomas, 208
Smith, Sir Thomas, *The Commonwealth of England*, 134
Smith, Col. Walter, 14
Smith, William, 124, 186; *General Idea of the College of Mirania*, 123
Smith, William, *History of New York*, 165
Smith, Colonel William, 20
Social clubs, 15, 114
Society, 33
Society for Promoting Christian Knowledge, 146
Society for the Propagation of the Gospel, 88, 95, 107, 111, 114, 115, 146, 147
Society Hill theater, 187
Society of the Woman in the Wilderness, 59
Somers, Sir George, 74
Sons of Liberty, 41

South Carolina, 3, 5, 13, 16, 20, 30, 91, 147, 169, 200, 201, 210, 241, 242, 244, 245; drama and other recreations, 183, 185, 187, 191, 193, 194, 195; education, 109, 113–114, 115; non-British elements, 52, 53, 54, 55, 60, 65, 67, 68, 69; religion, 87–88, 97; see also Aristocracy, Southern

South Carolina Gazette, 53, 113, 185, 187, 205, 206, 210, 244–245

South Sea Bubble, 11

Southern Colonies, 2–19, 27, 199; agrarian economy, 1, 2, 3, 4; planter class, 3–19, 44; small farmers, 4–5, 19–20, 28–29; see also Aristocracy, Southern

Southwark Theater, 185

Sower, Christopher, see Sauer

Spain, 32, 33, 73

Spanish in New Amsterdam, 47

Spanish threat to English settlements, 61, 91

Spanish Netherlands, 47

Spence, Dr., 231

Spenser, Edmund, 42, 142, 151

Spotswood, Alexander, Governor of Virginia, 9, 63

Stagg, Charles, 180

Stagg, Mary, 180

Stamp Act, 96, 246

Standish, Capt. Miles, 128, 129, 131

State House (Phila.), 201

Statute of Artificers, 27

Steele, Richard, Conscious Lovers, 182; The Tatler, 148, 244

Steen, Jan, 50

Sternhold, Thomas, Whole Book of Psalms, 192

Stevenson, Marmaduke, 83

Stiegel, Baron H. W., 63, 214–215

Stiles, Ezra, 171, 234; quoted, 64, 186

Stith, William, History of . . . Virginia, 168

Stoddard, Reverend Solomon, 119, 120

Strachey, William, History of Travel, 156–157; True Reportory, 156

Stuyvesant, Peter, 86, 87, 106, 209

Suetonius, works, 131, 132

Sugar industry 32, 33, 38

Sun Tavern, 193

Swedenborg, Emanuel, 211

Swedes in the colonies, 47, 50–51, 89, 197; in census of 1790, 46

Swedish Intelligencer, 133

Swiss settlers, 52, 55, 60, 61, 89

Switzerland, 51

Symmes, Benjamin, 100

Symmes Free School, 100

Tacitus, Annals, 148

Tailfer, Pat., 169

Taverns, 50, 178, 187, 193, 248

Taylor, Edward, 171

Taylor, Jeremy, sermons, 138

Teachers, 70, 100, 101, 102, 103, 105, 106, 109, 111, 112, 113, 114, 115, 122–123

Ten Broeck, Christina, 41

Tennent, Gilbert, 92, 94–95

Tennent, William, 92, 108, 121

Terence, 131, 132

Test Act, 66

Theaters, 178, 180, 181; New York, 183; Philadelphia, 89, 182–183, 184, 185; Williamsburg, 180, 181

Theus, Jeremiah, 210

Thomas, Gabriel, An Historical . . . Account, 165–166

Thomson, James, Masque of Alfred, 186

Thucydides, works, 131

Tillotson, Archbishop, 9

Timothée, Louis (Lewis Timothy), 53, 245

Tobacco, 2, 4, 5, 7, 8, 12, 14, 17, 33, 50, 69, 75, 118; as medicine, 217, 223

Tolles, Frederick, quoted, 42

Trade, 2–3, 240, 247, 251; foundation of colonial fortunes, 7, 11, 12–16, 17, 18, 21–22, 30–44; New England coasting ships, 7; with back country, 69

Transportation, 239–240, 248–250

Treadwell, Daniel, 122

Trinity Church, 87, 147

Trinity Church school, 107

True and Historical Narrative of . . . Georgia, 169

Truth and Delight, 38

Tryall, 33

Tuesday Club, 15

Tuffts, Thomas, 205
Tufts, John, *Very Plain and Easy Introduction*, 192
Twyne, Thomas, 131
Tyler, Moses Coit, quoted, 158

Ulster (Ire.), 65, 66, 108
Ulster Scots, 19, 20, 46, 65, 67, 68, 108
United Brethren, *see* Moravians
Universal Instructor . . . and Pennsylvania Gazette, 244
Upsall, Nicholas, 82
Urmstone, John, 115
Usselinx, Willem, 73

Vade Mecum for America, 249
Van Cortlandt, Anne, 41
Van Cortlandt, James, 41
Van Cortlandt, Oloff, 41
Van Cortlandt, Stephanus, 20
Van Dam, Rip, 181
Van Rensselaer, Kiliaen, 86
Van Twiller, Wouter, 86
Vassar family, 56
Vaughan, William, *Directions for Health*, 128
Virgil, works, 131, 132
Virginia, colony of, 2, 14, 16, 73, 155, 156, 158, 160, 196, 197, 198, 199, 201, 204, 207, 209, 218, 219, 230, 239, 240, 241, 250; education, 99–101, 111–113, 118–119; drama and other recreations, 3, 176, 177, 180, 182, 184, 188, 190, 191; literary efforts, 166–168, 169; literary taste, 127, 128, 130, 131, 132, 136, 137, 138; religion, 74–76, 96
Virginia Board of Trade, 166
Virginia Company of London, 46, 73, 74, 99, 156, 168
Virginia Council of State, 6, 9, 219
Virginia Declaration of Rights, 10
Virginia *Gazette*, 180, 187, 246
Virginia House of Burgesses, 6, 10, 75, 168
Vitruvius, 200

Wachovia (N.C.), 61
Wage regulation in colonies, 27, 28
Walker, Gov. Henderson, 55

Walloons in colonies, 47, 55, 85
Ware, Isaac, 200
Warner, William, *Albion's England*, 142
Watts, Isaac, *Hymns & Psalms*, 68, 193
Way to Wealth, 23–24
Weber, Max, on the rise of capitalism, 24
Weeks, Stephen B., quoted, 115
Welch, John, 213
Welde, Thomas, 170
Wesley, Charles, 90
Wesley, John, 90–91
West, Benjamin, 212
West Indies, 17, 32, 33, 36, 37, 38, 39, 40, 69, 206, 240, 241, 242, 247
Westchester County (N.Y.), 20, 21
Westover, 8, 9
Wheat production attempted by Robert Carter, 12
Wheelwright, John, 82
Whiskey, 69
Whitaker, Alexander, *Good News from Virginia*, 73, 74
White, John, 207
Whitefield, George, 91, 93–94, 115, 121, 163, 183
Whitelocke, Bulstrode, *Memorials of the English Affairs*, 134
Whitmarsh, Thomas, 245
Wickham, Goodwife, 104
Wigglesworth, Michael, 142; *Day of Doom*, 170–171
Willard, Josiah, 139
William III, 20, 54
Williams, Roger, 81–82, 84–85
Williams, William, 212
Williamsburg (Va.), 3, 5, 9, 12, 18, 119, 168, 170, 180, 181, 182, 184, 185, 187, 193, 202, 210, 224
Wilmington (Del.), 211
Wilmington (N.C.), 20
Wilson, Reverend John, 83
Winchester School, 100
Wine, colonial production hoped for, 46, 53, 55; imported, 32, 33
Wing, John, 178, 179
Winslow, Edward, 160; *Good News from New England*, 157
Winthrop, Fitz-John, 143
Winthrop, John, first governor of

Mass. Bay, 28, 34, 78, 82, 208;
Journal, 157, 158
Winthrop, John, Jr., 35, 117, 220,
221; scientific library, 135–136,
222, 223
Winthrop, John (IV), 225, 228
Winthrop family, 30
Winyaw Indigo Society school, 114
Wistar, Caspar, 63
Witherspoon, John, 70, 71, 112
Witt, Christopher, 193
*Wochentliche Philadelphische Staats-
bote, Der,* 246
Wood, George, 150
Wood, William, *New England's Pros-
pect,* 157
Woodbridge (N.J.), 245
Woodmason, Reverend Charles,
quoted on back-country Scots, 68n.
Woolen Act, 66

Work, gospel of, 23–44; epitomized in
Perkins' *Treatise,* 104; preached by
Franklin's *Way to Wealth,* 23–24
Wormeley, Ralph (II), 12, 54, 111,
130, 138
Wren, Sir Christopher, 202
Wroth, Lady Mary, *Countess of
Montgomery's Urania,* 144
Wycherley, William, 8

Yale, Elihu, 120
Yale College, 41, 94, 119–120, 121,
122, 124, 151–152, 172, 188, 202,
225–226, 232, 234
Yale University Library, 171
Yorktown (Va.), 182

Zenger, John Peter, 165, 245
Zinzendorf, Count, 61

Set in Intertype Baskerville
Format by D. F. Bradley
Manufactured by The Haddon Craftsmen, Inc.
Published by HARPER & BROTHERS, *New York*